Driver & Vehicle Standards Agency

The Official DVSA Theory Test for Car Drivers

London: TSO

Written and compiled by the Learning Materials section of the Driver and Vehicle Standards Agency (DVSA).

Questions and answers are compiled by DVSA.

Published with the permission of the Driver and Vehicle Standards Agency on behalf of the Keeper of the Public Record.

First published 1996
Nineteenth edition 2019
Second impression 2020

ISBN 978 0 11 553658 8

A CIP catalogue record for this book is available from the British Library.

Other titles in the Driving Skills series

The Official DVSA Guide to Driving – the essential skills
The Official DVSA Theory Test for Car Drivers (DVD-ROM)
The Official DVSA Guide to Learning to Drive
The Official DVSA Guide to Better Driving
The Official DVSA Guide to Hazard Perception (DVD-ROM)

The Official DVSA Theory Test Kit iPhone/Android App
The Official DVSA Highway Code iPhone App
The Official DVSA Hazard Perception Practice iPhone/Android App

The Official DVSA Guide to Riding – the essential skills
The Official DVSA Theory Test for Motorcyclists
The Official DVSA Theory Test for Motorcyclists (DVD-ROM)
The Official DVSA Guide to Learning to Ride
Better Biking – the official DVSA training aid (DVD)

The Official DVSA Guide to Driving Buses and Coaches
The Official DVSA Guide to Driving Goods Vehicles
The Official DVSA Theory Test for Drivers of Large Vehicles
The Official DVSA Theory Test for Drivers of Large Vehicles (DVD-ROM)
Driver CPC – the official DVSA guide for professional bus and coach drivers
Driver CPC – the official DVSA guide for professional goods vehicle drivers

The Official DVSA Guide to Tractor and Specialist Vehicle Driving Tests (eBook)

The Official DVSA Theory Test for Approved Driving Instructors (DVD-ROM)

Every effort has been made to ensure that the information contained in this publication is accurate at the time of going to press. The Stationery Office cannot be held responsible for any inaccuracies. Information in this book is for guidance only.

All metric and imperial conversions in this book are approximate.

Rules on driving and operating in the European Union (EU) may change during the Brexit transition. Check **www.gov.uk/transition** for the latest information.

We're turning over a new leaf.

100% recycled
This book is printed on 100% recycled paper

RECYCLED
Paper made from recycled material
FSC www.fsc.org
FSC® C002151

P003033508, J003693360

Find us online

GOV.UK – Simpler, clearer, faster

GOV.UK is the best place to find government services and information for

- car drivers
- motorcyclists
- driving licences
- driving and riding tests
- towing a caravan or trailer
- medical rules
- driving and riding for a living
- online services.

Visit **www.gov.uk** and try it out.

You can also find contact details for DVSA and other motoring agencies like DVLA at **www.gov.uk**

You'll notice that links to **GOV.UK**, the UK's central government site, don't always take you to a specific page. This is because this kind of site constantly adapts to what people really search for and so such static links would quickly go out of date. Try it out. Simply search what you need from your preferred search site or from **www.gov.uk** and you should find what you're looking for. You can give feedback to the Government Digital Service from the website.

Message from Mark Winn, the Chief Driving Examiner

Learning to drive is an exciting experience. As with acquiring any new skill, you may be nervous and it may be challenging at first. But, before long, you'll be ready to take the step towards getting your full licence and enjoying the freedom that comes with it.

A sound understanding of driving theory will help you to reach that stage. So, my advice is to take some practical lessons with a qualified instructor while you're studying for your theory test. Learning the theory and practical skills at the same time is the best approach; combining the two means you're more likely to understand and remember what you've learnt, something you'll be glad of on the day of your theory test!

I wish you a lifetime of safe driving.

Mark Winn
Chief Driving Examiner

Contents

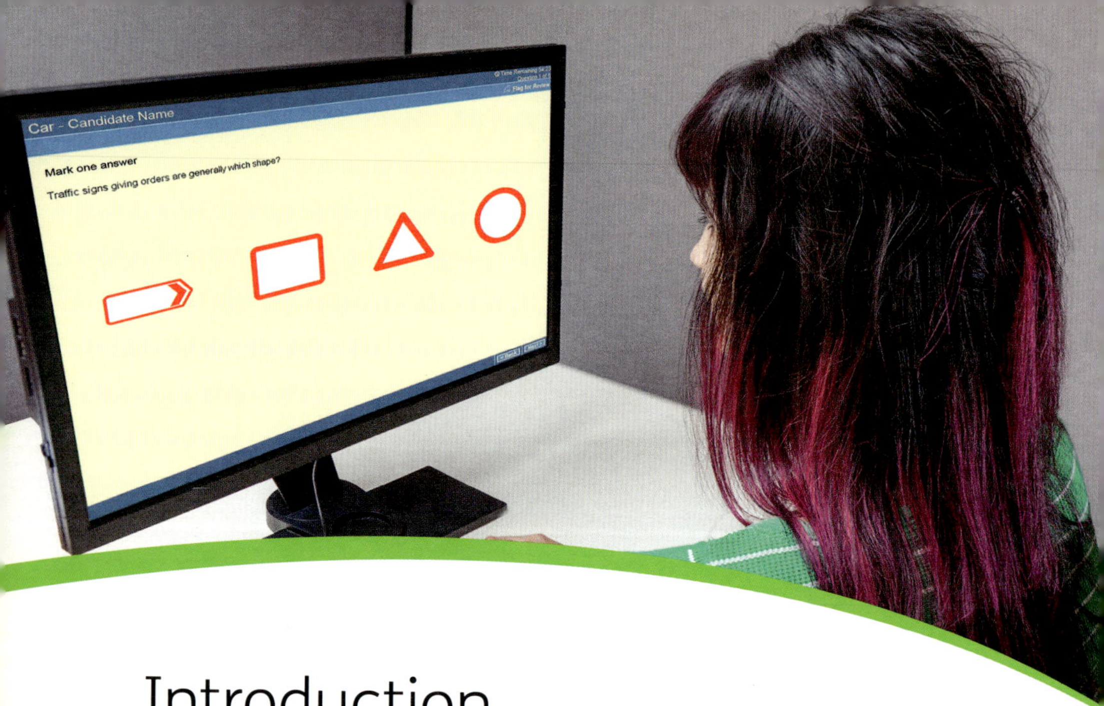

Introduction

About the theory test

In this section, you'll learn about

- how to use this book
- getting started
- the theory test
- after the theory test
- Pass Plus
- using the questions and answers sections
- using this book to learn and revise.

How to use this book

To prove that you have the right knowledge, understanding and attitude to be a safe and responsible driver, you'll need to pass the theory test.

It includes

- a multiple choice test, to assess your knowledge of driving theory
- a hazard perception test, to assess your hazard recognition skills.

This book contains hundreds of questions, which are very similar to the questions you'll be asked in the test and cover the same topics. It's easy to read, and explains why the answers are correct. References to the source material also appear with each question.

Everyone learns in different ways, so this book has features to help you understand driving theory whatever kind of learner you are, including

- bite-size chunks of information, which are easier to understand at your own pace
- lots of photographs and images to illustrate what you're learning
- fourteen topic-specific case studies and six mixed-topic ones, just like those you'll get in the test
- things to discuss and practise with your instructor, to put your learning about each topic into practice
- meeting the standards, to help you understand how each topic relates to the National Standard for Driving.

This book is designed to help you learn about the theory of driving and to practise for the test. To prepare thoroughly, you should also study the source materials that the questions are taken from. These are

The Official Highway Code
Know Your Traffic Signs
The Official DVSA Guide to Driving – the essential skills

There's always more you can learn, so keep your knowledge up to date throughout your driving career.

Getting started

Applying for your licence

You must be at least 17 years old to drive a car. As an exception, you can drive a car when you're 16 if you get, or have applied for, the enhanced rate of the mobility component of Personal Independence Payment (PIP). You must have a valid provisional driving licence before you can drive on the road.

Driving licences are issued by the Driver and Vehicle Licensing Agency (DVLA). You can apply online at **www.gov.uk**. Alternatively, you can apply by post. When applying by post, you'll need to fill in application form D1, which you can request from **www.gov.uk** or collect from certain post office branches. Send your form to the appropriate office, as shown on the form. You must enclose the required passport-type photographs, as all provisional licences are now photocard licences.

In Northern Ireland, the issuing authority is the Driver and Vehicle Agency (DVA; online at **nidirect.gov.uk/motoring**) and the form is a DL1. For more information, see **nidirect.gov.uk/information-and-services/motoring/learners-and-new-drivers**.

When you receive your provisional licence, check that all the details are correct before you drive on the road. If you need to contact DVLA, the telephone number is 0300 790 6801. (DVA's telephone number is 0300 200 7861.)

Residency requirements

You can't take a test or get a full licence unless you're normally resident in the United Kingdom. Normal residence means the place where you live because of personal or occupational (work) ties. However, if you moved to the United Kingdom having recently been permanently resident in another state of the EC/EEA (European Economic Area), you must have been normally resident in the UK for 185 days in the 12 months before you apply for a driving test or full driving licence.

Choosing an instructor

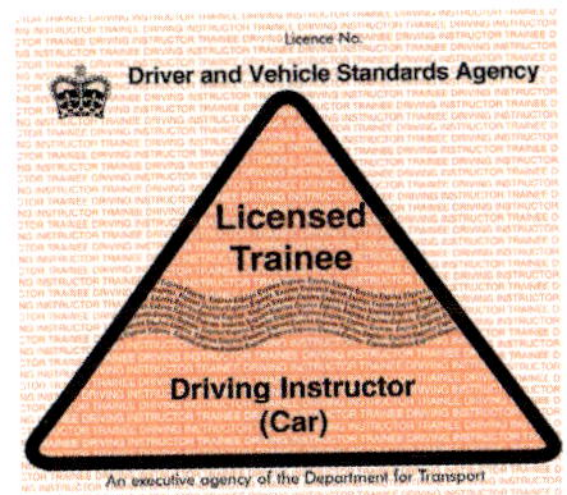

DVSA in Great Britain and DVA in Northern Ireland approve instructors, who are then able to teach learner drivers in return for payment. These instructors have their standards checked regularly.

Approved driving instructors (ADIs) must

- pass a series of difficult examinations
- reach a high standard of instruction
- be registered with DVSA or DVA
- display an ADI's certificate while giving professional driving instruction (except in Northern Ireland).

These professional driving instructors will give you guidance on

- your practical skills
- how to study and practise
- when you're ready for your tests
- further training after your practical test under the Pass Plus scheme (not applicable in Northern Ireland).

DVSA and DVA regulate ADIs, and both organisations place great emphasis on professional standards and business ethics. A code of practice (not applicable in Northern Ireland) has been created, within which all instructors should operate. To find your nearest fully qualified ADI, please visit **www.gov.uk**

About the theory test

You'll take the theory test on-screen in two parts. It's designed to test your knowledge of driving theory – in particular, the rules of the road and best driving practice.

The first part is a series of multiple choice questions. Some multiple choice questions will be presented as a case study. More information about this part of the test is given on pages 17–19. The revision questions are given in the main part of the book, beginning on page 30.

Each question has references to the learning materials; for example

DES s7, HC r128, KYTS p63

DES s indicates the section within *The Official DVSA Guide to Driving – the essential skills.*

HC r/HC p indicates the rule or page in *The Official Highway Code.*

KYTS p indicates the page in *Know Your Traffic Signs.*

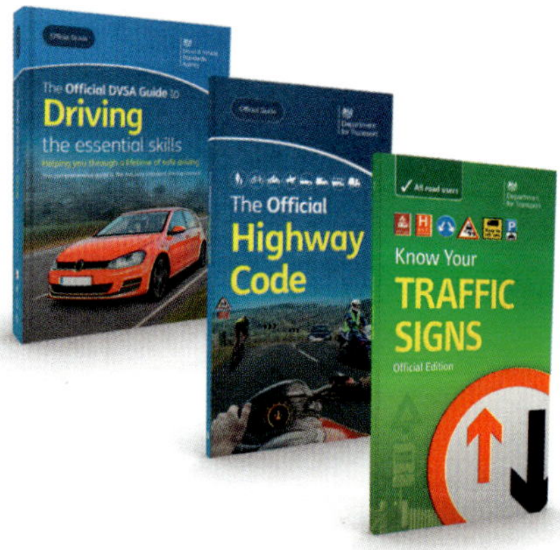

The second part of the theory test is the hazard perception part. More information about this is given on pages 19–20.

Can I take the practical test first?

No. You must pass your theory test before you can book a practical test.

Does everyone have to take the theory test?

Most people in the UK who are learning to drive will have to take the theory test. However, you won't have to if

- you're upgrading in the same category, eg B (car) to B+E (car with trailer)
- you already have a full B1 entitlement because you have a full motorcycle licence issued before 1 February 2001 (not applicable in Northern Ireland).

If you have any questions about whether you need to take a theory test, write to DVSA theory test enquiries, PO Box 381, Manchester M50 3UW. Tel 0300 200 1122 or email **customercare@pearson.com**

For Northern Ireland, contact the Driver Licensing Division, County Hall, Castlerock Road, Coleraine BT51 3TB. Tel 0300 200 7861.

Foreign licence holders: if you hold a foreign licence issued outside the EC/EEA, first check with DVLA (Tel 0300 790 6801; for Northern Ireland call 0300 200 7861), to see whether you can exchange your driving licence. If you can't, you'll need to apply for a provisional licence, then take a theory test and a practical driving test.

Preparing for your theory test

Although you must pass your theory test before you can take your practical test, it's best to start studying for your theory test as soon as possible – but don't actually take it until you have some practical experience of driving.

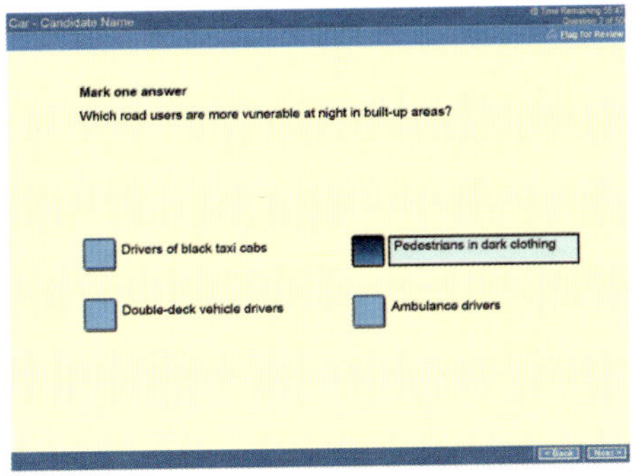

It's important that you study, not just to pass the test but to become a safer driver.

To prepare for the multiple choice part of the theory test, DVSA strongly recommends that you study the books from which the theory test questions are taken, as well as the questions you'll find in this book.

The Official Highway Code This is essential reading for all road users. It contains the very latest rules of the road and up-to-date legislation, as well as advice on road safety and best practice.

Know Your Traffic Signs This contains most of the signs and road markings that you're likely to see.

The Official DVSA Guide to Driving – the essential skills This is the official reference book, giving practical advice and best practice for all drivers.

These books will help you to answer the questions correctly and will also help you when studying for your practical test. The information in them will be relevant throughout your driving life, so make sure you always have an up-to-date copy.

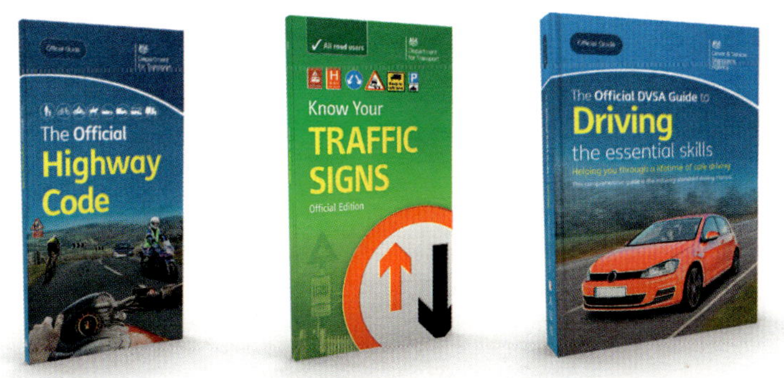

Other study aids

The Official DVSA Theory Test for Car Drivers (DVD-ROM) This is an alternative way of preparing for the multiple choice part of the theory test. It contains all the revision questions and answers, and also allows you to take mock tests.

The Official DVSA Guide to Hazard Perception (DVD-ROM) We strongly recommend that you use this, preferably with your instructor, to prepare for the hazard perception part of the test. The DVD-ROM is packed with useful tips, quizzes and expert advice. It also includes more than 100 interactive hazard perception clips, which you can use to test yourself and see if you're ready to take the real test.

The Official DVSA Complete Theory Test Kit for Car Drivers This contains the above two products, giving you all the information you need to prepare for the complete theory test, at a reduced price.

The Official DVSA Theory Test Kit App The ideal way to prepare for your test on the go, the Theory Test Kit covers both the multiple choice and hazard perception parts of the test. It's available for both iPhone and Android devices.

The Official DVSA Highway Code iPhone App All the latest rules of the road and traffic signs at your fingertips.

The Official DVSA Hazard Perception Practice iPhone/Android App A simple and convenient way to prepare for your hazard perception test on the go. The app is compatible with Android, iPhone and iPad, and contains 30 official interactive DVSA practice clips.

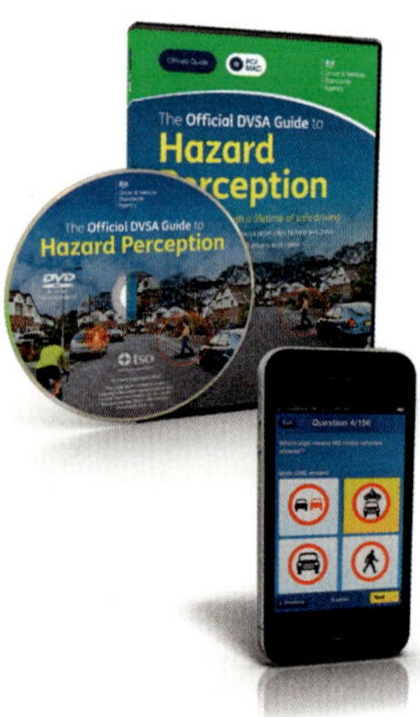

You can buy official DVSA learning materials online at **safedrivingforlife.info/shop** or by calling our expert publications team on **0333 200 2401**. The team can give you advice about learning materials and how to prepare for the tests and beyond. They can also help you select a suitable learning material if you have a special need; for example, if you have a learning disability or English isn't your first language.

DVSA publications are also available from bookshops and online retailers. DVSA apps can be downloaded from the iOS App Store, Google Play store and Amazon Appstore and eBooks are available from your device's eBook store.

Why do the questions change?

To make sure that all candidates are being tested fairly, questions and video clips are under continuous review. Some questions may be changed as a result of customer feedback. They may also be altered because of changes to legislation, and DVSA publications are updated so that the revision questions reflect these changes.

Can I take a mock test?

You can take a mock test for the multiple choice part of the theory test online at **safedrivingforlife.info/free-tests**

The theory test

Booking your theory test

Visit **www.gov.uk** to book your theory test online (for Northern Ireland, use **nidirect.gov.uk/motoring**).

If you have any special needs for the theory test, call 0300 200 1122 (0845 600 6700 for Northern Ireland). If you're a Welsh speaker, call 0300 200 1133.

If you have hearing or speech difficulties and use a minicom machine, call 0300 200 1166.

You'll need your

- DVLA or DVA driving licence number
- credit or debit card details (if you do this over the phone, the card holder must book the test). We accept Mastercard, Visa, Delta and Visa Electron.

You'll be given a booking number and you'll receive an appointment email on the same day if you book online.

If you book over the phone and don't provide an email address, you'll receive an appointment letter within 10 days.

Where can I take the test?

There are over 150 theory test centres throughout England, Scotland and Wales, and six in Northern Ireland. Most people have a test centre within 20 miles of their home, but this will depend on the density of population in your area. To find your nearest test centre, please visit **www.gov.uk**

What should I do if I don't receive an acknowledgement?

If you don't receive an acknowledgement within the time specified, please visit **www.gov.uk** or call the booking office to check that an appointment has been made. We can't take responsibility for postal delays. If you miss your test appointment, you'll lose your fee.

When are test centres open?

Test centres are usually open on weekdays, some evenings and some Saturdays.

How do I cancel or postpone my test?

You can cancel or postpone your test online by visiting **www.gov.uk** or by telephone. You should contact the booking office at least **three clear working days** before your test date, otherwise you'll lose your fee.

Short-notice cancellation and rebooking (not refund) is permitted in the following circumstances:

- if you're ill or injured and have a supporting medical certificate
- if you've been affected by a bereavement
- if you're sitting school examinations.

Booking by post If you prefer to book by post, you'll need to fill in an application form. You can download the form from **www.gov.uk**, or your instructor may have one.

You should normally receive confirmation of your appointment within 10 days of posting your application form. This will be by email if you've provided an email address or by post if not.

If you need support for special needs, please turn to page 16.

Taking your theory test

Arriving at the test centre You must make sure that when you arrive at the test centre you have all the relevant documents with you. If you don't have them, you won't be able to take your test and you'll lose your fee.

You'll need

- your signed photocard licence, or
- your signed old-style paper driving licence and valid passport (your passport doesn't have to be British).

No other form of identification is acceptable in England, Wales or Scotland.

Other forms of identification may be acceptable in Northern Ireland; please check **nidirect.gov.uk/motoring** or your appointment letter.

All documents must be original. We can't accept photocopies.

The test centre staff will check your documents and make sure that you take the right category of test.

Remember, if you don't bring your documents your test will be cancelled and you'll lose your fee.

Make sure you arrive in plenty of time so that you aren't rushed. If you arrive after the session has started, you may not be allowed to take the test.

Watch the 'Theory test 2020: official DVSA guide' video on DVSA's YouTube channel. This explains how to prepare for the theory test, what to expect on the day and what you need to do to pass.

youtube.com/dvsagovuk

Languages other than English

In Wales, and at theory test centres on the Welsh borders, you can take your theory test with Welsh text on-screen. A voiceover can also be provided in Welsh.

All Great Britain driving test candidates must take their theory test in either English or Welsh. Unless you're taking the test in Northern Ireland

- no voiceovers will be provided in any other language
- translators cannot attend the test with you to translate it from English into any other language.

Provision for special needs

We make every effort to ensure that the theory test can be taken by all candidates.

It's important that you state your needs when you book your test so that the necessary arrangements can be made.

Reading difficulties There's an English-language voiceover on a headset to help you if you have reading difficulties or dyslexia.

You can ask for up to twice the normal time to take the multiple choice part of the test.

You'll be asked to provide a letter from a suitable independent person who knows about your reading ability, such as a teacher or employer. Please check with the Special Needs section (call on the normal booking number; see page 13) if you're unsure who to ask.

We can't guarantee to return any original documents, so please send copies only.

Hearing difficulties If you're deaf or have other hearing difficulties, the multiple choice part and the introduction to the hazard perception part of the test can be delivered in British Sign Language (BSL) by an on-screen signer.

If you need a BSL interpreter, signer or lip speaker, please request one when you book your test. If you have any other requirements, please call the Special Needs section on the normal booking number (see page 13).

Physical disabilities If you have a physical disability that would make it difficult for you to use a mouse button in the theory test, please let us know when you book your test. We may be able to arrange for you to use a different method.

Multiple choice questions

The first part of the theory test consists of 50 multiple choice questions. Some of these will be in the form of a case study. You select your answers for this part of the test by using a mouse.

Before you start, you'll be given the chance to work through a practice session for up to 15 minutes to get used to the system. Staff at the test centre will be available to help you if you have any difficulties.

The questions will cover a variety of topics relating to road safety, the environment and documents. Only one question will appear on the screen at a time, and you'll be asked to mark one correct answer.

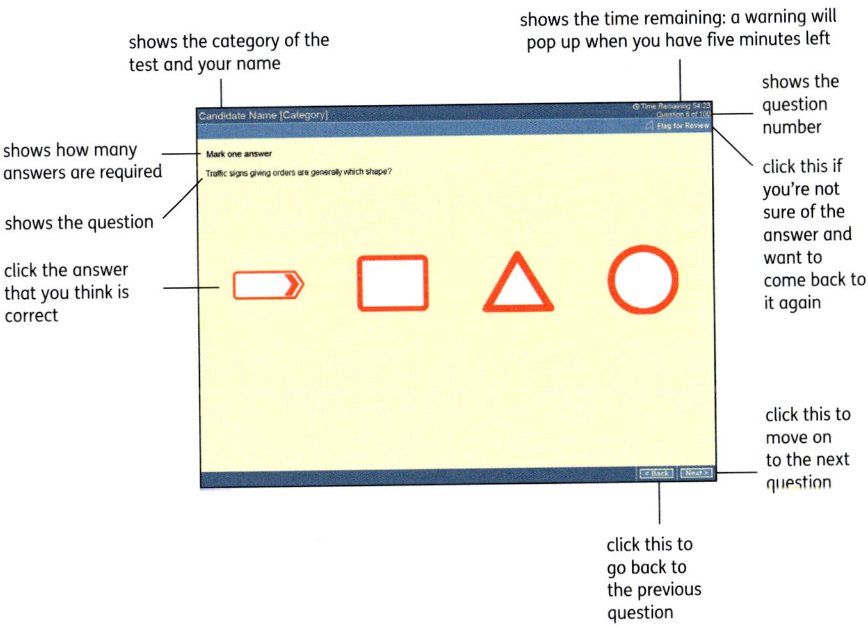

To answer, you need to click the box beside the answer you think is correct. If you change your mind and don't want that answer to be selected, click it again. You can then choose another answer.

Take your time and read the questions carefully. You're given 57 minutes for this part of the test, so relax and don't rush. Some questions will take longer to answer than others, but there are no trick questions. The time remaining is displayed on the screen.

You may be allowed extra time to complete the test if you have special needs and you let us know when you book your test.

You'll be able to move backwards and forwards through the questions and you can also 'flag' questions you'd like to look at again. It's easy to change your answer if you want to.

Try to answer all the questions. If you're well prepared, you shouldn't find them difficult.

At the end of this part of the test, you can use the 'review' feature to check your answers. If you click the 'review' button and then the 'end' button on the review screen, it will end your test. When you click the review button, you'll see the following screen.

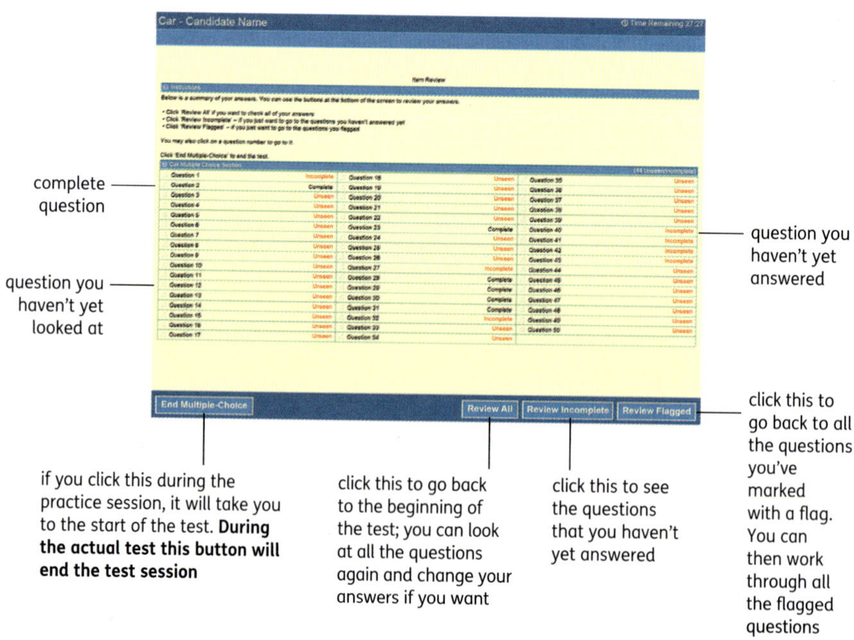

Case studies

Some of the multiple choice questions will be presented as part of a case study. Case studies are designed to test

- knowledge (recall of facts)
- comprehension (understanding)
- application (practical use of knowledge and understanding).

This is done by creating a set of circumstances that you may encounter in a real-life situation. You'll then be asked some questions relating to the scenario, and you'll have to decide how you would react or behave in each case. For an example of a case study, see page 459.

The case studies at the end of each section in this book set out scenarios and then ask you relevant questions. This is to help you test your knowledge in a format similar to the case studies in the theory test. However, the layout isn't the same as the theory test screens.

We'll soon be replacing the case study questions in the car theory test. Instead, after the multiple choice questions, you'll watch a computer-generated image (CGI) video clip. Then you'll have to answer three more multiple choice questions based on that clip. To see a sample clip and find out more, visit: **safedrivingforlife.info/driving-theory-test-booking-and-taking-your-test**

Hazard perception

After you've finished the multiple choice part, there's a break of up to three minutes before you start the hazard perception part of the test. You can't leave your seat during this break. This part of the test is a series of CGI video clips, shown from a driver's point of view. You'll be using a mouse for this part of the theory test.

Before you start this part of the test, you'll be shown a short CGI video that explains how the test works and gives you a chance to see a sample clip. This will help you to understand what you need to do. You can play this video again if you wish.

During the hazard perception part of the test, you'll be shown 14 CGI video clips. Each clip contains one or more developing hazards. You should press the mouse button **as soon as you see** a hazard developing that may need you, the driver, to take some action, such as changing speed or direction.

The earlier you notice a developing hazard and make a response, the higher your score. There are 15 hazards for which you can score points.

Your response won't change what happens in the scene in any way. However, a red flag will appear on the bottom of the screen to show that your response has been noted.

Before each clip starts, there'll be a 10-second pause to allow you to see the new road situation.

The hazard perception part of the test lasts about 20 minutes. For this part of the test no extra time is available, and you can't repeat any of the clips – you don't get a second chance to see a hazard when you're driving on the road.

Trial questions

We're constantly checking the questions and clips to help us decide whether to use them in future tests. After the hazard perception part of the test, you may be asked to try a few trial questions and clips. You don't have to do these if you don't want to, and if you answer them they won't count towards your final score.

Customer satisfaction survey

We want to make sure our customers are completely satisfied with the service they receive. At the end of your test you'll be shown some questions designed to give us information about you and how happy you are with the service you received from us.

Your answers will be treated in the strictest confidence. They aren't part of the test and they won't affect your final score or be used for marketing purposes. You'll be asked if you want to complete the survey, but you don't have to.

The result

You should receive your result at the test centre within 10 minutes of completing the test.

You'll be given a score for each part of the test (the multiple choice part and the hazard perception part). You'll need to pass both parts to pass the theory test. If you fail one of the parts, you'll have to take the whole test again.

Why do I have to retake both parts of the test if I only fail one?

It's really only one test. The theory test has always included questions relating to hazard awareness – the second part simply tests the same skills in a more effective way. The two parts are only presented separately in the theory test because different scoring methods are used.

What's the pass mark?

To pass the multiple choice part of the theory test, you must answer at least 43 out of 50 questions correctly. For learner car drivers and motorcyclists, the pass mark for the hazard perception part is 44 out of 75.

If I don't pass, when can I take the test again?

If you fail your test, you've shown that you're not fully prepared. You'll have to wait at least three clear working days before you can take the theory test again.

Good preparation will save you both time and money.

After the theory test

When you pass your theory test, you'll be given a certificate. Keep this safe, as you'll need it when you go for your practical test.

The certificate is valid for two years from the date of your test. This means that you have to take and pass the practical test within this two-year period. If you don't, you'll have to take and pass the theory test again before you can book your practical test.

Your practical driving test

To help you, DVSA has produced a book called *The Official DVSA Guide to Learning to Drive.*

This book explains the standards required to pass the practical driving test. It includes information about each of the 24 key skills examined within the test, with tips from the experts, and it explains what the examiner is looking for during the test.

Pass Plus

(not applicable in Northern Ireland)

During the year or so after passing your practical driving test, you're at greater risk of being involved in a road traffic incident than older, more experienced drivers. That risk is reflected in car insurance premiums.

There are likely to be many driving situations that you haven't experienced during your lessons. The Pass Plus scheme can help by showing you how to deal with these situations so that you can drive with confidence.

Pass Plus is aimed at improving your driving skills and making you a safer driver. It can also lead to insurance discounts. Pass Plus will take you through driving

- in town
- on rural roads
- in all weathers
- on dual carriageways and motorways
- in the dark.

The structured syllabus gives you the extra experience you need at a time when you're most likely to be involved in a collision. It builds on your existing skills and there's no test to take at the end.

The amount of money you save on insurance could cover the cost of the course. Many car insurers recognise the benefits of the scheme and will give you substantial discounts when you insure your car. To find out more about the Pass Plus scheme, insurance discounts and Pass Plus instructors in your area

- ask your driving instructor
- visit **www.gov.uk**
- call the Pass Plus hotline on **0115 936 6504**
- email **passplus@dvsa.gov.uk**

You can take the Pass Plus course at any time in your driving career, but it's mainly aimed at new drivers in the first year after passing their test.

Using the questions and answers sections

Sections 1 to 14 of this book contain the revision questions for the multiple choice part of the theory test. These are very similar to the questions you'll be asked in the test and cover the same topics.

For easy reference, the questions are divided into topics. Although this isn't how you'll find them in your test, it's helpful if you want to look at particular subjects.

At the start of each topic, before the questions, there are a few pages of useful information to help you learn more about each topic.

The questions are in the left-hand column with a choice of answers below.

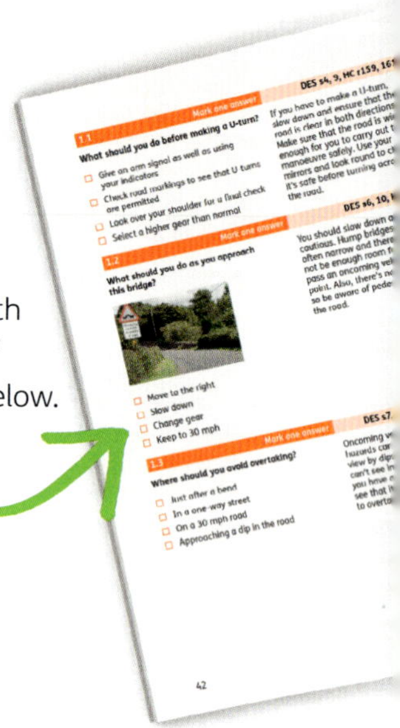

On the right-hand side of the page there's a brief explanation to help you understand the question. There'll also be some advice on correct driving procedures and some short references to the relevant source materials. These refer to the books listed on page 10.

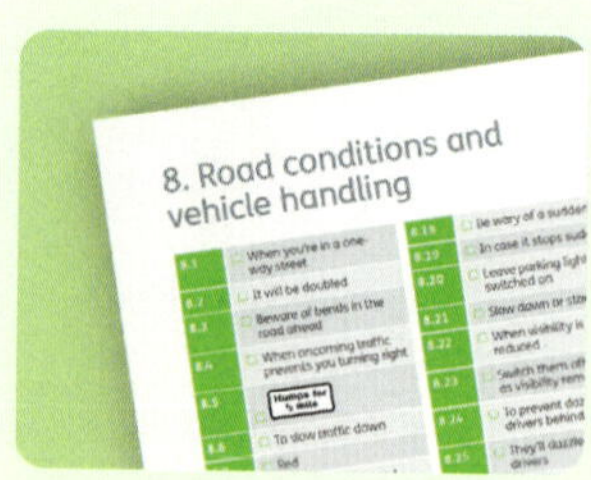

The correct answers are at the back of the book, in section 16.

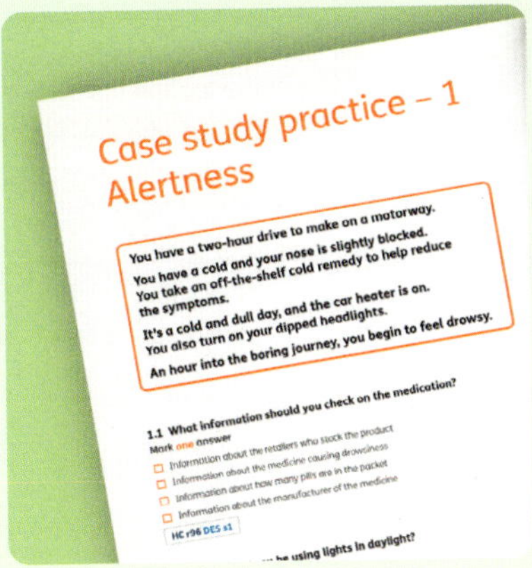

Case study practice – 1
Alertness

You have a two-hour drive to make on a motorway.

You have a cold and your nose is slightly blocked. You take an off-the-shelf cold remedy to help reduce the symptoms.

It's a cold and dull day, and the car heater is on. You also turn on your dipped headlights.

An hour into the boring journey, you begin to feel drowsy.

1.1 What information should you check on the medication?

Mark one answer

- [ ] Information about the retailers who stock the product
- [ ] Information about the medicine causing drowsiness
- [ ] Information about how many pills are in the packet
- [ ] Information about the manufacturer of the medicine

HC r96 DES s1

Don't just learn the answers; it's important that you know why they're correct. To help you do this, there's a short scenario at the end of each question section, with five questions to answer. This will give you an idea of how the case study part of the theory test will assess your understanding of the subject covered. This knowledge will help you with your practical skills and prepare you to become a safe and confident driver.

Taking exams or tests is rarely a pleasant experience, but you can make your test less stressful by being confident that you have the knowledge to answer the questions correctly.

Make studying more enjoyable by involving your friends and relatives. Take part in a question-and-answer game. Test those 'experienced' drivers who've had their licence a while: they might learn something too!

Some of the questions in this book won't be relevant to Northern Ireland theory tests. These questions are marked as follows: **NI EXEMPT**

Best wishes for your theory test. Once you're on the road, remember what you've learnt and be prepared to keep learning.

Using this book to learn and revise

We're all different. We like different foods, listen to different music and learn in different ways.

This book is designed to help you learn the important information that you'll need for the theory test in a variety of different formats, so you can find a way of learning that works best for you.

Features

A summary, at the start of each section, of what you'll learn.

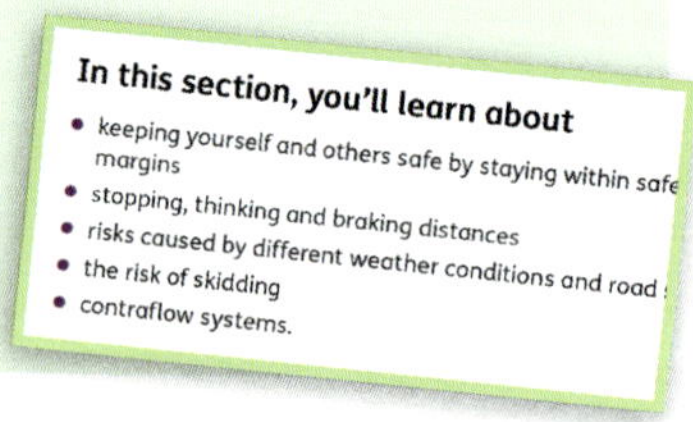

All the key information presented in bite-size chunks with clear headings.

Images to help you relate the information to the real world.

Diagrams and tables to help make information clear and summarise key points.

Self-reflection points to help you think about the way you drive.

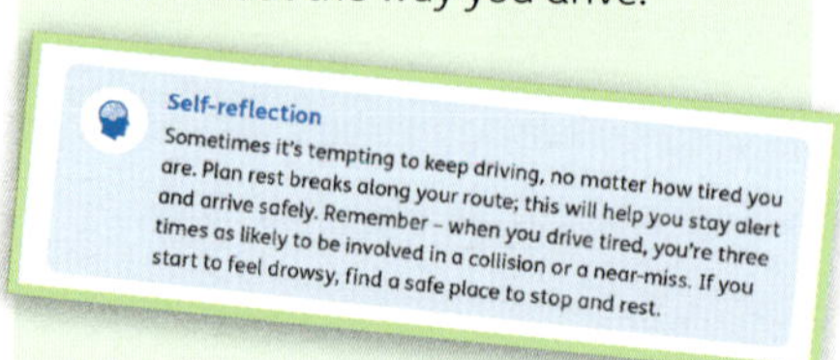

Links and QR codes to online videos and interactive activities, to further increase your knowledge and skills. Scan the QR code on your smartphone (you'll need a QR code reader app) to access the online content.

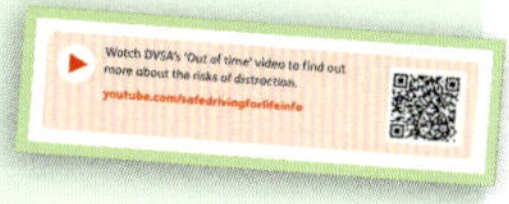

Links to other relevant publications, like *The Official Highway Code* and *The Official DVSA Guide to Driving – the essential skills.*

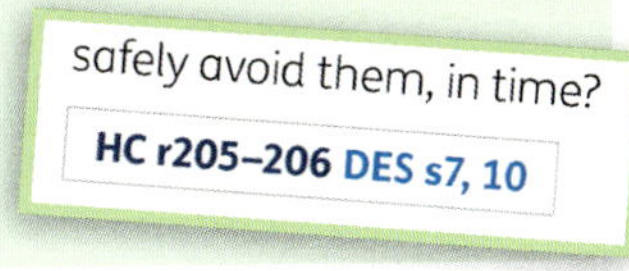

Tips containing useful extra information about driving safely.

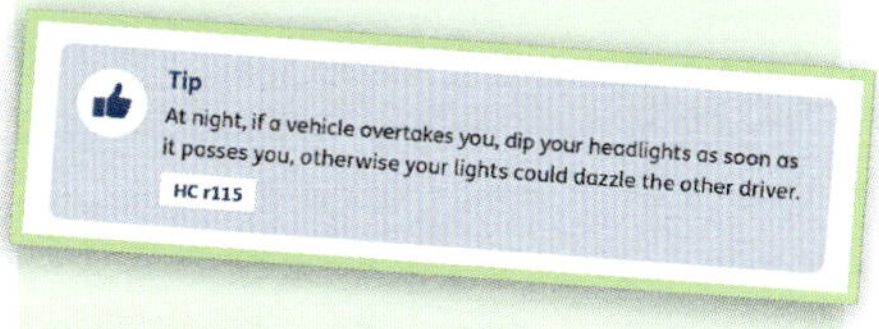

A summary, at the end of each section, of what you'll need to know and be able to do to meet the National Standard for Driving.

Pages for your own notes, with suggested things to think about.

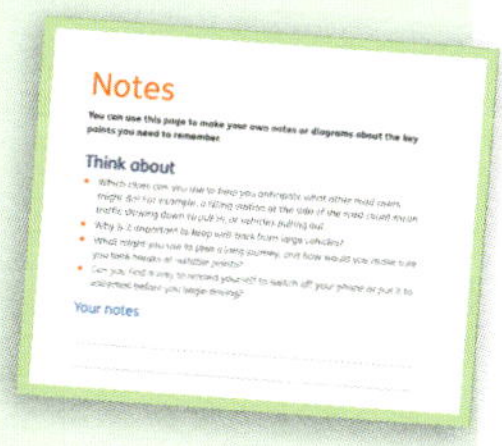

Ideas to discuss with your driving instructor and practise when driving.

Self-assessment – revision questions like the ones you'll get in the test.

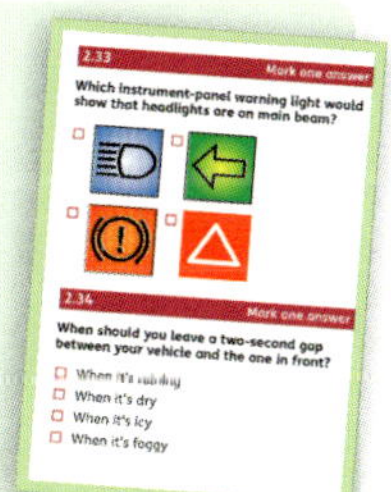

Case studies showing how the information might work in practice, and related questions.

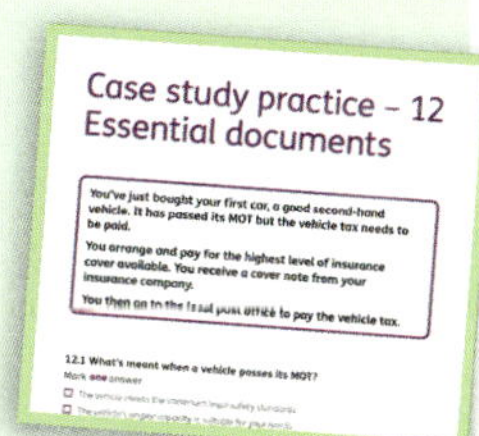

The theory test is just one part of the process of learning to drive. You need to learn the facts, but it's important to understand how they relate to real driving.

The combination of knowing driver theory and having good practical driving skills won't only help you pass your test; it will also help you through a lifetime of safe driving.

What kind of learner are YOU?

Ask yourself these questions

- Why are you doing this? What's motivating you?
- How have you learned best in the past? What helped you to remember what you needed to know?
- What are your strengths and weaknesses as a learner?

Think about the way that you learn best. You could try any combination of the following ideas.

I remember what I see or read

- Create flashcards with important facts or statistics
- Make diagrams and charts
- Use mind maps
- Use colour coding
- Watch the DVSA short films
- Make your own notes
- Cross-reference information using a variety of books, eg *The Official Highway Code*
- Draw your own diagrams to show key information.

I remember best when I physically do something

- Short study sessions
- Do things – create models or diagrams; make lists
- Use props
- Try the interactive activities
- Watch and copy what your driving instructor does
- Mime or act out different driving moves.

I remember what I hear

- Repeat rules out loud
- Use a voice recorder to make recordings of key information
- Work with others and discuss things
- Watch and listen to the DVSA video content.

Top tips

Remember your motivation

Think about the reason you're learning to drive. Is it for independence? For work? To drive a dream car? Remind yourself, from time to time, of your motivation for learning. Don't give up!

Relate to your personal experience

Information is more memorable when it's linked to what you already know. Try to picture yourself in the position of the driver. The case studies throughout the book can help you think about how the ideas would work in real life.

Use mnemonics

Mnemonics are little sayings, stories or techniques that help you remember something. A classic example is '**R**ichard **O**f **Y**ork **G**ave **B**attle **I**n **V**ain', which you can use to remember the colours of the rainbow (**r**ed, **o**range, **y**ellow, **g**reen, **b**lue, **i**ndigo, **v**iolet). You can use similar techniques to memorise statistics, facts or information to help you drive safely.

Question format

However you choose to learn the content, make certain you're familiar with the format of the test and how the questions will be presented. Go through the self-assessment questions in each chapter and see if you can answer them. Mark any you struggle with and try them again at a later date.

Plan your study

Set yourself timelines and targets. Try to set aside dedicated time for study, when you're feeling awake and are unlikely to be interrupted. The environment in which you study is important – try to find an area where you can concentrate.

Getting help

Think about the people you can speak with to ask questions, get advice or share experiences about driving – such as your driving instructor, parents, friends or colleagues at work.

Taking your test

Don't rush into the theory test before you're ready. You need to be confident with the information, and have enough practical experience to give you a deep understanding of the information too.

Section one

Alertness

In this section, you'll learn about

- observing what's going on around you
- being seen by other road users
- being aware of other road users
- anticipating what other road users are going to do
- keeping your concentration on the road
- avoiding distractions.

Alertness

Being alert to what's going on around you is vital to driving safely and will help you to avoid dangerous situations.

Observation and awareness

It's important to be aware of what's happening around you while you're driving, including

- other road users
- pedestrians
- signs and road markings
- weather conditions
- the area you're driving through.

Keep scanning the road ahead and to the sides, and assess the changing situations as you drive.

Before you move off, you should

use your mirrors to check how your actions will affect traffic behind you

look around for a final check, including checking the **blind spots** around your car

signal, if necessary.

HC r159–161 DES s4

blind spots

any areas that are hidden from the driver either by the car's bodywork or areas not covered by the mirrors.

Getting a clear view

If you can't see behind you when reversing, ask someone to guide you to make sure that you reverse safely.

If your view is blocked by parked cars when you're coming out of a junction, move forward slowly and carefully until you have a clear view.

Watch the 'Test your awareness' Transport for London (TfL) video.

youtube.com/watch?v=Ahg6qcgoay4

Overtaking

Observation is particularly important when you're overtaking another vehicle. Make sure you can see the road ahead clearly, looking out for

- vehicles coming towards you
- whether you're near a junction – vehicles could come out of the junction while you're overtaking
- whether the road gets narrower – there may not be enough space for you to overtake
- bends or dips in the road, which will make it difficult for you to see traffic coming towards you
- road signs that mean you **MUST NOT** overtake.

Before you overtake, check that

- it's safe, legal and necessary
- you have enough time to complete the overtaking manoeuvre.

HC r162–163, 165 DES s7 KYTS p64

Being seen by others

It's important for other road users to know you're there.

- Switch on your lights when it starts to get dark, even if the street lights aren't on.
- Where you can't be seen, such as at a hump bridge, you may need to use your horn.

HC r113–115

If you're following a large vehicle, stay well back. This will help the driver to see you in their mirrors. Staying back will also help you see the road ahead much more clearly. This is especially important if you're planning to overtake the vehicle.

HC r164

Tip

Remember, if you're following a large vehicle and can't see the vehicle's mirrors, the driver may not be able to see you or know you're there.

Anticipation

Anticipation can help you to avoid problems and incidents so that you can drive more safely. For example, a 'give way' sign warns you that a junction is ahead, so you can slow down in good time.

Look at the road signs and markings: these give you information about hazards. You should

- follow their advice
- slow down if necessary.

DES s6 KYTS p10, 62

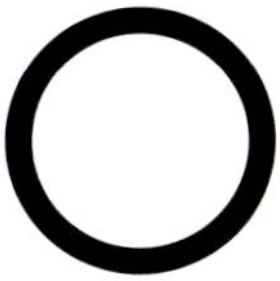

Circles
give orders

Triangles
give warnings

Rectangles
give information

When turning right onto a **dual carriageway**, check that the **central reservation** is wide enough for your vehicle to stop in, especially if you're towing a trailer. Do this in case you have to wait before joining the traffic. If there's not enough space for your vehicle, only emerge when it's clear both to the right and left.

dual carriageway
a road that has a central reservation to separate the carriageways

central reservation
an area of land that separates opposing lanes of traffic

If you're approaching traffic lights that have been green for some time, be prepared to stop because they may change.

Road conditions will affect how easy it is to anticipate what might happen. It's more difficult when you're not familiar with the route, and when your view ahead is reduced; for example, when

- the weather is very wet or windy
- the light is poor
- the traffic volume is heavy.

In these conditions, you need to slow down and be particularly aware of what's happening around you.

DES s7

Anticipating what other road users might do

Watch other road users. Try to anticipate their actions so that you're ready if you need to slow down or change direction.

Be aware of more vulnerable road users. Watch out for

pedestrians approaching a crossing, especially young, older or disabled people who may need more time to cross the road

cyclists – always pass them slowly and leave plenty of room, especially if the cyclist is young and may have little experience of dealing with traffic

motorcyclists, who may be difficult to see

horses, which may be startled by the noise of your vehicle – pass them slowly and leave plenty of room.

HC r204–218 DES s10

Always be ready to stop

However well prepared you are, you may still have to stop quickly in an emergency.

Keep both hands on the wheel as you brake to help you to keep control of your vehicle.

DES s5, 10

Staying focused

Driving safely takes a lot of concentration – as well as controlling the car, you need to be aware of what's happening on the road and what could happen next. Stay focused on driving and try not to get distracted.

Always plan your journey so that you

- know which route you need to take
- have regular rest stops.

Avoiding tiredness

You won't be able to concentrate properly if you're tired. It's particularly easy to feel sleepy when driving on a motorway, especially at night, so

- don't drive continuously for more than two hours
- keep fresh air circulating in the car
- if you start to feel drowsy, leave at the next exit. Find a safe and legal place to stop and take a break.

Tip

Stop in a safe place and have a cup of coffee or another caffeinated drink. Remember that this is only a short-term solution: it isn't a substitute for proper rest. If possible, take a short nap.

HC r91, 262 DES s1, 11

See the Think! road safety website for more information about driving and tiredness.

http://think.gov.uk/road-safety-laws/#fatigue

Self-reflection

Sometimes it's tempting to keep driving, no matter how tired you are. Plan rest breaks along your route; this will help you stay alert and arrive safely. Remember – when you drive tired, you're three times as likely to be involved in a collision or a near-miss. If you start to feel drowsy, find a safe place to stop and rest.

Distraction

It's easy to be distracted by what's happening in your car. Devices such as phones, music players and navigation systems can divide your concentration between the road ahead and what you're hearing.

Losing your concentration, or just taking your eyes off the road for a second, could be disastrous. At 60 mph, your vehicle will travel 27 metres in one second.

HC r149 DES s1

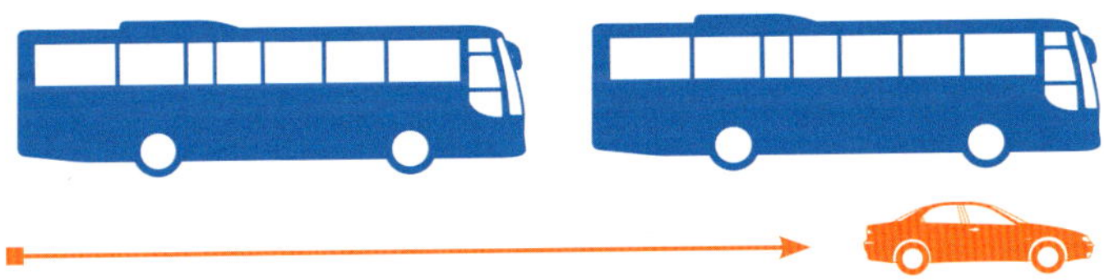

1 second at 60 mph = 27 metres/29.5 yards

Be careful that your passengers don't distract you. Joking about or having an argument can pull your attention away from the road for vital seconds.

DES s1

Watch DVSA's 'Out of time' video to find out more about the risks of distraction.

youtube.com/safedrivingforlifeinfo

Using a mobile phone while you're driving is illegal; it also drastically increases the chance of being involved in a collision. Even using a hands-free phone isn't safe because you can still be distracted from driving by making a call.

HC r149-150 DES s1

Be safe: switch your phone off or put it on voicemail. Wait until you're parked legally in a safe place before you use your mobile phone to

- retrieve any messages
- make any calls
- send or receive texts
- go online.

If you're driving on a motorway, you should leave the motorway and stop in a safe place before using your phone.

DES s11

See the Think! road safety website for more information about mobile phones and driving.

http://think.gov.uk/road-safety-laws/#mobile-phones

If you have a navigation system, stop in a safe place before programming the system.

You could also be distracted by something that has happened on the road, such as an incident on the other side of a motorway. Don't slow down or try to see what's happening; continue with your journey and keep your concentration on your driving.

Meeting the standards

The National Standard for Driving sets out the skills, knowledge and understanding that DVSA believes are required to be a safe and responsible driver. If you know, understand and are able to do the things described in the standard, then you'll not only be in a great position to pass your test but will also be well on your way to becoming a safe driver for life.

You can view the National Standard for Driving at **www.gov.uk**

You must be able to

decide if you're fit to drive. You shouldn't be

- too tired
- too ill
- too emotional
- under the influence of drugs or alcohol

manage your passengers so that they don't stop you driving safely

be aware of what's around you (nearby and far away) at all times

drive at such a speed that you can always stop in the clear space ahead of you.

You must know and understand

how a poor seating position and bad posture can make you tired

how to deal with passengers if they make it hard for you to concentrate on the road

that some cars have large pillars that block your view, and how to deal with this

how to read the road ahead and be prepared for the unexpected.

Notes

You can use this page to make your own notes or diagrams about the key points you need to remember.

Think about

- Which clues can you use to help you anticipate what other road users might do? For example, a filling station at the side of the road could mean traffic slowing down to pull in, or vehicles pulling out.
- Why is it important to keep well back from large vehicles?
- What might you use to plan a long journey, and how would you make sure you took breaks at suitable points?
- Can you find a way to remind yourself to switch off your phone or put it to voicemail before you begin driving?

Your notes

Things to discuss and practise with your instructor

These are just a few examples of what you could discuss and practise with your instructor. Read more about alertness to come up with your own ideas.

Discuss with your instructor

- what you need to take into account before overtaking, such as road markings, bends, etc
- what could distract you while driving; for example, friends, loud music, etc
- how to avoid getting bored while driving long distances.

Practise with your instructor

- your observation when making a turn in the road
- your alertness to other road users on narrow country lanes
- your ability to ignore your mobile phone. Arrange for someone to call you during your lesson so that you can practise your reaction. (Although *The Official Highway Code* advises you to turn your phone off while driving, sometimes you may forget.)

1.1 Mark one answer — DES s4, 9, HC r159, 161

What should you do before making a U-turn?

- ☐ Give an arm signal as well as using your indicators
- ☐ Check road markings to see that U-turns are permitted
- ☐ Look over your shoulder for a final check
- ☐ Select a higher gear than normal

If you have to make a U-turn, slow down and ensure that the road is clear in both directions. Make sure that the road is wide enough for you to carry out the manoeuvre safely. Use your mirrors and look round to check it's safe before turning across the road.

1.2 Mark one answer — DES s6, 10, HC r206

What should you do as you approach this bridge?

- ☐ Move to the right
- ☐ Slow down
- ☐ Change gear
- ☐ Keep to 30 mph

You should slow down and be cautious. Hump bridges are often narrow and there may not be enough room for you to pass an oncoming vehicle at this point. Also, there's no footpath, so be aware of pedestrians in the road.

1.3 Mark one answer — DES s7, HC r162, 163, 166

Where should you avoid overtaking?

- ☐ Just after a bend
- ☐ In a one-way street
- ☐ On a 30 mph road
- ☐ Approaching a dip in the road

Oncoming vehicles or other hazards can be hidden from view by dips in the road. If you can't see into the dip, wait until you have a clear view and can see that it's safe before starting to overtake.

1.4 **Mark one answer** **DES s7, HC r128, KYTS p63**

What does this curved arrow road marking mean?

- ☐ Heavy vehicles should take the next road on the left to avoid a weight limit
- ☐ The road ahead bends to the left
- ☐ Overtaking traffic should move back to the left
- ☐ The road ahead has a camber to the left

In this picture, the road marking shows that overtaking drivers or riders need to return to the left. These markings show the direction drivers must pass hatch markings or solid double white lines. They're also used to show the route that high vehicles should take under a low arched bridge.

1.5 **Mark one answer** **DES s1, HC r149, 270**

What should you do if your mobile phone rings while you're driving or riding?

- ☐ Stop immediately
- ☐ Answer it immediately
- ☐ Leave it until you have stopped in a safe place
- ☐ Pull up at the nearest kerb

It's illegal to use a hand-held mobile or similar device when driving or riding, except in a genuine emergency. The safest option is to switch off your mobile phone before you set off, and use a message service. If you've forgotten to switch your phone off and it rings, you should leave it. When you've stopped in a safe place, you can see who called and return the call if necessary.

1.6 Mark one answer DES s6, KYTS p68

Why are these yellow lines painted across the road?

- ☐ To help you choose the correct lane
- ☐ To help you keep the correct separation distance
- ☐ To make you aware of your speed
- ☐ To tell you the distance to the roundabout

These lines are often found on the approach to a roundabout or a dangerous junction. They give you extra warning to adjust your speed. Look well ahead and do this in good time.

1.7 Mark one answer DES s6

What should you do when you're approaching traffic lights that have been green for some time?

- ☐ Accelerate hard
- ☐ Maintain your speed
- ☐ Be ready to stop
- ☐ Brake hard

The longer traffic lights have been green, the sooner they'll change. Allow for this as you approach traffic lights that you know have been green for a while. They're likely to change soon, so you should be prepared to stop.

1.8 Mark one answer DES s4, HC r144, 161

What should you do before slowing down or stopping your vehicle?

- ☐ Sound the horn
- ☐ Use the mirrors
- ☐ Select a higher gear
- ☐ Flash the headlights

Before slowing down or stopping, check the mirrors to see what's happening behind you. Also assess what's ahead and make sure you give the correct signal if it will help other road users.

1.9	Mark one answer	DES s10, HC r221-222

You're following a large vehicle. Why should you stay a safe distance behind it?

- ☐ You'll be able to corner more quickly
- ☐ You'll help the large vehicle to stop more easily
- ☐ You'll give the driver a chance to see you in their mirrors
- ☐ You'll keep out of the wind better

If you're following a large vehicle but are so close to it that you can't see its exterior mirrors, the driver won't be able to see you. Keeping well back will also allow you to see the road ahead by looking past the large vehicle.

1.10	Mark one answer	DES s4, 10, HC r161

Why should you use your mirrors when you see a hazard ahead?

- ☐ Because you'll need to accelerate out of danger
- ☐ To assess how your actions will affect the traffic behind
- ☐ Because you'll need to brake sharply and stop
- ☐ To check what's happening on the road ahead

You should be constantly scanning the road for clues about what's going to happen next. Check your mirrors regularly, particularly as soon as you spot a hazard. What's happening behind may affect how you respond to hazards ahead.

1.11	Mark one answer	DES s8, 10

You're waiting to turn right at the end of a road. What should you do if your view is obstructed by parked vehicles?

- ☐ Stop and then move forward slowly and carefully for a clear view
- ☐ Move quickly to where you can see so you only block traffic from one direction
- ☐ Wait for a pedestrian to let you know when it's safe for you to emerge
- ☐ Turn your vehicle around immediately and find another junction to use

At junctions, your view is often restricted by buildings, trees or parked cars. You need to be able to see in order to judge a safe gap. Edge forward slowly and keep looking all the time. Don't cause other road users to change speed or direction as you emerge.

1.12 Mark one answer HC r89, p128

There are objects hanging from your interior mirror. Why could this be a hazard?

- ☐ Your view could be obstructed
- ☐ Your sun visor might get tangled
- ☐ Your radio reception might be affected
- ☐ Your windscreen could mist up more easily

Ensure that you can see clearly through the windscreen of your vehicle. Stickers or hanging objects could obstruct your view or draw your attention away from the road.

1.13 Mark one answer DES s1, HC r91, 262

You're on a long motorway journey. What should you do if you start to feel sleepy?

- ☐ Play some loud music
- ☐ Stop on the hard shoulder for a rest
- ☐ Drive faster to complete your journey sooner
- ☐ Leave the motorway and stop in a safe place

If you feel sleepy, you should leave the motorway at a service area or at the next exit and stop in a safe place to rest. A supply of fresh air can help to keep you alert before you reach the exit, but it isn't a substitute for stopping and resting.

1.14 Mark one answer DES s13, HC r115

Why should you switch your headlights on when it first starts to get dark?

- ☐ To make your dials easier to see
- ☐ So others can see you more easily
- ☐ So that you blend in with other drivers
- ☐ Because the street lights are lit

Your headlights and tail lights help others on the road to see you. It may be necessary to turn on your headlights during the day if visibility is reduced; for example, due to heavy rain. In these conditions, the light might fade before the street lights are timed to switch on. Be seen to be safe.

1.15 Mark one answer — DES s1, HC r149

What's most likely to distract you while you're driving?

- ☐ Using a mobile phone
- ☐ Using the windscreen wipers
- ☐ Using the demisters
- ☐ Using the mirrors

Except for emergencies, it's illegal to use a hand-held mobile phone while you're driving. Even using a hands-free kit can severely distract your attention.

1.16 Mark one answer — DES s1, HC r149

You're driving your car. When may you use a hand-held mobile phone?

- ☐ When you're receiving a call
- ☐ When you've parked safely
- ☐ When you're driving at less than 30 mph
- ☐ When your car has automatic transmission

It's illegal to use a hand-held mobile phone while you're driving, except in a genuine emergency. Even using a hands-free kit can distract your attention. Park in a safe and convenient place before receiving or making a call or using text messaging. Then you'll also be free to take notes or refer to papers.

1.17 Mark one answer — DES s5

You're driving on a wet road. What should you do if you have to stop your vehicle in an emergency?

- ☐ Apply the parking brake and footbrake together
- ☐ Keep both hands on the steering wheel
- ☐ Select reverse gear
- ☐ Give an arm signal

As you drive, look well ahead and all around so that you're ready for any hazards that might develop. If you have to stop in an emergency, react as soon as you can while keeping control of the vehicle. Keep both hands on the steering wheel so you can control the vehicle's direction of travel.

1.18 Mark one answer DES s4, 5, HC r159

What should you do when you move off from behind a parked car?

- ☐ Give a signal after moving off
- ☐ Look around before moving off
- ☐ Look around after moving off
- ☐ Use the exterior mirrors only

Before moving off, you should use both the interior and exterior mirrors to check that the road is clear. Look around to check the blind spots and, if necessary, give a signal to warn other road users of your intentions. Also look well ahead as you'll have to steer out into the road to pass the parked car.

1.19 Mark one answer DES s10, HC r212, 213

You're travelling along this road. How should you pass the cyclist?

- ☐ Sound your horn as you pass
- ☐ Keep close to them as you pass
- ☐ Leave them plenty of room as you pass
- ☐ Change down one gear before you pass

Allow the cyclist plenty of room in case they wobble or swerve around a pothole or raised drain. Look well ahead before you start to overtake, because you'll need to cross the hazard line. Look for entrances where vehicles could be waiting to pull out.

1.20 Mark one answer DES s5, 10

When do windscreen pillars cause a serious obstruction to your view?

- ☐ When you're driving on a motorway
- ☐ When you're driving on a dual carriageway
- ☐ When you're approaching a one-way street
- ☐ When you're approaching bends and junctions

Windscreen pillars can obstruct your view, particularly at bends and junctions. Look out for other road users – especially cyclists, motorcyclists and pedestrians who can easily be overlooked.

1.21 Mark one answer — DES s9, HC r202

What should you do if you can't see clearly behind when you're reversing?

- ☐ Open the window to look behind
- ☐ Open the door to look behind
- ☐ Look in the nearside mirror
- ☐ Ask someone to guide you

If you want to turn your car around, try to find a place where you have good all-round vision. If this isn't possible, and you're unable to see clearly, then get someone to guide you.

1.22 Mark one answer — DES s4, HC r159

What does the term 'blind spot' mean?

- ☐ An area covered by your right-hand mirror
- ☐ An area not covered by your headlights
- ☐ An area covered by your left-hand mirror
- ☐ An area not visible to the driver

Modern vehicles provide the driver with a good view of both the road ahead and behind using well-positioned mirrors. However, the mirrors can't see every angle of the scene behind and to the sides of the vehicle. It's essential that you know when and how to check the vehicle's blind spots, so that you're aware of any hidden hazards.

1.23 Mark one answer — DES s1, HC r149

What's likely to happen if you use a hands-free phone while you're driving?

- ☐ It will improve your safety
- ☐ It will increase your concentration
- ☐ It will reduce your view
- ☐ It will divert your attention

Talking to someone while you're driving can distract you and, unlike when someone is in the car with you, the person on the other end of a mobile phone is unable to see the traffic situations you're dealing with. They won't stop speaking to you even if you're approaching a hazardous situation. You need to concentrate on your driving at all times.

1.24 Mark one answer DES s8, HC r173

You're turning right onto a dual carriageway. What should you do before emerging?

- ☐ Stop, apply the parking brake and then select a low gear
- ☐ Position your vehicle well to the left of the side road
- ☐ Check that the central reservation is wide enough for your vehicle
- ☐ Make sure that you leave enough room for a vehicle behind

Before emerging right onto a dual carriageway, make sure that the central reservation is deep enough to protect your vehicle. If it isn't, you should treat the dual carriageway as one road and check that it's clear in both directions before pulling out. Neglecting to do this could place part or all of your vehicle in the path of approaching traffic and cause a collision.

1.25 Mark one answer DES s8, 10, HC r170

You're waiting to emerge from a junction. The windscreen pillar is restricting your view. What should you be particularly aware of?

- ☐ Lorries
- ☐ Buses
- ☐ Motorcyclists
- ☐ Coaches

Windscreen pillars can completely block your view of pedestrians, motorcyclists and cyclists. You should make a particular effort to look for these road users; don't just rely on a quick glance.

1.26 Mark one answer **DES s1, 18, HC r150**

How can you make sure that a satellite navigation (satnav) system doesn't distract you when you're driving?

- ☐ Turn it off while you're driving in built-up areas
- ☐ Choose a voice that you find calming
- ☐ Only set the destination when you're lost
- ☐ Set it before starting your journey

Satnavs can be useful when driving on unfamiliar routes. However, they can also distract you and cause you to lose control if you look at or adjust them while you're driving. Set the satnav before starting your journey, or pull up in a safe place before making any changes to it.

Case study practice – 1 Alertness

You have a two-hour drive to make on a motorway.

You have a cold and your nose is slightly blocked. You take an off-the-shelf cold remedy to help reduce the symptoms.

It's a cold and dull day, and the car heater is on. You also turn on your dipped headlights.

An hour into the boring journey, you begin to feel drowsy.

1.1 What information should you check on the medication?

Mark **one** answer

- ☐ Information about the retailers who stock the product
- ☐ Information about the medicine causing drowsiness
- ☐ Information about how many pills are in the packet
- ☐ Information about the manufacturer of the medicine

HC r96 DES s1

1.2 Why would you be using lights in daylight?

Mark **one** answer

- ☐ To observe other vehicles more clearly
- ☐ To improve your view of the road
- ☐ To catch sight of road signs easily
- ☐ To maximise your visibility to others

HC r115

Section two

Attitude

In this section, you'll learn about

- showing consideration and courtesy to other road users
- how to follow other road users safely
- giving priority to emergency vehicles, buses and pedestrians.

1.3 How does this journey affect you?

Mark **one** answer

- ☐ You feel happy
- ☐ You become drowsy
- ☐ You feel angry
- ☐ You become attentive

HC r262 DES s11

1.4 What should you do about your condition?

Mark **one** answer

- ☐ Keep driving, but slow down a little while taking a caffeinated drink
- ☐ Drive more slowly, turn the vehicle around and go back home
- ☐ Stop in a service area, drink a caffeinated drink and then rest
- ☐ Stop on the hard shoulder, recline the seat fully and rest

HC r91 DES s1

1.5 How could you help yourself stay alert in the short term?

Mark **one** answer

- ☐ Open the window
- ☐ Turn up the heater
- ☐ Turn on the radio
- ☐ Open a can of drink

DES s1

Attitude

Safe driving is all about developing the correct attitude and approach to road safety, together with a sound knowledge of driving techniques.

However modern, fast or expensive your vehicle, it's you, the driver, who determines how safe it is.

Good manners on the road

Be considerate to other road users. Other drivers, cyclists and horse riders have just as much right to use the road as you. If you drive in a competitive way, you'll make the road less safe for everyone using it.

DES s1

It's also important to be patient with other road users. Unfortunately, not everyone obeys the rules. Try to be calm and tolerant, however difficult it seems. For instance, if someone pulls out in front of you at a junction, slow down and don't get annoyed with them.

HC r147 DES s1

Self-reflection

Can you think of a time when driving made you impatient and angry? How did you react? Did you think about doing something dangerous? Ask yourself how your friends and family would feel if your driving created a serious incident. Is it worth taking the risk?

Helping other road users

You can help other road users know what you're planning to do by signalling correctly and moving to the correct position at junctions. For instance, if you want to turn right, get into the right-hand lane well before the junction. A badly positioned vehicle could obstruct traffic behind it.

HC r143 DES s7, 8

If you're driving a slow-moving vehicle, consider other drivers behind you. If there's a long queue, pull over as soon as you can do so safely and let the traffic pass. Think how you would feel if you were one of the drivers following behind you. They may not be as patient as you are.

HC r169 DES s10

Tip

If a large vehicle is trying to overtake you but is taking a long time, slow down and let it pass. It will need more time to pass you than a car would.

HC r168 DES s7

If you're travelling at the speed limit and a driver comes up behind flashing their headlights or trying to overtake, keep a steady course and allow them to overtake. Don't try to stop them – they could become more frustrated.

HC r168 DES s7, 11

Using your horn and lights

Only sound your horn if there's danger and you need to let others know you're there. Don't sound it through impatience.

HC r112 DES s5–8, 13

At night, don't dazzle other road users. Dip your lights when you're

following another vehicle

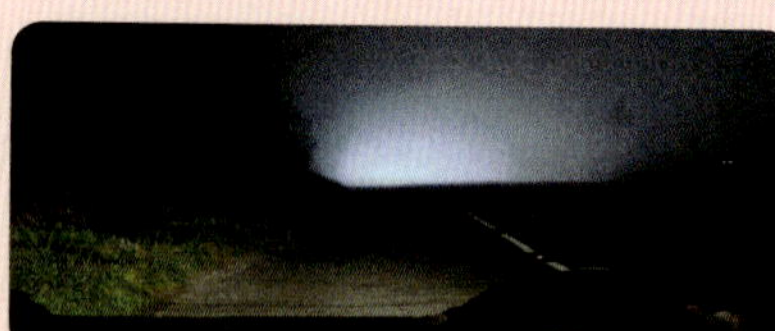

meeting another vehicle coming towards you.

HC r114 DES s13

If you're queuing in traffic at night, use your handbrake rather than keeping your foot on the brake, as your brake lights could dazzle drivers behind you.

Tip

You should only flash your headlights to show other road users you're there. It's not a signal to show priority, impatience or to greet others.

HC r110–111 DES s5, 10

Animals on the road

Horses can be frightened easily and a rider could lose control of their horse. When passing horses

- keep your speed down
- give them plenty of room.

HC r214–215 DES s10

See the Think! road safety website for more information about horses on the road.

http://think.gov.uk/road-safety-laws/#horses

Take care if there are animals, such as sheep, on the road. If the road is blocked by animals, or if you're asked to, stop and switch off your engine until the road is clear.

HC r214

Following safely

Driving too closely behind another vehicle – known as tailgating – is

- intimidating and distracting for the road user in front
- very dangerous, as it could cause an incident if the vehicle in front stops suddenly.

DES s10

Travelling too closely to another vehicle also means that you can see less of the road ahead, so keep well back, especially from large vehicles. You'll be able to see further down the road and spot any hazards ahead more easily.

DES s7, 10

Keep a safe distance from the vehicle in front.

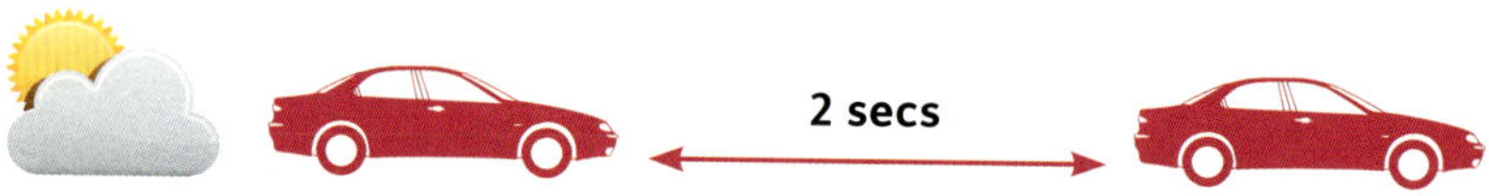

In good, dry conditions, leave a two-second gap.

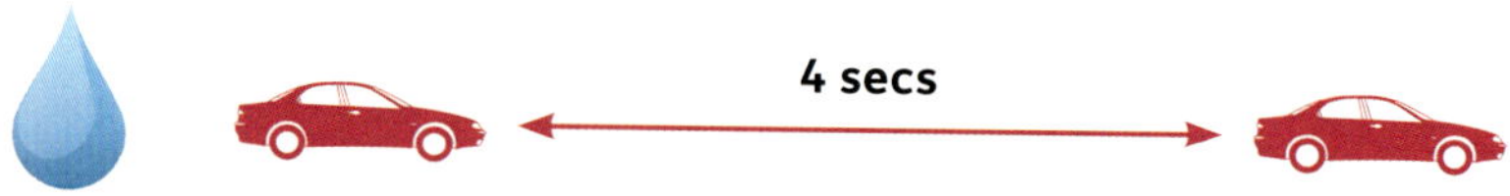

In wet weather, leave a four-second gap.

HC r126 DES s7, 10, 11

Tip

Use a fixed point, like a road sign, to help you measure the gap between you and the vehicle in front.

See section 4, Safety margins, for more information about the amount of space to leave between you and the vehicle in front.

When you're following large vehicles, you may see them move to the centre of the road before turning left – this is because they need more room to manoeuvre. Keep well back and don't try to pass on the left as the rear of the vehicle will cut in.

If the road user behind is following too closely, gradually slow down to increase the gap between you and the vehicle in front. This will give you a greater safety margin should traffic ahead slow down or stop suddenly. If another road user cuts in front of you, drop back until you've restored your safety margin.

HC r168

Giving priority to others

Who has priority on the road at any time can vary. Sometimes traffic going in one direction is given priority, and this is shown by a road sign. Having priority doesn't mean you can demand right of way. Be careful: the driver coming towards you may not have seen or understood the road sign.

Emergency vehicles

Always give priority to emergency vehicles. It's important for them to move quickly through traffic because someone's life might depend on it. Pull over to let them through as soon as you can do so legally and safely.

HC r219 DES s7

As well as fire, police and ambulance services, other emergency services (including those shown here) use a blue flashing light.

HM coastguard

Bomb disposal

Mountain rescue

Blood transfusion

Doctors' vehicles may use green flashing lights when answering an emergency call.

Watch the Blue Light Aware video to find out more about how to help emergency vehicles get through traffic.

bluelightaware.org.uk

Priority for buses

Give priority to buses pulling out from bus stops, as long as you can do so safely. In some areas, bus lanes allow buses to proceed quickly through traffic. Be aware of road signs and markings so that you don't use bus lanes while they're in operation.

HC r223 DES s6, 7, 10

Unmarked crossroads

At unmarked crossroads, no-one has priority. Slow down, look both ways and only emerge into the junction when you can do so safely.

Pedestrian crossings

Be particularly careful around pedestrian crossings so that you're ready to stop if necessary.

Type of crossing | **What you need to be aware of**

Zebra crossing

Watch out for pedestrians at or approaching a zebra crossing.

- Be ready to slow down and stop.
- Be patient if they cross slowly.
- Don't encourage them to cross by waving or flashing your headlights – there may be another vehicle coming.

HC r195 DES s7

Pelican crossing

If you're approaching a pelican crossing and the amber light is flashing

- give way to pedestrians on the crossing
- don't move off until the crossing is clear.

HC r196–198 DES s7

Type of crossing	What you need to be aware of
Puffin crossing 	Puffin crossings are electronically controlled. Sensors ensure that the red light shows until the pedestrian has safely crossed the road. These crossings don't have a flashing amber light; they have a steady amber light, like normal traffic lights. **HC r199 DES s7**
Toucan crossing 	Toucan crossings, which work in a similar way to puffin crossings, allow cyclists to cross at the same time as pedestrians. **HC r199 DES s7**

Meeting the standards

You must be able to

help other road users to understand what you intend to do by signalling correctly

support the signals that you make with the position of your vehicle. For example, if you're turning right, position the car in good time and use the right-turn lane if there is one

control your reaction to other road users. Try not to get annoyed or frustrated

give other road users enough time and space.

You must know and understand

what can happen if you wrongly use the headlights or the horn as a signal

what lane discipline is and why it's important

that it's an offence to drive

- without due care and attention
- without reasonable consideration for other road users.

Notes

You can use this page to make your own notes or diagrams about the key points you need to remember.

Think about

- Which vehicles do you need to give priority to?
- What would you do if someone was tailgating you?
- In what conditions should you keep a four-second distance between you and the vehicle in front?
- What problems might you cause if you're impatient and inconsiderate while driving?

Your notes

Things to discuss and practise with your instructor

These are just a few examples of what you could discuss and practise with your instructor. Read more about attitude to come up with your own ideas.

Discuss with your instructor

- the different crossings you may come across (puffin, toucan, etc) and who can use them
- which emergency vehicles you may see on the road (police, doctors, etc) and how to react to them
- what the 'two-second rule' means and how it may change in different weather conditions.

Practise with your instructor

- driving in an area with bus lanes, to practise how to react when they're in operation
- driving at night, to get used to using your dipped and main-beam headlights
- driving in heavy traffic, to get used to other vehicles that may be following you too closely.

2.1	Mark one answer	DES s7, HC r196

What must you do when the amber light is flashing at a pelican crossing?

- ☐ Stop and wait for the green light
- ☐ Stop and wait for the red light
- ☐ Give way to pedestrians waiting to cross
- ☐ Give way to pedestrians already on the crossing

Pelican crossings are signal-controlled crossings operated by pedestrians. Push-button controls change the signals. Pelican crossings have no red-and-amber stage before green; instead, they have a flashing amber light. This means you must give way to pedestrians who are on the crossing but if the crossing is clear you can continue.

2.2	Mark one answer	DES s7, HC r195

Why should you never wave people across at pedestrian crossings?

- ☐ Another vehicle may be coming
- ☐ They may not be looking
- ☐ It's safer for you to carry on
- ☐ They may not be ready to cross

If people are waiting to use a pedestrian crossing, slow down and be prepared to stop. Don't wave them across the road, because another driver may not have seen them, may not have seen your signal, and may not be able to stop safely.

2.3	Mark one answer	DES s10, 11, HC r126

Why is it dangerous to travel too close to the vehicle ahead?

- ☐ Your engine will overheat
- ☐ Your mirrors will need adjusting
- ☐ Your view of the road ahead will be restricted
- ☐ Your satnav will be confused

'Tailgating' is the term used when a driver or rider follows the vehicle in front too closely. It's dangerous because it restricts your view of the road ahead and leaves no safety margin if the vehicle in front needs to slow down or stop suddenly. Tailgating is often the underlying cause of rear-end collisions or multiple pile-ups.

2.4 Mark one answer | DES s7, 10, HC r222

What will happen if you follow this vehicle too closely?

- ☐ Your brakes will overheat
- ☐ Your fuel consumption will be increased
- ☐ Your engine will overheat
- ☐ Your view ahead will be reduced

Staying back will increase your view of the road ahead. This will help you to see any hazards that might occur and give you more time to react.

2.5 Mark one answer | DES s7, 10, 11, HC r126

What's the minimum time gap you should leave when following a vehicle on a wet road?

- ☐ One second
- ☐ Two seconds
- ☐ Three seconds
- ☐ Four seconds

Water will reduce your tyres' grip on the road. The safe separation gap of at least two seconds in dry conditions should be doubled, to at least four seconds, in wet weather.

2.6 Mark one answer | DES s7, HC r168

You're being overtaken by a long, heavily laden lorry. What should you do if it's taking a long time for it to overtake?

- ☐ Speed up
- ☐ Slow down
- ☐ Hold your speed
- ☐ Change direction

A long lorry with a heavy load will need more time to pass you than a car, especially on an uphill stretch of road. Slow down and allow the lorry to pass.

2.7 Mark one answer | DES s7

Which vehicle will use a blue flashing beacon?

- ☐ Motorway maintenance
- ☐ Bomb disposal
- ☐ Snow plough
- ☐ Breakdown recovery

Emergency vehicles use blue flashing lights. If you see or hear one, move out of its way as soon as it's safe and legal to do so.

2.8 Mark one answer | DES s7, HC r219

What should you do if you're being followed by an ambulance showing flashing blue lights?

- ☐ Pull over as soon as it's safe to do so
- ☐ Accelerate hard to get away from it
- ☐ Maintain your speed and course
- ☐ Brake harshly and stop well out into the road

Pull over in a place where the ambulance can pass safely. Check that there are no bollards or obstructions in the road that will prevent it from passing.

2.9 Mark one answer | DES s7, HC r219

What type of emergency vehicle is fitted with a green flashing beacon?

- ☐ Fire engine
- ☐ Road gritter
- ☐ Ambulance
- ☐ Doctor's car

A green flashing beacon on a vehicle means the driver or passenger is a doctor on an emergency call. Give way to them if it's safe to do so. Be aware that the vehicle may be travelling quickly or may stop in a hurry.

2.10 Mark one answer | DES s7, HC r300, KYTS p31

Who should obey diamond-shaped traffic signs?

- ☐ Tram drivers
- ☐ Bus drivers
- ☐ Lorry drivers
- ☐ Taxi drivers

These signs apply only to tram drivers, but you should know their meaning so that you're aware of the priorities and are able to anticipate the actions of the driver.

2.11 Mark one answer DES s7, HC r306

On a road where trams operate, which vehicles will be most at risk from the tram rails?

- ☐ Cars
- ☐ Cycles
- ☐ Buses
- ☐ Lorries

The narrow wheels of a bicycle can become stuck in the tram rails, causing the cyclist to stop suddenly, wobble or even lose balance altogether. The tramlines are also slippery, which could cause a cyclist to slide or fall off.

2.12 Mark one answer DES s3, 5, 10, HC r112

When should you use your vehicle's horn?

- ☐ To alert others to your presence
- ☐ To allow you right of way
- ☐ To greet other road users
- ☐ To signal your annoyance

You mustn't use your vehicle's horn between 11.30 pm and 7 am in a built-up area or when you're stationary, unless a moving vehicle poses a danger. Its function is to alert other road users to your presence.

2.13 Mark one answer DES s7, 8, HC r143

You're in a one-way street and want to turn right. Where should you position your vehicle when there are two lanes?

- ☐ In the right-hand lane
- ☐ In the left-hand lane
- ☐ In either lane, depending on the traffic
- ☐ Just left of the centre line

When you're in a one-way street and want to turn right, you should take up a position in the right-hand lane. This will allow other road users, not wishing to turn, to pass on the left. Indicate your intention and take up the correct position in good time.

2.14 Mark one answer DES s7, 8, HC r179

You wish to turn right ahead. Why should you take up the correct position in good time?

- ☐ To allow other drivers to pull out in front of you
- ☐ To give a better view into the road that you're joining
- ☐ To help other road users know what you intend to do
- ☐ To allow drivers to pass you on the right

If you wish to turn right into a side road, take up your position in good time. Move to the centre of the road when it's safe to do so. This will allow vehicles to pass you on the left. Early planning will show other traffic what you intend to do.

2.15 **Mark one answer** **DES s7, HC r25, KYTS p124**

Which type of crossing allows cyclists to ride across while pedestrians are also crossing?

- ☐ Toucan
- ☐ Puffin
- ☐ Pelican
- ☐ Zebra

A toucan crossing is designed to allow pedestrians and cyclists to cross at the same time. Look out for cyclists approaching the crossing at speed.

2.16 **Mark one answer** **DES s1, 11, HC r168**

You're travelling at the legal speed limit. What should you do if the vehicle behind approaches quickly, flashing its headlights?

- ☐ Accelerate to make a gap behind you
- ☐ Touch the brakes sharply to show your brake lights
- ☐ Maintain your speed to prevent the vehicle from overtaking
- ☐ Allow the vehicle to overtake

Don't enforce the speed limit by blocking another vehicle's progress. This will only cause frustration. Allow the other vehicle to pass when you can do so safely.

2.17 **Mark one answer** **DES s5, 10, HC r110–111**

When should you flash your headlights at other road users?

- ☐ When showing that you're giving way
- ☐ When showing that you're about to turn
- ☐ When telling them that you have right of way
- ☐ When letting them know that you're there

You should only flash your headlights to warn others of your presence. Don't use them to greet others, show impatience or give priority to other road users, because they could misunderstand your signal.

2.18 **Mark one answer** **DES s8, HC r146**

You're approaching an unmarked crossroads. How should you deal with the junction?

- ☐ Accelerate and keep to the middle
- ☐ Slow down and keep to the right
- ☐ Accelerate and look to the left
- ☐ Slow down and look both ways

Be cautious, especially when your view is restricted by hedges, bushes, walls, large vehicles, etc. In the summer months, these junctions can become more difficult to deal with, because growing foliage may further obscure your view.

2.19 Mark one answer — **DES s7, 10, 11, HC r126**

The conditions are good and dry. When should you use the 'two-second rule'?

- ☐ Before restarting the engine after it has stalled
- ☐ When checking your gap from the vehicle in front
- ☐ Before using the 'Mirrors – Signal – Manoeuvre' routine
- ☐ When traffic lights change to green

In good conditions, the 'two-second rule' can be used to check the distance between your vehicle and the one in front. This technique works on roads carrying faster traffic. Choose a fixed object, such as a bridge, sign or tree. When the vehicle ahead passes this object, say to yourself 'Only a fool breaks the two-second rule.' If you reach the object before you finish saying this, you're too close.

2.20 Mark one answer — **DES s7, HC r199**

Which colour follows the green signal at a puffin crossing?

- ☐ Steady red
- ☐ Flashing amber
- ☐ Steady amber
- ☐ Flashing green

Puffin crossings have infra-red sensors that detect when pedestrians are crossing and hold the red traffic signal until the crossing is clear. The use of a sensor means there's no flashing amber phase as there is with a pelican crossing.

2.21 Mark one answer — **DES s7, 10, 11, HC r126**

You're in a line of traffic. What action should you take if the driver behind is following very closely?

- ☐ Ignore the driver behind and continue to travel within the speed limit
- ☐ Slow down, gradually increasing the gap between you and the vehicle in front
- ☐ Signal left and wave the driver behind to come past
- ☐ Move over to a position just left of the centre line of the road

If the driver behind is following too closely, there's a danger they'll collide with the back of your vehicle if you stop suddenly. You can reduce this risk by slowing down and increasing the safety margin in front of you. This reduces the chance that you'll have to stop suddenly and allows you to spread your braking over a greater distance. This is an example of defensive driving.

2.22 Mark one answer

DES s13, HC r113-115

You're driving on a clear night. Which lights should you use if the national speed limit applies and there's a steady stream of oncoming traffic?

- ☐ Full-beam headlights
- ☐ Sidelights
- ☐ Dipped headlights
- ☐ Fog lights

Use the full-beam headlights only when you can be sure that you won't dazzle other road users.

2.23 Mark one answer

DES s10, HC r221

You're driving behind a large goods vehicle. What should you do if it signals left but steers to the right?

- ☐ Slow down and let the vehicle turn
- ☐ Drive on, keeping to the left
- ☐ Overtake on the right of it
- ☐ Hold your speed and sound your horn

Large, long vehicles need extra room when making turns at junctions. They may move out to the right in order to make a left turn. Keep well back and don't attempt to pass them on their left.

2.24 Mark one answer

DES s10, HC r168

You're driving along this road. What should you do if the red car cuts in close in front of you?

- ☐ Accelerate to get closer to the red car
- ☐ Give a long blast on the horn
- ☐ Drop back to leave the correct separation distance
- ☐ Flash your headlights several times

There are times when other drivers make incorrect or ill-judged decisions. Be tolerant and try not to retaliate or react aggressively. Always consider the safety of other road users, your passengers and yourself.

2.25 Mark one answer — DES s13, HC r114

You're waiting in a traffic queue at night. How can you avoid dazzling drivers behind you?

- ☐ Use the parking brake and release the footbrake
- ☐ Keep your foot on the footbrake
- ☐ Balance the clutch with the accelerator
- ☐ Use the parking brake and footbrake together

In queuing traffic, your brake lights can dazzle drivers behind you. If you apply your parking brake, you can take your foot off the footbrake. This will turn off the brake lights so that they can't dazzle the driver behind you.

2.26 Mark one answer — DES s10, HC r168

You're driving in traffic at the speed limit for the road. What should you do if the driver behind is trying to overtake?

- ☐ Move closer to the car ahead, so the driver behind has no room to overtake
- ☐ Wave the driver behind to overtake when it's safe
- ☐ Keep a steady course and allow the driver behind to overtake
- ☐ Accelerate to get away from the driver behind

Keep a steady course to give the driver behind an opportunity to overtake safely. If necessary, slow down. Reacting incorrectly to another driver's impatience can lead to danger.

2.27 Mark one answer — DES s6, HC r141, KYTS p32

What does it mean if the signs at a bus lane show no times of operation?

- ☐ The lane isn't in operation
- ☐ The lane is only in operation at peak times
- ☐ The lane is in operation 24 hours a day
- ☐ The lane is only in operation in daylight hours

Bus-lane signs show the vehicles allowed to use the lane and its times of operation. Where no times are shown, the bus lane is in operation 24 hours a day.

2.28 Mark one answer — DES s1, 10, HC r214

What should you do when a person herding sheep asks you to stop?

- ☐ Ignore them as they have no authority
- ☐ Stop and switch off your engine
- ☐ Continue on but drive slowly
- ☐ Try to get past quickly

If someone in charge of animals asks you to stop, you should do so and switch off your engine. Animals are unpredictable and startle easily; they could turn and run into your path or into the path of another moving vehicle.

2.29 Mark one answer — DES s10, HC r215

What should you do when you're overtaking a horse and rider?

- ☐ Sound your horn as a warning
- ☐ Go past as quickly as possible
- ☐ Flash your headlights as a warning
- ☐ Go past slowly and carefully

Horses can be startled by the sound of a car engine or the rush of air caused by a vehicle passing too closely. Keep well back and only pass when it's safe. Leave them plenty of room; you may have to use the other side of the road to go past safely.

2.30 Mark one answer — DES s7, HC r195

You're approaching a zebra crossing. What should you do if pedestrians are waiting to cross?

- ☐ Give way to older and infirm people only
- ☐ Slow down and prepare to stop
- ☐ Use your headlights to indicate they can cross
- ☐ Wave at them to cross the road

As you approach a zebra crossing, look for pedestrians waiting to cross. Where you can see them, slow down and prepare to stop. Be especially careful of children and older people, who may have difficulty judging when it's safe to cross.

2.31 Mark one answer — DES s8, HC r147

What should you do if a vehicle pulls out in front of you at a junction?

- ☐ Swerve past it and sound your horn
- ☐ Flash your headlights and drive up close behind
- ☐ Slow down and be ready to stop
- ☐ Accelerate past it immediately

Try to anticipate what other drivers might do. Look and plan ahead so that you're ready to respond safely if a hazard develops. Be tolerant of road users who make mistakes.

2.32 **Mark one answer** **DES s7, HC r199, KYTS p123**

You're approaching a red light at a puffin crossing. Pedestrians are on the crossing. When will the red light change?

- ☐ When you start to edge forward onto the crossing
- ☐ When the pedestrians have cleared the crossing
- ☐ When the pedestrians push the button on the far side of the crossing
- ☐ When a driver from the opposite direction reaches the crossing

A sensor will automatically detect that the pedestrians have reached a safe position. Don't drive on until the green light shows and it's safe for you to do so.

2.33 **Mark one answer** **DES s3**

Which instrument-panel warning light would show that headlights are on main beam?

☐ 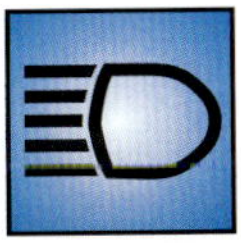

☐ 

☐ 

☐ 

You should be aware of all the warning lights and visual aids on the vehicle you're driving. If you're driving a vehicle for the first time, you should familiarise yourself with all the controls, warning lights and visual aids before you set off.

2.34 **Mark one answer** **DES s7, 10, HC r126**

When should you leave a two-second gap between your vehicle and the one in front?

- ☐ When it's raining
- ☐ When it's dry
- ☐ When it's icy
- ☐ When it's foggy

In good, dry conditions, a driver needs to keep a distance of at least two seconds from the car in front. This should allow enough space for you to stop if the driver in front has to stop suddenly.

2.35 Mark one answer DES s13, HC r113-115

You're driving at night on an unlit road. What should you do if you're following another vehicle?

- ☐ Flash your headlights
- ☐ Use dipped headlights
- ☐ Switch off your headlights
- ☐ Use full-beam headlights

If you follow another vehicle with your headlights on full beam, they could dazzle the driver. Leave a safe distance and make sure that the light from your dipped beam falls short of the vehicle in front.

2.36 Mark one answer DES s10, HC r169

What should you do if you're driving a slow-moving vehicle on a narrow winding road?

- ☐ Keep well out to stop vehicles overtaking dangerously
- ☐ Wave the vehicles behind to come past you if you think they can overtake quickly
- ☐ Pull in when you can, to let the vehicles behind overtake
- ☐ Give a left signal when it's safe for vehicles to overtake you

If you're driving a slow-moving vehicle along a narrow road, try not to hold up faster traffic. If you see vehicles following behind, pull over in a safe place and let the traffic pass before continuing. Don't wave other traffic past – this could be dangerous if you or they haven't noticed a hazard ahead.

2.37 Mark one answer DES s4, HC p130

You're driving a car that has a diesel engine. What can a loose filler cap on your fuel tank cause?

- ☐ It can make the engine difficult to start
- ☐ It can make the roads slippery for other road users
- ☐ It can improve your vehicle's fuel consumption
- ☐ It can increase the level of exhaust emissions

Diesel fuel can spill out if your filler cap isn't secured properly. This is most likely to occur on bends, junctions and roundabouts, where it will make the road slippery, especially if it's wet. At the end of a spell of dry weather, road surfaces may be especially slippery where diesel has been spilled but it hasn't been washed away by rain.

2.38 Mark one answer — DES s14, HC p130

What should you do to avoid fuel spillage?

- ☐ Check that your tank is only three-quarters full
- ☐ Check that you've used a locking filler cap
- ☐ Check that your fuel gauge is working
- ☐ Check that your filler cap is securely fastened

When learning to drive, it's a good idea to practise filling your car with fuel. Ask your instructor if you can use a petrol station and fill the fuel tank yourself. You need to know where the filler cap is on the car you're driving, so you know which side of the pump to park at. Take care not to overfill the tank and make sure you secure the filler cap correctly, so that no fuel leaks onto the road while you're driving.

2.39 Mark one answer — DES s1

What style of driving causes increased risk to everyone?

- ☐ Considerate
- ☐ Defensive
- ☐ Competitive
- ☐ Responsible

Competitive driving increases the risks to everyone and is the opposite of responsible, considerate and defensive driving. Defensive driving is about questioning the actions of other road users and being prepared for the unexpected. Don't be taken by surprise.

Case study practice – 2 Attitude

You're driving in heavy traffic.

It has rained, but now bright sun is causing glare on the wet road.

A car overtakes, then pulls back sharply into the traffic just in front of you.

Further on, there's a roundabout with two lanes on approach. You need to take the first exit, turning left. A large vehicle in front signals left but straddles both lanes.

The traffic is still heavy, and there's a zebra crossing up ahead. People are waiting to cross.

2.1 If affected by the road conditions, how should you react?

Mark **one** answer

- ☐ Slow down and, if necessary, stop
- ☐ Speed up to get out of the sunlight
- ☐ Turn around and go back home
- ☐ Turn on your hazard warning lights

HC r237 DES s12

2.2 What should you do about the overtaking vehicle?

Mark **one** answer

- ☐ Become upset, slow down and use the horn
- ☐ Stay focused, speed up and reduce the gap
- ☐ Remain calm, slow down and increase the gap
- ☐ Feel annoyed, speed up and use the horn

HC r147, 168 DES s1

2.3 How should you be positioned as you approach the roundabout?

Mark **one** answer

- [ ] In the right-hand lane while signalling right
- [ ] In the left-hand lane without signalling
- [ ] In the left-hand lane while signalling left
- [ ] In the right-hand lane without signalling

HC r186 DES s8

2.4 Why is the large vehicle taking this position?

Mark **one** answer

- [ ] The driver isn't sure which way to go
- [ ] The indicators aren't working properly
- [ ] The load being carried is extremely heavy
- [ ] The vehicle needs more room to turn

HC r187, 221 DES s8

2.5 What should you do at the zebra crossing?

Mark **one** answer

- [ ] Stop and then wave the pedestrians across
- [ ] Rev the engine until the pedestrians cross
- [ ] Stop and wait for the pedestrians to cross
- [ ] Inch forward slowly as the pedestrians cross

HC r195 DES s7

Section three

Safety and your vehicle

In this section, you'll learn about

- carrying out basic maintenance on your car
- what to do if your car has a fault
- using your car's safety equipment effectively
- making your car secure
- parking safely
- being aware of the environment
- avoiding congestion.

Safety and your vehicle

Look after your car and it will look after you, not only by being less likely to break down, but also by being more economical and lasting longer. Remember that an efficient engine is kinder to the environment.

Looking after your car

Regular maintenance should ensure that your car is safe and fit to be on the road. It will also help to make sure that your car uses fuel as efficiently as possible and keep its exhaust emissions to a minimum.

Lights, brakes, steering, the exhaust system, seat belts, horn, speedometer, wipers and washers must all be working properly.

HC p128–130 DES s12, 14

Check the following items on a regular basis.

The **windscreen** should be free of cracks and chips.

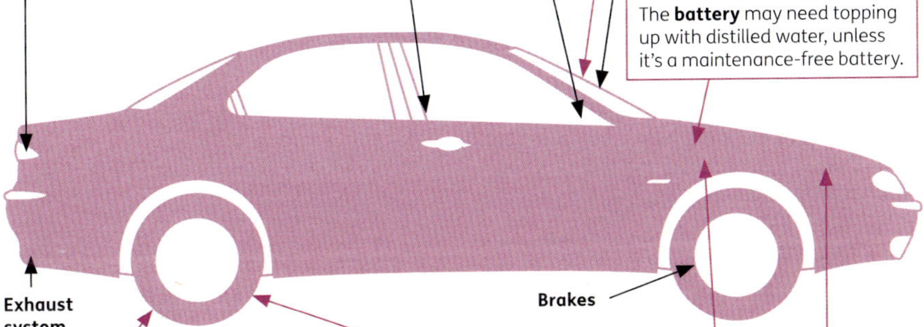

The **battery** may need topping up with distilled water, unless it's a maintenance-free battery.

Tyre condition: see the tyre-tread diagram on the next page. Uneven wear on the tyres can be caused by faults in the braking system, suspension or tracking. If the front wheels are unbalanced, they could make the steering vibrate.

Tyre pressures: check at least once a week, when the tyres are cold. This will ensure that you get an accurate reading. Under-inflated tyres can

- make the steering feel heavy
- increase fuel consumption
- increase your stopping distance.

HC p129 DES s12, 14

Brake fluid: if this is low, air may enter the system and the brakes won't work properly.

Oil and coolant levels: especially important before a long journey (be careful not to overfill with oil as this can cause oil leaks).

DES s14

The tread on car and trailer tyres must be at least 1.6 mm deep across the central three-quarters of the breadth of the tyre and around the entire circumference. It's illegal to drive with tyres that have cuts or defects in the side walls.

HC p129 DES s14

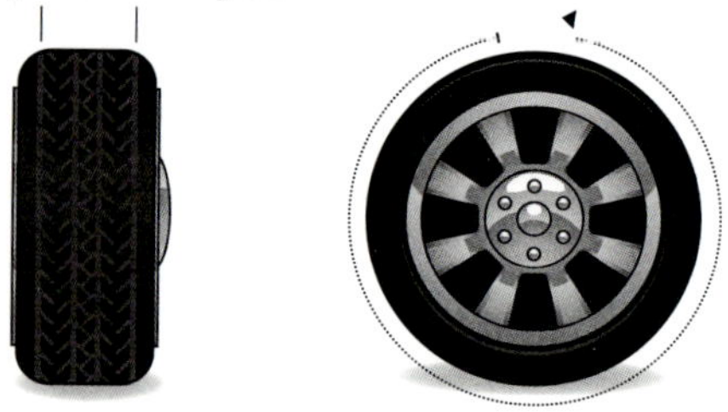

Find out more about tyre safety in this video.

tyresafe.org/tyre-safety/meet-the-mcintyres

Tip

Dry steering is when you turn the steering wheel while the car isn't moving. It can cause unnecessary wear to the tyres and steering mechanism.

DES s3

To check the condition of the shock absorbers, 'bounce' the vehicle. Push down hard over each wheel: there should be no more than one rebound when released.

HC p130 DES s14

Watch the 'Show me, tell me' videos on DVSA's YouTube channel.

youtube.com/dvsagovuk

Here's another useful summary of the maintenance checks you'll need to be able to do for your driving test.

youtube.com/watch?v=jxJERW-hN2I

Dealing with faults

A basic understanding of how your car works will help you recognise when there's a problem with it. It's important that your car is checked regularly by a qualified mechanic, especially the brakes and the steering.

Warning lights on the dashboard tell you about the performance of the engine and warn you of any faults.

- Check your vehicle handbook to make sure that you know what all the warning lights mean.
- Don't ignore a warning; it could affect your safety.

HC p128 DES s3, 14

The anti-lock braking system (ABS) warning light should go out when the car's travelling at 5–10 mph. If this doesn't happen, have the ABS checked by a qualified mechanic.

Tip

'Brake fade' is when the brakes become less effective because of overheating. It may happen if you use them continuously, such as on a long, steep downhill stretch of road. In this situation, use a lower gear to help you control the vehicle's speed.

DES s7

Visit a garage as soon as possible if

- the steering vibrates – you may need to have the **wheels balanced**
- the vehicle pulls to one side when you brake – your brakes may need adjusting.

DES s14

wheel balancing

making sure that the wheels and tyres are balanced to minimise any vibrations in the vehicle

Safety equipment

Modern cars are fitted with equipment designed to keep you as safe as possible, but you need to make sure that you use it correctly for it to be effective.

Seat belts and restraints

Always wear your seat belt and make sure your passengers wear theirs (unless exempt). The driver is responsible for making sure that children under 14 wear a suitable restraint.

HC r99, 100

Self-reflection

Not wearing a seat belt can have serious consequences for you, your passengers and other road users.

Have you ever driven without wearing a seat belt? How would you feel if you injured yourself – or someone else – in a road traffic incident?

Remember, if you're caught without wearing a seat belt you could be fined up to £500.

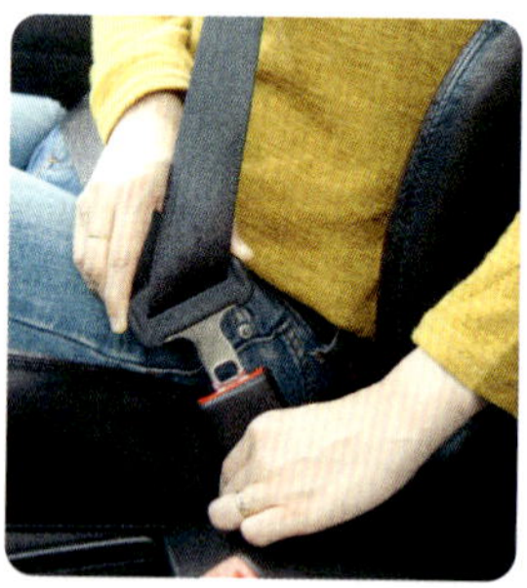

Adults, children aged 12 or over, and children over 1.35 metres (approx 4 feet 5 inches) in height **MUST** wear a seat belt unless exempt.

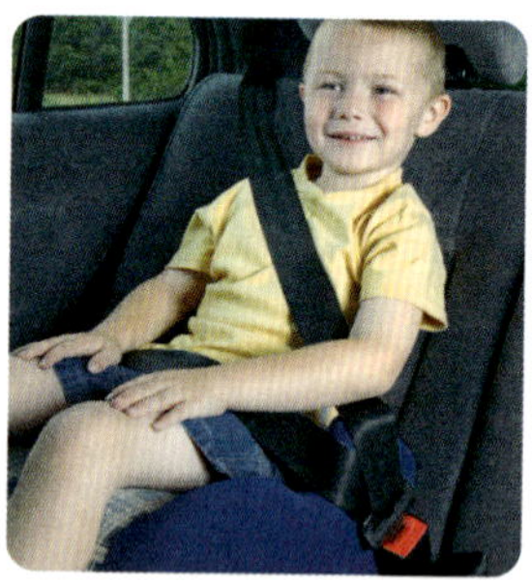

Children aged from 3 to 12 years, or up to 1.35 metres in height, **MUST** use a suitable child restraint. If a suitable child restraint isn't available in the rear seat for children aged 3 to 12, an adult seat belt **MUST** be used.

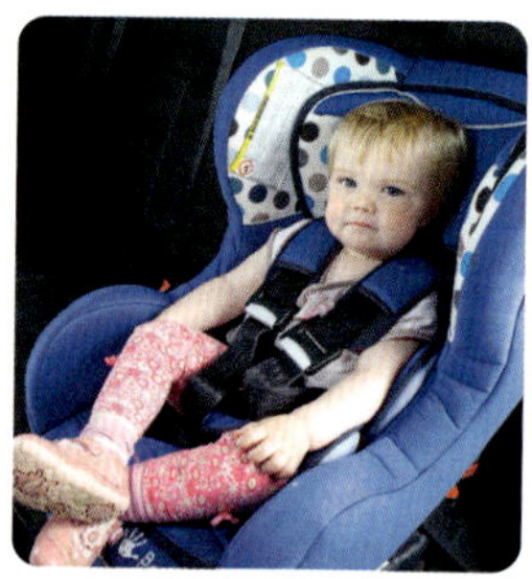

Children under 3 years of age **MUST** use a suitable child seat. Never fit a rear-facing baby seat in a seat protected by an active airbag. The airbag **MUST** be deactivated first.

HC r99–102 DES s2

Safety before you start driving

Make sure that you're safe and comfortable before you begin your journey.

When you get into the car

adjust the seat so that you can reach all the controls comfortably

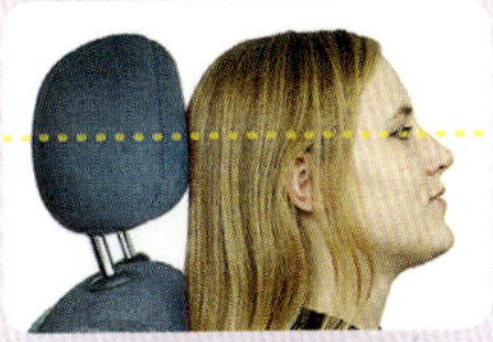

adjust the head restraint to help prevent neck injury in a collision

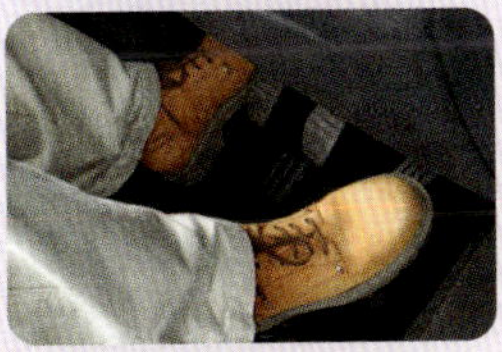

wear suitable shoes so that you can keep control of the pedals

adjust the mirrors so that you can see as clearly as possible all around. Convex mirrors give a wider view but can make vehicles look further away than they are. If you can't see behind you when you're reversing, get someone to guide you.

HC r97 DES s3, 4

See why it's important to adjust the head restraint correctly, and how to do it, in this video.

youtube.com/watch?v=wIYIPuRvwtM

Lights

If you're driving in poor visibility, such as fog or heavy rain, use dipped headlights. It's important for other road users to see you. If there's thick fog, use your fog lights but remember to switch them off when visibility improves.

HC r113–115, 226

When leaving your car on a two-way road at night, park in the direction of the traffic. If the speed limit is more than 30 mph (46 km/h), switch on your parking lights.

DES s12

Hazard warning lights are fitted so that you can warn road users of a hazard ahead, such as

- when you've broken down
- queuing traffic on a dual carriageway or motorway.

Don't use them as an excuse to park illegally, even for a short time.

HC r116, 274, 277–278 DES s3, 11

Security

Although it's impossible to make a car completely secure, the harder you make it for a potential thief to break in and steal your property or your car, the less likely you are to be targeted.

Tip

Always lock away valuable items, or anything that looks valuable, out of sight or take them with you.

Make it as difficult as you can for a thief to either break into your car or steal it.

Use a steering lock.

Remove the car keys and lock your car, even if you're only leaving it for a short time.

Lock any contents, especially valuables, out of sight, or take them with you if you can.

Don't leave the vehicle registration documents in the car; these documents would make it easy for a thief to sell the vehicle.

At night, park in a well-lit area.

HC p131 DES s20

To make it more difficult for an opportunist thief, you can

- fit an anti-theft alarm or immobiliser
- use a visible security device such as a steering lock or handbrake lock
- have the vehicle registration number etched on the windows; this makes it harder for a thief to sell a vehicle.

Stereos and other forms of in-car entertainment are prime targets for thieves. Install a security-coded stereo to deter thieves, or a removable one so you can lock it away or take it with you.

You **MUST NOT** leave your vehicle unattended with the engine running.

HC r123

Always switch off the engine and lock your car before leaving it.

Consider joining a Vehicle Watch scheme if there's one in your area. Contact the crime prevention officer at your local police station to find out more.

Use this link to find out more about thefts from vehicles.

crimestoppers-uk.org/keeping-safe/vehicle-safety

Parking safely

Where you park your car can affect the safety of other road users. Avoid parking where your car would block access or visibility for others, such as

- in front of a property entrance
- at or near a bus stop
- near the brow of a hill, where the limited view of the road ahead makes it difficult to see whether it's safe to pass the obstruction
- at a dropped kerb, as this is a place for wheelchair and mobility scooter users to get onto the road or pavement.

HC r243

You **MUST NOT** stop or park on the zigzag lines at a pedestrian crossing. This would block the view of pedestrians and road users, and endanger people trying to use the crossing.

HC r239–250, 291 DES s9

Being aware of the environment

Most cars burn petrol or diesel, which are both fossil fuels. Burning these fuels causes air pollution and damages the environment, while using up natural resources that can't be replaced.

You can help the environment by driving in a fuel-efficient manner. This will help to improve road safety, reduce exhaust emissions and reduce your fuel consumption, which will save you money.

DES s17

Fuel-efficient driving

Follow these guidelines to make your driving fuel efficient.

Reduce your speed. Vehicles travelling at 70 mph (112 km/h) use about 15% more fuel than those travelling at 50 mph (80 km/h).

Plan well ahead so that you can drive smoothly. Avoiding rapid acceleration and heavy braking can cut your fuel bill by up to 15%.

Change up as soon as you can so that you use the highest possible gear without making the engine struggle. Keeping the engine revs down uses less fuel.

Have your vehicle regularly serviced and tuned properly.

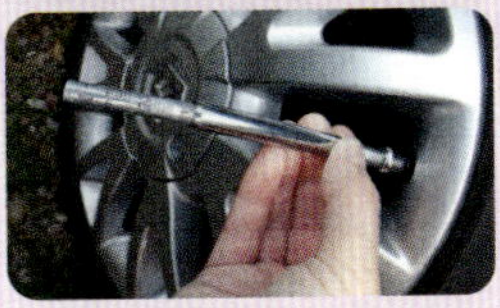

Make sure your tyres are correctly inflated.

DES s17

Avoid

- carrying unnecessary loads or leaving an empty roof rack on your car
- over-revving the engine in lower gears
- leaving the engine running unnecessarily – if your vehicle is stationary and likely to remain so for more than a few seconds, switch off the engine to reduce emissions and noise pollution.

HC r123 DES s17

Try not to use your car to make a lot of short journeys; consider walking or cycling instead. Using public transport or sharing a car can reduce the volume of traffic and vehicle emissions.

DES s17

Tip

In an automatic car, 'kick-down' is a mechanism that gives quick acceleration when needed; for example, to overtake. Excessive use of this will burn more fuel.

DES s22

Keeping your car in good condition

Having your car serviced regularly will keep its fuel consumption and exhaust emissions down. If your vehicle is over three years old (over four years old in Northern Ireland), it will have to pass an emissions test as part of the MOT test.

DES s17

The amount of vehicle tax you'll need to pay depends on the amount of carbon dioxide emitted by your car. Use this website to calculate vehicle tax rates.

www.gov.uk

If you service your own vehicle, dispose of old engine oil and batteries responsibly. Take them to a local-authority site or a garage. Don't pour oil down the drain.

Tip

Make sure your fuel filler cap is securely fastened. If it's loose, it could spill fuel, which wastes both fuel and money. Spilt diesel fuel makes the road slippery for other road users.

HC p130 DES s14

Noise pollution

Don't make excessive noise with your vehicle. In built-up areas, you **MUST NOT** use your car horn between 11.30 pm and 7.00 am unless another vehicle poses a danger.

HC r112 DES s3

Avoiding congestion

Sometimes it's impossible to avoid road congestion, but if you can it will make driving less stressful for you.

Always try to

- plan your route before starting out
- avoid driving at times when roads will be busy, if possible
- allow plenty of time for your journey, especially if you have an appointment to keep or a connection to make.

DES s18

Plan your route by

- looking at a map
- using satellite navigation equipment
- checking for roadworks or major events with a motoring organisation
- using a route planner on the internet.

Tip

In some towns and cities you may see red lines on the side of the road, which indicate 'Red Routes'. They help the traffic flow by restricting stopping on these routes.

HC p115 DES s6

If you're travelling on a new or unfamiliar route, it's a good idea to print out or write down the directions, and also to plan an alternative route in case your original route is blocked.

If you can avoid travelling at busy times, you'll

- be less likely to be delayed
- help to ease congestion for those who have to travel at these times.

In some areas, you may have to pay a congestion charge to use congested road space. In London, you may also have to pay the Ultra Low Emission Zone (ULEZ) and/or Low Emission Zone (LEZ) charges.

DES s18

Residents living within the London charging zone obtain a reduced rate but aren't exempt.

Find out more about congestion and emission zone charging in London using the Transport for London (TfL) website.

tfl.gov.uk/modes/driving/congestion-charge

tfl.gov.uk/modes/driving/low-emission-zone

tfl.gov.uk/modes/driving/ultra-low-emission-zone

Meeting the standards

You must be able to

check that all lights and reflectors are

- legal
- clean
- in good working order

make sure that all tyres (including any spare)

- are at the right pressure
- have enough tread depth

get to know the vehicle if it's the first time you've driven it

carry out pre-start checks on

- doors
- parking brake
- seat
- steering
- seat belt
- mirrors.

You must know and understand

that these must be kept clean at all times

- lights
- indicators
- reflectors
- number plates

how to check that tyres

- are correctly fitted
- are correctly inflated
- have enough tread depth
- are legal to use

how to check what sort of fuel your vehicle uses.

Notes

You can use this page to make your own notes or diagrams about the key points you need to remember.

Think about

- What maintenance does your car need each week, month and year?
- What should you do if a warning light appears on your dashboard while you're driving?
- Which security features does your car have? How could you improve your car's security?
- Are there more efficient alternative forms of transport available for your journey?
- How can you find out about local traffic congestion? (For example, local radio stations, websites and mobile phone apps.)

Your notes

Things to discuss and practise with your instructor

These are just a few examples of what you could discuss and practise with your instructor. Read more about safety and your vehicle to come up with your own ideas.

Discuss with your instructor

- the importance of the state of your tyres; for example, on safety, fuel consumption, vehicle handling, etc
- what the seat belt requirements are for different age groups and who's responsible for them
- how to keep your car and belongings safe while parked.

Practise with your instructor

- driving through built-up areas to get used to different methods of traffic calming
- parking in safe areas, both in daylight and at night
- planning your journey. Do this with your lesson route and see how you can avoid busy times and places. Prepare an alternative route as well.

3.1 **Mark one answer** **DES s14, HC p129**

How would under-inflated tyres affect your vehicle?

- ☐ The vehicle's stopping distance would increase
- ☐ The flash rate of the vehicle's indicators would increase
- ☐ The vehicle's gear change mechanism would become stiff
- ☐ The vehicle's headlights would aim high

Your tyres are your only contact with the road. To prevent problems with braking and steering, keep your tyres free from defects; they must have sufficient tread depth and be correctly inflated. Correct tyre pressures help reduce the risk of skidding and provide a safer and more comfortable drive or ride.

3.2 **Mark one answer** **DES s3, HC r112**

When are you not allowed to sound your vehicle's horn?

- ☐ Between 10.00 pm and 6.00 am in a built-up area
- ☐ At any time in a built-up area
- ☐ Between 11.30 pm and 7.00 am in a built-up area
- ☐ Between 11.30 pm and 6.00 am on any road

Every effort must be made to prevent excessive noise, especially in built-up areas at night. Don't rev your engine or sound the horn unnecessarily. It's illegal to sound your horn in a built-up area between 11.30 pm and 7.00 am, except when another road user poses a danger.

3.3 **Mark one answer** **DES s17**

What makes the vehicle in the picture 'environmentally friendly'?

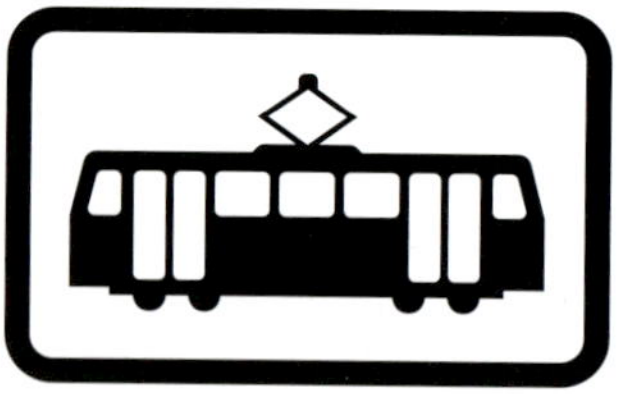

- ☐ It's powered by gravity
- ☐ It's powered by diesel
- ☐ It's powered by electricity
- ☐ It's powered by unleaded petrol

Trams are powered by electricity and therefore don't emit exhaust fumes. They ease traffic congestion by offering drivers an alternative to using their car, particularly in busy cities and towns.

3.4 **Mark one answer** **DES s18, HC p115**

Why have 'red routes' been introduced in major cities?

- ☐ To raise the speed limits
- ☐ To help the traffic flow
- ☐ To provide better parking
- ☐ To allow lorries to load more freely

Inconsiderate parking can obstruct the flow of traffic and so make traffic congestion worse. Red routes are designed to prevent this by enforcing strict parking restrictions. Driving slowly in traffic increases fuel consumption and causes a build-up of exhaust fumes.

3.5 **Mark one answer** **DES s6, HC r153**

What's the purpose of road humps, chicanes and narrowings?

- ☐ To separate lanes of traffic
- ☐ To increase traffic speed
- ☐ To allow pedestrians to cross
- ☐ To reduce traffic speed

Traffic-calming measures help to keep vehicle speeds low in congested areas where there are pedestrians and children. A pedestrian is much more likely to survive a collision with a vehicle travelling at 20 mph than they are with a vehicle travelling at 40 mph.

3.6 **Mark one answer** **DES s17**

What's the purpose of a catalytic converter?

- ☐ To reduce fuel consumption
- ☐ To reduce the risk of fire
- ☐ To reduce harmful exhaust gases
- ☐ To reduce engine wear

Catalytic converters reduce a large percentage of harmful exhaust emissions. They work more efficiently when the engine has reached its normal working temperature.

3.7 **Mark one answer** **DES s14, HC p129**

When should tyre pressures be checked?

- ☐ After any lengthy journey
- ☐ After travelling at high speed
- ☐ When tyres are hot
- ☐ When tyres are cold

Check the tyre pressures when the tyres are cold. This will give you a more accurate reading. The heat generated on a long journey will raise the pressure inside the tyre.

3.8 Mark one answer DES s17

When will your vehicle use more fuel?

- ☐ When its tyres are under-inflated
- ☐ When its tyres are of different makes
- ☐ When its tyres are over-inflated
- ☐ When its tyres are new

Check your tyre pressures frequently – normally once a week. If they're lower than those recommended by the manufacturer, there will be more 'rolling resistance'. The engine will have to work harder to overcome this, leading to increased fuel consumption.

3.9 Mark one answer DES s17

How should you dispose of a used vehicle battery?

- ☐ Bury it in your garden
- ☐ Put it in the dustbin
- ☐ Take it to a local-authority disposal site
- ☐ Leave it on waste land

Batteries contain acid, which is hazardous, and they must be disposed of safely. This means taking them to an appropriate disposal site.

3.10 Mark one answer DES s17

What's most likely to increase fuel consumption?

- ☐ Poor steering control
- ☐ Accelerating around bends
- ☐ Staying in high gears
- ☐ Harsh braking and accelerating

Accelerating and braking gently and smoothly will help to save fuel and reduce wear on your vehicle. This makes it better for the environment too.

3.11 Mark one answer DES s14

The fluid level in your battery is low. What fluid should you use to top it up?

- ☐ Battery acid
- ☐ Distilled water
- ☐ Engine oil
- ☐ Engine coolant

Some modern batteries are maintenance free. Check your vehicle handbook and, if necessary, make sure that the plates in each battery cell are covered with fluid.

3.12 Mark one answer — DES s13, HC r249

You're parked on the road at night. When must you use parking lights?

- ☐ When there are continuous white lines in the middle of the road
- ☐ When the speed limit exceeds 30 mph
- ☐ When you're facing oncoming traffic
- ☐ When you're near a bus stop

When parking at night, park in the direction of the traffic. This will enable other road users to see the reflectors on the rear of your vehicle. Use your parking lights if the speed limit is over 30 mph.

3.13 Mark one answer — DES s17

How can you reduce the environmental harm caused by your motor vehicle?

- ☐ Only use it for short journeys
- ☐ Don't service it
- ☐ Drive faster than normal
- ☐ Keep engine revs low

Engines that burn fossil fuels produce exhaust emissions that are harmful to health. The harder you make the engine work, the more emissions it will produce. Engines also use more fuel and produce higher levels of emissions when they're cold. Anything you can do to reduce your use of fossil fuels will help the environment.

3.14 Mark one answer — DES s14, HC p129

What can cause excessive or uneven tyre wear?

- ☐ A faulty gearbox
- ☐ A faulty braking system
- ☐ A faulty electrical system
- ☐ A faulty exhaust system

If you see that parts of the tread on your tyres are wearing before others, it may indicate a brake, suspension or wheel-alignment fault. Regular servicing will help to detect faults at an early stage and this will avoid the risk of minor faults becoming serious or even dangerous.

3.15 Mark one answer — DES s14

You need to top up your battery with distilled water. What level should you fill it to?

- ☐ The top of the battery
- ☐ Halfway up the battery
- ☐ Just below the cell plates
- ☐ Just above the cell plates

Top up the battery with distilled water and make sure each cell plate is covered.

3.16 Mark one answer — DES s18

Why is it a good idea to plan your journey to avoid busy times?

- ☐ You'll have an easier journey
- ☐ You'll have a more stressful journey
- ☐ Your journey time will be longer
- ☐ It will cause more traffic congestion

No-one likes to spend time in traffic queues. Try to avoid busy times related to school or work travel.

3.17 Mark one answer — DES s18

How will your journey be affected by travelling outside the busy times of day?

- ☐ Your journey will use more fuel
- ☐ Your journey will take longer
- ☐ Your journey will be more hazardous
- ☐ Your journey will have fewer delays

If possible, avoid the early morning, late afternoon and early evening 'rush hour'. Doing this should allow you to have a better journey, with fewer delays. This should help you to arrive at your destination feeling less stressed.

3.18 Mark one answer — DES s18

You plan your route before starting a journey. Why should you also plan an alternative route?

- ☐ Your original route may be blocked
- ☐ Your maps may have different scales
- ☐ You may find you have to pay a congestion charge
- ☐ You may get held up by a tractor

It can be frustrating and worrying to find your planned route is blocked by roadworks or diversions. If you've planned an alternative, you'll feel less stressed and more able to concentrate fully on your driving or riding. If your original route is mostly on motorways, it's a good idea to plan an alternative using non-motorway roads. Always carry a map with you just in case you need to refer to it.

3.19 Mark one answer — DES s18

You have to arrive on time for an appointment. How should you plan for the journey?

- ☐ Allow plenty of time for the trip
- ☐ Plan to travel at busy times
- ☐ Avoid roads with the national speed limit
- ☐ Prevent other drivers from overtaking

Always allow plenty of time for your journey in case of unforeseen problems. Anything can happen; for example, punctures, breakdowns, road closures, diversions and delays. You'll feel less stressed and less inclined to take risks if you aren't 'pushed for time'.

3.20 Mark one answer — DES s17

What can you expect if you drive using rapid acceleration and heavy braking?

- ☐ Reduced pollution
- ☐ Increased fuel consumption
- ☐ Reduced exhaust emissions
- ☐ Increased road safety

Using the controls smoothly can reduce fuel consumption by about 15%, as well as reducing wear and tear on your vehicle. Plan ahead and anticipate changes of speed well in advance. This will reduce the need to accelerate rapidly or brake sharply.

3.21 Mark one answer — HC p130

What could cause you to crash if the level is allowed to get too low?

- ☐ Anti-freeze level
- ☐ Brake-fluid level
- ☐ Battery-water level
- ☐ Radiator-coolant level

You should carry out frequent checks on all fluid levels but particularly brake fluid. As the brake pads or shoes wear down, the brake-fluid level will drop. If it drops below the minimum mark on the fluid reservoir, air could enter the hydraulic system and lead to a loss of braking efficiency or even complete brake failure.

3.22 Mark one answer — DES s14

What should you do if your anti-lock brakes (ABS) warning light stays on?

- ☐ Check the brake-fluid level
- ☐ Check the footbrake free play
- ☐ Check that the parking brake is released
- ☐ Have the brakes checked immediately

Consult the vehicle handbook or a garage before driving the vehicle any further. Only drive to a garage if it's safe to do so. If you aren't sure, get expert help.

3.23 **Mark one answer** **DES s3, HC p128**

What does it mean if this light comes on while you're driving?

- ☐ A fault in the braking system
- ☐ The engine oil is low
- ☐ A rear light has failed
- ☐ Your seat belt isn't fastened

If this light comes on, you should have the brake system checked immediately. A faulty braking system could have dangerous consequences.

3.24 **Mark one answer** **DES s1, HC r97**

Why is it important to wear suitable shoes when you're driving?

- ☐ To prevent wear on the pedals
- ☐ To maintain control of the pedals
- ☐ To enable you to adjust your seat
- ☐ To enable you to walk for assistance if you break down

When you're going to drive, make sure that you're wearing suitable clothing.

Comfortable shoes will ensure that you have proper control of the foot pedals.

3.25 **Mark one answer** **DES s3, HC r97**

If you're involved in a collision, what will reduce the risk of neck injury?

- ☐ An air-sprung seat
- ☐ Anti-lock brakes
- ☐ A collapsible steering wheel
- ☐ A properly adjusted head restraint

If you're involved in a collision, head restraints will reduce the risk of neck injury. They must be properly adjusted. Make sure they aren't positioned too low: in a crash, this could cause damage to the neck.

3.26 Mark one answer DES s14, HC p130

What does it mean if your vehicle keeps bouncing after you sharply press down and release on the bodywork over a wheel?

- ☐ The tyres are worn
- ☐ The tyres are under inflated
- ☐ The vehicle is on soft ground
- ☐ The shock absorbers are worn

If you find that your vehicle bounces as you drive around a corner or bend in the road, the shock absorbers might be worn. To test your shock absorbers, sharply press down and release above each wheel. If the vehicle continues to bounce, take it to be checked by a qualified mechanic.

3.27 Mark one answer DES s17

How will a roof rack affect your car?

- ☐ There will be less wind noise
- ☐ The engine will use more oil
- ☐ The car will accelerate faster
- ☐ Fuel consumption will increase

A roof rack increases your car's wind resistance. This will cause an increase in fuel consumption, so you should remove it when it isn't being used. An aerodynamically designed roof rack or box will help reduce wind resistance to a minimum, but the rack or box should still be removed when it isn't in use.

3.28 Mark one answer DES s14, HC r89, p129

What makes your tyres illegal?

- ☐ If they were bought second-hand
- ☐ If they have any large, deep cuts in the side wall
- ☐ If they're of different makes
- ☐ If they have different tread patterns

Your tyres may be of different treads and makes. They can even be second-hand, as long as they're in good condition. They must, however, be intact, without cuts or tears. When checking the side walls for cuts and bulges, don't forget to check the side of the tyre that's hidden from view, under the car.

3.29 Mark one answer DES s14, HC p129

What's the legal minimum depth of tread for car tyres?

- ☐ 1 mm
- ☐ 1.6 mm
- ☐ 2.5 mm
- ☐ 4 mm

Car tyres must have sufficient depth of tread to give them a good grip on the road surface. The legal minimum for cars is 1.6 mm. This depth should be across the central three-quarters of the breadth of the tyre and around the entire circumference.

3.30 Mark one answer DES s2, HC r100

You're carrying two 13-year-old children and their parents in your car. Who's responsible for seeing that the children wear seat belts?

- ☐ The children's parents
- ☐ You, the driver
- ☐ The front-seat passenger
- ☐ The children

Seat belts save lives and reduce the risk of injury. If you're carrying passengers under 14 years old, it's your responsibility as the driver to ensure that their seat belts are fastened or they're seated in an approved child restraint.

3.31 Mark one answer DES s17

How can drivers help the environment?

- ☐ By accelerating harshly
- ☐ By accelerating gently
- ☐ By using leaded fuel
- ☐ By driving faster

Rapid acceleration and heavy braking lead to increased

- fuel consumption
- wear on your vehicle.

Having your vehicle serviced regularly will maintain its efficiency, produce cleaner emissions and reduce the risk of a breakdown.

3.32 Mark one answer DES s17

How can you avoid wasting fuel?

- ☐ By having your vehicle serviced regularly
- ☐ By revving the engine in the lower gears
- ☐ By keeping an empty roof rack on your vehicle
- ☐ By driving at higher speeds where possible

If you don't have your vehicle serviced regularly, the engine will gradually become less efficient. This will cause increased fuel consumption and, in turn, an increase in the amount of harmful emissions it produces.

3.33 Mark one answer DES s17

What could you do to reduce the volume of traffic on the roads?

- ☐ Drive in a bus lane
- ☐ Use a car with a smaller engine
- ☐ Walk or cycle on short journeys
- ☐ Travel by car at all times

Try not to use your car as a matter of routine. For shorter journeys, consider walking or cycling instead – this is much better for both you and the environment.

3.34 Mark one answer — DES s17

What's most likely to waste fuel?

- ☐ Reducing your speed
- ☐ Driving on motorways
- ☐ Using different brands of fuel
- ☐ Under-inflated tyres

Wasting fuel costs you money and also causes unnecessary pollution. Ensuring your tyres are correctly inflated, avoiding carrying unnecessary weight and removing a roof rack that's not in use will all help to reduce your fuel consumption.

3.35 Mark one answer — DES s2, HC r89, p128

What part of the car does the law require you to keep in good condition?

- ☐ The gearbox
- ☐ The transmission
- ☐ The door locks
- ☐ The seat belts

Unless exempt, you and your passengers must wear a seat belt (or suitable child restraint). The seat belts in your car must be in good condition and working properly; they'll be checked during its MOT test.

3.36 Mark one answer — DES s17

How much more fuel will you use by driving at 70 mph, compared with driving at 50 mph?

- ☐ About 10%
- ☐ About 30%
- ☐ About 75%
- ☐ About 100%

Your vehicle will use less fuel if you avoid heavy acceleration. The higher the engine revs, the more fuel you'll use. Using the same gear, and covering the same distance, a vehicle travelling at 70 mph will use about 30% more fuel than it would at 50 mph. However, don't travel so slowly that you inconvenience or endanger other road users.

3.37 Mark one answer — DES s14

What should you do if your vehicle pulls to one side when you use the brakes?

- ☐ Increase the pressure in your tyres
- ☐ Have the brakes checked as soon as possible
- ☐ Change gear and pump the brake pedal
- ☐ Use your parking brake at the same time

The brakes on your vehicle must be effective and properly adjusted. If your vehicle pulls to one side when braking, take it to be checked by a qualified mechanic as soon as you can.

3.38	Mark one answer	DES s14

What will happen if your car's wheels are unbalanced?

- ☐ The steering will pull to one side
- ☐ The steering will vibrate
- ☐ The brakes will fail
- ☐ The tyres will deflate

If your wheels are out of balance, it will cause the steering to vibrate at certain speeds. This isn't a fault that will put itself right, so take your vehicle to a garage or tyre fitter to have the wheels rebalanced.

3.39	Mark one answer	DES s3

What can be damaged if you turn the steering wheel when the car isn't moving?

- ☐ The gearbox
- ☐ The engine
- ☐ The brakes
- ☐ The tyres

Turning the steering wheel when the car isn't moving is known as dry steering. It can cause unnecessary wear to the tyres and steering mechanism.

3.40	Mark one answer	DES s20, HC p131

What's the safest thing to do if you have to leave valuables in your car?

- ☐ Put them in a carrier bag
- ☐ Park near a school entrance
- ☐ Lock them out of sight
- ☐ Park near a bus stop

If you have to leave valuables in your car, lock them out of sight. This is the best way to deter an opportunist thief.

3.41	Mark one answer	DES s20, HC p131

What may help to deter a thief from stealing your car?

- ☐ Always keeping the headlights on
- ☐ Fitting reflective glass windows
- ☐ Always keeping the interior light on
- ☐ Etching the registration number on the windows

Having your car registration number etched on all your windows is a cheap and effective way to deter professional car thieves.

3.42 **Mark one answer** **DES s20, HC p131**

What should you remove from your car before leaving it unattended?

- ☐ The car dealer's details
- ☐ The owner's manual
- ☐ The service record
- ☐ The vehicle registration document

Never leave the vehicle registration document inside your car. This document would help a thief to dispose of your car more easily.

3.43 **Mark one answer** **DES s20, HC p131**

What should you do when leaving your vehicle parked and unattended?

- ☐ Park near a busy junction
- ☐ Park in a housing estate
- ☐ Lock it and remove the key
- ☐ Leave the left indicator on

An unlocked car is an open invitation to thieves. Leaving the keys in the ignition not only makes your car easy to steal but could also invalidate your insurance.

3.44 **Mark one answer** **DES s1, 17**

What will reduce fuel consumption?

- ☐ Driving more slowly
- ☐ Accelerating rapidly
- ☐ Late and heavy braking
- ☐ Staying in lower gears

Harsh braking, frequent gear changes and harsh acceleration increase fuel consumption. A car uses less fuel when travelling at a constant low speed in an appropriate high gear.

You need to look well ahead so you're able to anticipate hazards early. Easing off the accelerator and timing your approach at junctions, for example, can reduce the fuel consumption of your vehicle.

3.45 **Mark one answer** **DES s17**

You service your own vehicle. How should you dispose of the old engine oil?

- ☐ Take it to a local-authority site
- ☐ Pour it down a drain
- ☐ Tip it into a hole in the ground
- ☐ Put it in your dustbin

It's illegal to pour engine oil down any drain. Oil is a pollutant and harmful to wildlife. Dispose of it safely at an authorised site.

3.46 Mark one answer DES s17

Why do MOT tests include an exhaust emission test?

- ☐ To recover the cost of expensive garage equipment
- ☐ To help protect the environment against pollution
- ☐ To discover which fuel supplier is used the most
- ☐ To make sure diesel and petrol engines emit the same fumes

Emission tests are carried out to make sure your vehicle's engine is operating efficiently. This ensures the pollution produced by the engine is kept to a minimum. If your vehicle isn't serviced regularly, it may fail the MOT emissions test.

3.47 Mark one answer DES s17

How can you reduce the damage your vehicle causes to the environment?

- ☐ Use narrow side streets
- ☐ Brake heavily
- ☐ Use busy routes
- ☐ Anticipate well ahead

By looking well ahead and recognising hazards in good time, you can avoid late and heavy braking. Watch the traffic flow and look well ahead for potential hazards so you can control your speed in good time. Avoid over-revving the engine and accelerating harshly, as this increases wear to the engine and uses more fuel.

3.48 Mark one answer DES s14

How will you benefit from following the manufacturer's service schedule for your vehicle?

- ☐ Your vehicle will be cheaper to insure
- ☐ Your vehicle tax will be lower
- ☐ Your vehicle will remain reliable
- ☐ Your journey times will be reduced

All vehicles need to be serviced to keep working efficiently. An efficient engine uses less fuel and produces fewer harmful emissions than an engine that's running inefficiently. Keeping the vehicle serviced to the manufacturer's schedule should also keep it reliable and reduce the chance of it breaking down.

3.49 Mark one answer DES s6, HC r153

How should you drive when you're driving along a road that has road humps?

- ☐ Maintain a reduced speed throughout
- ☐ Accelerate quickly between the humps
- ☐ Always keep to the maximum legal speed
- ☐ Drive slowly at school times only

Road humps are there for a reason – to protect vulnerable road users by reducing the speed of traffic. Don't accelerate harshly between the humps. Put the safety of others first and maintain a reduced speed throughout the zone.

3.50 Mark one answer DES s14

When should you check the engine oil level?

- ☐ Before a long journey
- ☐ When the engine is hot
- ☐ Early in the morning
- ☐ Every time you drive the car

An engine can use more oil during long journeys than on shorter trips. Insufficient engine oil is potentially dangerous: it can lead to excessive wear, mechanical breakdown and expensive repairs.

Most cars have a dipstick to allow the oil level to be checked. If not, you should refer to the vehicle handbook.

3.51 Mark one answer HC r191, 240

You're having difficulty finding a parking space in a busy town. Can you park on the zigzag lines of a zebra crossing?

- ☐ No, not unless you stay with your car
- ☐ Yes, in order to drop off a passenger
- ☐ Yes, if you don't block people from crossing
- ☐ No, not under any circumstances

It's an offence to park on the zigzag lines of a zebra crossing. You'll be causing an obstruction by obscuring the view of both pedestrians and drivers.

3.52 Mark one answer
DES s20, HC r239, p131

What should you do when you leave your car unattended for a few minutes?

- ☐ Leave the engine running
- ☐ Switch the engine off but leave the key in
- ☐ Lock it and remove the key
- ☐ Park near a traffic warden

Always switch off the engine, remove the key and lock your car, even if you're only leaving it for a few minutes.

3.53 Mark one answer
DES s20, HC r239

Why should you try and park in a secure car park?

- ☐ It makes it easy to find your car
- ☐ It helps deter thieves
- ☐ It stops the car being exposed to bad weather
- ☐ It doesn't cost anything to park here

Whenever possible, leave your car in a secure car park. This will help deter thieves.

3.54 Mark one answer
DES s9, HC r243

Where would parking your vehicle cause an obstruction?

- ☐ Alongside a parking meter
- ☐ In front of a property entrance
- ☐ On your driveway
- ☐ In a marked parking space

Don't park your vehicle where it may obstruct access to a business or property. Think carefully before you slow down and stop. Look at road markings and signs to ensure that you aren't parking illegally.

3.55 Mark one answer
DES s3, HC r97

What's the most important reason for having a properly adjusted head restraint?

- ☐ To make you more comfortable
- ☐ To help you avoid neck injury
- ☐ To help you relax
- ☐ To help you maintain your driving position

In a collision, rapid deceleration will violently throw vehicle occupants forward and then backwards as the vehicle stops. Seat belts and airbags protect occupants against the forward movement. Head restraints should be adjusted so they give maximum protection to the head and neck during the backward movement.

3.56 **Mark one answer** **DES s17**

What can you do to reduce environmental damage caused by your vehicle?

- ☐ Avoid using the cruise control
- ☐ Use the air conditioning whenever you drive
- ☐ Use the gears to slow the vehicle
- ☐ Avoid making a lot of short journeys

Avoid using your car for short journeys. On a short journey, the engine is unlikely to warm up fully and will therefore be running less efficiently. This will result in the car using more fuel and emitting higher levels of harmful emissions.

3.57 **Mark one answer** **DES s17**

What can people who live or work in towns and cities do to help reduce urban pollution levels?

- ☐ Drive more quickly
- ☐ Over-rev in a low gear
- ☐ Walk or cycle
- ☐ Drive short journeys

Using a vehicle for short journeys means the engine doesn't have time to reach its normal operating temperature. When an engine is running below its normal operating temperature, it produces increased amounts of pollution. Walking and cycling don't create pollution and have health benefits as well.

3.58 **Mark one answer** **DES s20, HC p131**

How can you reduce the chances of your car being broken into when leaving it unattended?

- ☐ Take all valuables with you
- ☐ Park near a taxi rank
- ☐ Place any valuables on the floor
- ☐ Park near a fire station

When leaving your car, take all valuables with you if you can. Otherwise, lock them out of sight.

3.59 **Mark one answer** **DES s20**

How can you help to prevent your car radio being stolen?

- ☐ Park in an unlit area
- ☐ Leave the radio turned on
- ☐ Park near a busy junction
- ☐ Install a security-coded radio

A security-coded radio can deter thieves, as it's likely to be of little use when removed from the vehicle.

3.60 **Mark one answer** **DES s20**

How can you reduce the risk of your vehicle being broken into at night?

- ☐ Leave it in a well-lit area
- ☐ Park in a quiet side road
- ☐ Don't engage the steering lock
- ☐ Park in a poorly lit area

Having your vehicle broken into or stolen can be very distressing and inconvenient. Avoid leaving your vehicle unattended in poorly lit areas.

3.61 **Mark one answer** **DES s20**

What will help you to keep your car secure?

- ☐ Being a member of a vehicle breakdown organisation
- ☐ Registering with a Vehicle Watch scheme
- ☐ Passing an advanced driving test
- ☐ Taking car maintenance classes

The Vehicle Watch scheme helps to reduce the risk of your car being stolen. By displaying high-visibility Vehicle Watch stickers in your car, you're inviting the police to stop your vehicle if it's seen in use between midnight and 5 am.

3.62 **Mark one answer** **DES s14, 17**

On a vehicle, where would you find a catalytic converter?

- ☐ In the fuel tank
- ☐ In the air filter
- ☐ On the cooling system
- ☐ On the exhaust system

Although carbon dioxide is still produced, a catalytic converter fitted to the exhaust system reduces the toxic and polluting gases by up to 90%.

3.63 **Mark one answer** **DES s17**

What can you achieve if you drive smoothly?

- ☐ Reduction in journey times by about 15%
- ☐ Increase in fuel consumption by about 15%
- ☐ Reduction in fuel consumption by about 15%
- ☐ Increase in journey times by about 15%

By driving smoothly, you'll not only save about 15% of your fuel but will also reduce the amount of wear and tear on your vehicle and the level of pollution it produces. You're also likely to feel more relaxed and have a more pleasant journey.

3.64 Mark one answer — DES s17

Which driving technique can help you save fuel?

- ☐ Using lower gears as often as possible
- ☐ Accelerating sharply in each gear
- ☐ Using each gear in turn
- ☐ Missing out some gears

Missing out intermediate gears, when appropriate, helps to reduce the amount of time spent accelerating and decelerating – the times when your vehicle uses the most fuel.

3.65 Mark one answer — DES s17

How can driving in a fuel-efficient manner help protect the environment?

- ☐ Through the legal enforcement of speed regulations
- ☐ By increasing the number of cars on the road
- ☐ Through increased fuel bills
- ☐ By reducing exhaust emissions

Fuel-efficient driving is all about looking and planning further ahead. This helps raise your hazard awareness and reduces the need for late and heavy braking. This will make your journeys more comfortable, as well as considerably reducing your fuel bills and reducing emissions that can damage the environment.

3.66 Mark one answer — DES s17

What does fuel-efficient driving achieve?

- ☐ Increased fuel consumption
- ☐ Improved road safety
- ☐ Damage to the environment
- ☐ Increased exhaust emissions

The emphasis is on hazard awareness and planning ahead. By looking well ahead, you'll have plenty of time to deal with hazards safely and won't need to brake sharply. This will also reduce damage to the environment.

3.67 Mark one answer — DES s14, HC p129

What's the legal minimum tread depth for tyres on your trailer or caravan?

- ☐ 1 mm
- ☐ 1.6 mm
- ☐ 2 mm
- ☐ 2.6 mm

Trailers and caravans may be left in storage over the winter months, and tyres can deteriorate. It's important to check their tread depth and also their pressures and general condition. The legal tread depth of 1.6 mm applies to the central three-quarters of a tyre's breadth, over its entire circumference.

3.68 **Mark one answer** **DES s17**

When is fuel consumption at its highest?

- ☐ When you're braking
- ☐ When you're coasting
- ☐ When you're accelerating
- ☐ When you're turning sharply

Accelerating uses a lot of fuel, so always try to use the accelerator smoothly. Taking your foot off the accelerator allows the momentum of the car to take you forward, especially when going downhill. This can save a considerable amount of fuel without any loss of control over the vehicle.

3.69 **Mark one answer** **DES s2, HC r99**

When may a passenger travel in a car without wearing a seat belt?

- ☐ When they're under 14 years old
- ☐ When they're under 1.5 metres (5 feet) in height
- ☐ When they're sitting in the rear seat
- ☐ When they're exempt for medical reasons

If you have adult passengers, it's their responsibility to wear a seat belt, but you should still remind them to use one as they get in the car. It's your responsibility to make sure that all children in your car are secured with an appropriate restraint. Exemptions are allowed for those with a medical exemption certificate.

3.70 **Mark one answer** **DES s2, HC r100**

You're driving a friend's children home from school. They're both under 14 years old. Who's responsible for making sure they wear a seat belt or approved child restraint where required?

- ☐ An adult passenger
- ☐ The children
- ☐ You, the driver
- ☐ Your friend

Passengers should always be secured and safe. Children should be encouraged to fasten their seat belts or approved restraints themselves from an early age, so that it becomes a matter of routine. As the driver, you must check that they're fastened securely. It's your responsibility.

3.71 **Mark one answer** **DES s14**

What's likely to happen if you put too much oil in your engine?

- ☐ The clutch pedal will lock
- ☐ The air intake will become blocked
- ☐ The timing belt will slip
- ☐ The oil seals will leak

Too much oil will lead to increased pressure in the engine. This could damage oil seals and lead to oil leaks. Any excess oil should be drained off.

3.72 **Mark one answer** **DES s2, HC r99**

You have to make an unexpected journey. You're carrying a five-year-old child on the back seat of your car. They're under 1.35 metres (4 feet 5 inches) tall. How should you seat them if a correct child restraint isn't available?

- ☐ Behind the passenger seat
- ☐ Using an adult seat belt
- ☐ Sharing a belt with an adult
- ☐ Between two other children

In journeys of unexpected necessity, and when a correct child restraint isn't available, the child must sit on the rear seat and use an adult seat belt. In a collision, unrestrained objects and people can cause serious injury or even death.

3.73 **Mark one answer** **DES s2, HC r99**

You're carrying an 11-year-old child on the front seat of your car. They're under 1.35 metres (4 feet 5 inches) tall. What seat belt security must be in place?

- ☐ They must use an adult seat belt
- ☐ They must be able to fasten their own seat belt
- ☐ They must use a suitable child restraint
- ☐ They must be able to see clearly out of the front window

As the driver, it's your responsibility to make sure that children are secure and safe in your vehicle. Make yourself familiar with the rules. When children are carried on the back seat, there are a few very exceptional cases when an adult seat belt can be used instead of a correct child restraint.

3.74 Mark one answer DES s17, HC r123

You're stopped at the side of the road. What must you do if you'll be waiting there for some time?

- ☐ Switch off the engine
- ☐ Apply the steering lock
- ☐ Switch off the radio
- ☐ Use your headlights

If your vehicle is stationary and is likely to remain so for some time, you must switch off the engine unless you're stationary in traffic or diagnosing a fault.

3.75 Mark one answer DES s2, HC r101

You want to put a rear-facing baby seat on the front passenger seat. What must you do if the passenger seat is protected by a frontal airbag?

- ☐ Deactivate the airbag
- ☐ Turn the seat to face sideways
- ☐ Ask a passenger to hold the baby
- ☐ Put the child in an adult seat belt

It's illegal to fit a rear-facing baby seat into a passenger seat protected by an active frontal airbag. If the airbag activates, it could cause serious injury or even death to the child. You must secure it in a different seat or deactivate the relevant airbag. Follow the manufacturer's advice when fitting a baby seat.

3.76 **Mark one answer** **DES s17, HC r123**

You're leaving your vehicle parked on a road and unattended. When may you leave the engine running?

- ☐ If you'll be parking for less than five minutes
- ☐ If the battery keeps going flat
- ☐ When parked in a 20 mph zone
- ☐ Never if you're away from the vehicle

When you leave your vehicle parked on a road, switch off the engine and secure the vehicle. Make sure no valuables are visible, shut all the windows, lock the vehicle, and set the alarm if the vehicle has one.

3.77 **Mark one answer** **DES s5**

What does it mean if the electronic stability control (ESC) indicator lamp lights up while you're driving?

- ☐ The ESC system has activated
- ☐ The ESC system has a fault
- ☐ The ESC system is running a routine test
- ☐ The ESC system is switched off

ESC is a computer-controlled technology that detects reduced traction and automatically makes corrective adjustments to prevent loss of control. The ESC lamp comes on to alert the driver that the system has activated and the car is approaching its handling limits. It's a powerful driver aid but it can't save a car once its traction limits have been exceeded.

Case study practice – 3
Safety and your vehicle

You drive through the city centre, choosing to travel outside the rush hour.

In the city, there are double red lines along the roadside.

Later, you reach a major junction. The traffic lights aren't working but there are very few vehicles on the road.

At work, you have to park on the roadside. When parking, your steering feels a little heavy.

You pick up your laptop to take to work and lock the car. You leave your camera on the back seat.

3.1 What effect could your choice of travel time have on your journey?

Mark **one** answer

- ☐ Increased delays
- ☐ Reduced mileage
- ☐ Higher traffic volume
- ☐ Reduced travel time

DES s1, 18

3.2 What do the red lines mean?

Mark **one** answer

- ☐ No stopping at peak time
- ☐ No stopping at lunch time
- ☐ No stopping at any time
- ☐ No stopping at night time

HC r240, 247, p115 DES s18

3.3 What should you do at the traffic lights?

Mark **one** answer

- ☐ Stop and wait for the signals to start working again
- ☐ Proceed with care, as with an unmarked junction
- ☐ Continue on and assume you have right of way
- ☐ Drive across the junction as quickly as possible

HC r176

3.4 What could be affecting your steering?

Mark **one** answer

- ☐ Tyres that are over-inflated
- ☐ Tyres that are low on tread
- ☐ Tyres that are under-inflated
- ☐ Tyres that are non-matching

HC p129 DES s7

3.5 What should you do with your camera?

Mark **one** answer

- ☐ Leave it lying on the back seat
- ☐ Put it in a bag on the front seat
- ☐ Lock it away securely out of sight
- ☐ Cover it up with a thick blanket

HC p131 DES s20

Section four

Safety margins

In this section, you'll learn about

- keeping yourself and others safe by staying within safety margins
- stopping, thinking and braking distances
- risks caused by different weather conditions and road surfaces
- the risk of skidding
- contraflow systems.

Safety margins

Self-reflection

Your personal safety margin is the space you maintain around your vehicle. Think about your personal safety margin the next time you drive. Are you getting too close to other vehicles?

It's essential that you always keep in mind your safety, and that of your passengers and other road users, as you're driving.

You can reduce your chances of being involved in an incident on the road by knowing the safety margins and what can happen if you don't drive within them. Never take risks.

Keep control of your car by using the correct procedures. For instance, when you're travelling on a long downhill stretch of road, control your speed by selecting a lower gear and using your brakes carefully. Excessive braking on hills can cause your brakes to overheat and become less effective.

HC r160 DES s5, 7

Don't 'coast' – this means travelling in neutral or with the clutch disengaged (pressed down) – as this can reduce your control over the car.

HC r122

Stopping distance

Leave enough room between your vehicle and the one in front so that you can pull up safely if it slows down or stops suddenly.

Your overall stopping distance is the distance your car travels from the moment that you realise you must brake to the moment your car stops.

HC r126 DES s7

Thinking distance (distance travelled in the time it takes to react to a situation) + **Braking distance** (distance travelled from when you start to use the brakes to when your car completely stops) = **Stopping distance**

Typical stopping distances

Look at the typical stopping, thinking and braking distances given in *The Official Highway Code*. Remember that these are based on vehicles travelling

- with good tyres and brakes
- on a dry road
- in good conditions.

HC r126 DES s7

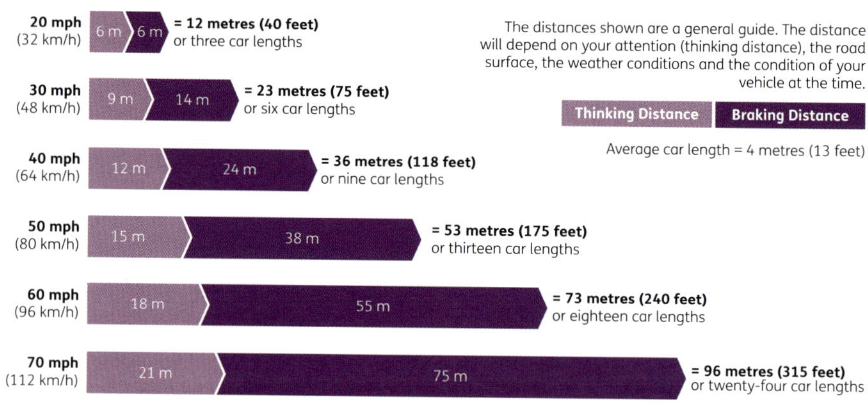

Watch the 'How fast can you stop?' video at this link.

youtu.be/JUd1vBee9SY

Don't just learn the stopping distance figures: you need to be able to judge the distance when you're driving.

HC r126 DES s12

Tip

In good conditions, leave a two-second gap between your car and the vehicle in front. Use a fixed point, like a road sign, to measure the time gap between your vehicle and the one in front. You can measure two seconds by saying the sentence 'Only a fool breaks the two-second rule.'

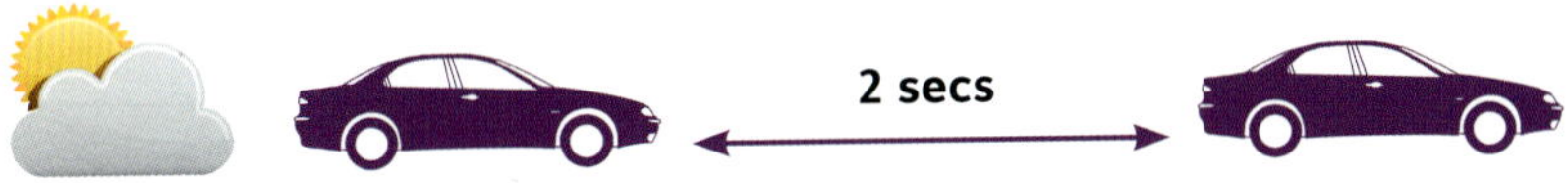

In good, dry conditions, leave a two-second gap.

In other conditions, you need to increase this distance.

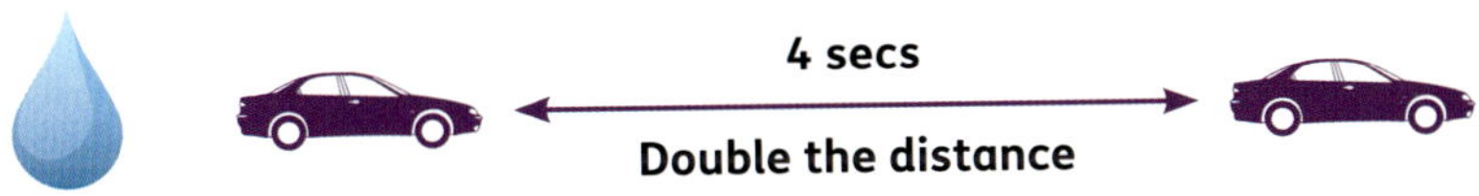

In wet weather, leave a four-second gap.

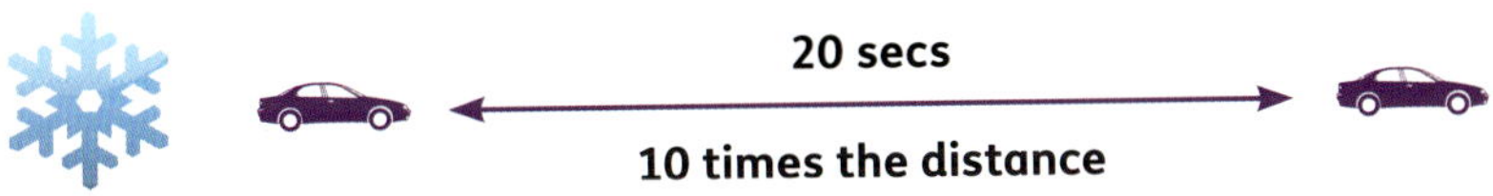

In icy weather, leave a 20-second gap.

Keeping a safe distance from the vehicle in front will help to lower your risk of having a collision. If someone overtakes you and pulls into the gap in front, drop back to keep a safe distance from them.

HC r126 DES s12

Weather conditions

Weather conditions have a major effect on your safety margins. If there's bad weather, such as snow, ice or thick fog, think about whether you really need to make your journey. Never underestimate the dangers.

HC r228–231

Find more information about winter driving at this website.

metoffice.gov.uk/barometer/advice/travel-advice

Weather	Actions to take
Heavy rain 	When there's heavy rainfall, water can collect on the road surface and may cause aquaplaning. This is where the tyres lift off the road surface and skate on a film of water. The steering becomes light. If this happens • ease off the accelerator • don't brake until your steering feels normal again. **HC r131, 227 DES s5, 7** If you've driven through deep water, such as a ford or a flood, test your brakes. You may need to dry them out by pressing lightly on the brake pedal as you drive. **HC r121 DES s5, 7**
Freezing 	Freezing conditions can make roads very slippery, which will make your car harder to control. Before starting a journey, clear ice and snow from your windows, lights, mirrors and number plates. **DES s7** When driving • keep your speed down • brake gently and in plenty of time • be prepared to stop and clean snow from your windscreen by hand if the wipers can't keep it clear. **HC r228–231**

Weather	Actions to take
Hot and/or bright 	Hot weather can also be dangerous. The road surface can become soft. This could affect your braking and steering. Bright sunlight can dazzle. Other drivers might not be able to see your indicators flashing. Give an arm signal if you think it will be helpful. **HC r237 DES s12**
Fog 	Fog reduces your visibility. Remember to • allow more time for your journey • slow down, because you can't see as far ahead as usual • increase the gap between your vehicle and the one in front of you • use dipped headlights, even in daylight. If visibility falls below 100 metres (328 feet), use fog lights if you've got them. You **MUST** switch them off when the fog lifts. **HC r234–236 DES s12**
Wind 	High wind can blow you off course, especially on an open stretch of road. It has an even greater effect on • high-sided vehicles • vehicles towing trailers or caravans • motorcyclists • cyclists. Take care and allow extra room if you pass these road users, as they may be blown off course by a sudden gust of wind. Check your left side as you pass them. **HC r232–233 DES s12**

Skidding

Skidding is when the tyres lose grip on the road, and it's caused by the driver. Road surface and tyre conditions can increase the risk of skidding, but skids are the result of how the driver controls acceleration, braking, speed and steering.

There's a greater risk of skidding in wet or icy conditions. Black ice can be a hazard in very cold weather and it isn't obvious until you feel the steering becoming light.

HC r119, 231 DES s5, 12

To reduce the risk of skidding in slippery conditions, drive

- at a low speed
- in the highest gear you can use effectively.

Drivers of vehicles equipped with anti-skid technology (see page 126) should check the vehicle handbook for the manufacturer's advice on getting the best out of its anti-skid system.

To reduce the risk of skidding, scan the road ahead for clues such as road signs and markings. You can then plan your driving so that you can

- slow down gradually before you reach a hazard, such as a bend
- avoid sudden steering movements.

HC r119, 231 DES s5

Anti-lock braking systems

An anti-lock braking system (ABS) is designed to prevent skidding caused by excessive braking. Wheel speed sensors anticipate when a wheel is about to lock, which could lead to skidding.

If you have to brake suddenly when you're driving a vehicle with ABS

- press the footbrake quickly and firmly
- don't release the brake pedal until your vehicle has stopped.

HC r120 DES s5, 12

ABS doesn't necessarily reduce your stopping distance, but you can keep steering while braking because the wheels are prevented from locking. It may not work as well if there's

- surface water, such as when there's been heavy rainfall
- a loose road surface, such as gravel.

Tip

ABS will help prevent skidding caused by braking too hard for the conditions; it won't reduce your car's stopping distance.

Anti-skid technology

Electronic stability control (ESC) is a computer-controlled system that combines the functions of ABS and traction control. It detects loss of traction and automatically makes corrective adjustments to prevent loss of control. When the system operates, the driver may be unaware of how close the car is to its handling limits. To alert the driver, the ESC indicator lamp will flash on when the ESC operates.

ESC can't overcome the laws of physics; if the driver is travelling too fast, there's a risk of losing control.

ESC is fitted to all new cars sold in the EU, but some manufacturers give it a different name; for example, Electronic Stability Programme (ESP®).

Contraflow systems

contraflow system
where one or more lanes have a direction of traffic against that of the rest of the carriageway

When you enter a **contraflow system**, you should

- reduce your speed in good time
- choose a suitable lane in good time: look for signs advising you to use a particular lane if you want to take an exit that will be coming up soon, or if you have a wide vehicle
- keep a safe distance behind the vehicle in front.

HC r290 DES s11

Meeting the standards

You must be able to
keep a safe distance from the vehicle in front
use the accelerator and brakes correctly to • regulate your speed • bring the vehicle to a stop safely
always use a safe, systematic approach to keep you and other road users safe. For example, mirrors, signal, manoeuvre, position, speed, look.

You must know and understand
the importance of keeping a safe separation distance in all weather and traffic conditions
about skidding • why a skid may occur • how to avoid skids • how to correct them if they do occur
the distance that a vehicle needs to stop • from different speeds • in different road conditions • in different weather conditions
how traffic and weather conditions may affect other road users and what to do. For example, their visibility may be reduced.

Notes

You can use this page to make your own notes or diagrams about the key points you need to remember.

Think about

- What are typical stopping distances and how do wet or icy roads affect them?
- What extra considerations or precautions might you need to take if the weather is
  - snowy or icy
  - wet
  - foggy
  - hot
  - bright and dazzling
  - windy?
- Does the car you're driving have ABS? How can you reduce the risk of skidding and what should you do if you start to skid?
- Picture yourself entering a contraflow system. What actions can you take to reduce risk?

Your notes

Things to discuss and practise with your instructor

These are just a few examples of what you could discuss and practise with your instructor. Read more about safety margins to come up with your own ideas.

Discuss with your instructor

- the causes of skidding and how to avoid it
- how to use your brakes and gears in snowy and icy weather
- stopping distances on dry, wet and icy roads.

Practise with your instructor

- driving in different weather conditions to practise vehicle handling
- driving up and down steep hills to practise your gear selection and control of the brakes
- driving through a ford to see how it will affect your brakes.

4.1 — Mark one answer — DES s12, RES s11, HC r230

How much can stopping distances increase in icy conditions?

- ☐ Two times
- ☐ Three times
- ☐ Five times
- ☐ Ten times

Tyre grip is greatly reduced in icy conditions. For this reason, you need to allow up to ten times the stopping distance you would allow on dry roads.

4.2 — Mark one answer — DES s12, RES s12, HC r232–233

What requires extra care when you're driving or riding in windy conditions?

- ☐ Using the brakes
- ☐ Moving off on a hill
- ☐ Turning into a narrow road
- ☐ Passing pedal cyclists

Always give cyclists plenty of room when overtaking them. You need to give them even more room when it's windy. A sudden gust could easily blow them off course and into your path.

4.3 — Mark one answer — DES s7, RES s9, HC r160

Why should you keep well to the left as you approach a right-hand bend?

- ☐ To improve your view of the road
- ☐ To overcome the effect of the road's slope
- ☐ To let faster traffic from behind overtake
- ☐ To be positioned safely if you skid

Keeping to the left as you approach right-hand bends will give you an earlier view around the bend and enable you to see any hazards sooner. It also reduces the risk of collision with any oncoming vehicle that may have drifted over the centre line while taking the bend.

4.4 **Mark one answer** **DES s12, RES s12, HC r121**

You've just gone through flood water. What should you do to make sure your brakes are working properly?

- ☐ Accelerate and keep to a high speed for a short time
- ☐ Go slowly while gently applying the brakes
- ☐ Avoid using the brakes at all for a few miles
- ☐ Stop for at least an hour to allow them time to dry

Water on the brakes will act as a lubricant, causing them to work less efficiently. Using the brakes lightly as you go along will quickly dry them out.

4.5 **Mark one answer** **DES s12, RES s12, HC r237**

What will be affected if the road surface becomes soft in very hot weather?

- ☐ The suspension
- ☐ The exhaust emissions
- ☐ The fuel consumption
- ☐ The tyre grip

If the road surface becomes very hot, it can soften. Tyres are unable to grip a soft surface as well as they can a firm dry one. Take care when cornering and braking.

4.6 **Mark one answer** **DES s12, HC r232**

Where is your vehicle most likely to be affected by side winds?

- ☐ On a narrow country lane
- ☐ On an open stretch of road
- ☐ On a busy stretch of road
- ☐ On a long, straight road

In windy conditions, care must be taken on exposed roads. A strong gust of wind can blow you off course. Watch out for other road users who are particularly likely to be affected, such as cyclists, motorcyclists, high-sided lorries and vehicles towing trailers.

4.7 **Mark one answer** **DES s10, HC r126**

You're following a vehicle on a wet road. You stay a safe distance behind it. What should you do if a driver overtakes you and pulls into the gap you've left?

- ☐ Flash your headlights as a warning
- ☐ Try to overtake safely as soon as you can
- ☐ Drop back to regain a safe distance
- ☐ Stay close to the other vehicle until it moves on

Wet weather will affect the time it takes for you to stop and can affect your control. Your speed should allow you to stop safely and in good time. If another vehicle pulls into the gap you've allowed, ease back until you've regained your stopping distance.

4.8 Mark one answer — DES s12, HC r233

What should you do when you're overtaking a motorcyclist on a windy day?

- ☐ Pass closely
- ☐ Pass very slowly
- ☐ Pass widely
- ☐ Pass immediately

In strong winds, riders of two-wheeled vehicles are particularly vulnerable. When you overtake them, allow plenty of room. Check to the left as you pass to make sure they're safe.

4.9 Mark one answer — DES s11, HC r126

You're travelling on the motorway. How can you lower the risk of a collision when the vehicle behind is following too closely?

- ☐ Increase your distance from the vehicle in front
- ☐ Brake sharply
- ☐ Switch on your hazard warning lights
- ☐ Move onto the hard shoulder and stop

On busy roads, traffic may still travel at high speeds. Don't follow the vehicle in front too closely. If a driver behind seems to be 'pushing' you, gradually increase your distance from the vehicle in front by slowing down gently. This will give you more space in front if you have to brake, and will reduce the risk of a collision involving several vehicles.

4.10 Mark one answer — DES s12, HC r235

You're following other vehicles in fog. You have your headlights on dipped beam. What else can you do to reduce the chances of being in a collision?

- ☐ Keep close to the vehicle in front
- ☐ Use main beam instead of dipped headlights
- ☐ Keep up with the faster vehicles
- ☐ Keep a safe distance from the vehicle in front

When it's foggy, use your headlights on dipped beam. This will help you see and be seen by other road users. If visibility is seriously reduced, consider using front and rear fog lights if you have them. Keep to a sensible speed and don't follow the vehicle in front too closely. If the road is wet and slippery, you'll need to allow twice the normal stopping distance.

4.11 **Mark one answer** **DES s11, HC r290**

What should you do when you're using a contraflow system?

- ☐ Choose an appropriate lane in good time
- ☐ Switch lanes to make better progress
- ☐ Increase speed to get through the contraflow more quickly
- ☐ Follow other motorists closely to avoid long queues

In a contraflow system, you'll be travelling close to oncoming traffic and sometimes in narrow lanes. You should get into the correct lane in good time, obey any temporary speed-limit signs and keep a safe separation distance from the vehicle ahead.

4.12 **Mark one answer** **DES s5, 12, HC r231**

How can you avoid wheelspin when you're driving on an icy road?

- ☐ Drive at a slow speed in the highest gear possible
- ☐ Use the parking brake if the wheels start to slip
- ☐ Brake gently and repeatedly
- ☐ Drive in a low gear at all times

If you're travelling on an icy road, extra caution will be required to avoid loss of control. Keeping your speed down and using the highest gear possible will reduce the risk of the tyres losing their grip on this slippery surface.

4.13 **Mark one answer** **DES s5, HC r119**

What's the main cause of skidding?

- ☐ The weather
- ☐ The driver
- ☐ The vehicle
- ☐ The road

Skidding is usually caused by driver error. You should always adjust your driving to take account of the road and weather conditions.

4.14 **Mark one answer** **DES s12, HC r231**

You're driving in freezing conditions. What should you do as you approach a sharp bend?

- ☐ Coast into the bend
- ☐ Apply your parking brake
- ☐ Firmly use your footbrake
- ☐ Slow down gently

Harsh use of the accelerator, brakes or steering is likely to lead to skidding, especially on slippery surfaces. Avoid steering and braking at the same time. In icy conditions, it's very important that you constantly assess what's ahead so that you can take appropriate action in plenty of time.

4.15 **Mark one answer** **DES s12, HC p128**

You're about to start a journey in freezing weather. What part of your vehicle should you clear of ice and snow?

- ☐ The aerial
- ☐ The windows
- ☐ The bumper
- ☐ The boot

Driving in bad weather increases your risk of having a collision. If you absolutely have to travel, clear your lights, mirrors, number plates and windows of any snow or ice, so that you can see and be seen.

4.16 **Mark one answer** **DES s12, HC r231**

What will help you to move off on a snowy surface?

- ☐ Using the car's lowest gear
- ☐ Using a higher gear than normal
- ☐ Using a high engine speed
- ☐ Using the parking brake and footbrake together

If you attempt to move off in a low gear, there'll be more torque (turning force) at the driven wheels than if you use a higher gear. More torque makes it easier for the tyres to lose grip and so spin the wheels.

4.17 **Mark one answer** **DES s12, HC r230**

What should you do when you're driving in snowy conditions?

- ☐ Brake firmly and quickly
- ☐ Be ready to steer sharply
- ☐ Use sidelights only
- ☐ Brake gently in plenty of time

In snowy conditions, be careful with the steering, accelerator and brakes. Braking sharply while you're driving on snow is likely to make your car skid.

4.18 **Mark one answer** **DES s22**

What's the main benefit of driving a four-wheel-drive vehicle?

- ☐ Improved grip on the road
- ☐ Lower fuel consumption
- ☐ Shorter stopping distances
- ☐ Improved passenger comfort

By driving all four wheels, the vehicle has maximum grip on the road. This grip is especially helpful when travelling on slippery or uneven surfaces. However, having four-wheel drive doesn't replace the skills you need to drive safely.

4.19 Mark one answer — DES s5, 7, HC r160

You're about to go down a steep hill. What should you do to control the speed of your vehicle?

- ☐ Select a high gear and use the brakes carefully
- ☐ Select a high gear and use the brakes firmly
- ☐ Select a low gear and use the brakes carefully
- ☐ Select a low gear and avoid using the brakes

When driving down a steep hill, gravity will cause your vehicle to speed up. This will make it more difficult for you to stop. To help keep your vehicle's speed under control, select a lower gear to give you more engine braking and make careful use of the brakes.

4.20 Mark one answer — DES s9, HC r252

What should you do when you park a car facing downhill?

- ☐ Turn the steering wheel towards the kerb
- ☐ Park close to the bumper of another car
- ☐ Park with two wheels on the kerb
- ☐ Turn the steering wheel away from the kerb

Turning the wheels towards the kerb will allow them to act as a chock, preventing any forward movement of the vehicle. It will also help to leave your car in gear, or select 'Park' if you have an automatic.

4.21 Mark one answer — DES s6, HC r153

You're driving in a built-up area that has traffic-calming measures. What should you do when you approach a road hump?

- ☐ Move across to the left-hand side of the road
- ☐ Wait for any pedestrians to cross
- ☐ Check your mirror and slow down
- ☐ Stop and check both pavements

Many towns have road humps as part of traffic-calming measures, designed to slow down traffic. Reduce your speed when driving over them. If you go too fast, you could lose control or damage your car. Look out for pedestrians or cyclists while you're driving in these areas.

4.22 Mark one answer DES s5

On what type of road surface may anti-lock brakes be ineffective?

- ☐ Dry
- ☐ Loose
- ☐ Firm
- ☐ Smooth

Poor contact with the road surface could cause one or more of the tyres to lose grip on the road. This is more likely to happen when braking in poor weather conditions and when the road has a loose, slippery or uneven surface.

4.23 Mark one answer DES s5, HC r120

You're driving a vehicle that has anti-lock brakes. How should you apply the footbrake when you need to stop in an emergency?

- ☐ Slowly and gently
- ☐ Slowly but firmly
- ☐ Rapidly and gently
- ☐ Rapidly and firmly

You may have to stop in an emergency due to a misjudgement by another driver or a hazard arising suddenly, such as a child running out into the road. If your vehicle has anti-lock brakes, you should apply the brakes immediately and keep them firmly applied until you stop.

4.24 Mark one answer DES s12, HC r121

You're driving along a country road. You see this sign. What should you do after dealing safely with the hazard?

- ☐ Check your tyre pressures
- ☐ Switch on your hazard warning lights
- ☐ Accelerate briskly
- ☐ Test your brakes

If your brakes have been thoroughly soaked, you should check that they're working properly before you build up speed again. Before you do this, remember to check your mirrors and consider what's behind you.

4.25 **Mark one answer** **DES s12, HC r231**

What would suggest you're driving on an icy road?

- ☐ There's less wind noise
- ☐ There's less tyre noise
- ☐ There's less transmission noise
- ☐ There's less engine noise

Drive extremely carefully when the roads are icy. When travelling on ice, tyres make virtually no noise and the steering feels light and unresponsive.

In icy conditions, be very gentle when braking, accelerating and steering.

4.26 **Mark one answer** **DES s12, HC r227**

You're driving along a wet road. How can you tell if your vehicle's tyres are losing their grip on the surface?

- ☐ The engine will stall
- ☐ The steering will feel very heavy
- ☐ The engine noise will increase
- ☐ The steering will feel very light

If you drive at speed in very wet conditions, your steering may suddenly feel lighter than usual. This means that the tyres have lifted off the surface of the road and are floating on the surface of the water. This is known as aquaplaning. Reduce speed but don't brake until your steering returns to normal.

4.27 **Mark one answer** **DES s12, HC r126**

In which conditions will your overall stopping distance increase?

- ☐ In the rain
- ☐ In fog
- ☐ At night
- ☐ In strong winds

Extra care should be taken in wet weather. On wet roads, your stopping distance could be double that in dry conditions.

4.28 **Mark one answer** **DES s7, HC r126**

You're driving on an open road in dry weather. What distance should you keep from the vehicle in front?

- ☐ A two-second time gap
- ☐ One car length
- ☐ Two metres (6 feet 6 inches)
- ☐ Two car lengths

One way of checking there's a safe distance between you and the vehicle in front is to use the two-second rule. To check for a two-second time gap, choose a stationary object ahead, such as a bridge or road sign. When the car in front passes the object, say 'Only a fool breaks the two-second rule'. If you reach the object before you finish saying the phrase, you're too close and need to increase the gap.

4.29 Mark one answer DES s7, HC r122, 160

How can you use your vehicle's engine as a brake?

- ☐ By changing to a lower gear
- ☐ By selecting reverse gear
- ☐ By changing to a higher gear
- ☐ By selecting neutral gear

When driving on downhill stretches of road, selecting a lower gear gives increased engine braking. This will prevent excessive use of the brakes, which become less effective if they overheat.

4.30 Mark one answer DES s5, HC r120

How should you use anti-lock brakes when you need to stop in an emergency?

- ☐ Keep pumping the footbrake to prevent skidding
- ☐ Brake normally but grip the steering wheel tightly
- ☐ Brake promptly and firmly until you've stopped
- ☐ Apply the parking brake to reduce the stopping distance

If you have ABS and need to stop in an emergency, keep your foot firmly on the brake pedal until the vehicle has stopped. When the ABS operates, you may hear a grating sound and feel vibration through the brake pedal. This is normal and you should maintain pressure on the brake pedal until the vehicle stops.

4.31 Mark one answer DES s12, HC r227

What lights should you use when you're driving on a wet motorway and vehicles are throwing up surface spray?

- ☐ Hazard warning lights
- ☐ Dipped headlights
- ☐ Rear fog lights
- ☐ Sidelights

When surface spray reduces visibility, switch on your headlights on dipped beam. This will help other road users to see you.

4.32 **Mark one answer** **DES s5, HC r122**

What can result when you travel for long distances in neutral (known as coasting)?

- ☐ Improvement in control
- ☐ Easier steering
- ☐ Reduction in control
- ☐ Increased fuel consumption

Coasting is the term used when the clutch is held down, or the gear lever is in neutral, and the vehicle is allowed to freewheel. This reduces the driver's control of the vehicle. When you coast, the engine can't drive the wheels to stabilise you through a corner, or give the assistance of engine braking to help slow the car.

4.33 **Mark one answer** **DES s12, HC r226, 235**

What should you do before starting a journey in foggy weather?

- ☐ Wear a hi-visibility jacket
- ☐ Have a caffeinated drink
- ☐ Allow more time
- ☐ Reduce your tyre pressures

Don't venture out if your journey isn't necessary. If you have to travel and someone is expecting you at the other end, let them know that you'll be taking longer than usual for your journey. This will stop them worrying if you don't turn up on time and will also take the pressure off you, so you don't feel you have to rush.

Case study practice – 4 Safety margins

You have a short but essential journey to make.

It's early morning and the roads are icy in places. It's very cold and snow is falling.

Your tyres are making almost no sound. On turning left, the back of your vehicle slides a little to the right.

Further on, there's a slow-moving vehicle spreading salt on the road.

4.1 What should you do in such weather conditions?

Mark **one** answer

- ☐ Allow more time
- ☐ Fill your fuel tank
- ☐ Put down your sun visor
- ☐ Reduce your tyre pressure

HC r228 DES s12

4.2 How should you brake under the conditions described?

Mark **one** answer

- ☐ Quickly and heavily
- ☐ Gently and quickly
- ☐ Slowly and heavily
- ☐ Gently and slowly

HC r231 DES s12

4.3 What does the lack of tyre noise indicate?

Mark **one** answer

- ☐ There could be grit
- ☐ There's new tarmac
- ☐ The road could be icy
- ☐ The road surface is worn

HC r231 DES s12

4.4 What should you do in the skid described?

Mark **one** answer

- ☐ Steer firmly to full right lock
- ☐ Steer gently to the left
- ☐ Steer firmly to full left lock
- ☐ Steer gently to the right

HC r119

4.5 What colour beacon would this slow-moving vehicle have?

Mark **one** answer

- ☐ Green
- ☐ Amber
- ☐ Blue
- ☐ White

HC r225

Section five

Hazard awareness

In this section, you'll learn about

- static hazards; for example, parked cars, junctions, roundabouts
- moving hazards, such as pedestrians, cyclists, drivers
- road and weather conditions
- physical conditions that make someone unfit to drive.

Hazard awareness

When you start learning to drive, you'll be concentrating on the basic controls of the car. As your skills improve, so will your ability to recognise hazards on the road.

A hazard is a situation that may require you to respond by taking action, such as braking or steering.

Hazards can be...

static, such as parked cars, junctions or roundabouts

moving, such as pedestrians, cyclists or drivers

road and weather conditions

you, if you aren't alert and fit to drive

Static hazards

There are many types of static hazard, including

- bends
- junctions
- roundabouts
- parked vehicles and obstructions in the road
- roadworks
- road surfaces
- different types of crossings
- traffic lights.

HC r153 DES s7, 8, 10

All of these may require you to respond in some way, so

- be aware that they're there
- slow down and be ready to stop if necessary.

Tip

At level crossings with traffic light signals, you MUST stop before the barrier when the red lights are flashing, even if the barrier isn't yet down.

HC r293

Road signs

Road signs and markings are there to give you clues about possible hazards, so it's vital that you learn their meanings. You can find them in *The Official Highway Code* (book, eBook, app and online) and *Know Your Traffic Signs* (book and online).

Watch out for signs and markings so that you can slow down in good time and be prepared for any action you may need to take. For example, if you see a sign for a bend, ask yourself 'What if there's a pedestrian or an obstruction around the bend – could I stop in time? Could I do it safely?'

HC p106–116 DES s6, 7, 10 KYTS p10–71, 77–93

Parked vehicles

In busy areas, parked cars can cause a hazard – especially if they're parked badly or even illegally, for example on the zigzag lines by a pedestrian crossing.

Watch out for

- children running out from between parked vehicles
- vehicle doors opening
- vehicles moving away.

Would you be able to stop, or safely avoid them, in time?

HC r205–206 DES s7, 10

Junctions

Your view is often reduced at junctions, especially in built-up areas (for example, in towns). Take extra care and pull forward slowly until you can see well into the road. You may also be able to see reflections of traffic in the windows of buildings, such as shops.

In queuing traffic, be careful not to block a junction. Leave it clear so that other vehicles can enter and emerge.

Where lanes are closed, be ready for vehicles cutting in front of you and keep a safe distance from the vehicle in front.

HC r151 DES s8, 10, 11

At a traffic-light-controlled junction where the lights aren't working, treat it as an unmarked junction and be prepared to stop. There may be police officers controlling traffic in these circumstances – make sure that you know and understand their signals.

HC r105, 176, p104 DES s6

Motorways and dual carriageways

If you're driving on a motorway or dual carriageway and see a hazard or obstruction ahead, such as a traffic jam, you may use your hazard warning lights briefly to warn the traffic behind.

HC r116

Slow-moving or stationary vehicles with a large arrow displayed on the back show where you need to change lanes as you approach roadworks.

Breakdowns

If your vehicle breaks down and is causing an obstruction, switch on your hazard warning lights to warn other road users.

HC r116 DES s11

Find out more about what to do if you break down on a motorway at this link.

survivegroup.org/pages/safety-information/stopping-on-the-hard-shoulder

Moving hazards

Moving hazards tend to be hazards caused by other types of road user.

Road user	What to do
Pedestrians 	If you see pedestrians crossing the road, be patient and don't try to make them rush. On country roads there may be no pavement, so look out for pedestrians walking along the road. They may be walking towards you on your side of the road. **HC r205–206 DES s7, 10**
Cyclists 	Be aware of cyclists and give them plenty of room. They may wobble or swerve to avoid drains or potholes. At junctions or traffic lights, give cyclists time to turn or pull away. When travelling in slow traffic, before you turn left, check for cyclists filtering through the traffic on your left. **HC r211–213 DES s10**
Motorcyclists 	Look out for motorcyclists, especially when you're • emerging from a junction • turning into a road on your right • changing lanes or moving out to overtake. **HC r211–213 DES s10**
Horse riders 	Horses can be unpredictable and easily spooked. Reduce your speed and give them plenty of room when you pass them. **HC r215 DES s10**

Road user	What to do
Drivers of large vehicles  	If you see a bus at a bus stop, remember that • people may get off and then cross the road • the bus may be about to move off. **HC r223 DES s10** School buses might stop at places other than bus stops. At some bridges, high vehicles may need to use the centre of the road to be able to pass underneath. **HC r221 DES s10** Large goods vehicles over 13 metres long have red and yellow markings at the back of the vehicle. **HC p117**
Drivers of vehicles carrying hazardous loads 	Some vehicles have information signs on the back, to show that they contain a hazardous load. Learn what the signs mean. **HC p117**
When you're being overtaken 	Watch out for vehicles, especially motorcyclists, overtaking you. If you need to, drop back to keep a safe distance from the vehicle in front. When turning right, don't forget to check to your right for overtaking vehicles before making the turn. **HC r211–213 DES s10**
Disabled people using powered vehicles 	Reduce your speed and be careful. People using these small vehicles are extremely vulnerable on the road because • they're difficult to see • they travel slowly.

Road user	What to do
Older drivers 	Older drivers may not react very quickly, so be patient with them. HC r216 DES s10

Find out about the hazard perception test on DVSA's YouTube channel.

youtube.com/dvsagovuk

Road and weather conditions

Different types of weather – rain, ice, fog and even bright sunlight – can create extra hazards by making it harder to see the road or affecting your control of the vehicle. Change the way you drive to suit the weather conditions, and be aware of the added dangers.

In these conditions...	remember to do this
Rain	Double your distance from the vehicle in front to four seconds.
Ice	Slow down and increase your separation distance. Allow up to 10 times the gap you'd leave in the dry.
Fog	Slow down and use dipped headlights.
Bright sunlight	Be aware that sunlight can dazzle you or other drivers.

HC r227 DES s11

Yourself

Don't allow yourself to become a hazard on the road. You need to be alert and concentrate on your driving at all times.

Awareness

Make sure you use your mirrors so that you're aware of what's going on around you at all times. These may be convex (curved outwards slightly) to give a wider field of vision.

HC r161

Tiredness

Don't drive if you're tired. Plan your journey so that you have enough rest and refreshment breaks. Try to stop at least once every two hours. Open a window so you have plenty of fresh air.

If you feel tired

- pull over at a safe and legal place to rest
- on a motorway, leave at the next exit or services.

HC r91 DES s1, 11

See the GEM Motoring Assist website for more information about driving and tiredness.

blog.motoringassist.com/road-safety/road-safety-general/dangers-fatigue/

Distractions

Your concentration can be affected by

- using a hands-free phone headset
- listening to loud music
- looking at navigation equipment
- how you're feeling.

Self-reflection

Switch off your phone and put it in the glove compartment before you drive. If you're carrying passengers, ask them to check that you've stored the phone out of reach. Remember: you can get six penalty points and a £200 fine if you use a hand-held phone when you're driving. You'll also lose your licence if you passed your driving test in the last two years.

It's important to avoid being distracted by these things while you're driving.

- Turn off your mobile phone or switch it to voicemail.
- Before setting or adjusting navigation equipment or using your phone, find somewhere safe and legal to stop.
- Keep music at a reasonable volume.
- Before looking at a map, find somewhere safe and legal to stop.
- If you're upset or angry, take time to calm down before you begin driving.

HC r91, 148–150 DES s1, 11

Alcohol

Never drive if you've been drinking alcohol; it's not worth taking a chance. If you're driving, don't drink. If you've had a drink, find another way to get home, such as public transport, taxi, walking or getting a lift.

HC r95

Did you know?

Alcohol can

- reduce your concentration, coordination and control
- give you a false sense of confidence
- reduce your judgement of speed
- slow down your reactions.

See the Think! road safety information on drink-driving.

http://think.gov.uk/road-safety-laws/#drink-driving

Medicines and drugs

You must be fit to drive. Some medicines can make you sleepy; check the label or ask your doctor or pharmacist if it's safe to drive after you've taken the medicine.

HC r90, 95–96 DES s1

Using illegal drugs is highly dangerous and the effects of some can last up to 72 hours. Never take them before driving.

If you've been convicted of driving while unfit through drink or drugs, the cost of your insurance will rise considerably. Driving while under the influence of drink or drugs may even invalidate your insurance.

DES s1

See the Think! road safety information on drug driving.

http://think.gov.uk/road-safety-laws/#drug-driving

Self-reflection

The consequences of drink- and drug-driving can be devastating. Talk to your friends before you go on a night out and ask them to choose a designated driver. Make the group responsible for everyone's safety by making sure that the driver doesn't drink or take drugs.

Eyesight

Your eyesight **MUST** be of the required legal standard to drive. If you need glasses or contact lenses to bring your eyesight up to this standard, you **MUST** wear them every time you drive. Tinted glasses can restrict your vision, so you mustn't wear them for driving at night.

You **MUST** tell the licensing authority if you suffer from any medical condition that may affect your driving.

HC r90, 92–94 DES s1

Find out about the eyesight rules for driving at this website.

www.gov.uk

Meeting the standards

You must be able to
use visual clues to prepare you for possible hazards; for example, reflections in shop windows
judge which possible hazards are most likely to affect you, so that you can plan what to do
respond to hazards safely.

You must know and understand

methods that you can use to scan around your vehicle, both close by and into the distance

which kinds of hazard you may find on different roads; for example

- tractors on country roads
- deer on forest roads
- children crossing near schools.

Notes

You can use this page to make your own notes or diagrams about the key points you need to remember.

Think about

- What are some examples of static hazards and why are they potentially dangerous?
- What kinds of moving hazards do you need to look out for when driving?
- What kinds of weather conditions can be hazardous and what can you do to reduce the risks?
- Think of the physical conditions that can make you unfit to drive. Have you experienced any? How did it affect you?

Your notes

Things to discuss and practise with your instructor

These are just a few examples of what you could discuss and practise with your instructor. Read more about hazard awareness to come up with your own ideas.

Discuss with your instructor

- the effects that alcohol and drugs can have on your driving
- how your driving is affected by tiredness and what you can do to stay alert
- how to deal with other people's bad driving behaviour.

Practise with your instructor

- driving through a busy town centre and identifying all the potential hazards; for example, wobbling cyclists, stationary buses, vans pulling out of junctions, etc
- driving
  - under low bridges
  - up to blind junctions
  - along roads where many vehicles are parked
- identifying road markings.

5.1	Mark one answer	HC p117

Where would you expect to see these markers?

- ☐ On a motorway sign
- ☐ On a railway bridge
- ☐ On a large goods vehicle
- ☐ On a diversion sign

These markers must be fitted to vehicles over 13 metres long, large goods vehicles, and rubbish skips placed in the road. They're reflective to make them easier to see in the dark.

5.2	Mark one answer	DES s10, HC r211–213

What's the main hazard shown in this picture?

- ☐ Vehicles turning right
- ☐ Vehicles doing U-turns
- ☐ The cyclist crossing the road
- ☐ Parked cars around the corner

Look at the picture carefully and try to imagine you're there. The cyclist in this picture appears to be trying to cross the road. You must be able to deal with the unexpected, especially when you're approaching a hazardous junction. Look well ahead to give yourself time to deal with any hazards.

5.3 Mark one answer — DES s7, HC r191

Which road user has caused a hazard?

- ☐ The parked car (arrowed A)
- ☐ The pedestrian waiting to cross (arrowed B)
- ☐ The moving car (arrowed C)
- ☐ The car turning (arrowed D)

The car arrowed A is parked within the area marked by zigzag lines at the pedestrian crossing. Parking here is illegal. It also

- blocks the view for pedestrians wishing to cross the road
- restricts the view of the crossing for approaching traffic.

5.4 Mark one answer — DES s7, HC r195

What should the driver of the car approaching the crossing do?

- ☐ Continue at the same speed
- ☐ Sound the horn
- ☐ Drive through quickly
- ☐ Slow down and get ready to stop

Look well ahead to see whether any hazards are developing. This will give you more time to deal with them in the correct way. The man in the picture is clearly intending to cross the road. You should be travelling at a speed that allows you to check your mirror, slow down and stop in good time. You shouldn't have to brake harshly.

5.5 **Mark one answer** **DES s7, 10, HC r205–206**

What should the driver of the grey car be especially aware of?

- ☐ The uneven road surface
- ☐ Traffic following behind
- ☐ Doors opening on parked cars
- ☐ Empty parking spaces

When passing parked cars, there's a risk that a driver or passenger may not check before opening the door into the road. A defensive driver will drive slowly and be looking for people who may be about to get out of their car.

5.6 **Mark one answer** **DES s6, HC p109, KYTS p11**

What should you expect if you see this sign ahead?

- ☐ The road will go steeply uphill
- ☐ The road will go steeply downhill
- ☐ The road will bend sharply to the left
- ☐ The road will bend sharply to the right

This sign indicates that the road will bend sharply to the left. Slow down in plenty of time and select the correct gear before you start to turn. Braking hard and late, while also sharply changing direction, is likely to cause a skid.

5.7 Mark one answer DES s10, HC r211–213

What should you do as you approach this cyclist?

- ☐ Try to overtake before the cyclist gets to the junction
- ☐ Flash your headlights at the cyclist
- ☐ Slow down and allow the cyclist to turn
- ☐ Rev your engine so the cyclist knows you're following behind

Keep well back and give the cyclist time and room to turn safely. Don't intimidate them by getting too close or trying to squeeze past.

5.8 Mark one answer DES s7, 10

Why must you take great care when emerging from this junction?

- ☐ The road surface is poor
- ☐ The footpath is narrow
- ☐ The kerbs are high
- ☐ The view is restricted

You may have to pull forward slowly until you can see up and down the road. Be aware that the traffic approaching the junction can't see you either. If you don't know that it's clear, don't go.

5.9 **Mark one answer** **DES s6, 10, KYTS p24**

Which type of vehicle should you be ready to give way to as you approach this bridge?

- ☐ Bicycles
- ☐ Buses
- ☐ Motorcycles
- ☐ Cars

A bus or high-sided lorry will have to take a position in the centre of the road to clear the bridge. There's normally a sign to show this. Look well ahead, past the bridge and be ready to stop and give way to large oncoming vehicles.

5.10 **Mark one answer** **DES s6, 10, KYTS p24**

What type of vehicle could you expect to meet in the middle of the road?

- ☐ Lorry
- ☐ Bicycle
- ☐ Car
- ☐ Motorcycle

The highest point of the bridge is in the centre, so a large vehicle might have to move to the centre of the road to have enough room to pass safely under the bridge.

5.11 **Mark one answer** **DES s6, 8, HC r171, KYTS p16**

What must you do at this junction?

- ☐ Stop behind the line, then edge forward to see clearly
- ☐ Stop beyond the line, at a point where you can see clearly
- ☐ Stop only if there's traffic on the main road
- ☐ Stop only if you're turning right

The 'stop' sign has been put here because the view into the main road is poor. You must stop because it won't be possible to take proper observation while you're moving.

5.12 **Mark one answer** **DES s1, HC r147**

What should you do if a driver pulls out of a side road in front of you, causing you to brake hard?

- ☐ Ignore the error and stay calm
- ☐ Flash your lights to show your annoyance
- ☐ Sound your horn to show your annoyance
- ☐ Overtake as soon as possible

Be tolerant if a vehicle emerges and you have to brake quickly. Anyone can make a mistake, so don't react aggressively. Be alert where there are side roads and be especially careful where there are parked vehicles, because these can make it difficult for emerging drivers to see you.

5.13 **Mark one answer** **DES s1, HC r216**

How would age affect an older person's driving ability?

- ☐ They won't be able to obtain car insurance
- ☐ They'll need glasses to read road signs
- ☐ They'll take longer to react to hazards
- ☐ They won't signal at junctions

As people age, their reaction time gets slower. The rate of decline varies from person to person but you can expect them to take longer to react to a hazard and they may be hesitant in some situations – for example, at a junction.

5.14 **Mark one answer** **DES s1, 11, HC r91**

Do you need to plan rest stops when you're planning a long journey?

- ☐ Yes, you should plan to stop every half an hour
- ☐ Yes, regular stops help concentration
- ☐ No, you'll be less tired if you get there as soon as possible
- ☐ No, only fuel stops will be needed

Try to plan your journey so that you can take rest stops. It's recommended that you take a break of at least 15 minutes after every two hours of driving or riding. This should help to maintain your concentration.

5.15 **Mark one answer** **DES s6, HC r293, p102, KYTS p27**

What should you do if the red lights start flashing as you approach a level crossing?

- ☐ Go over it quickly
- ☐ Go over it carefully
- ☐ Stop before the barrier
- ☐ Switch on your hazard warning lights

At level crossings, the red lights flash before and while the barrier is down. At most crossings, an amber light will precede the red lights. You must stop behind the white line unless you've already crossed it when the amber light comes on. Don't be tempted to zigzag around half-barriers.

5.16 **Mark one answer** **DES s6, HC r176**

You're approaching a crossroads. What should you do if the traffic lights have failed?

- ☐ Brake and stop only for large vehicles
- ☐ Brake sharply to a stop before looking
- ☐ Be prepared to brake sharply to a stop
- ☐ Be prepared to stop for any traffic

When approaching a junction where the traffic lights have failed, you should proceed with caution. Treat the situation as an unmarked junction and be prepared to stop.

5.17 Mark one answer — DES s10, HC r206–207

What should the driver of the red car (arrowed) do?

- ☐ Wave towards the pedestrians who are waiting to cross
- ☐ Wait for the pedestrian in the road to cross
- ☐ Quickly drive behind the pedestrian in the road
- ☐ Tell the pedestrian in the road she shouldn't have crossed

Some people might take a long time to cross the road. They may be older or have a disability. Be patient and don't hurry them by showing your impatience. If pedestrians are standing at the side of the road, don't signal or wave them to cross. Other road users might not have seen your signal and this could lead the pedestrians into a hazardous situation.

5.18 Mark one answer — DES s10, HC r167

You're following a slower-moving vehicle. What should you do if there's a junction just ahead on the right?

- ☐ Overtake after checking your mirrors and signalling
- ☐ Only consider overtaking when you're past the junction
- ☐ Accelerate quickly to overtake before reaching the junction
- ☐ Slow down and prepare to overtake on the left

You should never overtake as you approach a junction. If a vehicle emerged from the junction while you were overtaking, a dangerous situation could develop very quickly.

5.19 Mark one answer DES s6, 10

What should you do as you approach this overhead bridge?

- ☐ Move out to the centre of the road before going through
- ☐ Find another route; this one is only for high vehicles
- ☐ Be prepared to give way to large vehicles in the middle of the road
- ☐ Move across to the right-hand side before going through

Oncoming large vehicles may need to move to the middle of the road to pass safely under the bridge. There won't be enough room for you to continue, so you should be ready to stop and wait.

5.20 Mark one answer DES s4

Why are vehicle mirrors often slightly curved (convex)?

- ☐ They give a wider field of vision
- ☐ They totally cover blind spots
- ☐ They make it easier to judge the speed of the traffic behind
- ☐ They make the traffic behind look bigger

Although a convex mirror gives a wide view of the scene behind, you should be aware that it won't show you everything behind or to the side of your vehicle. Before you move off, you'll need to look over your shoulder to check for anything not visible in the mirrors.

5.21 **Mark one answer** **DES s11, HC p113, KYTS p135**

You're travelling on a three-lane motorway. How should you overtake a slow-moving lorry in the middle lane if it's showing this sign?

- ☐ Cautiously approach the lorry, then overtake on either side
- ☐ Follow the lorry until you can leave the motorway
- ☐ Use the right-hand lane and overtake the lorry normally
- ☐ Approach with care and overtake on the left of the lorry

This sign is found on slow-moving or stationary works vehicles. If you wish to overtake it, do so on the left, as indicated. Be aware that there might be people working in the area.

5.22 **Mark one answer** **HC r104, 167**

What should you do if you think the driver of the vehicle in front has forgotten to cancel their right indicator?

- ☐ Flash your lights to alert the driver
- ☐ Sound your horn before overtaking
- ☐ Overtake on the left if there's room
- ☐ Stay behind and don't overtake

Be cautious and don't attempt to overtake. The driver may be unsure of the location of a junction and may turn suddenly.

5.23 **Mark one answer** **DES s10, HC r223**

What's the main hazard the driver of the red car (arrowed) should be aware of?

- ☐ Glare from the sun may affect the driver's vision
- ☐ The black car may stop suddenly
- ☐ The bus may move out into the road
- ☐ Oncoming vehicles will assume the driver is turning right

If you can do so safely, give way to buses signalling to move off at bus stops. Try to anticipate the actions of other road users around you. The driver of the red car should be prepared for the bus pulling out. As you approach a bus stop, look to see how many passengers are waiting to board. If the last one has just got on, the bus is likely to move off.

5.24 **Mark one answer** **HC p117**

What type of vehicle displays this yellow sign?

- ☐ A broken-down vehicle
- ☐ A school bus
- ☐ An ice-cream van
- ☐ A private ambulance

Buses which carry children to and from school may stop at places other than scheduled bus stops. Be aware that they might pull over at any time to allow children to get on or off. This will normally be when traffic is heavy during rush hour.

5.25 **Mark one answer** **DES s10, HC r205–206**

What hazard should you be aware of when travelling along this street?

- ☐ Glare from the sun
- ☐ Lack of road markings
- ☐ Children running out between vehicles
- ☐ Large goods vehicles

On roads where there are many parked vehicles, you might not be able to see children between parked cars and they may run out into the road without looking.

5.26 **Mark one answer** **DES s10, HC r213**

What's the main hazard you should be aware of when following this cyclist?

- ☐ The cyclist may move to the left and dismount
- ☐ The cyclist may swerve into the road
- ☐ The cyclist may get off and push their bicycle
- ☐ The cyclist may wish to turn right at the end of the road

When following a cyclist, be aware that they have to deal with the hazards around them. They may wobble or swerve to avoid a pothole in the road or see a potential hazard and change direction suddenly. Don't follow them too closely or rev your engine impatiently.

5.27 **Mark one answer** **DES s1, HC r147**

A driver's behaviour has upset you. How can you get over this incident safely?

- ☐ Stop and take a break
- ☐ Shout abusive language
- ☐ Gesture to them with your hand
- ☐ Follow them, flashing your headlights

If you feel yourself becoming tense or upset, stop in a safe place and take a break. Tiredness can make things worse and may cause a different reaction to upsetting situations.

5.28 **Mark one answer** **DES s6, HC r153**

How should you drive or ride in areas with traffic-calming measures?

- ☐ At a reduced speed
- ☐ At the speed limit
- ☐ In the centre of the road
- ☐ With headlights on dipped beam

Traffic-calming measures such as road humps, chicanes and narrowings are intended to slow traffic down to protect vulnerable road users. Don't speed up until you reach the end of the traffic-calmed zone.

5.29 **Mark one answer** **DES s6, 10, HC r291, 293, KYTS p26**

Why should you slow down as you approach this hazard?

- ☐ Because of the level crossing
- ☐ Because it's hard to see to the right
- ☐ Because of approaching traffic
- ☐ Because of animals crossing

You should be slowing down and selecting the correct gear in case you have to stop at the level crossing. Look for the signals and be prepared to stop if necessary.

5.30 **Mark one answer** **DES s6, HC p116, KYTS p70**

Why are place names painted on the road surface?

- ☐ To restrict the flow of traffic
- ☐ To warn of oncoming traffic
- ☐ To help you select the correct lane in good time
- ☐ To prevent you from changing lanes

The names of towns and cities may be painted on the road at busy junctions and complex road systems. They guide you into the correct lane in good time, allowing traffic to flow more freely.

5.31 Mark one answer — DES s7, HC r135

Some two-way roads are divided into three lanes. Why are they particularly dangerous?

- ☐ Traffic in both directions can use the middle lane to overtake
- ☐ Traffic can travel faster in poor weather conditions
- ☐ Traffic can overtake on the left
- ☐ Traffic uses the middle lane for emergencies only

If you intend to overtake, you must consider that approaching traffic could be planning the same manoeuvre. When you've considered the situation and decided it's safe, indicate your intentions early. This will show the approaching traffic that you intend to pull out.

5.32 Mark one answer — DES s7, HC r225

What type of vehicle uses an amber flashing beacon on a dual carriageway?

- ☐ An ambulance
- ☐ A fire engine
- ☐ A doctor on call
- ☐ A tractor

An amber flashing beacon on a vehicle indicates that it's moving slowly or stopped and a possible hazard. Look well ahead on a dual carriageway and you should be able to see and respond to these vehicles in good time.

5.33 Mark one answer — HC p104

What does this signal from a police officer mean to oncoming traffic?

- ☐ Go ahead
- ☐ Stop
- ☐ Turn left
- ☐ Turn right

Police officers may need to direct traffic; for example, at a junction where the traffic lights have broken down. Check your copy of The Highway Code for the signals that they use.

5.34 Mark one answer — DES s10, HC r223

Why should you be cautious when going past this bus waiting at a bus stop?

- ☐ There's a zebra crossing ahead
- ☐ There are driveways on the left
- ☐ People may cross the road in front of it
- ☐ The road surface will be slippery

A bus at a bus stop can hide pedestrians who might try to cross the road just in front of it. Drive at a speed that will enable you to respond safely if you have to.

5.35 Mark one answer — DES s7, HC r167

Where would it be unsafe to overtake?

- ☐ On a single carriageway
- ☐ On a one-way street
- ☐ Approaching a junction
- ☐ Travelling up a long hill

You should overtake only when it's really necessary and you can see it's clear ahead. Look out for road signs and markings that show it's illegal or would be unsafe to overtake; for example, approaching junctions or bends. In many cases, overtaking is unlikely to significantly improve your journey time.

5.36 Mark one answer — DES s1, HC r95

How can drinking alcohol affect your ability to drive or ride?

- ☐ Your ability to judge speed will be reduced
- ☐ Your confidence will be reduced
- ☐ Your reactions will be faster
- ☐ Your awareness of danger will be improved

Alcohol will severely reduce your ability to drive or ride safely and there are serious consequences if you're caught over the drink-drive limit. It's known that alcohol can

- affect your judgement
- cause overconfidence
- reduce coordination and control.

5.37 **Mark one answer** **HC p114, KYTS p65**

What does the solid white line at the side of the road indicate?

- ☐ Traffic lights ahead
- ☐ Edge of the carriageway
- ☐ Footpath on the left
- ☐ Cycle path

The continuous white line shows the edge of the carriageway. It can be especially useful when visibility is restricted, such as at night or in bad weather. It's discontinued in some places; for example, at junctions, lay-bys, entrances or other openings.

5.38 **Mark one answer** **DES s6, HC r293, KYTS p27**

You're driving towards this level crossing. What would be the first warning of an approaching train?

- ☐ Both half-barriers down
- ☐ A steady amber light
- ☐ One half-barrier down
- ☐ Twin flashing red lights

The steady amber light will be followed by twin flashing red lights that mean you must stop. An alarm will also sound to alert you to the fact that a train is approaching.

5.39 **Mark one answer** **DES s10, HC r178**

You're behind this cyclist. When the traffic lights change, what should you do?

- ☐ Try to move off before the cyclist
- ☐ Allow the cyclist time and room
- ☐ Turn right but give the cyclist room
- ☐ Tap your horn and drive through first

Hold back and allow the cyclist to move off. Some junctions have special areas marked across the front of the traffic lane. These allow cyclists to wait for the lights to change and move off ahead of other traffic.

5.40 **Mark one answer** **DES s10, HC r178, 211–213**

You intend to turn left at the traffic lights. What should you do just before turning?

- ☐ Check your right mirror
- ☐ Move up closer to the car ahead
- ☐ Move out to the right
- ☐ Check for bicycles on your left

If you've been in a queue of traffic and are about to turn left, check your nearside for cyclists as they often filter past on the nearside of slow-moving or stationary vehicles.

5.41 **Mark one answer** **DES s8, HC p108, KYTS p10**

Why should you reduce your speed here?

☐ A staggered junction is ahead
☐ A low bridge is ahead
☐ The road surface changes ahead
☐ The road narrows ahead

Traffic could be turning off or pulling out ahead of you, to the left or right. Vehicles turning left will be slowing down before the junction, and any vehicles turning right may have to stop to allow oncoming traffic to clear. Be prepared for this, as you might have to slow down or stop behind them.

5.42 **Mark one answer** **DES s10, HC r134, p113, KYTS p129**

What might you expect to happen in this situation?

☐ Traffic will move into the right-hand lane
☐ Traffic speed will increase
☐ Traffic will move into the left-hand lane
☐ Traffic won't need to change position

Be courteous and allow the traffic to merge into the left-hand lane.

5.43	Mark one answer	HC p102, KYTS p121

You're driving on a road with several lanes. What do these signs above the lanes mean?

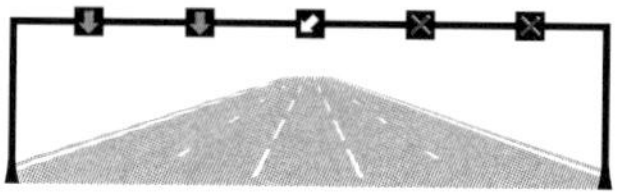

- ☐ The two right lanes are open
- ☐ The two left lanes are open
- ☐ Traffic in the left lanes should stop
- ☐ Traffic in the right lanes should stop

On some busy roads, lane control signals are used to vary the number of lanes available to give priority to the main traffic flow. A green arrow indicates that the lane is available to traffic facing the signal. A white diagonal arrow means that the lane is closed ahead and traffic should move to the next lane on the left. A red cross means that the lane is closed to traffic facing the signal.

5.44	Mark one answer	DES s1, HC r95

You're invited to a pub lunch. What should you do if you know that you'll have to drive in the evening?

- ☐ Avoid mixing your alcoholic drinks
- ☐ Don't drink any alcohol at all
- ☐ Have some milk before drinking alcohol
- ☐ Eat a hot meal with your alcoholic drinks

Alcohol will stay in your body for several hours and may make you unfit to drive later in the day. Drinking during the day will also affect your performance at work or study.

5.45	Mark one answer	DES s2, HC p128

What will become more expensive after you've been convicted of driving while unfit through drink or drugs?

- ☐ Road fund licence
- ☐ Insurance premiums
- ☐ Vehicle test certificate
- ☐ Driving licence

You've shown that you're a risk to yourself and others on the road. For this reason, insurance companies may charge you a higher premium.

5.46	Mark one answer	DES s1, HC r95

What advice should you give to a driver who has had a few alcoholic drinks at a party?

- ☐ Have a strong cup of coffee and then drive home
- ☐ Drive home carefully and slowly
- ☐ Go home by public transport
- ☐ Wait a short while and then drive home

Drinking black coffee or waiting a few hours won't make any difference. Alcohol takes time to leave the body.

A driver who has been drinking should go home by public transport or taxi. They might even be unfit to drive the following morning.

5.47 Mark one answer DES s1, HC r96

What should you do about driving if you've been taking medicine that causes drowsiness?

- ☐ Only drive if your journey is necessary
- ☐ Drive on quiet roads
- ☐ Ask someone to come with you
- ☐ Avoid driving and check with your doctor

You aren't fit to drive if you're taking medicine that makes you drowsy. Check with your doctor if you're unsure. You mustn't put other road users, your passengers or yourself at risk.

5.48 Mark one answer DES s1, HC r96

What should you do if a doctor prescribes drugs that are likely to affect your driving?

- ☐ Only drive if someone is with you
- ☐ Avoid driving on motorways
- ☐ Get someone else to drive
- ☐ Never drive at more than 30 mph

You shouldn't drive if you're taking medicine that could cause you to feel drowsy at the wheel. Ask someone else to drive or, if that isn't possible, find another way to get home.

5.49 Mark one answer DES s1, HC r96

What must you do if your ability to drive is impaired during a period of illness?

- ☐ See your doctor each time before you drive
- ☐ Take smaller doses of any medicines
- ☐ Stop driving until you're fit to drive again
- ☐ Take all your medicines with you when you drive

Only drive if you're fit to do so. Driving when you're ill or taking some medicines can affect your concentration and judgement. It may also cause you to become drowsy or even fall asleep.

5.50 Mark one answer DES s1, HC r91

What should you do if you begin to feel drowsy while you're driving?

- ☐ Stop and rest as soon as possible
- ☐ Turn the heater up to keep you warm and comfortable
- ☐ Close the car windows to help you concentrate
- ☐ Continue with your journey but drive more slowly

You'll be putting other road users at risk if you continue to drive when you're drowsy. Pull over and stop in a safe place for a rest. Caffeinated drinks and a short nap can temporarily help counter sleepiness. If you're driving a long distance, think about finding some accommodation so you can rest for longer before continuing your journey.

5.51 **Mark one answer** **DES s1, 11, HC r91**

What should you do if you become tired while you're driving on a motorway?

- ☐ Pull up on the hard shoulder and change drivers
- ☐ Leave the motorway at the next exit and rest
- ☐ Increase your speed and turn up the radio volume
- ☐ Close all your windows and set the heating to warm

If you feel yourself becoming tired or sleepy, you should leave the motorway at the next exit or services and stop for a rest. If you have to drive a long way, leave earlier and plan your journey to include rest stops. That way, you're less likely to become tired while driving and you'll still arrive in good time.

5.52 **Mark one answer** **DES s1, HC r90–91**

You're about to drive home. What should you do if you feel very tired and have a severe headache?

- ☐ Wait until you're fit and well before driving
- ☐ Drive home, but take a tablet for headaches
- ☐ Drive home if you can stay awake for the journey
- ☐ Wait for a short time, then drive home slowly

All of your concentration should be on your driving. Any pain you feel will distract you, and you should avoid driving when drowsy. The safest course of action is to wait until you've rested and are feeling better before starting your journey.

5.53 **Mark one answer** **DES s1, HC r91**

What can you do to help prevent tiredness on a long journey?

- ☐ Eat a large meal before driving
- ☐ Take regular refreshment breaks
- ☐ Play loud music in the car
- ☐ Complete the journey without stopping

Long-distance driving can be boring. This, coupled with a stuffy, warm vehicle, can make you feel tired and sleepy. Make sure you take rest breaks to help you stay awake and alert. Stop in a safe place before you get to the stage of fighting sleep.

5.54 Mark one answer — DES s1, HC r96

You take some cough medicine given to you by a friend. What should you do before driving your car?

- ☐ Ask your friend if taking the medicine affected their driving
- ☐ Drink some strong coffee one hour before driving
- ☐ Check the label to see if the medicine will affect your driving
- ☐ Drive a short distance to see if the medicine is affecting your driving

If you've taken medicine, never drive without first checking what the side effects might be; they might affect your judgement and perception, and therefore endanger lives.

5.55 Mark one answer — DES s7, HC r143

You're driving on a one-way street. What should you do if you realise you've taken the wrong route?

- ☐ Reverse out of the road
- ☐ Turn around in a side road
- ☐ Continue and find another route
- ☐ Reverse into a driveway

Never reverse or turn your vehicle around in a one-way street. It's illegal and could even cause a collision. If you've taken a wrong turn, carry on along the one-way street and find another route, checking the direction signs as you drive. Stop in a safe place if you need to check a map.

5.56 Mark one answer — DES s1, HC r148, 150

What will be a serious distraction while you're driving?

- ☐ Looking at road maps
- ☐ Switching on your demister
- ☐ Using your windscreen washers
- ☐ Looking in your door mirror

Looking at road maps while driving is very dangerous. If you aren't sure of your route, stop in a safe place and check the map. You must not allow anything to take your attention away from the road while you're driving.

5.57	Mark one answer	DES s5, 10, HC r112

What should you do if the vehicle starts reversing off the driveway?

- ☐ Move to the opposite side of the road
- ☐ Drive through as you have priority
- ☐ Sound your horn and be prepared to stop
- ☐ Speed up and drive through quickly

White lights at the rear of a car show that the driver has selected reverse gear. The driver is hidden from view so can't see you approaching. Sound your horn to warn of your presence, and be ready to stop if the car reverses into your path.

5.58	Mark one answer	DES s1

You've been involved in an argument that's made you feel angry. What should you do before starting your journey?

- ☐ Open a window
- ☐ Turn on your radio
- ☐ Have an alcoholic drink
- ☐ Calm down

If you're feeling upset or angry, you'll find it much more difficult to concentrate on your driving. You should wait until you've calmed down before starting a journey.

5.59	Mark one answer	DES s7, HC p113, KYTS p128-129

You're driving on this dual carriageway. Why may you need to slow down?

- ☐ There's a broken white line in the centre
- ☐ There are solid white lines on either side
- ☐ There are roadworks ahead of you
- ☐ There are no footpaths

Look well ahead and read any road signs as you drive. They're there to inform you of what's ahead. In this case, you may need to slow down and change direction.

Check your mirrors so you know what's happening around you before you change speed or direction.

5.60 Mark one answer — DES s10, HC r147

You've just been overtaken by this motorcyclist. What should you do if the rider cuts in sharply?

- ☐ Sound the horn
- ☐ Brake firmly
- ☐ Keep a safe gap
- ☐ Flash your lights

If another vehicle cuts in sharply, ease off the accelerator and drop back to allow a safe separation distance. Try not to overreact by braking sharply or swerving, as you could lose control. If vehicles behind you are too close or unprepared, it could lead to a crash.

5.61 Mark one answer — DES s1, HC r92

You're about to drive your car. What should you do if you can't find the glasses you need to wear?

- ☐ Drive home slowly, keeping to quiet roads
- ☐ Borrow a friend's glasses and use those
- ☐ Drive home at night, so that the lights will help you
- ☐ Find a way of getting home without driving

If you need to wear glasses for driving, it's illegal to drive without them. You must be able to see clearly when you're driving.

5.62 Mark one answer — DES s1, HC r95

How does drinking alcohol affect your driving behaviour?

- ☐ It improves judgement skills
- ☐ It increases confidence
- ☐ It leads to faster reactions
- ☐ It increases concentration

Alcohol can increase confidence to a point where your driving behaviour might become 'out of character'. Sensible behaviour might change to risk-taking behaviour. Never let yourself or your friends get into this situation.

5.63 Mark one answer — DES s1, HC r90, 96

Why should you check the information leaflet before taking any medicine?

- ☐ Drug companies want customer feedback on their products
- ☐ You may have to let your insurance company know about the medicine
- ☐ Some types of medicine can affect your ability to drive safely
- ☐ The medicine you take may affect your hearing

Always check the label or information leaflet for any medication you take. The medicine might affect your driving. If you aren't sure, ask your doctor or pharmacist.

5.64 Mark one answer — DES s1, HC r92

You need glasses to read a vehicle number plate at the required distance. When must you wear them?

- ☐ Only in bad weather conditions
- ☐ Whenever you're driving
- ☐ When you think it's necessary
- ☐ Only at night time

Have your eyesight tested before you start your practical training. Then, throughout your driving life, have checks periodically, as your vision may change.

5.65 Mark one answer — DES s13, HC r94

Which type of glasses would make driving at night more difficult?

- ☐ Half-moon
- ☐ Round
- ☐ Bifocal
- ☐ Tinted

If you're driving at night or in poor visibility, tinted lenses will reduce the efficiency of your vision by reducing the amount of light reaching your eyes.

5.66 Mark one answer — DES s1, HC r91, 95–96, 148

What can seriously reduce your ability to concentrate?

- ☐ Drugs
- ☐ Busy roads
- ☐ Tinted windows
- ☐ Weather conditions

Both recreational drugs and prescribed medicine can affect your concentration. It's also an offence to drive with certain drugs in your body and a positive test could lead to a conviction.

5.67 Mark one answer — DES s1, HC r90, 92

What must you do if your eyesight has become very poor and you're no longer able to meet the driver's eyesight requirements?

- ☐ Tell the driver licensing authority
- ☐ Tell your doctor
- ☐ Tell the police
- ☐ Tell your optician

Having very poor eyesight will have a serious effect on your ability to drive safely. If you can't meet the driver's eyesight requirements, you must tell DVLA (or DVA in Northern Ireland).

5.68 Mark one answer — DES s3, 15, HC r116, 274

When should you use hazard warning lights?

- ☐ When you're double-parked on a two-way road
- ☐ When your direction indicators aren't working
- ☐ When warning oncoming traffic that you intend to stop
- ☐ When your vehicle has broken down and is causing an obstruction

Hazard warning lights are an important safety feature and should be used if you've broken down and are causing an obstruction. Don't use them as an excuse to park illegally. You may also use them on motorways to warn traffic behind you of danger ahead.

5.69 Mark one answer — DES s8, 10, HC r170, 172

You want to turn left at this junction. What should you do if your view of the main road is restricted?

- ☐ Stay well back and wait to see if anything comes
- ☐ Build up your speed so that you can emerge quickly
- ☐ Stop and apply the parking brake even if the road is clear
- ☐ Approach slowly and edge out until you can see more clearly

You should slow right down, and stop if necessary, at any junction where your view is restricted. Edge forward until you can see properly. Only then can you decide whether it's safe to go.

5.70 | **Mark one answer** | **DES s22**

You're driving a car fitted with automatic transmission. When would you use 'kick down'?

- ☐ To engage cruise control
- ☐ To accelerate quickly
- ☐ To brake progressively
- ☐ To improve fuel economy

'Kick down' selects a lower gear, enabling the vehicle to accelerate faster.

5.71 | **Mark one answer** | **DES s7, 12, HC r126, 227**

What should you do if it's raining and you're following this lorry on a motorway?

- ☐ Allow a two-second separation gap
- ☐ Switch your headlights onto main beam
- ☐ Move into a lane that has less spray
- ☐ Be aware of spray reducing your vision

The usual two-second time gap increases to four seconds when the roads are wet. If you stay well back, you'll

- be able to see past the vehicle
- be out of the spray thrown up by the lorry's tyres
- give yourself more time to stop if the need arises
- increase your chances of being seen by the lorry driver.

5.72 | **Mark one answer** | **DES s10, HC r154**

You're driving towards this left-hand bend. What danger should you be anticipating?

- ☐ A vehicle overtaking you
- ☐ Mud on the road
- ☐ The road getting narrower
- ☐ Pedestrians walking towards you

Pedestrians walking on a road with no pavement should walk against the direction of the traffic. You can't see around this bend and if pedestrians are in the road you need to be able to deal with the situation safely. Always keep this in mind and give yourself time to react if a hazard does appear.

5.73 Mark one answer — DES s10, HC r288, 289

What should you do if the traffic in the left-hand lane is slowing?

- ☐ Slow down, keeping a safe separation distance
- ☐ Accelerate past the vehicles in the left-hand lane
- ☐ Pull up on the left-hand verge
- ☐ Move across and continue in the right-hand lane

Allow the traffic to merge into the left-hand lane. Leave enough room so that you can maintain a safe separation distance, even if vehicles pull in ahead of you.

5.74 Mark one answer — DES s3, HC r116, 274

When may you use hazard warning lights?

- ☐ When driving on a motorway to warn traffic behind of a hazard ahead
- ☐ When you're double-parked on a two-way road
- ☐ When your direction indicators aren't working
- ☐ When warning oncoming traffic that you intend to stop

Hazard warning lights are an important safety feature. Use them when driving on a motorway to warn traffic behind you of danger ahead.

You should also use them if your vehicle has broken down and is causing an obstruction.

5.75 Mark one answer — DES s7, 10

You're waiting to emerge at a junction. Your view is restricted by parked vehicles. What can help you to see traffic on the road you're joining?

- ☐ Looking for traffic behind you
- ☐ Reflections of traffic in windows
- ☐ Making eye contact with other road users
- ☐ Checking for traffic in your interior mirror

You must be completely sure it's safe to emerge. Try to look for traffic through the windows of the parked cars or in the reflections in windows. Keep looking in all directions as you slowly edge forwards until you can see it's safe.

5.76 Mark one answer — DES s1, HC r90

What must you do if poor health affects your driving?

- ☐ Inform your local police
- ☐ Avoid using motorways
- ☐ Always drive accompanied
- ☐ Inform the licensing authority

You must tell DVLA (or DVA in Northern Ireland) if your health is likely to affect your ability to drive. The licensing authority will investigate your situation and then make a decision on whether you're fit enough to drive safely.

5.77 Mark one answer HC r151

Why should the junction on the left be kept clear?

- ☐ To allow vehicles to enter and emerge
- ☐ To allow the bus to reverse
- ☐ To allow vehicles to make a U-turn
- ☐ To allow vehicles to park

You should always try to keep junctions clear. If you're in queuing traffic, make sure that when you stop you leave enough space for traffic to flow in and out of the junction.

5.78 Mark one answer DES s11, HC r91

What should you do if you start to feel drowsy while you're driving on a motorway?

- ☐ Stop on the hard shoulder for a sleep
- ☐ Open a window and stop as soon as it's safe and legal
- ☐ Speed up to arrive at your destination sooner
- ☐ Slow down and let other drivers overtake

Never stop on the hard shoulder to rest. If there's no service area for several miles, leave the motorway at the next exit and find somewhere safe and legal to pull over.

Case study practice – 5 Hazard awareness

You're waiting to turn right in the town centre. Cars are parked along the roadside, obstructing your view.

There are many shop windows. The area is busy with traffic and pedestrians.

Further on, a vehicle is unloading on the left and there are several oncoming cars.

A police officer is directing traffic where the traffic lights have stopped working. He's facing you with one hand straight up, his palm showing.

There's a bus lane, but no signs showing periods of operation or permitted use by other vehicles.

5.1 How could the shop windows help you here?

Mark **one** answer

- ☐ By showing reflections of any unseen vehicles approaching
- ☐ By letting you check that the vehicle's indicators are working
- ☐ By letting you check for any good bargains, sales or promotions
- ☐ By showing the number of cars parked on the main road

DES s7

5.2 What hazard do the parked cars create?

Mark **one** answer

- ☐ Empty parking spaces may be available
- ☐ The road surface would be difficult to see
- ☐ Pedestrians or cyclists could be hidden from view
- ☐ Traffic wardens may be working in the area

HC r205–206 DES s10

5.3 What should you do about the delivery vehicle?

Mark **one** answer

- ☐ Stop and wait until the vehicle pulls away
- ☐ Speed up and quickly pass the vehicle
- ☐ Stop and wait until the way is clear ahead
- ☐ Rev the engine and press the horn repeatedly

HC r163 DES s7, 10

5.4 What must you do in response to the officer's signal?

Mark **one** answer

- ☐ Travel through the junction as quickly as possible
- ☐ Drive carefully and slowly past the police officer
- ☐ Slow to a crawl, while flashing the headlights
- ☐ Stop and wait patiently until signalled to go on

HC r105, p104

5.5 When can you use the bus lane?

Mark **one** answer

- ☐ At any time
- ☐ Between 11.00 pm and 7.30 am
- ☐ Not at any time
- ☐ During the rush hour

HC r141 DES s6, 7

Section six

Vulnerable road users

In this section, you'll learn about

- who is particularly vulnerable on the road
- how to help keep other road users safe.

Vulnerable road users

As a car driver, you'll share the road with many other road users. Some of these are more vulnerable than you, because of their

- inexperience or lack of judgement
- size
- speed
- unpredictable behaviour.

In a car you're also surrounded by bodywork that's designed to protect you in a crash. Among the most vulnerable road users are

- pedestrians – especially children and older people
- cyclists
- motorcyclists
- horse riders.

Remember to treat all road users with courtesy and consideration. It's particularly important to be patient when there are children, older or disabled people using the road.

The most vulnerable drivers and riders are those who are still learning, inexperienced or older. Keep calm and make allowances for them.

Pedestrians

People walking on or beside the road – pedestrians – are vulnerable because they move more slowly than other road users and have no protection if they're involved in a collision. Everybody is a pedestrian at some time, but not every pedestrian has the understanding of how to use roads safely.

Pedestrians normally use a pavement or footpath. Take extra care if they have to walk in the road – for example, when the pavement is closed for repairs or on country roads where there's no pavement. Always check for road signs that indicate people may be walking in the road.

HC r206 DES s10 KYTS p13

On country roads, it's usually safest for pedestrians to walk on the right-hand side of the road, so that they're facing oncoming traffic and can see the vehicles approaching.

HC r2

A large group of people, such as those on an organised walk, may walk on the left-hand side. At night, the person at the front of the group should show a white light while the person at the back of the group should show a bright red light to help approaching drivers to see them.

HC r5

Watch out for pedestrians already crossing when you're turning into a side road. They have priority, so allow them to finish crossing.

HC r170 DES s8

Tip

When you see a bus stopped on the other side of the road, watch out for pedestrians who may come from behind the bus and cross the road, or dash across the road from your left to catch the bus.

HC r223 DES s10

Pedestrian crossings

Pedestrian crossings allow people to cross the road safely. Be ready to slow down and stop as you approach them. Make sure you know how different types of crossing work. See section 2, Attitude, for more details.

Remember that you should never park on or near a pedestrian crossing; for example, on the zigzag lines either side of a zebra crossing.

HC r195–199 DES s7

Tip

Look for tell-tale signs that someone is going to cross the road between parked cars, such as

- seeing their feet when looking between the wheels of the parked cars
- a ball bouncing out into the road
- a bicycle wheel sticking out between cars.

Slow down and be prepared to stop.

HC r205 DES s10

Children

Children are particularly vulnerable as road users because they can be unpredictable. They're less likely than other pedestrians to look before stepping into the road.

See this link for information on teaching road safety to children.

http://think.gov.uk/education-resources/

Drive carefully near schools.

There may be flashing amber lights under a school warning sign, to show that children are likely to be crossing the road on their way to or from school. Slow down until you're clear of the area.

Be prepared for a school crossing patrol to stop the traffic by stepping out into the road with a stop sign. You **MUST** obey the stop signal given by a school crossing patrol.

Drive carefully near schools.

Don't wait or park on yellow zigzag lines outside a school. A clear view of the crossing area outside the school is needed by

- drivers and riders on the road
- pedestrians on the pavement.

HC r208–210, 238 DES s6, 10 KYTS p56

Buses and coaches carrying schoolchildren show a special sign in the back. This tells you that they may stop often, and not just at normal bus stops.

HC r209, p117 DES s10

Older and disabled pedestrians

If you see older people about to cross the road ahead, be careful as they may have misjudged your speed.

If they're crossing, be patient and allow them to cross in their own time. They may need extra time to cross the road.

HC r207 DES s10

A pedestrian with hearing difficulties may have a dog with a distinctive yellow or burgundy coloured coat.

Take extra care as they may not be aware of vehicles approaching.

A person carrying a white stick with a red band is both deaf and blind. They may also have a guide dog with a red and white checked harness.

HC r207 DES s10

Cyclists

Cyclists should normally follow the same rules of the road as drivers, but they're slower and more vulnerable than other vehicles.

Find out about cycling safely at this link.

bikeability.org.uk

Cycle routes

In some areas there may be special cycle or shared cycle and pedestrian routes, which are marked by signs.

KYTS p35–36

At traffic lights, advanced stop lines are sometimes marked on the road so that cyclists can stop in front of other traffic. When the lights are red or about to become red, you should stop at the first white line.

HC r178

Overtaking cyclists

If you're overtaking a cyclist, give them as much room as you would a car. They may swerve

- to avoid an uneven road surface
- if a gust of wind blows them off course.

HC r211–213 DES s7, 10

A cyclist travelling at a low speed, or glancing over their shoulder to check for traffic, may be planning to turn right. Stay behind and give them plenty of room.

Never overtake a slow-moving vehicle just before you turn left. Hold back and wait until it has passed the junction before you turn.

Cyclists at junctions

When you're emerging from a junction, look carefully for cyclists. They're not as easy to see as larger vehicles. Also look out for cyclists emerging from junctions.

HC r77, 187 DES s8

Be aware of cyclists at a roundabout. They may decide to stay in the left-hand lane, whichever direction they're planning to take. Hold back and give them plenty of room.

Motorcyclists

Motorcyclists can be hard to see because their vehicles are smaller than cars. They're usually fast-moving too, so they can be very vulnerable in a collision.

Remember to leave enough room while overtaking a motorcycle; the rider may swerve to avoid an uneven surface or be affected by a gust of wind. Look carefully for motorcyclists at junctions too, as they may be easily hidden by other vehicles, **street furniture** or other roadside features, such as trees.

street furniture
objects and pieces of equipment on roads and pavements; for example, street lights and signs, bus stops, benches, bollards, etc.

Before you turn right, always check for other traffic, especially motorcyclists, that may be overtaking.

HC r180

When you're moving in queues of traffic, be aware that motorcyclists may

- filter between lanes
- cut in just in front of you
- pass very close to you.

Check your mirrors for motorcycles approaching from behind and give them space if possible.

If there's a slow-moving motorcyclist ahead and you're not sure what the rider is going to do, stay behind them in case they change direction suddenly.

HC r180

To improve their visibility, motorcyclists often wear bright clothing and ride with dipped headlights, even during the day.

HC r86

Motorcyclists also wear safety equipment, such as a helmet, to protect themselves. If there's been an accident and you find a motorcyclist has been injured, get medical assistance. Don't remove their helmet unless it's essential.

HC r283 DES s16

Tip

If you have a collision, you **MUST** stop. By law, you **MUST** stop at the scene of the incident if damage or injury is caused to any other person, vehicle, animal or property.

HC r286 DES s16

Watch this DVSA video to see how difficult it can be for a car driver at a junction to see a motorcyclist approaching.

youtube.com/watch?v=tcNT83m4VGU

Animals

Horses and other animals can behave in unpredictable ways on the road because they get frightened by the noise and speed of vehicles. Always drive carefully if there are animals on the road.

- Stay well back.
- Don't rev your engine or sound your horn near horses as this may startle them.
- Go very slowly and be ready to stop.

When it's safe to overtake

- drive past slowly
- leave plenty of room.

HC r214–215 DES s10

Take extra care when approaching a roundabout. Horse riders, like cyclists, may keep to the left, even if they're signalling right. Stay well back.

HC r187, 215 DES s8

See the Think! road safety advice about horses on the road.

http://think.gov.uk/road-safety-laws/#horses

Visit this web page for more advice on passing horses safely.

bhs.org.uk/our-work/safety/dead-slow

Other drivers

Other drivers, especially those who are inexperienced or older, may not react as quickly as you to what's happening on the road. Learner drivers may make mistakes, such as stalling at a junction. Be patient and be ready to slow down or stop if necessary.

HC r216–217 DES s1

Tip

A flashing amber beacon on the top of a vehicle means it's a slow-moving vehicle. A powered wheelchair or mobility scooter MUST have a flashing amber light when travelling on a dual carriageway with a speed limit that exceeds 50 mph.

HC r220

If you find another vehicle is following you too closely in fast-moving traffic, slow down gradually to increase your distance from the vehicle in front. This gives you more room to slow down gradually or stop if necessary, and so reduces the risk of the vehicle behind crashing into you because the driver hasn't left enough room to stop safely.

Learner drivers and newly qualified drivers

Statistics show that 17- to 25-year-olds are the most likely to be involved in a road traffic incident. Over-confidence, lack of experience and poor judgement are the main causes of incidents for young and new drivers and motorcyclists.

Anyone can teach you to drive providing they

- are over 21
- have held, and still hold, a full licence for that category of vehicle for at least three years
- don't charge – even petrol money – unless they're an approved driving instructor (ADI).

However, you're strongly advised to take lessons with an ADI to make sure you're taught the correct procedures from the start.

DES s1

For more information, read *The Official DVSA Guide to Learning to Drive*, which includes lots of advice for those helping learners to practise.

Find driving schools and lessons using this website.

www.gov.uk

Meeting the standards

You must be able to

look out for the effect of starting your engine near vulnerable road users. Passing cyclists or pedestrians may be affected

look for vulnerable road users at junctions, roundabouts and crossings. For example

- cyclists
- motorcyclists
- horse riders.

You must know and understand

when other road users are vulnerable and how to allow for them

the rules that apply to vulnerable road users, like cyclists and motorcyclists, and the position that they may select on the road as a result

how vulnerable road users may act on the road. For example

- cyclists may wobble
- children may run out
- older people may take longer to cross the road.

Notes

You can use this page to make your own notes or diagrams about the key points you need to remember.

Think about

- Which types of pedestrian crossing might you see, and what are the differences between them?
- When might you need to watch out for children near the road?
- Which disability might a person have if they're walking with a dog that has a red and white checked harness?
- What might a cyclist or motorcyclist be about to do if they're checking over their shoulder?
- What mustn't you do when driving near horses or other animals on the road?

Your notes

Things to discuss and practise with your instructor

These are just a few examples of what you could discuss and practise with your instructor. Read more about vulnerable road users to come up with your own ideas.

Discuss with your instructor

- which sticks are used by people with different disabilities; for example, a white stick with a red band
- the times when motorcyclists may be particularly vulnerable and how you should behave towards them
- what you think a cyclist's experience of driving through traffic may be. How can you make them feel safer?

Practise with your instructor

- driving near schools at times when students and parents are likely to be arriving or leaving
- driving down country lanes where you may encounter horse riders or pedestrians walking along the road
- identifying the signs warning you of vulnerable road users, such as a red triangle with a picture of a bicycle.

6.1	Mark one answer	HC p109, KYTS p13

Which sign means that there may be people walking along the road?

- [ ] 
- [ ] 
- [ ] 
- [ ] 

Always check the road signs. Triangular signs are warning signs: they inform you about hazards ahead and help you to anticipate any problems. There are a number of different signs showing pedestrians. Learn the meaning of each one.

6.2	Mark one answer	DES s8, HC r170

What should you do if you want to turn left at a junction where pedestrians have started to cross?

- [ ] Go around them, leaving plenty of room
- [ ] Stop and wave at them to cross
- [ ] Sound your horn and proceed
- [ ] Give way to them

When you're turning into a side road, pedestrians who are crossing have priority. You should wait to allow them to finish crossing safely. Be patient if they're slow or unsteady. Don't try to rush them by sounding your horn, flashing your lights, revving your engine or giving any other inappropriate signal.

6.3	Mark one answer	DES s8, HC r170

What hazard should you be especially aware of if you're turning left into a side road?

- [ ] One-way street
- [ ] Pedestrians
- [ ] Traffic congestion
- [ ] Parked vehicles

Make sure that you've reduced your speed and are in the correct gear for the turn. Look into the road before you turn and always give way to any pedestrians who are crossing.

6.4 Mark one answer — DES s10, HC r211

Why should you check for motorcyclists just before turning right into a side road?

- ☐ They may be overtaking on your left
- ☐ They may be following you closely
- ☐ They may be emerging from the side road
- ☐ They may be overtaking on your right

Never attempt to change direction to the right without first checking your right-hand mirror and blind spot. A motorcyclist might not have seen your signal and could be hidden by other traffic. This observation should become a matter of routine.

6.5 Mark one answer — DES s7, HC r25

Why is a toucan crossing different from other crossings?

- ☐ Moped riders can use it
- ☐ It's controlled by a traffic warden
- ☐ It's controlled by two flashing lights
- ☐ Cyclists can use it

Toucan crossings are shared by pedestrians and cyclists, who are permitted to cycle across. They're shown the green light together. The signals are push-button-operated and there's no flashing amber phase.

6.6 Mark one answer — DES s10, HC r210

How will a school crossing patrol signal you to stop?

- ☐ By pointing to children waiting to cross
- ☐ By displaying a red light
- ☐ By displaying a 'stop' sign
- ☐ By giving you an arm signal

If a school crossing patrol steps out into the road with a 'stop' sign, you must stop. Don't wave anyone across the road and don't get impatient or rev your engine.

6.7 Mark one answer HC p117

Where would you see this sign?

- ☐ In the window of a car taking children to school
- ☐ At the side of the road
- ☐ At playground areas
- ☐ On the rear of a school bus or coach

Vehicles that are used to carry children to and from school will be travelling at busy times of the day. If you're following a vehicle with this sign, be prepared for it to make frequent stops. It might pick up or set down passengers in places other than normal bus stops.

6.8 Mark one answer KYTS p36

What does this sign mean?

- ☐ No route for pedestrians and cyclists
- ☐ A route for pedestrians only
- ☐ A route for cyclists only
- ☐ A route for pedestrians and cyclists

This sign shows a shared route for pedestrians and cyclists: when it ends, the cyclists will be rejoining the main road.

6.9 Mark one answer DES s10, HC r207

You see a pedestrian carrying a white stick that also has a red band. What does this mean?

- ☐ They have limited mobility
- ☐ They're deaf
- ☐ They're blind
- ☐ They're deaf and blind

When someone is deaf as well as blind, they may carry a white stick with a red reflective band or bands. They may not be aware that you're approaching and they may not be able to hear anything; so, for example, your horn would be ineffective as a warning to them.

6.10 Mark one answer DES s10, HC r207

What would you do if you see older people crossing the road ahead?

- ☐ Wave them across so they know that you've seen them
- ☐ Be patient and allow them to cross in their own time
- ☐ Rev the engine to let them know that you're waiting
- ☐ Tap the horn in case they're hard of hearing

Be aware that older people might take a long time to cross the road. They might also be hard of hearing and not hear you approaching. Don't hurry older people across the road by getting too close to them or revving your engine.

6.11 Mark one answer — DES s10, HC r207

What should you do when you see an older person about to cross the road ahead?

- ☐ Expect them to wait for you to pass
- ☐ Speed up to get past them quickly
- ☐ Stop and wave them across the road
- ☐ Be careful; they may misjudge your speed

Older people may have impaired hearing, vision, concentration and judgement. They may also walk slowly and so could take a long time to cross the road.

6.12 Mark one answer — DES s8, HC r187

You're approaching a roundabout. What should you do if a cyclist ahead is signalling to turn right?

- ☐ Overtake on the right
- ☐ Give a warning with your horn
- ☐ Signal the cyclist to move across
- ☐ Give the cyclist plenty of room

If you're following a cyclist who's signalling to turn right at a roundabout, leave plenty of room. Give them space and time to get into the correct lane.

6.13 Mark one answer — DES s10, HC r163

Which vehicle should you allow extra room as you overtake them?

- ☐ Lorry
- ☐ Tractor
- ☐ Bicycle
- ☐ Road-sweeper

Don't pass cyclists too closely, as they may

- need to veer around a pothole, drain or other hazard
- be buffeted by side wind
- be made unsteady by your vehicle.

Always leave as much room as you would for a car, and don't cut in front of them.

6.14 Mark one answer — DES s10, HC r211

Why should you look carefully for motorcyclists and cyclists at junctions?

- ☐ They may want to turn into the side road
- ☐ They may slow down to let you turn
- ☐ They're harder to see
- ☐ They might not see you turn

Cyclists and motorcyclists are smaller than other vehicles and so are more difficult to see. They can easily be hidden from your view by cars parked near a junction.

6.15 Mark one answer — DES s10, HC r211

You're waiting to come out of a side road. Why should you look carefully for motorcycles?

- ☐ Motorcycles are usually faster than cars
- ☐ Police patrols often use motorcycles
- ☐ Motorcycles can easily be hidden behind obstructions
- ☐ Motorcycles have right of way

If you're waiting to emerge from a side road, look carefully for motorcycles: they can be difficult to see. Be especially careful if there are parked vehicles or other obstructions restricting your view.

6.16 Mark one answer — HC r86

Why do motorcyclists use dipped headlights in daylight?

- ☐ So that the rider can be seen more easily
- ☐ To stop the battery overcharging
- ☐ To improve the rider's vision
- ☐ The rider is inviting you to proceed

A motorcycle can be lost from sight behind another vehicle. The use of headlights helps to make it more conspicuous and therefore more easily seen.

6.17 Mark one answer — HC r86

Why do motorcyclists wear bright clothing?

- ☐ They must do so by law
- ☐ It helps keep them cool in summer
- ☐ The colours are popular
- ☐ To make them more visible

Motorcycles and scooters are generally smaller than other vehicles and can be difficult to see. Wearing bright clothing makes it easier for other road users to see a motorcyclist approaching, especially at junctions.

6.18 Mark one answer — HC r212

Why do motorcyclists often look round over their right shoulder just before turning right?

- ☐ To listen for traffic behind them
- ☐ Motorcycles don't have mirrors
- ☐ It helps them balance as they turn
- ☐ To check for traffic in their blind area

When you see a motorcyclist take a glance over their shoulder, they're probably about to change direction. Recognising a clue like this helps you to anticipate their next action. This can improve road safety for you and others.

6.19	Mark one answer	DES s8, 10, HC r207, 211

Which is the most vulnerable road user?

- ☐ Car driver
- ☐ Tractor driver
- ☐ Lorry driver
- ☐ Motorcyclist

Pedestrians and riders on two wheels can be harder to see than other road users. Make sure you look for them, especially at junctions. Effective observation, coupled with appropriate action, can save lives.

6.20	Mark one answer	DES s10, HC r187, 214-215

You're approaching a roundabout. What should you do if there are horses being ridden in front of you?

- ☐ Sound your horn as a warning
- ☐ Treat them like any other vehicle
- ☐ Give them plenty of room
- ☐ Accelerate past as quickly as possible

Horse riders often keep to the outside of the roundabout even if they're turning right. Give them plenty of room and remember that they may have to cross lanes of traffic.

6.21	Mark one answer	DES s10, HC r194, 207

As you approach a pelican crossing, the lights change to green. What should you do if older people are still crossing?

- ☐ Wave them to cross as quickly as they can
- ☐ Rev your engine to make them hurry
- ☐ Flash your lights in case they haven't noticed you
- ☐ Wait patiently while they cross

If the lights turn to green, wait for any pedestrians to clear the crossing. Allow them to finish crossing the road in their own time, and don't try to hurry them by revving your engine.

6.22 Mark one answer DES s6, 10, HC r208

What action should you take when you see flashing amber lights under a school warning sign?

- ☐ Reduce speed until you're clear of the area
- ☐ Keep up your speed and sound the horn
- ☐ Increase your speed to clear the area quickly
- ☐ Wait at the lights until they stop flashing

The flashing amber lights are switched on to warn you that children may be crossing near a school. Slow down and take extra care, as you may have to stop.

6.23 Mark one answer DES s6, HC r238, KYTS p56

Why should these road markings be kept clear?

- ☐ To allow children to be dropped off at school
- ☐ To allow teachers to park
- ☐ To allow children to be picked up after school
- ☐ To allow children to see and be seen when they're crossing the road

The markings are there to show that the area should be kept clear. This is to allow an unrestricted view for

- approaching drivers and riders
- children wanting to cross the road.

6.24 Mark one answer **HC p117**

Where would you see this sign?

- ☐ Near a school crossing
- ☐ At a playground entrance
- ☐ On a school bus
- ☐ At a 'pedestrians only' area

School buses can stop to pick up or drop off schoolchildren at places that aren't designated bus stops. Watch out for children crossing the road to catch the bus or from the far side of the bus if they've just been dropped off.

6.25 Mark one answer **DES s8, 10, HC r77, 187**

You're following two cyclists as they approach a roundabout in the left-hand lane. Where would you expect the cyclists to go?

- ☐ Left
- ☐ Right
- ☐ Any direction
- ☐ Straight ahead

Cyclists approaching a roundabout in the left-hand lane may be turning right but may not have been able to get into the correct lane due to heavy traffic. They may also feel safer keeping to the left all the way around the roundabout. Be aware of them and give them plenty of room.

6.26 Mark one answer **DES s8, HC r187, 211**

You're travelling behind a moped. What should you do if you want to turn left a short distance ahead?

- ☐ Overtake the moped before the junction
- ☐ Pull alongside the moped and stay level until just before the junction
- ☐ Sound your horn as a warning and pull in front of the moped
- ☐ Stay behind until the moped has passed the junction

Passing the moped and turning into the junction could mean that you cut across the front of the rider. This might force them to slow down, stop or even lose control. Stay behind the moped until it has passed the junction and then you can turn without affecting the rider.

6.27 Mark one answer — DES s8, HC r187, 215

You see a horse rider as you approach a roundabout. What should you do if they're signalling right but keeping well to the left?

- ☐ Proceed as normal
- ☐ Keep close to them
- ☐ Cut in front of them
- ☐ Stay well back

Allow the horse rider to enter and exit the roundabout in their own time. They may feel safer keeping to the left all the way around the roundabout. Don't get up close behind or alongside them, because that would probably upset the horse and create a dangerous situation.

6.28 Mark one answer — DES s1, HC r217

How should you react to inexperienced drivers?

- ☐ Sound your horn to warn them of your presence
- ☐ Be patient and prepare for them to react more slowly
- ☐ Flash your headlights to indicate that it's safe for them to proceed
- ☐ Overtake them as soon as possible

Learners might not have confidence when they first start to drive. Allow them plenty of room and don't react adversely to their hesitation. We all learn from experience, but new drivers will have had less practice in dealing with all the situations that might occur.

6.29 Mark one answer — DES s1, HC r217

What should you do when you're following a learner driver who stalls at a junction?

- ☐ Be patient, as you expect them to make mistakes
- ☐ Stay very close behind and flash your headlights
- ☐ Start to rev your engine if they take too long to restart
- ☐ Immediately steer around them and drive on

Learning to drive is a process of practice and experience. Try to understand this and tolerate those who make mistakes while they're learning.

6.30 Mark one answer — DES s10, HC r2, 154

You're travelling on a country road that has no pavement. What should you anticipate finding on your side of the road?

- ☐ Motorcycles
- ☐ Bicycles
- ☐ Pedestrians
- ☐ Horse riders

On a quiet country road, always be aware that there may be a hazard just around the next bend, such as a slow-moving vehicle or pedestrians. Pedestrians are advised to walk on the right-hand side of the road if there's no pavement, so they may be walking towards you on your side of the road.

6.31 Mark one answer — DES s8, HC r182, 212

You're following a cyclist. What should you do when you wish to turn left a short distance ahead?

- ☐ Overtake the cyclist before you reach the junction
- ☐ Pull alongside the cyclist and stay level until after the junction
- ☐ Hold back until the cyclist has passed the junction
- ☐ Go around the cyclist on the junction

Make allowances for cyclists, and give them plenty of room. Don't overtake and then immediately turn left. Be patient and turn behind them when they've passed the junction.

6.32 Mark one answer — DES s8, HC r187, 215

A horse rider is in the left-hand lane approaching a roundabout. Where should you expect the rider to go?

- ☐ In any direction
- ☐ To the right
- ☐ To the left
- ☐ Straight ahead

Horses and their riders move more slowly than other road users. They might not have time to cut across heavy traffic to take up a position in the right-hand lane. For this reason, a horse and rider may approach a roundabout in the left-hand lane even though they're turning right.

6.33 **Mark one answer** **DES s10, HC r220**

Powered vehicles used by disabled people are small and can be hard to see. What must they display if they're travelling on a dual carriageway?

- ☐ Flashing red beacon
- ☐ Flashing green beacon
- ☐ Flashing blue beacon
- ☐ Flashing amber beacon

Powered vehicles used by disabled people are small and low making them hard to see on the road. They also travel very slowly. On an unrestricted dual carriageway, they must display a flashing amber beacon to warn other road users of their presence.

6.34 **Mark one answer** **DES s7, 12, HC r225**

What does it mean when a moving vehicle is showing a flashing amber beacon?

- ☐ The vehicle is slow moving
- ☐ The vehicle has broken down
- ☐ The vehicle is a doctor's car
- ☐ The vehicle belongs to a school crossing patrol

Different coloured beacons warn of different types of vehicle needing special attention. Blue beacons are used on emergency vehicles that need priority. Green beacons are found on doctors' cars. Amber beacons generally denote slower moving vehicles, which are often large. These vehicles are usually involved in road maintenance or local amenities and make frequent stops.

6.35 **Mark one answer** **HC p107, KYTS p35**

What does this sign mean?

- ☐ Contraflow cycle lane
- ☐ With-flow cycle lane
- ☐ Cycles and buses only
- ☐ No cycles or buses

Usually, a picture of a cycle will also be painted on the road, and sometimes the lane will have a different coloured surface. Leave these areas clear for cyclists and don't pass too closely when you overtake.

6.36 Mark one answer DES s10, HC r215

What should you do when you see these horse riders in front?

- ☐ Pull out to the middle of the road
- ☐ Slow down and be ready to stop
- ☐ Switch on your hazard warning lights
- ☐ Give a right-turn signal

Be particularly careful when approaching horse riders – slow down and be prepared to stop. Always pass wide and slowly, and look out for signals given by the riders. Horses are unpredictable: always treat them as potential hazards and take great care when passing them.

6.37 Mark one answer DES s6, HC r208, 238, KYTS p56

What's the purpose of these road markings?

- ☐ To ensure children can see and be seen when they're crossing the road
- ☐ To enable teachers to have clear access to the school
- ☐ To ensure delivery vehicles have easy access to the school
- ☐ To enable parents to pick up or drop off children safely

These markings are found on the road outside schools. Don't stop or park on them, even to set down or pick up children. The markings are there to ensure that drivers, riders, children and other pedestrians have a clear view of the road in all directions.

6.38 Mark one answer DES s10, HC r2, 206

What should you do if the left-hand pavement is closed due to street repairs?

- ☐ Watch out for pedestrians walking in the road
- ☐ Use your right-hand mirror more often
- ☐ Speed up to get past the roadworks more quickly
- ☐ Position close to the left-hand kerb

Where street repairs have closed off pavements, proceed carefully and slowly, as pedestrians might have to walk in the road.

6.39 Mark one answer DES s10, HC r213

What should you do when you're following a motorcyclist along a road that has a poor surface?

- ☐ Follow closely so they can see you in their mirrors
- ☐ Overtake immediately to avoid delays
- ☐ Allow extra room in case they swerve to avoid potholes
- ☐ Allow the same room as normal to avoid wasting road space

To avoid being unbalanced, a motorcyclist might swerve to avoid potholes and bumps in the road. Be prepared for this and allow them extra space.

6.40 Mark one answer HC p109, KYTS p36

What does this sign mean?

- ☐ No cycling
- ☐ Cycle route ahead
- ☐ Cycle parking only
- ☐ End of cycle route

More people are cycling today and cycle routes are being extended in our towns and cities to provide safe cycling routes. Respect the presence of cyclists on the road and give them plenty of room if you need to pass.

6.41 **Mark one answer** **DES s8, 10, HC r77, 187**

You're approaching this roundabout. What should you do when a cyclist is keeping to the left while signalling to turn right?

- ☐ Sound your horn
- ☐ Overtake them
- ☐ Assume they're turning left
- ☐ Allow them space to turn

Cycling in today's heavy traffic can be hazardous. Some cyclists may not feel safe crossing the path of traffic to take up a position in an outside lane. Be aware of this and understand that, although they're in the left-hand lane, the cyclist might be turning right.

6.42 **Mark one answer** **DES s7, HC r195–199**

What should you do when you're approaching this crossing?

- ☐ Prepare to slow down and stop
- ☐ Stop and wave the pedestrians across
- ☐ Speed up and pass by quickly
- ☐ Continue unless the pedestrians step out

Be courteous and prepare to stop. Don't wave people across, because this could be dangerous if another vehicle is approaching the crossing.

6.43 Mark one answer — DES s10, HC r207

What does it mean if you see a pedestrian with a dog that has a yellow or burgundy coat?

- ☐ The pedestrian is an older person
- ☐ The pedestrian is a dog trainer
- ☐ The pedestrian is colour-blind
- ☐ The pedestrian is deaf

Dogs trained to help deaf people have a yellow or burgundy coat. If you see one, you should take extra care, as the pedestrian may not be aware of vehicles approaching.

6.44 Mark one answer — DES s7, HC r25

Who may use toucan crossings?

- ☐ Motorcyclists and cyclists
- ☐ Motorcyclists and pedestrians
- ☐ Only cyclists
- ☐ Cyclists and pedestrians

There are some crossings where cycle routes lead cyclists to cross at the same place as pedestrians. These are called toucan crossings. Always look out for cyclists, as they're likely to be approaching faster than pedestrians.

6.45 Mark one answer — DES s6, HC r178

This junction, controlled by traffic lights, has a marked area between two stop lines. What's this for?

- ☐ To allow taxis to position in front of other traffic
- ☐ To allow people with disabilities to cross the road
- ☐ To allow cyclists and pedestrians to cross the road together
- ☐ To allow cyclists to position in front of other traffic

These are known as advanced stop lines. When the lights are red (or about to become red), you should stop at the first white line. However, if you've crossed that line as the lights change, you must stop at the second line even if it means you're in the area reserved for cyclists.

6.46 Mark one answer — DES s7, 10, HC r211–213

You're about to overtake a cyclist. Why should you leave them as much room as you would give to a car?

- ☐ The cyclist might speed up
- ☐ The cyclist might get off their bicycle
- ☐ The cyclist might be unsettled if you pass too near them
- ☐ The cyclist might have to make a left turn

Before overtaking, assess the situation. Look well ahead to see whether the cyclist will need to change direction. Be especially aware of a cyclist approaching parked vehicles, as they'll need to alter course. Don't pass too closely or cut in sharply as this could unsettle the rider.

6.47 Mark one answer — DES s10, HC r214

What should you do when you're passing loose sheep on the road?

- ☐ Briefly sound your horn
- ☐ Go very slowly
- ☐ Pass quickly but quietly
- ☐ Herd them to the side of the road

Slow down and be ready to stop if you see animals in the road ahead. Animals are easily frightened by noise and vehicles passing too close to them. Stop if you're signalled to do so by the person in charge.

6.48 Mark one answer — HC r5

At night, what does it mean if you see a pedestrian wearing reflective clothing and carrying a bright red light?

- ☐ You're approaching roadworks
- ☐ You're approaching an organised walk
- ☐ You're approaching a slow-moving vehicle
- ☐ You're approaching a traffic danger spot

The people on the walk should be keeping to the left, but don't assume this. Pass carefully, making sure you have time to do so safely. Be aware that the pedestrians have their backs to you and may not know that you're there.

6.49 Mark one answer — DES s1, HC p134

You've just passed your driving test. How can you reduce your risk of being involved in a collision?

- ☐ By always staying close to the vehicle in front
- ☐ By never going over 40 mph
- ☐ By staying in the left-hand lane on all roads
- ☐ By taking further training

New drivers and riders are often involved in a collision or incident early in their driving career. Due to a lack of experience, they may not react to hazards appropriately. Approved training courses are offered by driver and rider training schools for people who have passed their test but want extra training.

6.50 Mark one answer — DES s9, HC r202

You want to reverse into a side road. What should you do if you aren't sure that the area behind your car is clear?

- ☐ Look through the rear window only
- ☐ Get out and check
- ☐ Check the mirrors only
- ☐ Carry on, assuming it's clear

If you can't tell whether there's anything behind you, it's always safest to check before reversing. There may be a small child or a low obstruction close behind your car.

6.51 Mark one answer — DES s5,9, HC r202

You're about to reverse into a side road. What should you do if a pedestrian is waiting to cross behind your car?

- ☐ Wave to the pedestrian to stop
- ☐ Give way to the pedestrian
- ☐ Sound your horn to warn the pedestrian
- ☐ Reverse before the pedestrian starts to cross

If you need to reverse into a side road, try to find a place that's free from traffic and pedestrians. Look all around before and during the manoeuvre. Stop and give way to any pedestrians who want to cross behind you. Avoid waving them across, sounding the horn, flashing your lights or giving any signals that could mislead them and create a dangerous situation.

6.52 Mark one answer — DES s9, HC r202

Which road users are most difficult to see when you're reversing your car?

- ☐ Motorcyclists
- ☐ Car drivers
- ☐ Cyclists
- ☐ Children

It may not be possible to see a small child through the rear windscreen of your vehicle. Be aware of this before you reverse. If there are children about, get out and check that it's clear before reversing.

6.53 Mark one answer DES s8, 10, HC r152, 232

You want to turn right from a junction. What should you do if your view is restricted by parked vehicles?

- ☐ Move out quickly, but be prepared to stop
- ☐ Sound your horn and pull out if there's no reply
- ☐ Stop, then move forward slowly until you have a clear view
- ☐ Stop, get out and look along the main road to check

If you want to turn right from a junction and your view is restricted, stop. Ease forward until you can see – something might be approaching.

If you don't know, don't go.

6.54 Mark one answer DES s8, HC r180

You're at the front of a queue of traffic waiting to turn right into a side road. Why is it important to check your right mirror just before turning?

- ☐ To look for pedestrians about to cross
- ☐ To check for overtaking vehicles
- ☐ To make sure the side road is clear
- ☐ To check for emerging traffic

A motorcyclist could be riding along the outside of the queue. Always check your mirror before turning, as situations behind you can change while you've been waiting to turn.

6.55 Mark one answer DES s7, HC r196

You've driven up to a pelican crossing. What must you do while the amber light is flashing?

- ☐ Signal the pedestrian to cross
- ☐ Always wait for the green light before proceeding
- ☐ Give way to any pedestrians on the crossing
- ☐ Wait for the red-and-amber light before proceeding

The flashing amber light allows pedestrians already on the crossing to get to the other side before a green light shows to the traffic. Be aware that some pedestrians, such as older people and young children, need longer to cross. Let them do this at their own pace.

6.56 **Mark one answer** **DES s7, HC r198**

You've stopped at a pelican crossing. What should you do if a disabled person is crossing slowly in front of you and the lights change to green?

- ☐ Wait for them to finish crossing
- ☐ Drive in front of them
- ☐ Edge forward slowly
- ☐ Sound your horn

At a pelican crossing, the green light means you may proceed as long as the crossing is clear. If someone hasn't finished crossing, be patient and wait for them, whether they're disabled or not.

6.57 **Mark one answer** **DES s10, HC r205**

You're driving past a line of parked cars. What should you do if a ball bounces out into the road ahead?

- ☐ Continue driving at the same speed and sound your horn
- ☐ Continue driving at the same speed and flash your headlights
- ☐ Slow down and be prepared to stop for children
- ☐ Stop and wave the children across to fetch their ball

Beware of children playing in the street and running out into the road. If a ball bounces out from the pavement, slow down and be prepared to stop. Don't encourage anyone to retrieve it. Other road users may not see your signal and you might lead a child into a dangerous situation.

6.58 **Mark one answer** **DES s8, HC r180**

You want to turn right from a main road into a side road. What should you do just before turning?

- ☐ Cancel your right-turn signal
- ☐ Select first gear
- ☐ Check for traffic overtaking on your right
- ☐ Stop and set the parking brake

In some circumstances, your indicators may be difficult to see and another road user may not realise you're about to turn. A final check in your mirror and blind spot can help you to see an overtaking vehicle, so that you can avoid turning across their path.

6.59 Mark one answer — DES s10, HC r211

You're driving in a slow-moving queue of traffic. What should you do just before changing lane?

- ☐ Sound the horn and flash your lights
- ☐ Look for motorcyclists filtering through the traffic
- ☐ Give a 'slowing down' arm signal
- ☐ Change down to first gear

In queuing traffic, motorcyclists could be passing you on either side. Use your mirrors and check your blind area before changing lanes or changing direction.

6.60 Mark one answer — DES s10, HC r223

You're driving in town. Why should you be careful if there's a bus at a bus stop on the other side of the road?

- ☐ The bus might have broken down
- ☐ Pedestrians might come from behind the bus
- ☐ The bus might move off suddenly
- ☐ The bus might remain stationary

If you see a bus ahead, watch out for pedestrians. They might not be able to see you if they're behind the bus.

6.61 Mark one answer — DES s7, 10, HC r215

How should you overtake horse riders?

- ☐ Drive up close and overtake as soon as possible
- ☐ Speed isn't important but allow plenty of room
- ☐ Use your horn just once to warn them
- ☐ Drive slowly and leave plenty of room

When you decide to overtake a horse rider, make sure you can do so safely before you move out. Leave them plenty of room and pass slowly. Passing too close could startle the horse and unseat the rider.

6.62 Mark one answer — DES s10, HC r232

Why should you allow extra room while overtaking a motorcyclist on a windy day?

- ☐ The rider may turn off suddenly to get out of the wind
- ☐ The rider may be blown in front of you
- ☐ The rider may stop suddenly
- ☐ The rider may be travelling faster than normal

If you're driving in high winds, be aware that the conditions might make a motorcyclist (or cyclist) swerve or wobble. Take this into consideration if you're following or wish to overtake a two-wheeled vehicle.

6.63 Mark one answer — DES s8, 10, HC r170, 211

Where should you take particular care to look for motorcyclists and cyclists?

- ☐ On dual carriageways
- ☐ At junctions
- ☐ At zebra crossings
- ☐ On one-way streets

Motorcyclists and cyclists are often more difficult to see at junctions. They're easily hidden from view and you may not be able to see them approaching a junction if your view is partially blocked; for example, by other traffic.

6.64 Mark one answer — DES s6, HC r208, 238, KYTS p56

The road outside this school is marked with yellow zigzag lines. What do these lines mean?

- ☐ You may park on the lines when dropping off schoolchildren
- ☐ You may park on the lines when picking up schoolchildren
- ☐ You shouldn't wait or park your vehicle here
- ☐ You must stay with your vehicle if you park here

Parking here would block other road users' view of the school entrance and would endanger the lives of children on their way to and from school.

6.65 Mark one answer DES s10, HC r211

You're driving past parked cars. What should you do if you see a bicycle wheel sticking out between the cars?

- ☐ Accelerate past quickly and sound your horn
- ☐ Slow down and wave the cyclist across
- ☐ Brake sharply and flash your headlights
- ☐ Slow down and be prepared to stop for a cyclist

Scan the road as you drive. Try to anticipate hazards by being aware of the places where they're likely to occur. You'll then be able to react in good time.

6.66 Mark one answer DES s4

You're driving at night. What should you do if you're dazzled by a vehicle behind you?

- ☐ Set your mirror to the anti-dazzle position
- ☐ Set your mirror to dazzle the other driver
- ☐ Brake sharply to a stop
- ☐ Switch your rear lights on and off

The interior mirror of most vehicles can be set to an anti-dazzle position. You'll still be able to see the lights of the traffic behind you, but the dazzle will be greatly reduced.

6.67 **Mark one answer** **DES s7, 10, HC r195, 207**

You're driving towards a zebra crossing. What should you do if a person in a wheelchair is waiting to cross?

- ☐ Continue on your way
- ☐ Wave to the person to cross
- ☐ Wave to the person to wait
- ☐ Be prepared to stop

You should slow down and be prepared to stop, as you would for an able-bodied person. Don't wave them across, as other traffic may not stop.

Case study practice – 6 Vulnerable road users

You're driving behind a cyclist. The road has potholes and cracks.

Further ahead, there's a roundabout. A horse rider is approaching it in the left-hand lane.

In a built-up area with street lights, you see a school sign with a flashing amber signal. There are no speed-limit signs.

Later, you stop at a pedestrian crossing where the lights are red. The person crossing carries a red-banded white stick and has a guide dog wearing a red-and-white checked harness.

6.1 What might the cyclist need to do on this road surface?

Mark **one** answer

- ☐ Swerve
- ☐ Speed up
- ☐ Turn left
- ☐ Turn round

HC r213 DES s10

6.2 What should you expect the horse rider to do next?

Mark **one** answer

- ☐ Make a right-hand turn
- ☐ Go in any direction
- ☐ Make a left-hand turn
- ☐ Proceed straight on

HC r187 DES s8, 10

6.3 What does this flashing amber signal mean?

Mark **one** answer

- ☐ Children may be playing in the road
- ☐ Parents may be standing in the road
- ☐ Children may be crossing the road
- ☐ Vehicles may be turning in the road

HC r208 DES s6, 7 KYTS p14

6.4 What would the speed limit be in the built-up area?

Mark **one** answer

- ☐ 10 mph
- ☐ 20 mph
- ☐ 30 mph
- ☐ 40 mph

HC r124, p40 DES s6

6.5 What can you tell about the person at the pedestrian crossing?

Mark **one** answer

- ☐ They're partially deaf
- ☐ They're blind and mute
- ☐ They're partially blind
- ☐ They're deaf and blind

HC r207 DES s10

Section seven

Other types of vehicle

In this section, you'll learn about

- different types of vehicle
- safety when driving towards or following other types of vehicle.

Other types of vehicle

When you're driving towards or following another type of vehicle, such as a motorcycle or a lorry, you need to be aware of that vehicle's capabilities and how they differ from those of your car.

Motorcycles

Windy weather has a big effect on motorcyclists. They can be blown into your path, so

- if you're overtaking a motorcyclist, allow extra room
- if a motorcyclist in front of you is overtaking a high-sided vehicle, keep well back, as they could be blown off course
- be particularly aware of motorcyclists where there are side wind warning signs.

HC r232–233, p109 DES s12

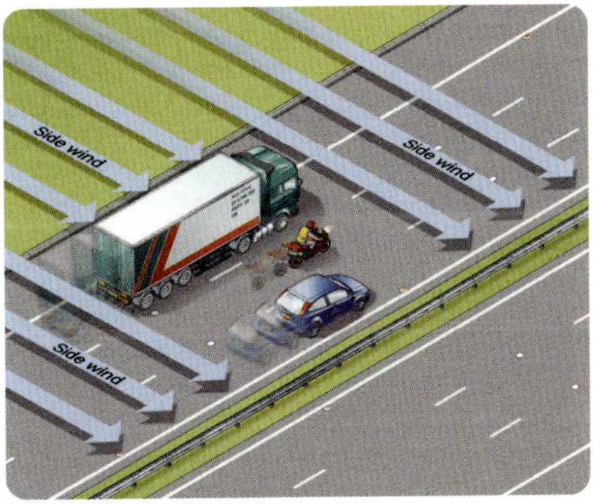

Tip

Side winds are likely to affect

- cyclists
- motorcyclists
- drivers towing caravans or trailers
- drivers of high-sided vehicles

more than car drivers. If you're following or overtaking, be aware that these vehicles might be blown off course, and give them extra room.

DES s12

Motorcyclists may swerve to avoid uneven or slippery surfaces, so if you're following a motorcyclist allow plenty of space. Metal drain covers in wet weather are particularly hazardous for two-wheeled vehicles.

HC r213 DES s10

See the Think! road safety information about driving safely near motorcyclists.

think.gov.uk/advice-for-road-users/#drivers

Large vehicles

Large vehicles can make it difficult for you to see the road ahead. Keep well back if you're following a large vehicle, especially if you're planning to overtake. If another vehicle fills the gap you've left, drop back further. This will improve your view of the road ahead.

HC r164, 222 DES s7

Overtaking a large vehicle is risky because it takes more time to overtake than a car.

Keep well back until you can see that the road ahead is clear. This also helps the driver of the large vehicle to see you in their mirrors.

HC r164 DES s7, 12

Never begin to overtake unless you're sure that you can complete the manoeuvre safely.

In wet weather, large vehicles throw up a lot of spray. This can make it difficult for you to see, so drop back further until you can see clearly. If the conditions make it difficult for you to be seen by other road users, use dipped headlights. If visibility is reduced to less than 100 metres (328 feet), you may use fog lights.

HC r226 DES s11, 12

> **Tip**
>
> If you're driving downhill and a large vehicle coming uphill needs to move out to pass a parked car, slow down and give way if possible. It's much more difficult for large vehicles to stop and then start up again if they're going uphill.
>
> DES s7

Stay well back and give large vehicles plenty of room as they approach or negotiate

- road junctions
- crossroads
- mini-roundabouts.

To get around a corner, long vehicles may need to move in the opposite direction to the one they're indicating. If they want to turn left, they may indicate left but move over to the right before making the turn, and vice versa.

HC r221 DES s8

If you're waiting to turn left from a minor road and a large vehicle is approaching from the right, think. It may seem as if there's time to turn but there could be an overtaking vehicle hidden from view.

Buses

Bus drivers need to make frequent stops to pick up and set down passengers. If a bus pulls up at a bus stop, watch out for pedestrians who may get off and cross the road in front of or behind the bus. Be prepared to give way to a bus that's trying to move off from a bus stop, as long as it's safe to do so.

HC r223 DES s10

Trams

Some cities have trams. Take extra care around them because they

- are very quiet
- move quickly
- can't steer to avoid you.

HC r223–224 DES s7

In these cities there may be extra white light signals at some traffic lights, which are for tram drivers.

Powered vehicles used by disabled people

Powered vehicles used by disabled people, such as wheelchairs and mobility scooters, have a maximum speed limit of 8 mph (12 km/h) when used on the road.

HC r36, 220

Meeting the standards

You must be able to

look out for other road users and predict what they may do

monitor and manage your own reactions to other road users.

You must know and understand

the rules that apply to other road users and the positions they may select on the road as a result. For example

- drivers of large vehicles
- bus and coach drivers
- cyclists
- motorcyclists.

Notes

You can use this page to make your own notes or diagrams about the key points you need to remember.

Think about

- What conditions could make a motorcyclist swerve unexpectedly?
- When do you need to give large vehicles plenty of space?
- What should you watch out for when a bus has stopped at the side of the road?
- What do you need to be aware of when driving in an area that has trams?

Your notes

Things to discuss and practise with your instructor

These are just a few examples of what you could discuss and practise with your instructor. Read more about other types of vehicle to come up with your own ideas.

Discuss with your instructor

- how windy weather can affect the way motorcyclists ride. What can you do to allow for this?
- the maximum speed of powered wheelchairs and how you should behave when you need to overtake one
- how trams operate and what to look out for if you encounter a tram system.

Practise with your instructor

- driving around an industrial estate, or somewhere you're likely to encounter large vehicles
- overtaking large vehicles and noting how this differs from overtaking a car
- driving in different weather conditions and making sure that you can be seen by other road users, eg in the rain, in the fog, etc.

7.1 Mark one answer | DES s10, s12, HC r213, p109, KYTS p12

You're about to overtake a slow-moving motorcyclist. Which sign would make you take special care?

☐ 

☐ 

☐ 

☐ 

In windy weather, watch out for motorcyclists and also cyclists, as they can be blown sideways into your path. When you pass them, leave plenty of room and check their position in your mirror before pulling back in.

7.2 Mark one answer | DES s8, HC r222

You're waiting to turn right out of a minor road. It's clear to the left but a lorry is coming from the right. Why should you wait, even if you have enough time to turn?

☐ Anything overtaking the lorry will be hidden from view

☐ The lorry could suddenly speed up

☐ The lorry might be slowing down

☐ The load on the lorry might be unstable

Large vehicles can hide other vehicles that are overtaking – especially motorcycles. You need to be aware of the possibility of hidden vehicles and not assume that it's safe to turn.

7.3 Mark one answer | DES s8, HC r221

You're following a long vehicle as it approaches a crossroads. What should you do if it signals left but moves out to the right?

☐ Get closer in order to pass it quickly

☐ Stay well back and give it room

☐ Assume the signal is wrong and that it's turning right

☐ Overtake it as it starts to slow down

A long vehicle may need to swing out in the opposite direction as it approaches a turn, to allow the rear wheels to clear the kerb. Don't try to filter through if you see a gap; as the lorry turns, the gap will close.

7.4	Mark one answer	DES s8, HC r221

You're following a long vehicle approaching a crossroads. What should you do if the driver signals right but moves close to the left-hand kerb?

- ☐ Warn the driver about the wrong signal
- ☐ Wait behind the long vehicle
- ☐ Report the driver to the police
- ☐ Overtake on the right-hand side

When a long vehicle is going to turn right, it may need to keep close to the left-hand kerb. This is to prevent the rear end of the trailer cutting the corner. You need to be aware of how long vehicles behave in such situations. Don't overtake the lorry, because it could turn as you're alongside. Stay behind and wait for it to turn.

7.5	Mark one answer	DES s8, HC r187, r221

You're approaching a mini-roundabout. What should you do if a long vehicle in front signals left but positions over to the right?

- ☐ Sound your horn
- ☐ Overtake on the left
- ☐ Follow the same course as the lorry
- ☐ Keep well back

At mini-roundabouts, there isn't much room for a long vehicle to manoeuvre. It will have to swing out wide so that it can complete the turn safely. Keep well back and don't try to move up alongside it.

7.6	Mark one answer	DES s7, HC r164, 222

You're travelling on a single carriageway road. Why should you keep well back while you're following a large vehicle?

- ☐ To give yourself acceleration space if you decide to overtake
- ☐ To get the best view of the road ahead
- ☐ To leave a gap in case the vehicle stops and rolls back
- ☐ To offer other drivers a safe gap if they want to overtake you

When following a large vehicle, keep well back. If you're too close, you won't be able to see the road ahead and the driver of the long vehicle might not be able to see you in their mirrors.

7.7 Mark one answer DES s7, 10, HC r223

You're travelling behind a bus. What should you do if it pulls up at a bus stop?

- ☐ Accelerate past the bus
- ☐ Look for pedestrians
- ☐ Sound your horn
- ☐ Pull in closely behind the bus

People may be running to catch the bus or passengers leaving the bus might wish to cross the road in front of the bus. Look out for them if you intend to go past it. Consider how many people are waiting to get on the bus – check the queue if you can. The bus might move off straight away if no-one is waiting to get on.

If a bus is signalling to pull out, give it priority if it's safe to do so.

7.8 Mark one answer DES s12, HC r222, 227

You're following a lorry on a wet road. What should you do when spray makes it difficult to see the road ahead?

- ☐ Drop back until you can see better
- ☐ Put your headlights on full beam
- ☐ Keep close to the lorry, away from the spray
- ☐ Speed up and overtake quickly

Large vehicles can throw up a lot of spray when it's wet. This makes it difficult for drivers behind to see the road ahead. You'll be able to see more by dropping back further, out of the spray. This will also increase your separation distance, giving you more room to stop if you have to.

7.9 Mark one answer DES s7, 10, HC r164, 168

You're leaving a safe gap as you follow a large vehicle. What should you do if a car moves into this gap?

- ☐ Sound your horn
- ☐ Drop back further
- ☐ Flash your headlights
- ☐ Start to overtake

Sometimes your separation distance is shortened by a driver moving into the gap you've allowed. When this happens, react positively, stay calm and drop further back to re-establish a safe following distance.

7.10 Mark one answer — DES s10, HC r223

What should you do when you're approaching a bus that's signalling to move away from a bus stop?

- ☐ Get past before it moves
- ☐ Allow it to pull away, if it's safe to do so
- ☐ Flash your headlights as you approach
- ☐ Signal left and wave the bus on

Try to give way to buses if you can do so safely, especially when the driver signals to pull away from a bus stop. Look out for people getting off the bus or running to catch it, because they may cross the road without looking. Don't accelerate to get past the bus, and don't flash your lights, as this could mislead other road users.

7.11 Mark one answer — DES s7, HC r164

What should you do if you want to overtake a long, slow-moving vehicle on a busy road?

- ☐ Follow it closely and keep moving out to see the road ahead
- ☐ Flash your headlights for the oncoming traffic to give way
- ☐ Stay behind until the driver waves you past
- ☐ Keep well back so that you get a good view of the road ahead

When you're following a long vehicle, stay well back so that you can get a better view of the road ahead. The closer you get, the less you'll be able to see of the road. Be patient and don't take a gamble. Only overtake when you're certain that you can complete the manoeuvre safely.

7.12 Mark one answer — DES s12, HC r232–233

Which vehicles are least likely to be affected by side wind?

- ☐ Cyclists
- ☐ Motorcyclists
- ☐ High-sided vehicles
- ☐ Cars

Although cars are the least likely to be affected, side winds can take anyone by surprise. This is most likely to happen after overtaking a large vehicle, when passing gaps between hedges or buildings, and on exposed sections of road.

7.13 Mark one answer DES s8, HC r221

What should you do as you approach this lorry?

- ☐ Slow down and be prepared to wait
- ☐ Make the lorry wait for you
- ☐ Flash your lights at the lorry
- ☐ Move to the right-hand side of the road

When turning, long vehicles need much more room on the road than other vehicles. At junctions, they may take up the whole of the road space, so be patient and allow them the room they need.

7.14 Mark one answer DES s8, HC r221

You're following a large vehicle as it approaches a crossroads. What should you do if the driver signals to turn left?

- ☐ Overtake if you can leave plenty of room
- ☐ Overtake if there are no oncoming vehicles
- ☐ Wait for the driver to cancel his signal
- ☐ Wait for the vehicle to finish turning

Hold back and wait until the vehicle has turned before proceeding. Don't overtake, because the vehicle turning left could hide another vehicle emerging from the same junction.

7.15 Mark one answer DES s7, HC r164

Why is it more difficult to overtake a large vehicle than a car?

- ☐ It will take longer to overtake a large vehicle
- ☐ A large vehicle will be fitted with a speed limiter
- ☐ A large vehicle will have air brakes
- ☐ It will take longer for a large vehicle to accelerate

Depending on relative speed, it will usually take you longer to pass a lorry than other vehicles. Hazards to watch for include oncoming traffic, junctions ahead, bends or dips that could restrict your view, and signs or road markings that prohibit overtaking. Make sure you can see that it's safe to complete the manoeuvre before you start to overtake.

7.16 Mark one answer **DES s12, HC r232–233**

It's very windy. What should you do if you're behind a motorcyclist who's overtaking a high-sided vehicle?

- ☐ Overtake the motorcyclist immediately
- ☐ Keep well back
- ☐ Stay level with the motorcyclist
- ☐ Keep close to the motorcyclist

Windy weather affects motorcyclists more than other vehicles. In windy conditions, high-sided vehicles cause air turbulence. You should keep well back, as the motorcyclist could be blown off course.

7.17 Mark one answer **DES s10, HC r223**

What should you do if there's a bus at a bus stop ahead of you?

- ☐ Flash your lights to warn the driver of your presence
- ☐ Continue at the same speed but sound your horn as a warning
- ☐ Watch carefully for the sudden appearance of pedestrians
- ☐ Pass the bus as quickly as you possibly can

As you approach, look out for any signal the driver might make. If you pass the vehicle, watch out for pedestrians attempting to cross the road from behind the bus. They'll be hidden from view until the last moment.

7.18 Mark one answer **DES s8, HC r221**

What should you be prepared to do in this situation?

- ☐ Sound your horn and continue
- ☐ Slow down and give way
- ☐ Report the driver to the police
- ☐ Squeeze through the gap

Sometimes, large vehicles may need more space than other road users. If a vehicle needs more time and space to turn, be prepared to stop and wait.

7.19 Mark one answer DES s7, HC r224

Why should drivers be more careful on roads where trams also operate?

- ☐ Because trams don't have a horn
- ☐ Because trams can't stop for cars
- ☐ Because trams don't have lights
- ☐ Because trams can't steer to avoid obstructions

You should take extra care when you first encounter trams. You'll have to get used to dealing with a different traffic system.

Be aware that trams can accelerate and travel very quickly, and they can't change direction to avoid obstructions.

7.20 Mark one answer DES s19

You're towing a caravan. Which is the safest type of rear-view mirror to use?

- ☐ Interior wide-angle mirror
- ☐ Extended-arm side mirrors
- ☐ Ordinary door mirrors
- ☐ Ordinary interior mirror

Towing a large trailer or caravan can greatly reduce your view of the road behind. You may need to fit extended-arm side mirrors so that you can see clearly behind and down both sides of the caravan or trailer.

7.21 Mark one answer | DES s12, HC r226, 236

You're driving in heavy traffic on a wet road. Which lights should you use if there's a lot of surface spray?

- ☐ Main-beam headlights
- ☐ Sidelights only
- ☐ Rear fog lights if visibility is more than 100 metres (328 feet)
- ☐ Dipped headlights

You must make sure that other road users can see you, but you don't want to dazzle them. Use your dipped headlights during the day if visibility is poor. If visibility falls below 100 metres (328 feet), you may use your rear fog lights, but don't forget to turn them off when the visibility improves.

7.22 Mark one answer | DES s12, HC r232

What should you do if you overtake a cyclist when it's very windy?

- ☐ Overtake very slowly
- ☐ Keep close as you pass
- ☐ Sound your horn repeatedly
- ☐ Allow extra room

Cyclists, and motorcyclists, are very vulnerable in high winds. They can easily be blown well off course and veer into your path. Always allow plenty of room when overtaking them. Passing too close could cause a draught and unbalance the rider.

Case study practice – 7
Other types of vehicle

It's dry but very windy. On the motorway, you see a car towing a large caravan in the middle lane.

You then move onto a long, open stretch of single carriageway, where you pass a motorcyclist.

Later, you're travelling behind a long vehicle and want to overtake.

Once in town, there are trams directed by traffic lights and you have to drive across their tracks.

Further on, a bus is signalling its intention to pull out from a bus stop.

7.1 What's the national motorway speed limit for the vehicle and caravan?

Mark **one** answer

- ☐ 40 mph
- ☐ 50 mph
- ☐ 60 mph
- ☐ 70 mph

HC p40

7.2 What could happen to the motorcyclist in these weather conditions?

Mark **one** answer

- ☐ They may have to turn around
- ☐ They may travel faster than usual
- ☐ They could be blown off course
- ☐ They could have engine trouble

HC r232–233 DES s12

7.3 What should you do when following the long vehicle?

Mark **one** answer

- ☐ Get closer so that you can overtake more quickly
- ☐ Drop back so you can see more of the road ahead
- ☐ Slow down until the long vehicle moves out of sight
- ☐ Keep pressing the horn to get the driver's attention

HC r164 DES s7

7.4 Why is it important not to obstruct these tracks?

Mark **one** answer

- ☐ Electric power to the tram may be disrupted
- ☐ The wheels of your vehicle could get stuck
- ☐ Your tyre treads could be seriously damaged
- ☐ Trams are unable to steer round obstructions

HC r224, 302 DES s7

7.5 What should you do about the bus?

Mark **one** answer

- ☐ Speed up and pass it before it pulls out
- ☐ Drive past slowly so the driver can see you
- ☐ Give way as long as it's safe to do so
- ☐ Stop and switch on hazard warning lights

HC r223 DES s10

Section eight

Road conditions and vehicle handling

In this section, you'll learn about

- how to drive safely in different weather conditions
- driving at night
- keeping control of your vehicle
- traffic-calming measures and different road surfaces.

Road conditions and vehicle handling

As well as being aware of other road users, you need to think about the conditions you're driving in and how they might affect your safety. The weather, the time of day, hills, traffic calming and different road surfaces can all change the way you need to drive.

Weather conditions

The weather makes a big difference to how you drive and how your vehicle handles.

Rain and wet conditions

When it's raining or the road is wet, leave at least double the normal stopping distance between you and the vehicle in front. If you're following a vehicle at a safe distance and another vehicle pulls into the gap you've left, drop back until you're at a safe distance again. See section 4, Safety margins, for more information on stopping distances.

If visibility is poor during the day, such as when it's raining or misty, use dipped headlights to help other road users see you. If visibility becomes seriously reduced, you **MUST** use dipped headlights. 'Seriously reduced' means you can't see for more than about 100 metres (328 feet).

HC r226 DES s12

When there's been heavy rainfall, a ford is likely to flood and become difficult to cross. There may be a depth gauge to help you decide whether you should go through. If you decide to cross it

- use a low gear
- drive through slowly
- test your brakes afterwards: wet brakes are less effective.

HC r121 DES s12

Fog

When visibility is seriously reduced, you **MUST** use headlights and you may also use fog lights if you have them.

Remember to switch off your fog lights when conditions improve. Never use front or rear fog lights unless visibility is seriously reduced because

- they can dazzle other road users
- road users behind you won't be able to see your brake lights clearly, so they may not react in time to stop safely
- road users behind you may mistake your fog lights for brake lights and slow unnecessarily.

In foggy weather, you can't see as far as you can in good conditions, so always keep your speed down. Increase your distance from the vehicle in front in case it stops or slows suddenly.

HC r114, 126, 226 DES s12

Tip

Always allow more time for your journey in bad weather.

When driving on motorways in fog, reflective studs help you to see the road ahead and also help you to know which lane you're in.

- Red studs mark the left-hand edge of the carriageway.
- Amber studs mark the central reservation.

For more details, see section 9, Motorway driving.

HC r132 DES s6

If you're parking on the road in foggy conditions, leave the parking lights on.

Very bad weather

In very bad weather, such as heavy snow or thick fog, don't travel unless your journey is essential. If you must travel, take great care and allow plenty of time.

Before you start your journey, make sure

- your lights are working
- your windows are clean.

HC r228–235 DES s12

In deep snow, it's a good idea to fit snow chains to your wheels to help grip and prevent skidding.

When you're on the road, keep well back from the vehicle in front in case it stops suddenly. In icy conditions your stopping distance can be 10 times further than it would be in dry conditions.

Tip

If it's very cold and the road looks wet, listen for noise from your tyres. If they're making very little noise suspect black ice. Keep your speed down and use the highest gear possible to reduce the risk of skidding.

See this website for winter driving advice.

motoringassist.com/winter

Windy weather

Windy weather can affect all vehicles, but high-sided vehicles, cyclists, motorcyclists and cars towing caravans are likely to be the worst affected: a sudden gust can blow them off course. Look out for these vehicles, particularly when they're

- passing a large vehicle on a dual carriageway or motorway
- driving on exposed stretches of road
- passing gaps between buildings or hedges.

HC r232 DES s11, 12

Driving at night

When you're driving at night, you need to think about how clearly you can see and be seen, as well as how your lights might affect other road users.

Make sure that your headlights don't dazzle the vehicle you're following or any oncoming traffic. If you're dazzled by the headlights of an oncoming vehicle, slow down or stop if necessary.

HC r114–115 DES s13

Tip

If you meet other road users at night, including cyclists and pedestrians, dip your headlights so that you don't dazzle them.

When you overtake at night, you can't see a long way ahead and there may be bends in the road or other unseen hazards.

On a motorway, use

- dipped headlights, even if the road is well lit
- sidelights if you've broken down and are stopped on the hard shoulder. This will help other road users to see you.

DES s11, 15

Keeping control of your vehicle

You need to have full control of your vehicle at all times. Driving with the clutch down or in neutral for any length of time (called coasting) reduces your control of the car, especially steering and braking. This is particularly dangerous when you're travelling downhill, as your vehicle will speed up when there's no **engine braking** to hold it back.

HC r122 DES s5, 7

> **engine braking**
> using the engine's resistance to help slow the vehicle

You can use your vehicle's engine to help control your speed: for example, if you select a lower gear when you're driving down a steep hill, the engine will act as a brake. This helps avoid your brakes overheating and becoming less effective.

When you're driving up a steep hill, the engine has to work harder. If you take your foot off the accelerator to reduce speed, you'll slow down sooner than usual. Changing down to a lower gear will help prevent the engine struggling as it delivers the power needed to climb the hill.

DES s7

On single-track roads, be aware of the limited space available. If you see a vehicle coming towards you, pull into (or opposite) a passing place.

HC r155

> See the Brake.org website for more advice on driving on country roads.
>
> **brake.org.uk/rsw/15-facts-a-resources/facts/1257-speed-country-roads**

Always adjust your driving to suit the road and weather conditions. Your stopping distance will be affected by several factors, including

- your speed
- the condition of your tyres
- the road surface
- the weather.

DES s10

In wet or icy conditions, try to avoid skidding; it can be hard to get your car back under control once you've started skidding. If you don't have anti-lock brakes and your vehicle begins to skid when you're braking on a wet road

- release the footbrake
- if the rear wheels begin to skid, steer into the skid by turning the steering wheel in the same direction.

HC r119 DES s5

Traffic calming and road surfaces

Traffic calming is used to slow traffic and make the roads safer for vulnerable road users, especially pedestrians. One of the most common measures is road humps (sometimes called speed humps). Make sure that you stay within the speed limit and don't overtake other moving vehicles within traffic-calmed areas.

HC r153 DES s6

Rumble devices (raised markings across the road) may be used to warn you of a hazard, such as a roundabout, and to encourage you to reduce your speed.

KYTS p68, 75

In cities where trams operate, the areas used by the trams may have a different surface texture or colour, which may be edged with white line markings.

HC r300 KYTS p31

Tip

If it rains after a long, dry hot spell, the road surface can become unusually slippery. Loose chippings can also increase the risk of skidding, so slow down and be aware of the increased skid risk in these conditions.

HC r237 DES s12

Meeting the standards

You must be able to

use the accelerator smoothly to reach and keep to a suitable speed

change gear smoothly and in good time

coordinate the use of gears with braking and acceleration

steer the vehicle safely and responsibly in all road and traffic conditions.

You must know and understand

why it's best not to over-rev your engine when moving away and while stationary

the benefits of changing gear at the right time when going up and down hills

that different vehicles may have different numbers of gears with different ratios

how to keep control of the steering wheel.

Notes

You can use this page to make your own notes or diagrams about the key points you need to remember.

Think about

- By how much must visibility be reduced before you can use fog lights?
- Why must you make sure that your fog lights are turned off when visibility improves again?
- In which weather conditions should you increase the distance between your vehicle and the one in front?
- Which road users are most likely to be affected by very windy weather?
- When can you use engine braking, and why is it a good idea?
- What are rumble devices used for?

Your notes

Things to discuss and practise with your instructor

These are just a few examples of what you could discuss and practise with your instructor. Read more about road conditions and vehicle handling to come up with your own ideas.

Discuss with your instructor

- your stopping distances in different weather conditions
- when you may use your front fog lights
- the purpose of speed humps and how you should behave on the roads where they're found.

Practise with your instructor

- going out at night to get used to driving with reduced visibility
- using your brakes in heavy rain
- your gear selection and clutch control while driving downhill.

8.1 **Mark one answer** **DES s7, HC r143**

When may you overtake another vehicle on their left?

- ☐ When you're in a one-way street
- ☐ When approaching a motorway slip road where you'll be turning off
- ☐ When the vehicle in front is signalling to turn left
- ☐ When a slower vehicle is travelling in the right-hand lane of a dual carriageway

You may pass slower vehicles on their left while travelling along a one-way street. Be aware of drivers who may need to change lanes and may not expect faster traffic passing on their left.

8.2 **Mark one answer** **DES s12, HC r227**

You're travelling in very heavy rain. How is this likely to affect your overall stopping distance?

- ☐ It will be doubled
- ☐ It will be halved
- ☐ It will be ten times greater
- ☐ It will be no different

The road will be very wet and spray from other vehicles will reduce your visibility. Tyre grip will also be reduced, increasing your stopping distance. You should at least double your separation distance to make sure you can stop safely in the space you've allowed.

8.3 **Mark one answer** **DES s13**

What should you do when you're overtaking at night?

- ☐ Wait until a bend so that you can see oncoming headlights
- ☐ Sound your horn twice before moving out
- ☐ Go past slowly so that you can react to unseen hazards
- ☐ Beware of bends in the road ahead

Don't overtake if there's a possibility of a road junction, bend or brow of a bridge or hill ahead. There are many hazards that are difficult to see in the dark. Only overtake if you're certain that the road ahead is clear. Don't take a chance.

8.4 Mark one answer **DES s6, HC r174, KYTS p67**

When may you wait in a box junction?

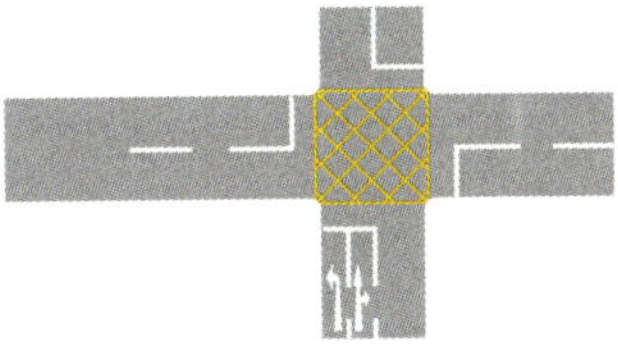

- ☐ When you're stationary in a queue of traffic
- ☐ When approaching a pelican crossing
- ☐ When approaching a zebra crossing
- ☐ When oncoming traffic prevents you turning right

The purpose of a box junction is to keep the junction clear by preventing vehicles from stopping in the path of crossing traffic.

You mustn't enter a box junction unless your exit is clear. However, you may enter the box and wait if you want to turn right and are only prevented from doing so by oncoming traffic.

8.5 Mark one answer **HC p109, KYTS p72**

Which plate may appear with this road sign?

☐ 

☐ 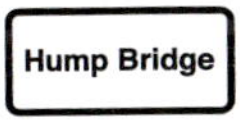

☐ 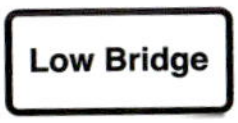

☐ 

Road humps are used to slow down traffic. They're found in places where there are often pedestrians, such as

- shopping areas
- near schools
- residential areas.

Watch out for people close to the kerb or crossing the road.

8.6 Mark one answer — DES s6, HC r153

What's the reason for traffic-calming measures?

- ☐ To stop road rage
- ☐ To make overtaking easier
- ☐ To slow traffic down
- ☐ To make parking easier

Traffic-calming measures make the roads safer for vulnerable road users, such as cyclists, pedestrians and children. These can be designed as chicanes, road humps or other obstacles that encourage drivers and riders to slow down.

8.7 Mark one answer — DES s11, HC r132

What colour are the reflective studs along the left-hand edge of the motorway?

- ☐ Green
- ☐ Amber
- ☐ Red
- ☐ White

Reflective studs are used to help you in poor visibility. Different colours are used so that you'll know which lane you're in. These are

- red on the left-hand edge of the carriageway
- white between lanes
- amber on the right-hand edge of the carriageway
- green between the carriageway and slip roads.

8.8 Mark one answer — KYTS p75

What's a rumble device designed to do?

- ☐ Give directions
- ☐ Prevent cattle escaping
- ☐ Alert you to low tyre pressure
- ☐ Alert you to a hazard

A rumble device consists of raised markings or strips, designed to give drivers an audible, visual and tactile warning. These devices are used in various locations, including in the line separating the hard shoulder and the left-hand lane on the motorway and on the approach to some hazards, to alert drivers to the need to slow down.

8.9 Mark one answer — DES s12

What should you do if you have to make a journey in foggy conditions?

- ☐ Follow other vehicles' tail lights closely
- ☐ Avoid using dipped headlights
- ☐ Leave plenty of time for your journey
- ☐ Keep two seconds behind the vehicle ahead

If you're planning to make a journey when it's foggy, listen to the weather reports. If visibility is very poor, avoid making unnecessary journeys. If you do travel, leave plenty of time – and if someone is waiting for you to arrive, let them know that your journey will take longer than normal. This will also take off any pressure you may feel to rush.

8.10 Mark one answer — DES s13, HC r114–115

What must you do when you're overtaking a car at night?

- ☐ Flash your headlights before overtaking
- ☐ Select a higher gear
- ☐ Switch your headlights to main beam before overtaking
- ☐ Make sure you don't dazzle other road users

To prevent your headlights from dazzling the driver of the car in front, wait until you've passed them before switching to main beam.

8.11 Mark one answer — HC r153

You're travelling on a road that has road humps. What should you do when the driver in front is travelling more slowly than you?

- ☐ Sound your horn
- ☐ Overtake as soon as you can
- ☐ Flash your headlights
- ☐ Slow down and stay behind

Be patient and stay behind the car in front. You shouldn't normally overtake other vehicles in areas subject to traffic calming. If you overtake here, you may easily exceed the speed limit, defeating the purpose of the traffic-calming measures.

8.12 Mark one answer — KYTS p68

What's the purpose of the yellow lines painted across the road?

- ☐ To show a safe distance between vehicles
- ☐ To keep the area clear of traffic
- ☐ To make you aware of your speed
- ☐ To warn you to change direction

These lines may be painted on the road on the approach to a roundabout, a village or a particular hazard. The lines are raised and painted yellow, and their purpose is to make you aware of your speed. Reduce your speed in good time so that you avoid having to brake harshly over the last few metres before reaching the junction.

8.13 Mark one answer — DES s10, HC r155

What should you do when you meet an oncoming vehicle on a single-track road?

- ☐ Reverse back to the main road
- ☐ Carry out an emergency stop
- ☐ Stop at a passing place
- ☐ Switch on your hazard warning lights

Take care when using single-track roads. It can be difficult to see around bends, because of hedges or fences, so expect to meet oncoming vehicles. Drive carefully and be ready to pull into or stop opposite a passing place, where you can pass each other safely.

8.14 Mark one answer — HC r213

The road is wet. Why would a motorcyclist steer around drain covers while they were cornering?

- ☐ To avoid puncturing the tyres on the edge of the drain covers
- ☐ To prevent the motorcycle sliding on the metal drain covers
- ☐ To help judge the bend using the drain covers as marker points
- ☐ To avoid splashing pedestrians on the pavement

Other drivers or riders may have to change course due to the size or characteristics of their vehicle. Understanding this will help you to anticipate their actions. Motorcyclists and cyclists will be checking the road ahead for uneven or slippery surfaces, especially in wet weather. They may need to move across their lane to avoid surface hazards such as potholes and drain covers.

8.15 Mark one answer — DES s12, HC r121

Why should you test your brakes after this hazard?

- ☐ You'll be on a slippery road
- ☐ Your brakes will be wet
- ☐ You'll be going down a long hill
- ☐ You'll have just crossed a long bridge

A ford is a crossing over a stream that's shallow enough to drive or ride through. After you've gone through a ford or deep puddle, your brakes will be wet and they won't work as well as usual. To dry them out, apply a light brake pressure while moving slowly. Don't travel at normal speeds until you're sure your brakes are working properly again.

8.16 Mark one answer — DES s12, HC r234

Why should you reduce your speed when you're driving or riding in fog?

- ☐ The brakes don't work as well
- ☐ You'll be dazzled by other headlights
- ☐ The engine will take longer to warm up
- ☐ It's more difficult to see what's ahead

You won't be able to see as far ahead in fog as you can on a clear day. You'll need to reduce your speed so that, if a hazard looms out of the fog, you have the time and space to take avoiding action.

Travelling in fog is hazardous. If you can, try to delay your journey until it has cleared.

8.17 Mark one answer — DES s7

What will happen to your car when you drive up a steep hill?

- ☐ The high gears will pull better
- ☐ The steering will feel heavier
- ☐ Overtaking will be easier
- ☐ The engine will work harder

The engine will need more power to pull the vehicle up the hill. When approaching a steep hill you should select a lower gear to help maintain your speed. You should do this without hesitation, so that you don't lose too much speed before engaging the lower gear.

8.18	Mark one answer	DES s11, 12, HC r232-233

You're driving on the motorway in windy conditions. What should you do as you overtake a high-sided vehicle?

- ☐ Increase your speed
- ☐ Be wary of a sudden gust
- ☐ Drive alongside very closely
- ☐ Expect normal conditions

The draught caused by other vehicles – particularly those with high sides – could be strong enough to push you out of your lane. Be prepared for a sudden gust of wind as you overtake large vehicles. Keep both hands on the steering wheel to help you keep full control.

8.19	Mark one answer	DES s12, HC r235

You're driving in fog. Why should you keep well back from the vehicle in front?

- ☐ In case it changes direction suddenly
- ☐ In case its fog lights dazzle you
- ☐ In case it stops suddenly
- ☐ In case its brake lights dazzle you

If you're following another road user in fog, stay well back. The driver in front won't be able to see hazards until they're close and might need to brake suddenly. Also, the road surface is likely to be wet and could be slippery.

8.20	Mark one answer	DES s12, HC r251

What should you do if you park on the road when it's foggy?

- ☐ Leave parking lights switched on
- ☐ Leave dipped headlights and fog lights switched on
- ☐ Leave dipped headlights switched on
- ☐ Leave main-beam headlights switched on

If you have to park your vehicle in foggy conditions, try to find a place to park off the road. If this isn't possible, park on the road facing in the same direction as the traffic. Leave your parking lights switched on and make sure they're clean.

8.21	Mark one answer	DES s13, HC r115

You're driving at night. What should you do if you're dazzled by headlights coming towards you?

- ☐ Pull down your sun visor
- ☐ Slow down or stop
- ☐ Flash your main-beam headlights
- ☐ Shade your eyes with your hand

If the headlights of an oncoming vehicle dazzle you, slow down or, if necessary, stop. Don't close your eyes or swerve, as you'll increase your chances of having a collision. Don't flash your headlights either, as this could dazzle other drivers and make the situation worse.

8.22 Mark one answer

DES s3, 12, HC r114, 226, 236

When may front fog lights be used?

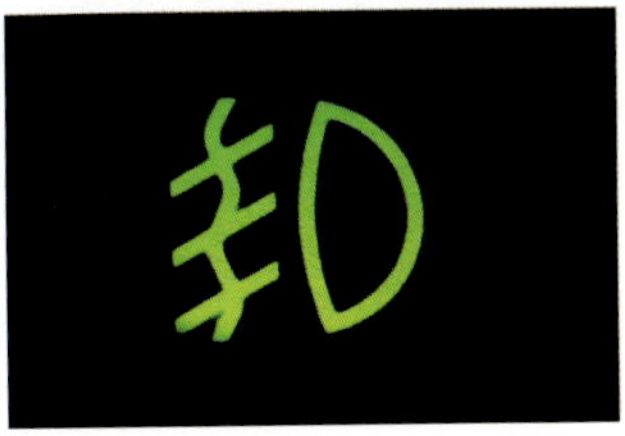

- ☐ When visibility is seriously reduced
- ☐ When they're fitted above the bumper
- ☐ When they aren't as bright as the headlights
- ☐ When an audible warning device is used

Your fog lights must only be used when visibility is reduced to 100 metres (328 feet) or less. You need to be familiar with the layout of your dashboard so you're aware if your fog lights have been switched on in error, or you've forgotten to switch them off.

8.23 Mark one answer

DES s3, 12, HC r114, 226, 236

You're driving with your front fog lights switched on. What should you do if the fog has cleared?

- ☐ Leave them on if other drivers have their lights on
- ☐ Switch them off as long as visibility remains good
- ☐ Flash them to warn oncoming traffic that it's foggy
- ☐ Drive with them on instead of your headlights

Switch off your fog lights if the weather improves, but be prepared to use them again if visibility reduces to less than 100 metres (328 feet).

8.24 Mark one answer

DES s3, 12, HC r114, 226, 236

Why should you switch off your rear fog lights when the fog has cleared?

- ☐ To allow your headlights to work
- ☐ To stop draining the battery
- ☐ To stop the engine losing power
- ☐ To prevent dazzling drivers behind

Don't forget to switch off your fog lights when the weather improves. You could be prosecuted for driving with them on in good visibility. The high intensity of rear fog lights can dazzle drivers behind and make your brake lights difficult to notice.

8.25 Mark one answer | DES s3, 12, HC r114, 226, 236

What will happen if you use rear fog lights in good conditions?

- ☐ They'll make it safer when towing a trailer
- ☐ They'll protect you from larger vehicles
- ☐ They'll dazzle other drivers
- ☐ They'll make drivers behind keep back

Rear fog lights shine more brightly than normal rear lights, so that they show up in reduced visibility. When the visibility improves, you must switch them off; this stops them dazzling the driver behind.

8.26 Mark one answer | DES s12

Why would you fit chains to your wheels?

- ☐ To help prevent damage to the road surface
- ☐ To help prevent wear to the tyres
- ☐ To help prevent skidding in deep snow
- ☐ To help prevent the brakes locking

Chains can be fitted to your wheels in snowy conditions. They can help you to move off without wheelspin, or to keep moving in deep snow. You'll still need to adjust your driving to suit these conditions.

8.27 Mark one answer | DES s5, 7, HC r160

How can you use your vehicle's engine to control your speed?

- ☐ By changing to a lower gear
- ☐ By selecting reverse gear
- ☐ By changing to a higher gear
- ☐ By selecting neutral

You should brake and slow down before selecting a lower gear. The gear can then be used to keep the speed low and help you control the vehicle. This is particularly helpful on long downhill stretches, where brake fade can occur if the brakes overheat.

8.28 Mark one answer | DES s5, HC r122

Why could it be dangerous to keep the clutch down, or select neutral, for long periods of time while you're driving?

- ☐ Fuel spillage will occur
- ☐ Engine damage may be caused
- ☐ You'll have less steering and braking control
- ☐ It will wear tyres out more quickly

Letting your vehicle roll or coast in neutral reduces your control over steering and braking. This can be dangerous on downhill slopes, where your vehicle could pick up speed very quickly.

8.29 Mark one answer — DES s12, HC r230

You're driving on an icy road. What distance from the car in front should you drive?

- ☐ Four times the normal distance
- ☐ Six times the normal distance
- ☐ Eight times the normal distance
- ☐ Ten times the normal distance

Don't travel in icy or snowy weather unless your journey is essential.

Drive extremely carefully when roads are or may be icy. Stopping distances can be ten times greater than on dry roads.

8.30 Mark one answer — DES s11

Which lights must you use if you're driving on a well-lit motorway at night?

- ☐ Use only your sidelights
- ☐ Use your headlights
- ☐ Use rear fog lights
- ☐ Use front fog lights

If you're driving on a motorway at night or in poor visibility, you must always use your headlights, even if the road is well lit. Other road users must be able to see you, but you should avoid causing dazzle.

8.31 Mark one answer — DES s11

You're driving on a motorway at night. Which lights should you have on if there are other vehicles just ahead of you?

- ☐ Front fog lights
- ☐ Main-beam headlights
- ☐ Sidelights only
- ☐ Dipped headlights

If you're driving behind other traffic on the motorway at night, use dipped headlights. Main-beam headlights will dazzle the other drivers. Your headlights' dipped beam should fall short of the vehicle in front.

8.32 Mark one answer — DES s7, HC r126

What will affect your vehicle's stopping distance?

- ☐ The speed limit
- ☐ The street lighting
- ☐ The time of day
- ☐ The condition of the tyres

Having tyres correctly inflated and in good condition will ensure they have maximum grip on the road; how well your tyres grip the road has a significant effect on your car's stopping distance.

8.33 Mark one answer — DES s5, 7

When will you feel the effects of engine braking?

- ☐ When you only use the parking brake
- ☐ When you're in neutral
- ☐ When you change to a lower gear
- ☐ When you change to a higher gear

When you take your foot off the accelerator, engines have a natural resistance to turn, caused mainly by the cylinder compression. Changing to a lower gear requires the engine to turn faster and so it will have greater resistance than when it's made to turn more slowly. When going downhill, changing to a lower gear will therefore help to keep the vehicle's speed in check.

8.34 Mark one answer — DES s12, HC r115

Which lights should you switch on when daytime visibility is poor but not seriously reduced?

- ☐ Headlights and fog lights
- ☐ Front fog lights
- ☐ Dipped headlights
- ☐ Rear fog lights

Only use your fog lights when visibility is seriously reduced. Use dipped headlights in poor conditions because this helps other road users to see you without the risk of causing dazzle.

8.35 Mark one answer — DES s12

Why are vehicles fitted with rear fog lights?

- ☐ To make them more visible when driving at high speed
- ☐ To show when they've broken down in a dangerous position
- ☐ To make them more visible in thick fog
- ☐ To warn drivers following closely to drop back

Rear fog lights make it easier to spot a vehicle ahead in foggy conditions. Avoid the temptation to use other vehicles' lights as a guide, as they may give you a false sense of security.

8.36 Mark one answer **DES s12, HC r228**

There's been a heavy fall of snow. What should you consider before driving in these conditions?

- ☐ Whether you should fit an amber flashing beacon to your car
- ☐ Whether you should drive without wearing your seat belt
- ☐ Whether you should wear sunglasses to reduce the glare
- ☐ Whether your journey is essential

Consider whether the increased risk is worth it. If the weather conditions are bad and your journey isn't essential, then don't drive. If you have to drive, make sure you're well prepared in case you get stuck.

8.37 Mark one answer **DES s12**

What should you check before you start a journey in foggy weather?

- ☐ The radiator has enough anti-freeze
- ☐ You have a warning triangle in the vehicle
- ☐ The windows and lights are clean and clear
- ☐ You have a mobile phone with you

If you have to drive in fog, switch your dipped headlights on and keep all your windows clear. You should always be able to pull up within the distance you can see ahead.

8.38 Mark one answer **DES s3, 12, HC r114, 226, 236**

You've been driving in fog. What must you do when the visibility improves?

- ☐ Switch off your fog lights
- ☐ Keep your rear fog lights switched on
- ☐ Keep your front fog lights switched on
- ☐ Leave your fog lights switched on in case the fog returns

You must turn off your fog lights if visibility is more than 100 metres (328 feet). Be prepared for the fact that the fog may be patchy and you may need to turn them on again if the fog returns.

8.39 Mark one answer — DES s12, HC r114, 226

Why is it dangerous to leave rear fog lights switched on after the fog has cleared?

- ☐ They may be confused with brake lights
- ☐ The bulbs would fail
- ☐ Electrical systems could be overloaded
- ☐ Direction indicators may not work properly

If your rear fog lights are left on when it isn't foggy, the glare they cause makes it difficult for road users behind to know whether you're braking or you've just forgotten to turn off your rear fog lights. This can be a particular problem on wet roads and on motorways. If you leave your rear fog lights on at night, road users behind you are likely to be dazzled and this could put them at risk.

8.40 Mark one answer — DES s5, HC r122

What will happen if you hold the clutch pedal down or roll in neutral for too long?

- ☐ It will use more fuel
- ☐ It will cause the engine to overheat
- ☐ It will reduce your control
- ☐ It will improve tyre wear

Holding the clutch down or staying in neutral for too long will cause your vehicle to freewheel. This is known as 'coasting' and it's dangerous because it reduces your control of the vehicle.

8.41 Mark one answer — DES s5, HC r122

Why is it bad technique to coast when you're driving downhill?

- ☐ The fuel consumption will increase
- ☐ The engine will overheat
- ☐ The tyres will wear more quickly
- ☐ The vehicle will gain speed more quickly

Coasting is when you allow the vehicle to freewheel in neutral or with the clutch pedal depressed. When travelling downhill, this will cause the vehicle to gain speed more quickly as you lose the benefits of engine braking; it may even lead to a loss of control. You shouldn't coast, especially when approaching hazards such as junctions or bends and when travelling downhill.

8.42 **Mark one answer** **DES s12, HC r121**

What should you do when dealing with this hazard?

- ☐ Switch on your hazard warning lights
- ☐ Use a low gear and drive slowly
- ☐ Use a high gear to prevent wheelspin
- ☐ Switch on your windscreen wipers

In normal conditions, a ford can be crossed quite safely by driving through it slowly. The water may affect your brakes, so when you're clear of the ford, test them before you resume normal driving.

8.43 **Mark one answer** **DES s5, HC r122**

Why is travelling in neutral for long distances (known as coasting) bad driving technique?

- ☐ It will cause the car to skid
- ☐ It will make the engine stall
- ☐ The engine will run faster
- ☐ There won't be any engine braking

Try to look and plan well ahead. Plan your approach to hazards and select the correct gear in good time. This will help give you the control you need to deal with anything unexpected that may occur.

8.44 **Mark one answer** **DES s12, HC r115, 226**

When must you use dipped headlights during the day?

- ☐ All the time you're driving
- ☐ When you're driving along narrow streets
- ☐ When you're driving in poor visibility
- ☐ When you're parking

You must use dipped headlights when daytime visibility is seriously reduced, generally to 100 metres (328 feet) or less. You may also use front or rear fog lights, but they must be switched off when visibility improves.

Case study practice – 8 Road conditions and vehicle handling

You're driving in very thick fog and the road surface is also rather damp.

You're using fog lights as well as headlights.

You leave a larger gap than normal between your vehicle and the one in front.

Later, a drain is being unblocked and the pumping vehicle is obstructing the road on your side.

Further on still, there are rumble devices on the approach to a roundabout.

8.1 How might the road condition affect your stopping distance?
Mark **one** answer

- ☐ It may be improved
- ☐ It could be doubled
- ☐ It remains unaffected
- ☐ It should be halved

DES s12

8.2 Why would you be using your fog lights?

Mark **one** answer

- ☐ Visibility is below 100 metres
- ☐ Visibility is below 150 metres
- ☐ Visibility is below 200 metres
- ☐ Visibility is below 250 metres

HC r226 DES s12

8.3 Why would you leave a larger gap between your vehicle and the one in front?

Mark **one** answer

- ☐ You may need to stop suddenly
- ☐ Other vehicles' lights may dazzle you
- ☐ The vehicle ahead may stop suddenly
- ☐ Your vehicle's lights might cause glare

HC r235 DES s12

8.4 What should you do before overtaking the pumping vehicle?

Mark **one** answer

- ☐ Use the horn and drive past quickly
- ☐ Wait until the vehicle stops work
- ☐ Pass slowly with hazard warning lights on
- ☐ Wait until the road ahead is clear

HC r163 DES s7

8.5 What information would the rumble devices provide to help you?

Mark **one** answer

- ☐ A routine test of your car's suspension
- ☐ A caution to check your tyre pressures
- ☐ A reminder to make you aware of your speed
- ☐ A warning about the road surface condition

DES s6 KYTS p75

Section nine

Motorway driving

In this section, you'll learn about

- how to drive safely on motorways
- the speed limits that apply on motorways and how they're used to avoid congestion
- the markings used on motorway lanes
- what to do if your car breaks down on the motorway.

Motorway driving

Motorways are designed to help traffic travel at constant, higher speeds than on single carriageways. Due to the traffic's speed, situations on motorways can change more quickly than on other roads, so you need to be especially alert at all times.

Check your vehicle thoroughly before starting a long motorway journey. Driving at high speeds for long periods of time may increase the risk of your vehicle breaking down. See section 3, Safety and your vehicle, for more information about what to check.

DES s11

Tip

Learner drivers may have driving lessons on motorways but only with an approved driving instructor (ADI) and in a car fitted with dual controls that's clearly displaying L plates (D plates in Wales).

HC r253

Pedestrians and horse riders can't use a motorway. The following vehicles can't be used on a motorway

- bicycles
- motorcycles under 50 cc
- most powered wheelchairs/mobility scooters
- agricultural vehicles
- some slow-moving vehicles.

HC r253

Driving on the motorway

When you join the motorway from a slip road

- adjust your speed to match the speed of the traffic already on the motorway
- give way to traffic already on the motorway.

HC r259 DES s11

All traffic, whatever its speed, should normally use the left-hand lane of the motorway. Use the middle and right-hand lanes only for overtaking other vehicles and return to the left lane when you've finished overtaking.

HC r264, 267 DES s11

You should normally only overtake on the right. However, you may overtake on the left if traffic is moving slowly in queues and the queue on your right is moving more slowly than the one you're in.

HC r268 DES s11

Where the motorway goes uphill steeply, there may be a separate lane for slow-moving vehicles. This helps the faster-moving traffic to flow more easily.

HC r139 DES s11

If you're travelling in the left-hand lane and traffic is joining from a slip road, move to another lane if you're able to do so safely. This helps the flow of traffic joining the motorway, especially at peak times.

DES s11

Countdown markers on the left-hand verge show that you're approaching the next exit. If you want to leave the motorway, try to get into the left-hand lane in plenty of time. If you accidentally go past the exit you wanted, carry on to the next one. Never try to stop and reverse.

HC r272 DES s11

Self-reflection

Does the thought of driving on motorways make you anxious? Your instructor will only take you on a motorway when you're ready. They'll be able to help you prepare by

- talking through the practical driving skills you'll need to drive on motorways
- giving you techniques to help you to manage your anxiety and stay focused on the road.

Speed limits

The national speed limit for cars and motorcycles on a motorway is 70 mph (112 km/h). This limit applies to all lanes. Obey any signs showing a lower speed limit.

HC r261, p40 DES s11

A vehicle towing a trailer

- is restricted to a lower speed limit of 60 mph (96 km/h)
- isn't allowed to travel in the right-hand lane of a motorway with three or more lanes, unless there are lane closures
- in Northern Ireland shouldn't use the right-hand lane of a three-lane motorway.

Tip

You can use your hazard lights to warn traffic behind you that the traffic ahead is slowing down or stopping suddenly. Switch them off as soon as following traffic has reacted to your signal.

HC r116 DES s11

When you're approaching roadworks, watch for lower speed limits, especially if there's a contraflow system. You should

- obey all speed limits
- keep a safe distance from the vehicle ahead.

HC r289–290 DES s11

See section 4, Safety margins, for more information about contraflow systems.

Reducing congestion

Active traffic management (ATM), also known as 'smart motorways', tries to reduce congestion and make journey times more reliable. Where this is in use, **mandatory speed limit** signs will show on the gantries. The speed limit helps to keep the traffic speed constant so that traffic is less likely to bunch up and journey times can be improved.

DES s18

mandatory speed limit
the maximum speed at which you may travel, shown inside a red circle

In ATM areas, the hard shoulder is sometimes used as a normal traffic lane. You'll know when you can use this because a speed-limit sign will be shown above all lanes, including the hard shoulder. A red cross showing above the hard shoulder means that you shouldn't travel in this lane and it should be used only in an emergency or breakdown.

Emergency refuge areas have been built in these areas for use in cases of emergency or breakdown.

Find out more about ATM here.

www.gov.uk/guidance/how-to-drive-on-a-smart-motorway

Traffic officers operate in England and Wales, covering motorways and some 'A' class roads. They

- can stop and direct anyone on a motorway or an 'A' road
- respond to calls made on roadside emergency telephones.

HC r105, 108 DES s18

Lane markings

Reflective studs help you to see where you are on the carriageway, especially at night or in fog. Different colours are used in different places.

HC r132 DES s11

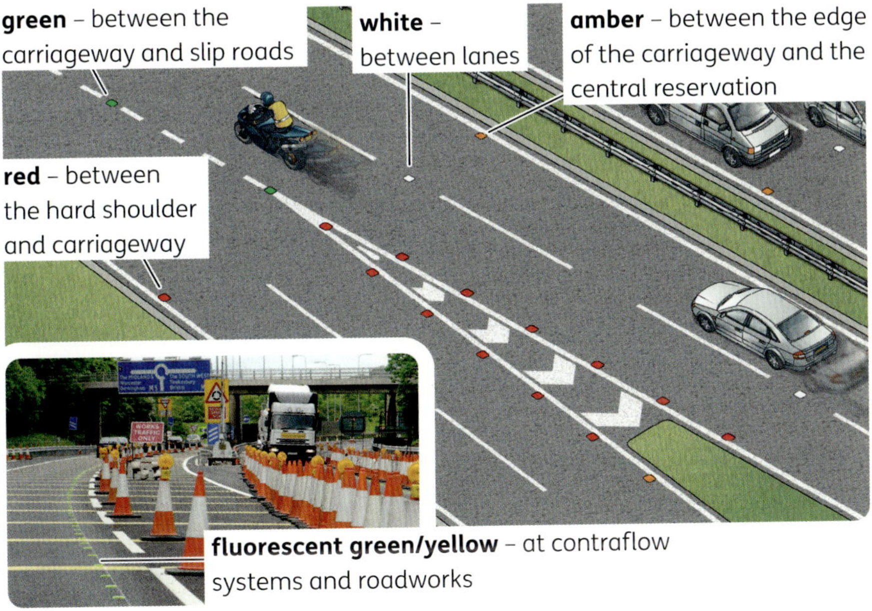

Stopping and breakdowns

Motorways are designed to keep traffic moving, so you mustn't stop on the motorway unless you have to.

Only stop on the motorway

- if flashing red lights show above every lane
- when told to do so by the police, Driver and Vehicle Standards Agency (DVSA) officers or traffic officers
- in a traffic jam
- in an emergency or breakdown.

Move over if signals on the overhead gantries advise you to do so.

HC r258, 270 DES s11 KYTS p90

Should you need to stop for any other reason, such as to have a rest, make a phone call or look at a map, either leave at the next exit or go to a service area.

HC r270 DES s11

If your vehicle breaks down or a tyre has a puncture, try to get onto the hard shoulder and call for help. If you can, use one of the emergency telephones. These are

- normally at one-mile intervals. Marker posts at 100-metre intervals point you in the direction of the nearest phone
- connected directly to a control centre, where the operator will deal with your call and direct the appropriate services to help you.

HC r275 DES s15

When you're using an emergency phone, stand facing the oncoming traffic so that you can see any hazards approaching – for example, the draught from a large vehicle driving past could take you by surprise.

If you decide to use your mobile phone

- make a note of your location (the number on the nearest marker post) before you make the call
- give this information to the emergency services.

HC r275 DES s15

Having parked your car on the hard shoulder

- switch on your hazard lights to warn other drivers that you've broken down
- switch on the sidelights at night or if visibility is poor
- don't open the offside doors (those nearest the carriageway)
- you and your passengers should leave the vehicle by the nearside doors, away from the traffic
- wait on the embankment near your vehicle, but away from the hard shoulder, in case another vehicle crashes into yours.

DES s15

When you're ready to return to the carriageway, drive along the hard shoulder to gain speed before rejoining the main carriageway by moving into a safe gap in the traffic.

HC r276 DES s15

If you can't get onto the hard shoulder when you break down

- switch on your hazard warning lights
- leave your vehicle only when you can get off the carriageway safely.

HC r277 DES s15

Meeting the standards

You must be able to

join a motorway or dual carriageway safely and responsibly from the left or the right

allow for other road users joining or leaving the motorway

change lanes safely and responsibly.

You must know and understand

that you mustn't stop on a motorway except in an emergency

that you mustn't

- pick anybody up on a motorway
- set anybody down on a motorway
- walk on a motorway, except in an emergency

the need to look well ahead for other road users joining or leaving the motorway or for queuing traffic

that some stretches of motorway may have

- local, active traffic management (sometimes called smart motorways)
- control systems installed, which will change speed limits and the direction of flow in particular lanes.

You must obey the instructions given by these systems.

Notes

You can use this page to make your own notes or diagrams about the key points you need to remember.

Think about

- At what speed should you be driving when you join the motorway?
- What should you do if you miss the exit that you want to take off the motorway?
- What information do the marker posts give you?
- What should you do if your car breaks down on the motorway?

Your notes

Things to discuss and practise with your instructor

These are just a few examples of what you could discuss and practise with your instructor. Read more about motorway driving to come up with your own ideas.

Discuss with your instructor

- how you should join the motorway and what to look out for as you do so
- the different national speed limits for various vehicles on the motorway, and in which lanes these vehicles may travel
- what you should do if you break down on the motorway
- what ATM stands for and its purpose on the motorway.

Practise with your instructor

Until you hold a full driving licence you won't be able to drive on the motorway, so practising your driving there won't be possible. Instead, practise with your instructor

- on a dual carriageway, as some of the techniques are the same as driving on the motorway; for example, joining from a slip road, lane discipline and driving at higher speeds
- identifying motorway signs, signals and road markings from *Know Your Traffic Signs* and *The Official Highway Code*.

9.1 **Mark one answer** **DES s11, HC r259**

You're joining a motorway from a slip road. How should you deal with traffic already on the motorway?

- ☐ Carry on along the hard shoulder until you see a safe gap
- ☐ Stop at the end of the slip road and look for a safe gap
- ☐ Use the slip road to accelerate until you're moving much faster than the motorway traffic
- ☐ Match your speed to traffic in the left-hand lane and filter into a safe gap

You should give way to traffic already on the motorway. Where possible, traffic may move over to let you in, but don't force your way into the traffic stream. Traffic could be travelling at high speed, so try to match your speed to filter in without affecting the traffic flow.

9.2 **Mark one answer** **HC r261, p40**

What's the national speed limit on motorways for cars and motorcycles?

- ☐ 30 mph
- ☐ 50 mph
- ☐ 60 mph
- ☐ 70 mph

Travelling at the national speed limit doesn't allow you to hog the right-hand lane. Always use the left-hand lane whenever possible. When leaving a motorway, get into the left-hand lane well before your exit. Reduce your speed on the slip road and look out for sharp bends or curves and traffic queuing at roundabouts.

9.3 **Mark one answer** **DES s11, HC r264**

Which vehicles should use the left-hand lane on a three-lane motorway?

- ☐ Any vehicle that isn't overtaking
- ☐ Large vehicles only
- ☐ Emergency vehicles only
- ☐ Slow vehicles only

On a motorway, all traffic should use the left-hand lane unless overtaking. When overtaking a number of slower vehicles, move back to the left-hand lane when you're safely past. Check your mirrors frequently and don't stay in the middle or right-hand lane if the left-hand lane is free.

9.4 Mark one answer DES s11, HC r265

Which vehicles aren't allowed to use the right-hand lane of a three-lane motorway?

- ☐ Small delivery vans
- ☐ Motorcycles
- ☐ Vehicles towing a trailer
- ☐ Motorcycle and sidecar outfits

On the motorway, any vehicle towing a trailer is restricted to 60 mph. It isn't allowed in the right-hand lane, as it might hold up faster-moving traffic that wishes to overtake in that lane.

9.5 Mark one answer DES s15, HC r275, 283

Your vehicle breaks down on a motorway and you need to call for help. Why might it be better to use an emergency roadside telephone rather than a mobile phone?

- ☐ It connects you to a local garage
- ☐ Using a mobile phone will distract other drivers
- ☐ It allows easy location by the emergency services
- ☐ Mobile phones don't work on motorways

On a motorway, it's best to use a roadside emergency telephone so that the emergency services are able to find you easily. The location of the nearest telephone is shown by an arrow on marker posts at the edge of the hard shoulder. If you use a mobile, find out the number on the nearest marker post before you call. This number will let the operator know where you are and in which direction you're travelling.

9.6 Mark one answer DES s15, HC r276

Your vehicle broke down on the hard shoulder of a motorway, but has now been repaired. How should you rejoin the main carriageway?

- ☐ Move out onto the carriageway, then build up your speed
- ☐ Move out onto the carriageway using your hazard warning lights
- ☐ Gain speed on the hard shoulder before moving out onto the carriageway
- ☐ Wait on the hard shoulder until someone flashes their headlights at you

Signal your intention and build up sufficient speed on the hard shoulder so that you can filter into a safe gap in the traffic. Don't push your way into a small gap or cause other traffic to alter speed or direction.

9.7 **Mark one answer** **DES s11**

You're travelling along a motorway. Where would you find a crawler or climbing lane?

- ☐ On a steep gradient
- ☐ Before a service area
- ☐ Before a junction
- ☐ Along the hard shoulder

Large, slow-moving vehicles can hinder the progress of other traffic. On a steep gradient, an extra crawler lane may be provided for slow-moving vehicles to allow faster-moving traffic to flow more easily.

9.8 **Mark one answer** **DES s11, HC p112, KYTS p79**

What do these motorway signs mean?

- ☐ They're countdown markers to a bridge
- ☐ They're distance markers to the next telephone
- ☐ They're countdown markers to the next exit
- ☐ They warn of a police control ahead

The exit from a motorway is indicated by countdown markers. These are positioned 90 metres (100 yards) apart, the first being 270 metres (300 yards) from the start of the slip road. Move into the left-hand lane well before you reach the start of the slip road.

9.9 Mark one answer — DES s11, HC r132

Where are amber reflective studs found on a motorway?

- ☐ Between the hard shoulder and the carriageway
- ☐ Between the acceleration lane and the carriageway
- ☐ Between the central reservation and the carriageway
- ☐ Between each pair of lanes

On motorways, reflective studs of various colours are fixed in the road between the lanes. These help you to identify which lane you're in when it's dark or in poor visibility. Amber-coloured studs are found on the right-hand edge of the main carriageway, next to the central reservation.

9.10 Mark one answer — DES s11, HC r132

What colour are the reflective studs between the lanes on a motorway?

- ☐ Green
- ☐ Amber
- ☐ White
- ☐ Red

White studs are found between the lanes on motorways. They reflect back the light from your headlights. This is especially useful in bad weather, when visibility is restricted.

9.11 Mark one answer — DES s11, HC r132

What colour are the reflective studs between a motorway and a slip road?

- ☐ Amber
- ☐ White
- ☐ Green
- ☐ Red

The studs between the carriageway and the hard shoulder are normally red. These change to green where there's a slip road, helping you to identify slip roads when visibility is poor or when it's dark.

9.12 Mark one answer — DES s15, HC r275

Your vehicle has broken down on a motorway. In which direction should you walk to find the nearest emergency telephone?

- ☐ With the traffic flow
- ☐ Facing oncoming traffic
- ☐ In the direction shown on the marker posts
- ☐ In the direction of the nearest exit

Along the hard shoulder there are marker posts at 100-metre intervals. These will direct you to the nearest emergency telephone.

9.13 Mark one answer | DES s11, HC r259

Why is it important to make full use of the slip road as you join a motorway?

- ☐ Because there's space available to turn round if you need to
- ☐ To allow you direct access to the overtaking lanes
- ☐ To allow you to fit safely into the traffic flow in the left-hand lane
- ☐ Because you can continue on the hard shoulder

Try to join the motorway without affecting the progress of the traffic in the left-hand lane and always give way to traffic already on the motorway. At busy times, you may have to slow down to merge into slow-moving traffic.

9.14 Mark one answer | DES s15, HC r275

How should you position yourself when you use the emergency telephone on a motorway?

- ☐ Stay close to the carriageway
- ☐ Face the oncoming traffic
- ☐ Keep your back to the traffic
- ☐ Stand on the hard shoulder

Traffic is passing you at speed. If the draught from a large lorry catches you by surprise, it could blow you off balance and even onto the carriageway. By facing the oncoming traffic, you can see approaching lorries and so be prepared for their draught. You'll also be in a position to see any other hazards approaching.

9.15 Mark one answer | DES s11, HC r132

What colour are the reflective studs between the hard shoulder and the left-hand lane of a motorway?

- ☐ Green
- ☐ Red
- ☐ White
- ☐ Amber

Red studs are placed between the edge of the carriageway and the hard shoulder. Where slip roads leave or join the motorway, the studs are green.

9.16 Mark one answer | DES s11, HC r264

On a three-lane motorway, which lane should you use if there's no traffic ahead?

- ☐ Left
- ☐ Right
- ☐ Centre
- ☐ Either the right or centre

On a three-lane motorway, you should travel in the left-hand lane unless you're overtaking. This applies regardless of the speed at which you're travelling.

9.17 Mark one answer **DES s11, HC r290**

What should you do when going through a contraflow system on a motorway?

- ☐ Use dipped headlights
- ☐ Keep a good distance from the vehicle ahead
- ☐ Switch lanes to keep the traffic flowing
- ☐ Stay close to the vehicle ahead to reduce queues

At roadworks, and especially where a contraflow system is operating, a speed restriction is likely to be in place. Keep to the lower speed limit and don't

- switch lanes
- get too close to the vehicle in front of you.

Be aware that there will be no permanent barrier between you and the oncoming traffic.

9.18 Mark one answer **DES s11, HC r132**

You're on a three-lane motorway. Which lane are you in if there are red reflective studs on your left and white ones to your right?

- ☐ In the right-hand lane
- ☐ In the middle lane
- ☐ On the hard shoulder
- ☐ In the left-hand lane

The colours of the reflective studs on the motorway and their locations are

- red – between the hard shoulder and the carriageway
- white – between lanes
- amber – between the carriageway and the central reservation
- green – along slip-road exits and entrances
- bright green/yellow – at roadworks and contraflow systems.

9.19 Mark one answer — DES s11, HC r288, 289

What should you do when you're approaching roadworks on a motorway?

- ☐ Speed up to clear the area quickly
- ☐ Always use the hard shoulder
- ☐ Obey the speed limit
- ☐ Stay very close to the vehicle in front

Be aware of reduced speed limits at roadworks. Speed limits shown inside a red circle are mandatory and cameras are often used to enforce the reduced limit. Slow down in good time and keep your distance from the vehicle in front.

9.20 Mark one answer — DES s2, HC r253

Which vehicles are prohibited from using the motorway?

- ☐ Powered mobility scooters
- ☐ Motorcycles over 50 cc
- ☐ Double-deck buses
- ☐ Cars with automatic transmission

Motorways mustn't be used by pedestrians, cyclists, motorcycles under 50 cc, certain slow-moving vehicles without permission, and powered wheelchairs/mobility scooters.

9.21 Mark one answer — DES s11, HC r254

What should you do while you're driving or riding along a motorway?

- ☐ Look much further ahead than you would on other roads
- ☐ Travel much faster than you would on other roads
- ☐ Maintain a shorter separation distance than you would on other roads
- ☐ Concentrate more than you would on other roads

Traffic on motorways usually travels faster than on other roads. You need to be looking further ahead to give yourself more time to react to any hazard that may develop.

9.22 Mark one answer — DES s11, HC r259, 264

What should you do immediately after joining a motorway?

- ☐ Try to overtake
- ☐ Re-adjust your mirrors
- ☐ Position your vehicle in the centre lane
- ☐ Stay in the left-hand lane

When you've just joined a motorway, stay in the left-hand lane long enough to get used to the higher speeds of motorway traffic before considering overtaking.

9.23 Mark one answer DES s11, HC r267

When would you use the right-hand lane on a three-lane motorway?

- ☐ When you're turning right
- ☐ When you're overtaking
- ☐ When you're travelling above the speed limit
- ☐ When you're trying to save fuel

The right-hand lane of the motorway is for overtaking. Sometimes you may be directed into a right-hand lane as a result of roadworks or a traffic incident. This will be indicated by signs or officers directing the traffic.

9.24 Mark one answer DES s11, 15, HC r269, 270

You're on a motorway that isn't subject to smart motorway regulations. When should you use the hard shoulder?

- ☐ When you're stopping in an emergency
- ☐ When you're leaving the motorway
- ☐ When you're stopping for a rest
- ☐ When you're joining the motorway

Don't use the hard shoulder for stopping unless it's an emergency. If you want to stop for any other reason, go to the next exit or service area.

9.25 Mark one answer HC p102, KYTS p90

You're in the right-hand lane of a three-lane motorway. What do these overhead signs mean?

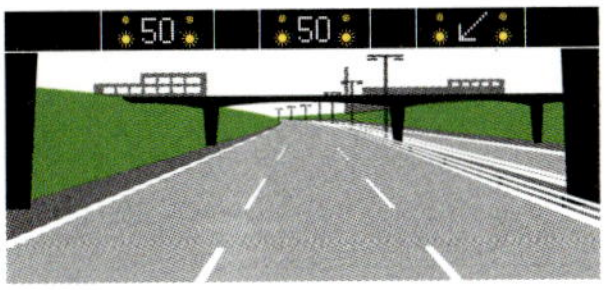

- ☐ Move to the left and reduce your speed to 50 mph
- ☐ There are roadworks 50 metres (55 yards) ahead
- ☐ Use the hard shoulder until you've passed the hazard
- ☐ Leave the motorway at the next exit

You must obey these signs even if there appear to be no problems ahead. There could be queuing traffic or another hazard that you can't see yet.

9.26 Mark one answer — DES s11, HC r270

When are you allowed to stop on a motorway?

- ☐ When you need to walk and get fresh air
- ☐ When you wish to pick up hitchhikers
- ☐ When you're signalled to do so by traffic signals
- ☐ When you need to use a mobile telephone

You must stop if overhead gantry signs show a red cross above every lane on the motorway. If any of the other lanes doesn't show a red cross, you may move into that lane and continue if it's safe to do so.

9.27 Mark one answer — DES s11

You're travelling in the left-hand lane of a three-lane motorway. How should you react to traffic joining from a slip road?

- ☐ Increase your speed to ensure they join behind you
- ☐ Adjust your speed or change lane if you can do so safely
- ☐ Maintain a steady speed
- ☐ Switch on your hazard warning lights

Plan well ahead when approaching a slip road. If you see traffic joining the motorway, be prepared to adjust your speed or move to another lane if it's safe to do so. This can help the flow of traffic joining the motorway, especially at peak times.

9.28 Mark one answer — DES s11, HC r264

How should you use the lanes on a motorway?

- ☐ Use the lane that has the least traffic
- ☐ Keep to the left-hand lane unless you're overtaking
- ☐ Overtake using the lane that's clearest
- ☐ Stay in one lane until you reach your exit

You should normally travel in the left-hand lane unless you're overtaking a slower-moving vehicle. When you've finished overtaking, move back into the left-hand lane, but don't cut across in front of the vehicle that you've overtaken.

9.29 Mark one answer — DES s11, HC r268

You're travelling along a motorway. When are you allowed to overtake on the left?

- ☐ When you can see well ahead that the hard shoulder is clear
- ☐ When the traffic in the right-hand lane is signalling right
- ☐ When you warn drivers behind by signalling left
- ☐ When in queues and traffic to your right is moving more slowly than you are

Never overtake on the left, unless the traffic is moving in queues and the queue on your right is moving more slowly than the one you're in.

9.30 **Mark one answer** **DES s11, HC r269**

When would you use an emergency refuge area on a smart motorway?

- ☐ In cases of emergency or breakdown
- ☐ If you think you'll be involved in a road rage incident
- ☐ To stop and check where you are
- ☐ To make a private phone call

On smart motorways, emergency refuge areas are built at the side of the hard shoulder. If you break down, try to get your vehicle into the refuge, where there's an emergency telephone. The phone connects directly to a control centre. Remember to take care when rejoining the motorway, especially if the hard shoulder is being used as a running lane.

9.31 **Mark one answer** **DES s11, HC r108, p105**

Traffic officers operate on motorways and some primary routes in England and Wales. What are they authorised to do?

- ☐ Stop and arrest drivers who break the law
- ☐ Repair broken-down vehicles on the motorway
- ☐ Issue fixed penalty notices
- ☐ Stop and direct anyone on a motorway

Traffic officers don't have enforcement powers but are able to stop and direct people on motorways and some 'A' class roads. They operate in England and Wales and work in partnership with the police at incidents, providing a highly trained and visible service. They're recognised by an orange-and-yellow jacket and their vehicle has yellow-and-black markings.

9.32 Mark one answer DES s11, HC r258, 269

You're on a smart motorway. What does it mean when a red cross is displayed above the hard shoulder?

- ☐ Pull up in this lane to answer your mobile phone
- ☐ Use this lane as a running lane
- ☐ This lane can be used if you need a rest
- ☐ You shouldn't travel in this lane

Some motorways have been redesigned as smart motorways. At certain times, the hard shoulder will be open as a running lane. However, a red cross above the hard shoulder shows that it isn't open as a running lane and should only be used for emergencies and breakdowns.

9.33 Mark one answer DES s11, HC r269

You're on a smart motorway. What does it mean when a mandatory speed limit is displayed above the hard shoulder?

- ☐ You shouldn't travel in this lane
- ☐ The hard shoulder can be used as a running lane
- ☐ You can park on the hard shoulder if you feel tired
- ☐ You can pull up in this lane to answer a mobile phone

A mandatory speed-limit sign above the hard shoulder shows that this part of the road can be used as a running lane between junctions. You must stay within the speed limit. Look out for vehicles that may have broken down and could be blocking the hard shoulder.

9.34 Mark one answer **DES s11, HC r261**

How do smart motorways prevent traffic bunching?

- ☐ By using higher speed limits
- ☐ By using advisory speed limits
- ☐ By using minimum speed limits
- ☐ By using variable speed limits

When a smart motorway is operating, you must follow the mandatory signs on the gantries above each lane, including the hard shoulder. Variable speed limits help keep the traffic moving and also help to prevent bunching.

9.35 Mark one answer **DES s11, HC r261**

What helps to reduce traffic bunching on a motorway?

- ☐ Variable speed limits
- ☐ Contraflow systems
- ☐ National speed limits
- ☐ Lane closures

Congestion can be reduced by keeping traffic at a constant speed. At busy times, maximum speed limits are displayed on overhead gantries. These can be varied quickly, depending on the amount of traffic. By keeping to a constant speed on busy sections of motorway, overall journey times are normally improved.

9.36 Mark one answer **DES s11, HC r270**

When may you stop on a motorway?

- ☐ If you have to read a map
- ☐ When you're tired and need a rest
- ☐ If your mobile phone rings
- ☐ In an emergency or breakdown

You shouldn't normally stop on a motorway, but there may be occasions when you need to do so. If your vehicle breaks down or there's an emergency, stop on the hard shoulder and use the emergency telephones to call for assistance.

9.37 Mark one answer **HC r261, p40**

What's the national speed limit for a car or motorcycle on a motorway?

- ☐ 50 mph
- ☐ 60 mph
- ☐ 70 mph
- ☐ 80 mph

The national speed limit for a car or motorcycle on a motorway is 70 mph. Lower speed limits may be in force; for example, at roadworks. Variable speed limits also operate in some areas when the motorway is very busy. Cars or motorcycles towing trailers are subject to a lower speed limit.

9.38 Mark one answer DES s11, HC r258, p102, KYTS p89

You're on a motorway. What must you do if there's a red cross showing above every lane?

- ☐ Pull onto the hard shoulder
- ☐ Slow down and watch for further signals
- ☐ Leave at the next exit
- ☐ Stop and wait

A red cross signal above all lanes means you must stop and wait. Don't change lanes and don't try to continue any further along the motorway.

9.39 Mark one answer DES s11, HC r269

You're on a smart motorway. What does it mean if a red cross is showing above the hard shoulder and mandatory speed limits above all other lanes?

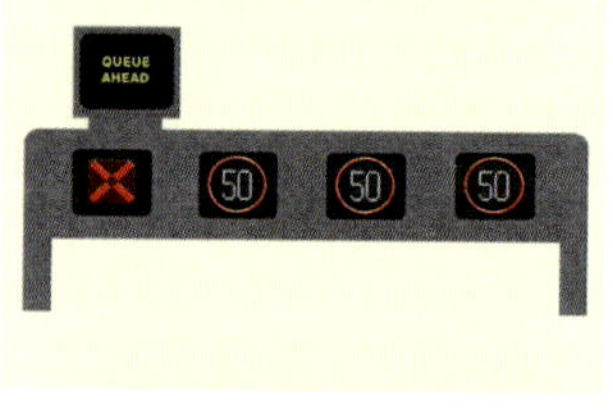

- ☐ The hard shoulder can be used as a rest area if you feel tired
- ☐ The hard shoulder is for emergency or breakdown use only
- ☐ The hard shoulder can be used as a normal running lane
- ☐ The hard shoulder has a speed limit of 50 mph

A red cross above the hard shoulder shows that it's closed as a running lane and should only be used for emergencies or breakdowns. On a smart motorway, the hard shoulder may be used as a running lane at busy times. This will be shown by a mandatory speed limit on the gantry above the hard shoulder.

9.40 Mark one answer DES s11, HC r269

On a smart motorway, what does this sign mean?

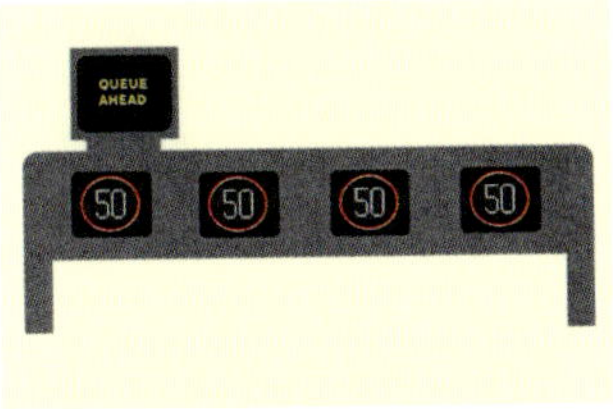

- ☐ Use any lane except the hard shoulder
- ☐ Use the hard shoulder only
- ☐ Use the three right-hand lanes only
- ☐ Use all the lanes, including the hard shoulder

You must obey mandatory speed-limit signs above motorway lanes, including the hard shoulder. In this case, you can use the hard shoulder as a running lane but you should look for any vehicles that may have broken down and may be blocking the hard shoulder.

9.41 Mark one answer DES s11, HC r91

Where should you stop to rest if you feel tired while you're travelling along a motorway?

- ☐ On the hard shoulder
- ☐ At the nearest service area
- ☐ On a slip road
- ☐ On the central reservation

If you feel tired, stop at the nearest service area. If that's too far away, leave the motorway at the next exit and find a safe place to stop. You mustn't stop on the carriageway or hard shoulder of a motorway except in an emergency, when in a traffic queue, or when signalled to do so by a police officer, a traffic officer or traffic signals. Plan your journey so that you have regular rest stops.

9.42 Mark one answer DES s19, HC r261, p40

What's the speed limit for a car towing a trailer on a motorway?

- ☐ 40 mph
- ☐ 50 mph
- ☐ 60 mph
- ☐ 70 mph

If you're towing a small, light trailer, it won't reduce your vehicle's performance by very much and it may not be visible in your mirrors. However, strong winds or buffeting from large vehicles might cause the trailer to snake from side to side. Be aware of your speed and don't exceed the reduced speed limit imposed on vehicles towing trailers.

9.43 Mark one answer — DES s11, HC r264

When should you use the left-hand lane of a motorway?

- ☐ When your vehicle breaks down
- ☐ When you're overtaking slower traffic in the other lanes
- ☐ When you're making a phone call
- ☐ When the road ahead is clear

You should drive in the left-hand lane whenever possible. Only use the other lanes for overtaking or when directed to do so by signals. Using other lanes when the left-hand lane is empty can frustrate drivers behind you.

9.44 Mark one answer — DES s11, HC r116

You're driving on a motorway and have to slow down suddenly due to a hazard ahead. How can you warn drivers behind of the hazard?

- ☐ Switch on your hazard warning lights
- ☐ Switch on your headlights
- ☐ Sound your horn
- ☐ Flash your headlights

Using your hazard warning lights, as well as your brake lights, will give the traffic behind an extra warning of the problem ahead. Only use them for long enough for your warning to be seen.

9.45 Mark one answer — DES s15, HC r275

Your car gets a puncture while you're driving on the motorway. What should you do when you've stopped on the hard shoulder?

- ☐ Carefully change the wheel yourself
- ☐ Use an emergency telephone and call for help
- ☐ Try to wave down another vehicle for help
- ☐ Only change the wheel if you have a passenger to help you

Park as far to the left as you can and leave the vehicle by the nearside door. Don't attempt even simple repairs. Instead, walk to an emergency telephone on your side of the road and phone for help. While waiting for help to arrive, stay by your car, keeping well away from the carriageway and hard shoulder.

9.46 Mark one answer — DES s11, HC r263

What should you do if you're driving on a motorway and you miss the exit that you wanted to take?

- ☐ Carefully reverse along the hard shoulder
- ☐ Carry on to the next exit
- ☐ Carefully reverse in the left-hand lane
- ☐ Make a U-turn at the next gap in the central reservation

It's illegal to reverse, cross the central reservation or drive against the traffic flow on a motorway. If you miss your exit, carry on until you reach the next one. Ask yourself why you missed your exit – if you think that your concentration is fading, take a break before continuing your journey.

9.47 **Mark one answer** **DES s15, HC r277**

Your vehicle has broken down on a motorway. What should you do if you aren't able to get onto the hard shoulder?

- ☐ Switch on your hazard warning lights
- ☐ Stop the traffic behind and ask for help
- ☐ Attempt to repair your vehicle quickly
- ☐ Stand behind your vehicle to warn others

If you can't get your vehicle onto the hard shoulder, use your hazard warning lights to warn others. Leave your vehicle only when you can safely get clear of the carriageway. Don't try to repair the vehicle or attempt to place any warning device on the carriageway.

9.48 **Mark one answer** **DES s11**

Why is it particularly important to check your vehicle before making a long motorway journey?

- ☐ You'll have to do more harsh braking on motorways
- ☐ Motorway services areas don't deal with breakdowns
- ☐ The road surface will wear down the tyres faster
- ☐ Continuous high speeds increase the risk of your vehicle breaking down

Before you start your journey, make sure that your vehicle can cope with the demands of high-speed driving. You should check a number of things; the main ones being fuel, oil, water and tyres. You also need to plan rest stops if you're making a long journey.

9.49 **Mark one answer** **DES s11, HC r116**

You're driving on a motorway. What does it mean if the car in front shows its hazard warning lights for a short time?

- ☐ The driver wants you to overtake
- ☐ The other car is going to change lanes
- ☐ Traffic ahead is slowing or stopping suddenly
- ☐ There's a police speed check ahead

If the vehicle in front shows its hazard warning lights, there may be an incident, stopped traffic or queuing traffic ahead. By keeping a safe distance from the vehicle in front, you're able to look beyond it and see any hazards well ahead.

9.50 Mark one answer — DES s11, HC r272

You're driving on the motorway. Which lane should you get into well before you reach your exit?

- ☐ The middle lane
- ☐ The left-hand lane
- ☐ The hard shoulder
- ☐ The right-hand lane

You'll see the first advance direction sign one mile from a motorway exit. If you're travelling at 60 mph in the right-hand lane, you'll only have about 50 seconds before you reach the countdown markers. There'll be another sign at the half-mile point. Don't cut across lanes of traffic at the last moment – move to the left-hand lane in good time.

9.51 Mark one answer — DES s2, HC r253

What restrictions apply to people who have a provisional driving licence?

- ☐ They can't drive over 30 mph
- ☐ They can't drive at night
- ☐ They can't drive unaccompanied
- ☐ They can't drive with more than one passenger

You won't be able to drive unaccompanied until you've passed your practical driving test. If you haven't driven on the motorway while you were learning, ask your instructor to take you for a lesson on the motorway when you've passed your test. Alternatively, you could take part in the Pass Plus scheme. This has been created for new drivers and includes motorway driving. Ask your instructor for details.

9.52 Mark one answer — DES s15, HC r283

Your vehicle breaks down on a motorway and you manage to stop on the hard shoulder. What should you do if you use your mobile phone to call for help?

- ☐ Stand at the rear of the vehicle while making the call
- ☐ Phone a friend and ask them to come and collect you
- ☐ Wait in the car for the emergency services to arrive
- ☐ Check your location from the nearest marker posts beside the hard shoulder

You should use an emergency telephone when you break down on the motorway; only use your mobile if this isn't possible. The emergency services need to know your exact location so they can reach you as quickly as possible. Look for a number on the nearest marker post beside the hard shoulder. Give this number when you call the emergency services.

9.53 NI EXEMPT **Mark one answer** **DES s19, HC r265**

You're towing a trailer along a three-lane motorway. When may you use the right-hand lane?

- ☐ When there are lane closures
- ☐ When there's slow-moving traffic
- ☐ When you can maintain a high speed
- ☐ When large vehicles are in the left and centre lanes

If you're towing a caravan or trailer, you mustn't use the right-hand lane of a motorway with three or more lanes except in certain specified circumstances, such as when lanes are closed.

9.54 **Mark one answer** **DES s11, HC r290**

What would you expect to find at a contraflow system on a motorway?

- ☐ Temporary traffic lights
- ☐ Lower speed limits
- ☐ Wider lanes than normal
- ☐ Road humps

When approaching a contraflow system, reduce speed in good time and obey all speed limits. You may be travelling in a narrower lane than normal, with no permanent barrier between you and the oncoming traffic. Be aware that the hard shoulder may be used for traffic and the road ahead could be obstructed by slow-moving or broken-down vehicles.

Case study practice – 9 Motorway driving

You're towing a small trailer behind your car and joining the motorway from a slip road. The motorway is busy with morning traffic.

Further along the motorway, the central reservation is coned off for repair. Lanes have been narrowed for some distance, using cones and temporary reflective studs.

Once past the roadworks, traffic speeds up and the left-hand lane becomes clear.

You then realise that you've gone past the exit you need.

9.1 Who has priority at the motorway/slip-road junction?

Mark **one** answer

- ☐ Vehicles already travelling in the left-hand lane
- ☐ Vehicles joining the motorway from the slip road
- ☐ Vehicles travelling along on the hard shoulder
- ☐ Vehicles leaving the motorway via the slip road

HC r259 DES s11

9.2 What colours would these studs be?

Mark **one** answer

- ☐ Blue/yellow
- ☐ Red/yellow
- ☐ Green/yellow
- ☐ Orange/yellow

HC r132 DES s11

9.3 Which lane should you use after the roadworks?

Mark **one** answer

- ☐ The middle lane
- ☐ The right-hand lane
- ☐ The hard shoulder
- ☐ The left-hand lane

HC r264 DES s11

9.4 What's the national motorway speed limit for your vehicle and trailer?

Mark **one** answer

- ☐ 50 mph
- ☐ 60 mph
- ☐ 70 mph
- ☐ 80 mph

HC p40 DES s19

9.5 What should you do about leaving the motorway?

Mark **one** answer

- ☐ Continue on until you reach the next exit
- ☐ Reverse back to the exit you've just missed
- ☐ Go on until you reach the end of the motorway
- ☐ Wait on the hard shoulder for traffic officers

HC r272 DES s11

Section ten

Rules of the road

In this section, you'll learn about

- the speed limits that you need to obey
- how to use junctions and lanes safely
- rules about overtaking and reversing
- driving over pedestrian crossings and level crossings
- where you can stop and park safely and legally.

Rules of the road

It's important that everyone knows and follows the rules of the road. Some are legal requirements and some are recommended best practice, but they all help to make the roads safer.

Speed limits

You **MUST NOT** drive faster than the speed limit for the road you're on or your vehicle type. Where no other limit is shown, the national speed limit for cars and motorcycles is

- 60 mph (96 km/h) on a single carriageway road
- 70 mph (112 km/h) on a dual carriageway or motorway.

There are lower speed limits for these vehicles when towing a trailer or caravan

- 50 mph (80 km/h) on a single carriageway road
- 60 mph (96 km/h) on a dual carriageway or motorway.

HC r124, p40

Where there are street lights, there's normally a 30 mph (48 km/h) speed limit for all vehicles unless signs show otherwise.

HC r124, p40

On some roads you may see a sign showing a minimum speed limit. You should travel above the limit shown on the sign unless it's not safe to do so.

HC p107

Self-reflection

Do you sometimes go over the speed limit? Ask your instructor to help you identify correct speed limits. Talk to them about how to keep to a speed that's appropriate for the driving conditions. Remember, the speed limit is the absolute maximum. It doesn't mean that it's safe to drive at that speed whatever the conditions. Driving at speeds too fast for the road and traffic conditions is dangerous.

Speed limits

Type of vehicle	Built-up areas*	Single carriage-ways	Dual carriage-ways	Motorways
	mph (km/h)	mph (km/h)	mph (km/h)	mph (km/h)
 **Cars and motorcycles** (including car-derived vans up to 2 tonnes maximum laden weight)	30 (48)	60 (96)	70 (112)	70 (112)
 **Cars towing caravans or trailers** (including car-derived vans and motorcycles)	30 (48)	50 (80)	60 (96)	60 (96)
 **Buses, coaches and minibuses** (not exceeding 12 metres in overall length)	30 (48)	50 (80)	60 (96)	70 (112)
 **Goods vehicles** (not exceeding 7.5 tonnes maximum laden weight)	30 (48)	50 (80)	60 (96)	70† (112)
 **Goods vehicles** (exceeding 7.5 tonnes maximum laden weight) in England and Wales	30 (48)	50 (80)	60 (96)	60 (96)
 **Goods vehicles** (exceeding 7.5 tonnes maximum laden weight) in Scotland	30 (48)	40 (64)	50 (80)	60 (96)

*The 30 mph limit usually applies to all traffic on all roads with street lighting unless signs show otherwise.
†60 mph (96 km/h) if articulated or towing a trailer.

Be aware that large vehicles may have speed limiters – buses and coaches are restricted to 62 mph and large goods vehicles to 56 mph.

Always drive with care and take account of the road and weather conditions. If you're driving along a street where cars are parked, keep your speed down and beware of

pedestrians (especially children) stepping out from behind parked vehicles

vehicles pulling out

drivers' doors opening.

HC r152 DES s10

At roadworks, there may be temporary speed limits to slow traffic. These are mandatory speed limits and may be enforced by cameras.

HC r288 KYTS p90

The Think! road safety website has more advice on speed and speed limits.

http://think.gov.uk/road-safety-laws/#speed

Lanes and junctions

Some roads have lanes reserved for specific vehicles, such as cycles, buses, trams or, in some places, motorcycles. These are marked by signs and road markings, and should be used only by those vehicles during the lanes' hours of operation, unless signs indicate otherwise.

HC r141

Never drive or park in a cycle lane marked by a solid white line during its hours of operation. Don't drive or park in a cycle lane marked by a broken line unless it's unavoidable.

HC r140–141 KYTS p32–36

You should only drive over a footpath when it's necessary in order to reach a property.

HC r145

On a dual carriageway, the right-hand lane is only for turning right or overtaking. The same rule applies to three-lane dual carriageways.

Tip

If you want to turn right onto a dual carriageway that has a central reservation that's too narrow to fit the length of your vehicle, wait until the road is clear in both directions before you emerge. If you emerge into the central reservation but your vehicle is too long, it could obstruct traffic coming from your right.

HC r173 DES s8

Always be careful at junctions. As you approach a junction, move into the correct position in plenty of time.

When you're turning left, keep well to the left as you approach the junction. In slow-moving traffic, remember to check for cyclists to your left before you turn.

HC r181–183 DES s8

If you're on a busy road and you find you're travelling in the wrong direction, or you're in the wrong lane at a busy junction, keep going until you can find somewhere safe, such as a quiet side road, where you can turn around.

HC r200 DES s9

A box junction is marked by yellow hatched lines, and should be kept clear. Only enter it if your exit road is clear – otherwise, wait on your side of the junction. You can, however, wait in the box if you want to turn right and are waiting for a gap in the oncoming traffic before you can turn.

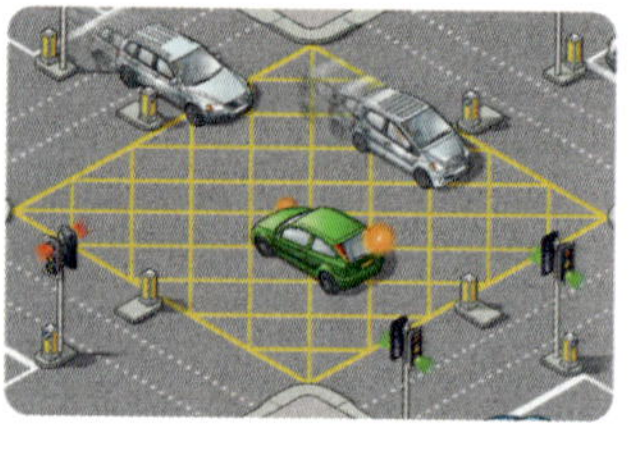

HC r174 DES s6

Tip

If something is blocking your side of the road, such as a parked car, you should give way to oncoming traffic if there isn't room for you both to continue safely.

DES s7

Crossroads

If you're turning right at a crossroads when an oncoming driver is also turning right, it's normally safer to keep the other vehicle to your right and turn behind it. If you have to pass in front of the other vehicle, take extra care as your view may be blocked.

HC r181

At crossroads where there aren't any signs or markings, no-one has priority. Check very carefully in all directions before you drive into the junction.

HC r146 DES s8

Roundabouts

Roundabouts are designed to help traffic flow smoothly. Follow signs and road markings as you approach and drive around them. Normally, if you're going straight ahead

- don't signal as you approach
- signal left just after you pass the exit before the one you want.

HC r185–186 DES s8

Some vehicles may not follow the normal rules.

- Cyclists and horse riders may stay in the left-hand lane even if they're turning right.
- Long vehicles may take up a different position to stop the rear of the vehicle hitting the kerb.

HC r187

Self-reflection

Safety at roundabouts and junctions takes good judgement and excellent control of your vehicle. If you're finding this a challenge, chat to your instructor about the barriers you're facing. Ask them to help you practise by choosing quiet junctions and roundabouts. Remember – waiting for a safe gap is no reflection on your driving skills. It may take some time to judge the speed of the traffic, but this is a critical part of knowing when it's safe to go.

Overtaking

Overtaking can be dangerous. Ask yourself if you really need to do it, and never overtake if you're in any doubt as to whether it's safe.

HC r163 DES s7

You should normally overtake other vehicles on the right, but in a one-way street you can pass slower traffic on the left. Take extra care if you're overtaking on a dual carriageway, as the right-hand lane can also be used by traffic turning right.

HC r137–138 DES s7

Tip

At night, if a vehicle overtakes you, dip your headlights as soon as it passes you, otherwise your lights could dazzle the other driver.

HC r115

Reversing

Never reverse

- for longer than you have to
- from a side road into a main road.

HC r200–203 DES s9

When reversing into a side road, always check road and traffic conditions in all directions. You can undo your seat belt while reversing if it helps you to get a better view. You **MUST** refasten the belt once you've completed the manoeuvre.

If you're not sure whether it's safe, get out and check before you start to reverse. The front of your vehicle swings out as you turn and this may create a hazard for passing traffic.

Pedestrian crossings

If someone is standing on the pavement waiting to cross at a zebra crossing, stop and let them cross if it's safe to do so.

Pelican crossings are controlled by traffic lights. When the red light changes to flashing amber, wait for any pedestrians to finish crossing before you move off.

On toucan crossings, cyclists are allowed to cycle across at the same time as pedestrians.

HC r195–199 DES s7 KYTS p124

For more information on pedestrian crossings, see section 6, Vulnerable road users.

Level crossings

A level crossing is where a railway line crosses the road.

It may have countdown markers to warn you if the crossing is hidden, such as around a bend.

Controlled crossings have traffic-light signals with twin flashing red lights, plus a warning alarm for pedestrians.

Crossings may or may not have barriers.

	If this happens …	you should do this
	The warning lights come on as you're approaching the crossing.	Stop. You **MUST** obey the red lights, by law.
	You're already on the crossing when the warning lights come on or a bell rings.	Keep going and clear the crossing.
	You're waiting at a level crossing and a train has passed but the red lights keep flashing.	You **MUST** wait: there may be another train coming.

HC r293, p109 DES s6 KYTS p26–29

Some types of level crossing don't have lights. These include crossings with user-operated gates or barriers, and open crossings. Be careful at all level crossings.

HC r295–299 DES s7

See the Network Rail guide to using level crossings safely.

networkrail.co.uk/running-the-railway/looking-after-the-railway/level-crossings

Stopping and parking

Always think carefully about where you stop and park your car, to make sure it's safe and legal.

At night, the safest place to park your vehicle is in your garage, if you have one. If you're away from home, try to find a secure car park or park in a well-lit area.

HC r239, p131 DES s9

If you have to park on a road at night, you **MUST** leave your parking lights on if the speed limit on that road is over 30 mph (48 km/h). You should normally park on the left-hand side of the road so that other road users can see your reflectors, but in a one-way street you can park on either side.

HC r248–250 DES s13

You **MUST NOT** stop on a **clearway**. On an urban clearway, you may stop, but only to drop off and pick up passengers. On a road marked with double white lines (even where one of the lines is broken), you may stop, but only to drop off and pick up passengers or to load/unload goods.

HC r240 DES s6

clearway

a stretch of road or street where stopping isn't allowed

Don't park where you would cause a danger or get in the way of other road users, such as

- on or near the brow of a hill
- at a bus stop
- opposite a traffic island
- in front of someone else's drive
- near a school entrance
- opposite or within 10 metres (32 feet) of a junction (in Northern Ireland, within 15 metres or 48 feet of a junction), unless there's an authorised parking space.

HC r242–243

You also need to make sure that you don't cause an obstruction by stopping or parking where there are restrictions shown by signs and yellow lines. In a controlled parking zone, you'll have to pay to park. Make sure you park within marked bays on the days and times shown on the zone entry signs.

HC r238, 245 DES s6 KYTS p39–50

Only park in a disabled parking space if you, or your passenger, are a disabled badge holder. Remember to display the badge when you leave the vehicle.

KYTS p45

By law, you **MUST** stop

- if you're involved in a road traffic incident
- at a red traffic light
- when signalled to do so by a police officer, traffic warden, Driver and Vehicle Standards Agency (DVSA) officer, traffic officer or school crossing patrol.

HC r105, 109, 286

Smoking in your car

It's illegal to smoke in a private enclosed vehicle if one or more of the occupants is under 18.

This means that it's an offence

- for a person of any age to smoke in a private vehicle that's carrying someone under 18
- for a driver (including a provisional driver) not to stop someone smoking if one of the occupants is under 18.

The rules don't apply to e-cigarettes.

Meeting the standards

You must be able to

apply a safe, systematic procedure to safely and responsibly negotiate

- junctions
- roundabouts
- crossings

turn left and right and go ahead safely and responsibly

emerge safely and responsibly into streams of traffic

cross the path of traffic safely when turning right.

You must know and understand

the rules that apply to particular junctions and roundabouts; for example, priority rules

the rules about

- merging into a stream of traffic
- crossing the path of an approaching stream of traffic
- all types of pedestrian crossing
- train and tram crossings

how to work out the speed limit where you can't see speed-limit signs.

Notes

You can use this page to make your own notes or diagrams about the key points you need to remember.

Think about

- Where might you see a minimum-speed-limit sign?
- When can you drive in a bus lane?
- What's a box junction? What mustn't you do at one of these junctions?
- When are you allowed to undo your seat belt while driving?
- If you've just driven onto a level crossing and the warning lights start flashing, what should you do?
- How close to a junction are you allowed to park?

Your notes

Things to discuss and practise with your instructor

These are just a few examples of what you could discuss and practise with your instructor. Read more about the rules of the road to come up with your own ideas.

Discuss with your instructor

- what the 'national speed limit applies' sign looks like. What does this mean in mph on different roads and for different vehicles?
- what the speed limit will usually be if there are street lights along the road
- what the different lanes are used for on
  - a two-lane dual carriageway
  - a three-lane dual carriageway
  - a motorway.

Practise with your instructor

- roundabouts with several lanes on approach
- driving in areas with changing speed limits
- entering, exiting and overtaking on busy dual carriageways.

10.1 **Mark one answer** **HC p106, KYTS p20**

What's the meaning of this sign?

- ☐ Local speed limit applies
- ☐ No waiting on the carriageway
- ☐ National speed limit applies
- ☐ No entry for vehicles

This sign doesn't tell you the speed limit in figures. You should know the speed limit for the type of road that you're on and the type of vehicle that you're driving or riding. Study your copy of The Highway Code.

10.2 **Mark one answer** **HC p40**

What's the national speed limit for cars and motorcycles on a dual carriageway?

- ☐ 30 mph
- ☐ 50 mph
- ☐ 60 mph
- ☐ 70 mph

Make sure that you know the speed limit for the road that you're on. The speed limit on a dual carriageway or motorway is 70 mph for cars and motorcycles, unless signs indicate otherwise. The speed limits for different types of vehicle are listed in The Highway Code.

10.3 **Mark one answer** **HC r124**

There are no speed-limit signs on the road. How is a 30 mph limit generally indicated?

- ☐ By hazard warning lines
- ☐ By street lighting
- ☐ By pedestrian islands
- ☐ By double or single yellow lines

There's a 30 mph speed limit where there are street lights unless signs show another limit.

10.4 **Mark one answer** **HC r124**

What will the speed limit usually be where you can see street lights but no speed-limit signs?

- ☐ 30 mph
- ☐ 40 mph
- ☐ 50 mph
- ☐ 60 mph

The presence of street lights generally indicates that there's a 30 mph speed limit, unless signs tell you otherwise.

10.5 **Mark one answer** **KYTS p21**

What does this sign mean?

- ☐ Minimum speed 30 mph
- ☐ End of maximum speed
- ☐ End of minimum speed
- ☐ Maximum speed 30 mph

The red slash through the sign indicates that the restriction has ended. In this case, the restriction was a minimum speed limit of 30 mph.

10.6 **Mark one answer** **DES s7, HC r163**

What should you do if you want to overtake a tractor but aren't sure that it's safe?

- ☐ Follow another vehicle as it overtakes the tractor
- ☐ Sound your horn to make the tractor driver pull over
- ☐ Speed past, flashing your lights at oncoming traffic
- ☐ Stay behind it if you're in any doubt

Following a tractor can be frustrating, but never overtake if you're unsure whether it's safe. Ask yourself: 'Can I see far enough down the road to ensure that I can complete the manoeuvre safely?' It's better to be delayed for a minute or two than to take a chance that may cause a collision.

10.7 Mark one answer HC r187

Which vehicle is most likely to take an unusual course at a roundabout?

- ☐ Estate car
- ☐ Milk float
- ☐ Delivery van
- ☐ Long vehicle

Long vehicles might have to take a slightly different position when approaching the roundabout or going around it. This is to stop the rear of the vehicle cutting in and mounting the kerb.

10.8 Mark one answer KYTS p55

When may you stop on a clearway?

- ☐ Never
- ☐ When it's busy
- ☐ In the rush hour
- ☐ During daylight hours

Clearways are in place so that traffic can flow without the obstruction of parked vehicles. Just one parked vehicle can cause an obstruction for all other traffic. You mustn't stop where a clearway is in force, not even to pick up or set down passengers.

10.9 Mark one answer KYTS p54

What's the meaning of this sign?

- ☐ No entry
- ☐ Waiting restrictions
- ☐ National speed limit
- ☐ School crossing patrol

This sign indicates that there are waiting restrictions. It's normally accompanied by details of when the restrictions are in force.

Details of most signs in common use are shown in The Highway Code. For more comprehensive coverage, see Know Your Traffic Signs.

10.10 Mark one answer — DES s13

You're looking for somewhere to park at night. When may you park on the right-hand side of the road?

- ☐ When you're in a one-way street
- ☐ When you have your sidelights on
- ☐ When you're more than 10 metres (32 feet) from a junction
- ☐ When you're under a lamppost

Red rear reflectors show up when headlights shine on them. These are useful when you're parked at night, but they'll only reflect if you park in the same direction as the traffic flow. Normally you should park on the left, but in a one-way street you may also park on the right-hand side of the road.

10.11 Mark one answer — DES s11, HC r137–138

When should you use the right-hand lane of a three-lane dual carriageway?

- ☐ When you're overtaking only
- ☐ When you're overtaking or turning right
- ☐ When you're using cruise control
- ☐ When you're turning right only

You should normally use the left-hand lane on any dual carriageway unless you're overtaking or turning right.

When overtaking on a dual carriageway, look for vehicles ahead that are turning right. They may be slowing or stopped. You need to see them in good time so that you can take appropriate action.

10.12 Mark one answer — DES s5, 9

You're approaching a busy junction. What should you do when, at the last moment, you realise you're in the wrong lane?

- ☐ Continue in that lane
- ☐ Force your way into the lane you need
- ☐ Stop until the area has cleared
- ☐ Use arm signals to help you change lane

There are times when road markings are obscured by queuing traffic, or you're unsure which lane to use. If, at the last moment, you find you're in the wrong lane, don't cut across or bully other drivers to let you in. Follow the lane you're in and find somewhere safe to turn around and rejoin your route.

10.13	Mark one answer	DES s7, HC r143

Where may you overtake on a one-way street?

- ☐ Only on the left-hand side
- ☐ Overtaking isn't allowed
- ☐ Only on the right-hand side
- ☐ On either the right or the left

You can overtake other traffic on either side when travelling in a one-way street. Make full use of your mirrors and ensure it's clear all around before you attempt to overtake. Look for signs and road markings, and use the most suitable lane for your destination.

10.14	Mark one answer	DES s8, HC r186

What signal should you give when you're going straight ahead at a roundabout?

- ☐ Signal left before leaving the roundabout
- ☐ Don't signal at any time
- ☐ Signal right when you're approaching the roundabout
- ☐ Signal left when you're approaching the roundabout

When going straight ahead at a roundabout, don't signal as you approach it. Signal left just after passing the exit before the one you wish to take.

10.15	Mark one answer	DES s8, HC r187

Which vehicle might have to take a different course from normal at a roundabout?

- ☐ Sports car
- ☐ Van
- ☐ Estate car
- ☐ Long vehicle

A long vehicle may have to straddle lanes either on or approaching a roundabout so that the rear wheels don't mount the kerb.

If you're following a long vehicle, stay well back and give it plenty of room.

10.16 **Mark one answer** **DES s6, HC r174**

When may you enter a box junction?

- ☐ When there are fewer than two vehicles ahead
- ☐ When signalled by another road user
- ☐ When your exit road is clear
- ☐ When traffic signs direct you

Yellow box junctions are marked on the road to prevent the road becoming blocked. Don't enter the box unless your exit road is clear. You may wait in the box if you want to turn right and your exit road is clear but oncoming traffic or other vehicles waiting to turn right are preventing you from making the turn.

10.17 **Mark one answer** **DES s6, HC r174**

When may you stop and wait in a box junction?

- ☐ When oncoming traffic prevents you from turning right
- ☐ When you're in a queue of traffic turning left
- ☐ When you're in a queue of traffic going ahead
- ☐ When you're on a roundabout

The purpose of yellow box markings is to keep junctions clear of queuing traffic. You may only wait in the marked area when you're turning right and your exit lane is clear but you can't complete the turn because of oncoming traffic or other traffic waiting to turn right.

10.18 **Mark one answer** **HC r105–109**

Who is authorised to signal you to stop?

- ☐ A motorcyclist
- ☐ A pedestrian
- ☐ A police officer
- ☐ A bus driver

You must obey signals to stop given by police and traffic officers, traffic wardens and school crossing patrols. Failure to do so is an offence and could lead to prosecution.

10.19 **Mark one answer** **DES s7, HC r195**

What should you do if you see a pedestrian waiting at a zebra crossing?

- ☐ Go on quickly before they step onto the crossing
- ☐ Stop before you reach the zigzag lines and let them cross
- ☐ Be ready to slow down or stop to let them cross
- ☐ Ignore them as they're still on the pavement

By standing on the pavement, the pedestrian is showing an intention to cross. By looking well ahead, you'll give yourself time to see the pedestrian, check your mirrors and respond safely.

10.20 **Mark one answer** **DES s7, HC r199**

Which road users benefit from toucan crossings?

- ☐ Car drivers and motorcyclists
- ☐ Cyclists and pedestrians
- ☐ Bus and lorry drivers
- ☐ Tram and train drivers

Toucan crossings are similar to pelican crossings but there's no flashing amber phase. Cyclists share the crossing with pedestrians and are allowed to cycle across when the green cycle symbol is shown.

10.21 **Mark one answer** **DES s7, HC r196**

You're waiting at a pelican crossing. What does it mean when the red light changes to flashing amber?

- ☐ Give way to pedestrians on the crossing
- ☐ Move off immediately without any hesitation
- ☐ Wait for the green light before moving off
- ☐ Get ready and go when the continuous amber light shows

This light allows pedestrians already on the crossing to get to the other side in their own time, without being rushed. Don't rev your engine or start to move off while they're still crossing.

10.22 Mark one answer HC r240

You see these double white lines along the centre of the road. When may you park on the left?

- ☐ If the line nearest to you is broken
- ☐ When there are no yellow lines
- ☐ To pick up or set down passengers
- ☐ During daylight hours only

You mustn't park or stop on a road marked with double white lines (even where one of the lines is broken) except to pick up or set down passengers.

10.23 Mark one answer HC r181

You're turning right at a crossroads. An oncoming driver is also turning right. What's the advantage of turning behind the oncoming vehicle?

- ☐ You'll have a clearer view of any approaching traffic
- ☐ You'll use less fuel because you can stay in a high gear
- ☐ You'll have more time to turn
- ☐ You'll be able to turn without stopping

When turning right at a crossroads where oncoming traffic is also turning right it's generally safer to turn behind the approaching vehicle. This allows you a clear view of approaching traffic and is called turning offside to offside. However some junctions, usually controlled by traffic light filters, are marked for vehicles to turn nearside to nearside.

10.24 Mark one answer DES s10, HC r152

You're travelling along a residential street. There are parked vehicles on the left-hand side. Why should you keep your speed down?

- ☐ So that oncoming traffic can see you more clearly
- ☐ You may set off car alarms
- ☐ There may be delivery lorries on the street
- ☐ Children may run out from between the vehicles

Travel slowly and carefully near parked vehicles. Beware of

- vehicles pulling out, especially bicycles and motorcycles
- pedestrians, especially children, who may run out from between cars
- drivers opening their doors.

10.25 **Mark one answer** **DES s7**

What should you do when there's an obstruction on your side of the road?

- ☐ Carry on, as you have priority
- ☐ Give way to oncoming traffic
- ☐ Wave oncoming vehicles through
- ☐ Accelerate to get past first

Take care if you have to pass an obstruction, such as a parked vehicle, on your side of the road. Give way to oncoming traffic if there isn't enough room for you both to continue safely.

10.26 **Mark one answer** **HC r137**

When would you use the right-hand lane of a two-lane dual carriageway?

- ☐ When you're turning right or overtaking
- ☐ When you're passing a side road on the left
- ☐ When you're staying at the minimum allowed speed
- ☐ When you're travelling at a constant high speed

Normally you should travel in the left-hand lane and only use the right-hand lane for overtaking or turning right. Move back into the left lane as soon as it's safe but don't cut in across the path of the vehicle you've just passed.

10.27 **Mark one answer** **DES s8, HC r146**

Who has priority at an unmarked crossroads?

- ☐ The larger vehicle
- ☐ No-one has priority
- ☐ The faster vehicle
- ☐ The smaller vehicle

Practise good observation in all directions before you emerge or make a turn. Proceed only when you're sure it's safe to do so.

10.28 **NI EXEMPT** **Mark one answer** **HC r243**

What's the nearest you may park to a junction?

- ☐ 10 metres (32 feet)
- ☐ 12 metres (39 feet)
- ☐ 15 metres (49 feet)
- ☐ 20 metres (66 feet)

Don't park within 10 metres (32 feet) of a junction (unless in an authorised parking place). This is to allow drivers emerging from, or turning into, the junction a clear view of the road they're joining. It also allows them to see hazards such as pedestrians or cyclists at the junction.

10.29 NI EXEMPT Mark one answer HC r243

You're looking for somewhere to safely park your vehicle. Where would you choose to park?

- ☐ At or near a bus stop
- ☐ More than 10 metres (33 feet) from a junction
- ☐ Near the brow of a hill
- ☐ On the approach to a level crossing

It may be tempting to park where you shouldn't while you run a quick errand. Careless parking is a selfish act and could endanger other road users.

10.30 Mark one answer DES s6, HC r293, KYTS p27

You're waiting at a level crossing. What must you do if a train passes but the lights keep flashing?

- ☐ Carry on waiting
- ☐ Phone the signal operator
- ☐ Edge over the stop line and look for trains
- ☐ Park and investigate

If the lights at a level crossing keep flashing after a train has passed, you should continue to wait, because another train might be coming. Time seems to pass slowly when you're held up in a queue. Be patient and wait until the lights stop flashing.

10.31 Mark one answer HC p112, KYTS p54

What does this sign mean?

- ☐ No through road
- ☐ End of traffic-calming zone
- ☐ Free-parking zone ends
- ☐ End of controlled parking zone

This sign shows that you're leaving a controlled parking zone and those restrictions no longer apply.

10.32 Mark one answer HC r288, KYTS p139

What must you do if you come across roadworks that have a temporary speed limit displayed?

- ☐ Obey the speed limit
- ☐ Obey the limit, but only during rush hour
- ☐ Ignore the displayed limit
- ☐ Use your own judgement; the limit is only advisory

Where there are extra hazards, such as at roadworks, it's often necessary to slow traffic by imposing a lower speed limit. These speed limits aren't advisory; they must be obeyed.

10.33 Mark one answer — HC r115

You're in a built-up area at night and the road is well lit. Why should you use dipped headlights?

- ☐ So that you can see further along the road
- ☐ So that you can go at a much faster speed
- ☐ So that you can switch to main beam quickly
- ☐ So that you can be easily seen by others

You may be difficult to see when you're travelling at night, even on a well-lit road. If you use dipped headlights rather than sidelights, other road users should be able to see you more easily.

10.34 Mark one answer — DES s8, HC r173

You're turning right onto a dual carriageway. What should you do if the central reservation is too narrow to contain your vehicle?

- ☐ Proceed to the central reservation and wait
- ☐ Wait until the road is clear in both directions
- ☐ Stop in the first lane so that other vehicles give way
- ☐ Emerge slightly to show your intentions

When the central reservation is narrow, it may not be able to contain your vehicle. In this case, you should treat a dual carriageway as one road. Wait until the road is clear in both directions before emerging to turn right. If you try to treat it as two separate roads and wait in the middle, your vehicle will stick out and cause an obstruction that may lead to a collision.

10.35 Mark one answer — HC p40

What's the national speed limit on a single carriageway road for cars and motorcycles?

- ☐ 30 mph
- ☐ 50 mph
- ☐ 60 mph
- ☐ 70 mph

Exceeding the speed limit is dangerous and can result in you receiving penalty points on your licence. It isn't worth it. You should know the speed limit for the road that you're on by observing the road signs. Different speed limits apply if you're towing a trailer.

10.36 Mark one answer — DES s13, HC r249

What should you do when you park at night on a road that has a 40 mph speed limit?

- ☐ Park facing the traffic
- ☐ Leave parking lights switched on
- ☐ Leave dipped headlights switched on
- ☐ Park near a street light

You must use parking lights when parking at night on a road or in a lay-by on a road with a speed limit greater than 30 mph. You must also park in the direction of the traffic flow and not close to a junction.

10.37 Mark one answer — KYTS p27

Where will you see these red and white markers?

- ☐ Approaching the end of a motorway
- ☐ Approaching a concealed level crossing
- ☐ Approaching a concealed speed-limit sign
- ☐ Approaching the end of a dual carriageway

If there's a bend just before a level crossing, you may not be able to see the level-crossing barriers or waiting traffic. These signs give you an early warning that you may find these hazards just around the bend.

10.38 Mark one answer — DES s18, HC r108

You're travelling on a motorway in England. When must you stop your vehicle?

- ☐ When signalled to stop by a roadworks supervisor
- ☐ When signalled to stop by a traffic officer
- ☐ When signalled to stop by a pedestrian on the hard shoulder
- ☐ When signalled to stop by a driver who has broken down

You'll find traffic officers on motorways and some primary routes in England and Wales. They work in partnership with the police, helping to keep traffic moving and helping to make your journey as safe as possible. It's an offence not to comply with the directions given by a traffic officer.

10.39 Mark one answer — DES s8, HC r186

How should you signal if you're going straight ahead at a roundabout?

- ☐ Signal right on the approach and then left to leave the roundabout
- ☐ Signal left after you leave the roundabout and enter the new road
- ☐ Signal right on thc approach to the roundabout and keep the signal on
- ☐ Signal left just after you pass the exit before the one you're going to take

To go straight ahead at a roundabout, you should normally approach in the left-hand lane, but check the road markings. At some roundabouts, the left lane on approach is marked 'left turn only', so make sure you use the correct lane to go ahead. You won't normally need to signal as you approach, but signal before you leave the roundabout, as other road users need to know your intentions.

10.40 **Mark one answer** **HC r145**

When may you drive over a pavement?

- ☐ To overtake slow-moving traffic
- ☐ When the pavement is very wide
- ☐ If there are no pedestrians nearby
- ☐ To gain access to a property

It's illegal to drive on or over a pavement, except to gain access to a property. If you need to cross a pavement, give priority to pedestrians.

10.41 **Mark one answer** **HC p40**

A single carriageway road has this sign. What's the maximum permitted speed for a car towing a trailer?

- ☐ 30 mph
- ☐ 40 mph
- ☐ 50 mph
- ☐ 60 mph

When you're towing a trailer, a reduced speed limit also applies on dual carriageways and motorways. These lower speed limits apply to vehicles pulling all sorts of trailers, including caravans and horse boxes.

10.42 **Mark one answer** **HC p40**

What's the speed limit for a car towing a caravan on a dual carriageway?

- ☐ 50 mph
- ☐ 40 mph
- ☐ 70 mph
- ☐ 60 mph

The speed limit for cars towing caravans or trailers on dual carriageways or motorways is 60 mph. Due to the increased weight and size of the combination, you should plan further ahead. Take care in windy weather, as a strong side wind can make a caravan or large trailer unstable.

10.43 Mark one answer KYTS p44

You want to park and you see this sign. What should you do on the days and times shown?

- ☐ Park in a bay and not pay
- ☐ Park on yellow lines and pay
- ☐ Park on yellow lines and not pay
- ☐ Park in a bay and pay

Parking restrictions apply in a variety of places and situations. Make sure you know the rules and understand where and when restrictions apply. Controlled parking areas will be indicated by signs and road markings. Parking in the wrong place could cause an obstruction and danger to other traffic. It can also result in a fine.

10.44 Mark one answer DES s6, HC r140

A cycle lane, marked by a solid white line, is in operation. What does this mean for car drivers?

- ☐ They may park in the lane
- ☐ They may drive in the lane at any time
- ☐ They may use the lane when necessary
- ☐ They mustn't drive along the lane

While it's in operation, other vehicles must not use this part of the carriageway except to pick up or set down passengers. At other times, when the lane isn't in operation, you should still be aware that there may be cyclists using the lane. Give them plenty of room as you pass and allow for their movement from side to side, especially in windy weather or on a bumpy road.

10.45 — Mark one answer — DES s8

You're going to turn left from a main road into a minor road. What should you do as you approach the junction?

- ☐ Keep just left of the middle of the road
- ☐ Keep in the middle of the road
- ☐ Swing out to the right just before turning
- ☐ Keep well to the left of the road

Your road position can help other road users to anticipate your actions. Keep to the left as you approach a left turn and don't swing out into the centre of the road in order to make the turn easier. This could endanger oncoming traffic and may cause other road users to misunderstand your intentions.

10.46 — Mark one answer — DES s6, HC r293, KYTS p27

You're waiting at a level crossing. What should you do if the red warning lights continue to flash after a train has passed by?

- ☐ Get out and investigate
- ☐ Telephone the signal operator
- ☐ Continue to wait
- ☐ Drive across carefully

At a level crossing, flashing red lights mean you must stop. If the train passes but the lights keep flashing, wait. Another train may be coming.

10.47 Mark one answer DES s6, HC r293

What should you do if the amber lights come on and a warning sounds while you're driving over a level crossing?

- ☐ Get everyone out of the vehicle immediately
- ☐ Stop and reverse back to clear the crossing
- ☐ Keep going and clear the crossing
- ☐ Stop immediately and use your hazard warning lights

Keep going; don't stop on the crossing. If the warning sounds and the amber lights come on as you're approaching the crossing, you must stop unless it's unsafe to do so. Red flashing lights together with the audible warning mean you must stop.

10.48 Mark one answer DES s9, HC r200

You're driving on a busy main road. What should you do if you find that you're driving in the wrong direction?

- ☐ Turn into a side road on the right and reverse into the main road
- ☐ Make a U-turn in the main road
- ☐ Make a 'three-point' turn in the main road
- ☐ Turn around in a side road

Don't turn around in a busy street or reverse from a side road into a main road. Find a quiet side road and choose a place to turn around where you won't obstruct an entrance or exit. Look out for pedestrians and cyclists as well as other traffic.

10.49 Mark one answer DES s9

When may you drive without wearing your seat belt?

- ☐ When you're carrying out a manoeuvre that includes reversing
- ☐ When you're moving off on a hill
- ☐ When you're testing your brakes
- ☐ When you're driving slowly in queuing traffic

You may remove your seat belt while you're carrying out a manoeuvre that includes reversing. However, you must remember to put it back on again before you resume driving.

10.50	Mark one answer	DES s9, HC r203

How far are you allowed to reverse?

- ☐ No further than is necessary
- ☐ No more than a car's length
- ☐ As far as it takes to reverse around a corner
- ☐ The length of a residential street

You mustn't reverse further than is necessary. You may decide to turn your vehicle around by reversing into an opening or side road. When you reverse, always look all around you and watch for pedestrians. Don't reverse from a side road into a main road.

10.51	Mark one answer	DES s9

What should you do when you're unsure whether it's safe to reverse your vehicle?

- ☐ Sound your horn
- ☐ Rev your engine
- ☐ Get out and check
- ☐ Reverse slowly

A small child could be hidden directly behind you, so, if you can't see all around your vehicle, get out and have a look. You could also ask someone reliable outside the vehicle to guide you.

10.52	Mark one answer	DES s9, HC r201

Why could it be dangerous to reverse from a side road into a main road?

- ☐ Your reverse sensors will beep
- ☐ Your view will be restricted
- ☐ Your reversing lights will be hidden
- ☐ Your mirrors will need adjusting

Don't reverse into a main road from a side road because your view will be restricted. The main road is likely to be busy and the traffic on it moving quickly.

10.53	Mark one answer	DES s6, HC r174

You want to turn right at a box junction. What should you do if there's oncoming traffic?

- ☐ Wait in the box junction if your exit is clear
- ☐ Wait before the junction until it's clear of all traffic
- ☐ Drive on; you can't turn right at a box junction
- ☐ Drive slowly into the box junction when signalled by oncoming traffic

You can wait in the box junction as long as your exit is clear. At some point there'll be a gap in the oncoming traffic, or the traffic lights will change, allowing you to proceed.

10.54 Mark one answer — DES s9

You're reversing into a side road. When would your vehicle be the greatest hazard to passing traffic?

- ☐ After you've completed the manoeuvre
- ☐ Just before you begin to manoeuvre
- ☐ After you've entered the side road
- ☐ When the front of your vehicle swings out

Always check in all directions before reversing. Keep a good lookout throughout the manoeuvre and remember that the front will swing out as you reverse into the side road. Act on what you see and wait if necessary.

10.55 Mark one answer — DES s9

Where's the safest place to park your vehicle at night?

- ☐ In a garage
- ☐ On a busy road
- ☐ In a quiet car park
- ☐ Near a red route

If you have a garage, use it. Your vehicle is less likely to be a victim of car crime if it's in a garage. Also, in winter, the windows will be kept free from ice and snow.

10.56 Mark one answer — HC p107, KYTS p55

When may you stop on an urban clearway?

- ☐ To set down and pick up passengers
- ☐ To use a mobile telephone
- ☐ To ask for directions
- ☐ To load or unload goods

Urban clearways have their times of operation clearly signed. You may only stop to pick up or set down passengers.

10.57 Mark one answer — HC r241, KYTS p47

You're looking for somewhere to park your vehicle. What should you do if the only free spaces are marked for disabled drivers?

- ☐ Use one of these spaces
- ☐ Park in one of these spaces but stay with your vehicle
- ☐ Use one of the spaces as long as one is kept free
- ☐ Wait for a regular parking space to become free

It's illegal to park in a space reserved for disabled drivers unless you're permitted to do so. These spaces are provided for people with limited mobility, who may need extra space to get in and out of their vehicle.

10.58 **Mark one answer** **DES s10, HC r155**

You're on a road that's only wide enough for one vehicle. What should you do if a car is coming towards you?

- ☐ Pull into a passing place on your right
- ☐ Force the other driver to reverse
- ☐ Pull into a passing place if your vehicle is wider
- ☐ Pull into a passing place on your left

Pull into the nearest passing place on the left if you meet another vehicle on a narrow road. If the nearest passing place is on the right, wait opposite it.

10.59 **Mark one answer** **DES s13**

You're driving at night with your headlights on main beam. A vehicle is overtaking you. When should you dip your headlights?

- ☐ Some time after the vehicle has passed you
- ☐ Before the vehicle starts to pass you
- ☐ Only if the other driver dips their headlights
- ☐ As soon as the vehicle passes you

On main beam, your lights could dazzle the driver in front. Dip your headlights as soon as the driver passes you and drop back so that the dipped beam falls short of the vehicle in front.

10.60 **Mark one answer** **KYTS p32**

When may you drive a car in this bus lane?

- ☐ Outside its hours of operation
- ☐ To get to the front of a traffic queue
- ☐ You may not use it at any time
- ☐ To overtake slow-moving traffic

Some bus lanes operate only during peak hours and other vehicles may use them outside these hours. Make sure you check the sign for the hours of operation before driving in a bus lane.

10.61 Mark one answer — DES s5

Other than direction indicators, how can you give signals to other road users?

- ☐ By using brake lights
- ☐ By using sidelights
- ☐ By using fog lights
- ☐ By using interior lights

Your brake lights will give an indication to traffic behind that you're slowing down. Good anticipation will allow you time to check your mirrors before slowing.

10.62 Mark one answer — DES s9, HC r200

You're parked in a busy high street. What's the safest way to turn your vehicle around so you can drive in the opposite direction?

- ☐ Turn around in a quiet side road
- ☐ Drive into a side road and reverse out into the main road
- ☐ Ask someone to stop the traffic
- ☐ Carry out a U-turn

Make sure you carry out the manoeuvre without causing a hazard to other vehicles. Choose a place to turn that's safe and considers other road users.

10.63 Mark one answer — DES s20

Where should you park your vehicle at night?

- ☐ Near a police station
- ☐ In a quiet road
- ☐ On a red route
- ☐ In a well-lit area

When you're parking at night, park in a well-lit area. This can help deter criminals from targeting your vehicle.

10.64 **Mark one answer** **DES s11, HC r288–289**

You're driving in the right-hand lane of a dual carriageway. What should you do if you see a sign showing that the right-hand lane is closed 800 yards ahead?

- ☐ Keep in that lane until you reach the queue
- ☐ Move to the left immediately
- ☐ Wait and see which lane is moving faster
- ☐ Move to the left in good time

Keep a lookout for traffic signs. If you're directed to change lanes, do so in good time. Don't

- push your way into traffic in another lane
- try to gain advantage by delaying changing lanes.

10.65 **Mark one answer** **HC r140**

You're driving on a road that has a cycle lane. What does it mean if the lane is marked by a broken white line?

- ☐ You shouldn't drive in the lane unless it's unavoidable
- ☐ There's a reduced speed limit for motor vehicles using the lane
- ☐ Cyclists can travel in both directions in that lane
- ☐ The lane must be used by motorcyclists in heavy traffic

Cycle lanes are marked with either a solid or a broken white line. If the line is solid, you should check the times of operation shown on the signs, and not drive or park in the lane during those times. If the line is broken, you shouldn't drive or park in the lane unless it's unavoidable.

10.66 Mark one answer — DES s9, HC r241

When are you allowed to park in a parking bay for disabled drivers?

- ☐ When you have a Blue Badge
- ☐ When you have a wheelchair
- ☐ When you have an advanced driver certificate
- ☐ When you have an adapted vehicle

Don't park in a space reserved for disabled people unless you or your passenger are a Blue Badge holder. The badge must be displayed on the dashboard or fascia panel, where it can be clearly read through the front windscreen.

10.67 Mark one answer — HC r105–109, 286

When must you stop your vehicle?

- ☐ If you're involved in an incident that causes damage or injury
- ☐ At a junction where there are 'give way' lines
- ☐ At the end of a one-way street
- ☐ Before merging onto a motorway

You must stop your vehicle when signalled to do so by a

- police, DVSA or traffic officer
- traffic warden
- school crossing patrol
- red traffic light.

You must also stop if you're involved in an incident that causes damage or injury to any other person, vehicle, animal or property.

Case study practice – 10 Rules of the road

It's early evening and the street lamps are lit.

You're driving home at 30 mph, although there are no speed-limit signs. The road is a single carriageway and you're alone in your vehicle.

Sleet is falling steadily and it's cold. Ahead, a vehicle is spreading salt on the road.

In town there are high-occupancy vehicle lanes, which you don't use.

Your home is level with a zebra crossing but you park beyond its markings, further down the road.

10.1 How have you identified a 30 mph speed limit?

Mark **one** answer

- ☐ There are many retail outlets still open in the town
- ☐ There are regularly spaced street lights in the area
- ☐ There are yellow lines painted on the road surface
- ☐ There are plenty of pedestrians and cyclists around

HC r124, p40

10.2 What would the normal centre white-line markings be on this road?

Mark **one** answer

- ☐ Short dashes with short spaces
- ☐ Long dashes with short spaces
- ☐ Short dashes with long spaces
- ☐ Long dashes with long spaces

HC r127, p114

10.3 What colour flashing beacon would the salting vehicle have?

Mark **one** answer

- ☐ White
- ☐ Green
- ☐ Red
- ☐ Amber

HC r225

10.4 Why would you not use the high-occupancy lane on your journey?

Mark **one** answer

- ☐ It's for vehicles of all types, but only at certain times
- ☐ It's for vehicles that have two or more occupants
- ☐ It's for vehicles of as many types and sizes as possible
- ☐ It's for vehicles that have flashing amber beacons

HC p112 DES s6 KYTS p140–141

10.5 Why don't you park level with your home?

Mark **one** answer

- ☐ Because your parking permit has expired
- ☐ Because you mustn't park there
- ☐ Because you don't want to park there
- ☐ Because you haven't paid your vehicle tax

HC r240 DES s7

Section eleven

Road and traffic signs

In this section, you'll learn about

- what the shapes of road sign can tell you
- what road markings mean
- the sequence and meaning of traffic lights
- motorway warning lights
- the signals used by other drivers and by police officers.

Road and traffic signs

Road and traffic signs give important information to keep you safe on the road, so it's essential that you know what they mean and what you need to do when you see them.

Signs

The shape and colour of a road sign tell you about its meaning.

Circular sign give orders.

Blue circles give an instruction or show which sort of road user can use a route, eg cyclists, pedestrians, trams.

Red rings or circles tell you what you mustn't do.

Triangular signs give warnings.

Rectangular signs give information.

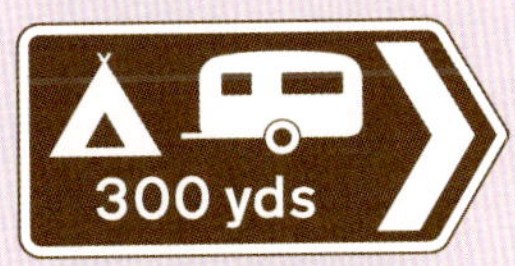

Signs with a brown background give tourist information.

KYTS p9, 84, 100–104

The exception to the shape rule is the 'stop' sign: this is octagonal so that it stands out and can be understood even if it's partly covered; for example, by snow.

HC r109 DES s6 KYTS p9

Maximum speed limits are shown inside red circles: you **MUST NOT** go faster than the speed shown. Where no speed limit is shown, the national speed limits (given on page 304) apply. Speed-limit signs may be combined with other signs, such as those indicating a traffic-calmed area.

HC p106 KYTS p20

It's impossible to mention all the signs here. *Know Your Traffic Signs* shows all the signs you're likely to see and *The Official Highway Code* contains important advice, information on current laws in Great Britain, and best practice in road safety. It's important that you get to know these to make sure that you don't break the law.

Test your knowledge of signs using the activity on the Safe Driving for Life website.

safedrivingforlife.info/road-signs-quiz

Road markings

Markings on the road give information, orders or warnings. As a general rule, the more paint there is, the more important the message.

HC r127–131 DES s8 KYTS p62–64

There are three types of road markings.

Along the middle of the road

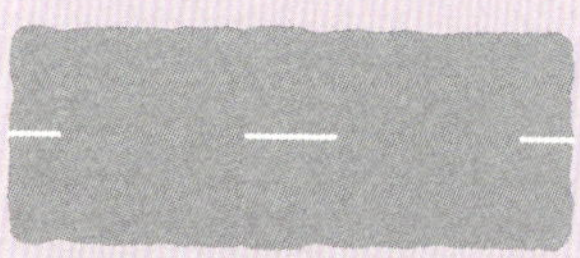

Short broken white lines mark the centre of the road.

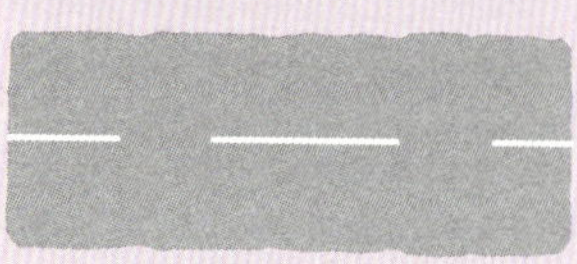

Longer broken white lines are hazard warning lines: only overtake if you can see that the road ahead is clear.

Along the middle of the road

You **MUST NOT** cross or straddle double white lines with a solid white line on your side of the road unless

- you're turning into a junction or an entrance
- you need to pass a stationary vehicle
- you need to overtake a cyclist, horse or road maintenance vehicle if they're moving at 10 mph or less.

White diagonal stripes or chevrons separate lanes of traffic or protect traffic turning right.

Sometimes red tarmac is used within a block of white lines or diagonals. This highlights the area that separates traffic flowing in opposite directions.

HC p114 DES s6 KYTS p62–64

Along the side of the road

A white line shows the edge of the carriageway.

Yellow lines show waiting and stopping restrictions.

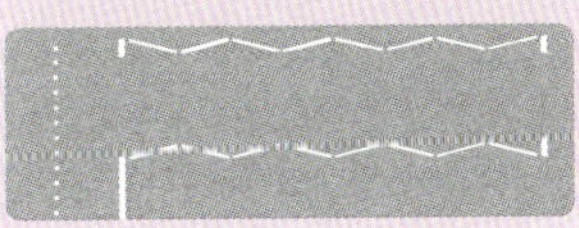

White zigzag lines at pedestrian crossings mean no stopping or parking at any time.

HC p115, 116 DES s6 KYTS p39–44, 56, 65, 122

Lines on or across the road

Broken lines across the road mean 'give way'.

A single solid line means 'stop'.

Various markings on the road, for example 'give way' triangles, road-hump markings and rumble devices, warn of a hazard.

HC p114–116 KYTS p62–75

As with signs, you should look at *Know Your Traffic Signs* and *The Official Highway Code* to learn more about road markings.

You may see reflective studs on motorways and other roads. These are especially useful at night and when visibility is poor, as they help to make the lanes and edges of the road easier to see. Different coloured studs are used on motorways to help drivers identify which lane they're using. See section 9, Motorway driving, for more details.

HC r132

Traffic lights and warning lights

Traffic lights work in a sequence.

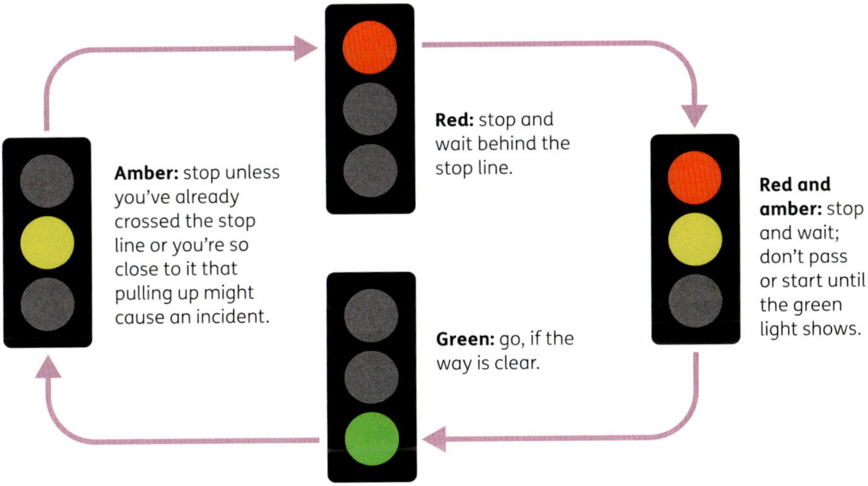

HC p102 DES s6 KYTS p119–120

On some traffic lights there's a green filter arrow. This means you can go in the direction of the arrow, even if the main light isn't showing green.

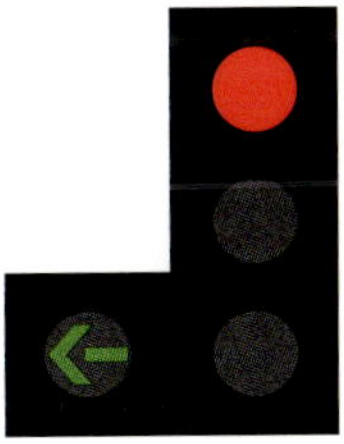

If a set of traffic lights is out of order, drive very carefully: nobody has priority. There may be a sign telling you that the lights aren't working.

DES s6

Red flashing lights are used at level crossings and other locations, such as lifting bridges and outside some fire stations. You **MUST** stop when these show.

HC r293, p102 KYTS p13, 26–29, 120

At roadworks, traffic can be controlled by

- a police officer
- traffic lights
- a 'stop/go' board.

HC r288 KYTS p136

On motorways, signals on the overhead gantries or at the roadside may also have flashing lights.

Amber warns you of a hazard (eg lane closures, to leave at the next exit, fog) or a temporary maximum speed advised for the conditions.

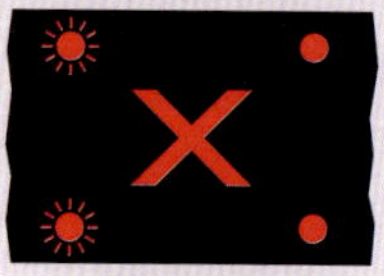

If red lights flash on a signal and a red X is showing, you **MUST NOT** drive in the lane shown as closed beyond the signal.

If red lights flash on a signal in the central reservation or on the side of the road and the lane closed sign is showing, you **MUST NOT** go beyond the signal in any lane. If red lights flash at the start of a slip road, you **MUST NOT** enter the slip road or try and join the motorway at that junction.

HC r255–258, p102 KYTS p89–91

Signals given by drivers and the police

Road users normally signal where they're intending to turn by using their indicators. Make sure that your indicators are cancelled after you've turned, to avoid confusing other road users. Be aware that another driver may have left their indicator on by mistake.

If you're emerging from a junction and a driver coming along the main road from the right is close to you and indicating left, wait until the vehicle starts to turn before you emerge.

HC r103–104 DES s5

You may need to use an arm signal to strengthen or clarify the message given by your indicators, such as when you're signalling to turn right in busy traffic.

If you're slowing down and stopping just after a junction, wait to signal until you're passing the junction, or just after it.

You can use the horn to warn others that you're there. You **MUST NOT** use it between 11.30 pm and 7.00 am when driving in a built-up area, except when another road user puts you in danger. You **MUST NOT** use your horn when stationary unless another vehicle is likely to cause a danger.

The only reason you should flash your headlights is to warn other road users that you're there.

HC r110–112 DES s5

Tip

If you're driving on a motorway or unrestricted dual carriageway, you can briefly use your hazard warning lights to warn drivers behind you when there's an obstruction ahead.

HC r116 DES s3, 11

Police or traffic officers may signal to you if they're directing traffic. Make sure that you know all the official arm signals they might use in case you need to react to them.

HC p103–105

A police or traffic officer following you in a patrol vehicle may flash their headlights, indicate left and point to the left to direct you to stop. Pull up on the left as soon as it's safe to do so.

HC r106

Remember, you **MUST** obey any signals given by police or traffic officers, traffic wardens and signs used by school crossing patrols.

HC r105–108, p104–105

Road lanes

Contraflow lanes are lanes that flow in the opposite direction to most of the traffic. Bus and cycle contraflow lanes may be found in one-way streets. They'll be signed and marked on the road. Don't try to drive against the flow of traffic in these lanes.

HC r140–141, 143 DES s6

You may also see contraflow lanes at roadworks. When you see the signs

- reduce your speed and comply with any temporary speed limits
- choose an appropriate lane in good time
- keep the correct distance from the vehicle in front.

DES s11 KYTS p128–133

The centre and right-hand lanes of a three-lane motorway are overtaking lanes. Always move back to a lane on your left after overtaking, to allow other vehicles to overtake. On a free-flowing motorway or dual carriageway, you mustn't overtake other vehicles on their left.

HC r264, 268 DES s11

Meeting the standards

You must be able to

respond correctly to all

- permanent traffic signals, signs and road markings
- temporary traffic signals, signs and road markings.

You must know and understand

the meaning of all mandatory traffic signs and how to respond to them

the meaning of all warning signs and how to respond to them

the meaning of all road markings and how to respond to them.

Notes

You can use this page to make your own notes or diagrams about the key points you need to remember.

Think about

- When are you allowed to cross double white lines along the centre of the road?
- What must you never do on zigzag lines?
- What shape is the 'stop' sign?
- What should you do at an amber traffic light?
- When might you need to use arm signals?

Your notes

Things to discuss and practise with your instructor

These are just a few examples of what you could discuss and practise with your instructor. Read more about road and traffic signs to come up with your own ideas.

Discuss with your instructor

- which is the only octagonal road sign and why it's unique
- what these shapes of sign tell you
  - round
  - triangular
  - rectangular
- what different patterns of road markings mean, eg double white lines, yellow boxes, etc.

Practise with your instructor

- identifying signs from *The Official Highway Code* and *Know Your Traffic Signs*
- driving through a busy town centre and identifying all the warning signs that you see
- driving to a level crossing and identifying the signs and signals that you find there.

11.1 Mark one answer DES s6, HC p106, KYTS p9, 16

How can you identify traffic signs that give orders?

- ☐ They're rectangular with a yellow border
- ☐ They're triangular with a blue border
- ☐ They're square with a brown border
- ☐ They're circular with a red border

There are three basic types of traffic sign: those that warn, those that inform and those that give orders. Generally, triangular signs warn, rectangular signs give information or directions and circular signs give orders. An exception is the eight-sided 'stop' sign.

11.2 Mark one answer DES s6, HC p106, KYTS p9, 16

What shape are traffic signs giving orders?

☐  ☐ 

☐  ☐ 

Road signs in the shape of a circle give orders. Those with a red circle are mostly prohibitive. The 'stop' sign is octagonal to give it greater prominence. Signs giving orders must always be obeyed.

11.3 Mark one answer DES s6, HC p106, KYTS p9, 16

Which type of sign tells you what you must not do?

☐  ☐ 

☐  ☐ 

Signs in the shape of a circle give orders. A sign with a red circle means that you aren't allowed to do something. Study Know Your Traffic Signs to ensure that you understand what the different traffic signs mean.

11.4 **Mark one answer** **DES s6, HC p106, KYTS p20**

What does this sign mean?

- ☐ Maximum speed limit with traffic calming
- ☐ Minimum speed limit with traffic calming
- ☐ '20 cars only' parking zone
- ☐ Only 20 cars allowed at any one time

If you're in a place where there are likely to be pedestrians (for example, outside a school, near a park, in a residential area or in a shopping area), you should be cautious and keep your speed down.

Many local authorities have taken steps to slow traffic down by creating traffic-calming measures such as road humps. They're there for a reason; slow down.

11.5 **Mark one answer** **DES s6, HC p106, KYTS p20**

What does this sign mean?

- ☐ New speed limit 20 mph
- ☐ No vehicles over 30 tonnes
- ☐ Minimum speed limit 30 mph
- ☐ End of 20 mph zone

Where you see this sign, the 20 mph restriction ends and a 30 mph restriction starts. Check all around for possible hazards and only increase your speed if it's safe to do so.

11.6 Mark one answer — DES s6, HC p106, KYTS p17

What does this sign mean?

- ☐ No overtaking
- ☐ No motor vehicles
- ☐ Clearway (no stopping)
- ☐ Cars and motorcycles only

A sign will indicate which types of vehicles are prohibited from certain roads. Make sure that you know which signs apply to the vehicle you're using.

11.7 Mark one answer — DES s6, HC p106, KYTS p17

What does this sign mean?

- ☐ No parking
- ☐ No road markings
- ☐ No through road
- ☐ No entry

'No entry' signs are used in places such as one-way streets to prevent vehicles driving against the traffic. To ignore one would be dangerous, both for yourself and for other road users, as well as being against the law.

11.8 Mark one answer — DES s6, HC p106, KYTS p18

What does this sign mean?

- ☐ Bend to the right
- ☐ Road on the right closed
- ☐ No traffic from the right
- ☐ No right turn

The 'no right turn' sign may be used to warn road users that there's a 'no entry' prohibition on a road to the right ahead.

11.9 **Mark one answer** **DES s6, HC p106, KYTS p17**

Which sign means 'no entry'?

- ☐ 
- ☐ 
- ☐ 
- ☐ 

Look for and obey traffic signs. Disobeying or not seeing a sign could be dangerous. It may also be an offence for which you could be prosecuted.

11.10 **Mark one answer** **DES s6, HC p107, KYTS p30**

What does this sign mean?

- ☐ Route for trams only
- ☐ Route for buses only
- ☐ Parking for buses only
- ☐ Parking for trams only

Avoid blocking tram routes. Trams are fixed on their route and can't manoeuvre around other vehicles or pedestrians. Modern trams travel quickly and are quiet, so you might not hear them approaching.

11.11 **Mark one answer** **DES s6, HC p106, KYTS p23**

Which type of vehicle does this sign apply to?

- ☐ Wide vehicles
- ☐ Long vehicles
- ☐ High vehicles
- ☐ Heavy vehicles

The triangular shapes above and below the dimensions indicate a height restriction that applies to the road ahead.

11.12	Mark one answer	DES s6, HC p106, KYTS p17

Which sign means no motor vehicles allowed?

- ☐ 
- ☐ 
- ☐ 
- ☐ 

This sign is used to enable pedestrians to walk free from traffic. It's often found in shopping areas.

11.13	Mark one answer	DES s6, HC p106, KYTS p18

What does this sign mean?

- ☐ You have priority
- ☐ No motor vehicles
- ☐ Two-way traffic
- ☐ No overtaking

Road signs that prohibit overtaking are placed in locations where passing the vehicle in front is dangerous. If you see this sign, don't attempt to overtake. The sign is there for a reason; you must obey it.

11.14	Mark one answer	DES s6, HC p107, KYTS p54

What does this sign mean?

- ☐ Waiting restrictions apply
- ☐ Waiting permitted
- ☐ National speed limit applies
- ☐ Clearway (no stopping)

There'll be a plate or additional sign to tell you when the restrictions apply.

11.15 **Mark one answer** **DES s6, HC p112, KYTS p54**

What does this sign mean?

- ☐ End of restricted speed area
- ☐ End of restricted parking area
- ☐ End of clearway
- ☐ End of cycle route

Even though you've left the restricted area, make sure that you park where you won't endanger other road users or cause an obstruction.

11.16 **Mark one answer** **DES s6, HC p107, KYTS p55**

Which sign means 'no stopping'?

☐  ☐ 

☐  ☐ 

Stopping where this clearway restriction applies is likely to cause congestion. Allow the traffic to flow by obeying the signs.

11.17 **Mark one answer** **DES s6, HC p107, KYTS p55**

What does this sign mean?

- ☐ National speed limit applies
- ☐ Waiting restrictions apply
- ☐ No stopping
- ☐ No entry

This is the sign for a clearway. Clearways are stretches of road where you aren't allowed to stop unless it's an emergency. Stopping where these restrictions apply may be dangerous and is likely to cause an obstruction. Restrictions might apply for several miles and this may be indicated on the sign.

11.18 Mark one answer DES s6, KYTS p115

What does this sign mean?

- ☐ Distance to parking place ahead
- ☐ Distance to public telephone ahead
- ☐ Distance to public house ahead
- ☐ Distance to passing place ahead

If you intend to stop and rest, this sign allows you time to reduce speed and pull over safely.

11.19 Mark one answer DES s6, KYTS p50

What does this sign mean?

- ☐ Vehicles may not park on the verge or footway
- ☐ Vehicles may park on the left-hand side of the road only
- ☐ Vehicles may park fully on the verge or footway
- ☐ Vehicles may park on the right-hand side of the road only

In order to keep roads free from parked cars, there are some areas where you're allowed to park on the verge. Only do this where you see the sign. Parking on verges or footways anywhere else could lead to a fine.

11.20 **Mark one answer** **DES s6, HC p106, KYTS p18**

What does this traffic sign mean?

- ☐ No overtaking allowed
- ☐ Give priority to oncoming traffic
- ☐ Two-way traffic
- ☐ One-way traffic only

Priority signs are normally shown where the road is narrow and there isn't enough room for two vehicles to pass. Examples are narrow bridges, roadworks and where there's a width restriction.

Make sure you know who has priority; don't force your way through. Show courtesy and consideration to other road users.

11.21 **Mark one answer** **DES s6, HC p113, KYTS p73**

What's the meaning of this traffic sign?

- ☐ End of two-way road
- ☐ Give priority to vehicles coming towards you
- ☐ You have priority over vehicles coming towards you
- ☐ Bus lane ahead

Don't force your way through. Show courtesy and consideration to other road users. Although you have priority, make sure oncoming traffic is going to give way before you continue.

11.22 **Mark one answer** **DES s6, HC p106, KYTS p16**

What shape is a 'stop' sign?

- ☐ 
- ☐ 
- ☐ 
- ☐ 

To make it easy to recognise, the 'stop' sign is the only sign of this shape. You must stop and take effective observation before proceeding.

11.23 **Mark one answer** **DES s6, HC p106, KYTS p16**

In winter, road signs can become covered by snow. What does this sign mean?

- ☐ Crossroads
- ☐ Give way
- ☐ Stop
- ☐ Turn right

The 'stop' sign is the only road sign that's octagonal. This is so that it can be recognised and obeyed even if it's obscured (for example, by snow).

11.24 **Mark one answer** **DES s6, HC p107, KYTS p21**

What does this sign mean?

- ☐ Service area 30 miles ahead
- ☐ Maximum speed 30 mph
- ☐ Minimum speed 30 mph
- ☐ Lay-by 30 miles ahead

This sign is shown where slow-moving vehicles would impede the flow of traffic; for example, in tunnels. However, if you need to slow down or even stop to avoid an incident or potential collision, you should do so.

11.25 **Mark one answer** **DES s6, HC p107, KYTS p19**

What does this sign mean?

- ☐ Give way to oncoming vehicles
- ☐ Approaching traffic passes you on both sides
- ☐ Turn off at the next available junction
- ☐ Pass either side to get to the same destination

These signs are often seen in one-way streets that have more than one lane. When you see this sign, use the route that's the most convenient and doesn't require a late change of direction.

11.26 Mark one answer

DES s6, HC p107, KYTS p30

What does this sign mean?

- ☐ Route for trams
- ☐ Give way to trams
- ☐ Route for buses
- ☐ Give way to buses

Take extra care when you encounter trams. Look out for road markings and signs that alert you to them. Modern trams are very quiet and you may not hear them approaching.

11.27 Mark one answer

DES s6, HC p107, KYTS p9

What messages are given by circular traffic signs that have a blue background?

- ☐ They give temporary directions during a diversion
- ☐ They give directions to car parks
- ☐ They give motorway information
- ☐ They give mandatory instructions

Signs with blue circles generally give mandatory instruction. These are often found in urban areas and include signs for mini-roundabouts and directional arrows.

11.28 Mark one answer

DES s6, HC p107, KYTS p33, 35

Where would you see a contraflow bus lane?

- ☐ On a dual carriageway
- ☐ On a roundabout
- ☐ On an urban motorway
- ☐ On a one-way street

The traffic permitted to use a contraflow lane travels in the opposite direction to traffic in the other lanes on the road.

11.29 Mark one answer DES s6, HC p107, KYTS p33

What does this sign mean?

- ☐ Bus station on the right
- ☐ Contraflow bus lane
- ☐ With-flow bus lane
- ☐ Give way to buses

There will also be markings on the road surface to indicate the bus lane. You mustn't use this lane for parking or overtaking.

11.30 Mark one answer DES s6, KYTS p84

What does a sign with a brown background show?

- ☐ Tourist directions
- ☐ Primary roads
- ☐ Motorway routes
- ☐ Minor roads

Signs with a brown background give directions to places of interest. They're often seen on a motorway, directing you along the easiest route to the attraction.

11.31 Mark one answer DES s6, KYTS p100

What does this sign mean?

- ☐ Tourist attraction
- ☐ Beware of trains
- ☐ Level crossing
- ☐ Beware of trams

These signs indicate places of interest and are designed to guide you by the easiest route. They're particularly useful when you're unfamiliar with the area.

11.32 Mark one answer **DES s6, HC p108, KYTS p10**

What's the purpose of triangular shaped signs?

- ☐ To give warnings
- ☐ To give information
- ☐ To give orders
- ☐ To give directions

Triangular signs warn you of hazards ahead. Make sure you look at each sign that you pass on the road, so that you don't miss any vital instructions or information.

11.33 Mark one answer **DES s6, HC p108, KYTS p10**

What does this sign mean?

- ☐ Turn left ahead
- ☐ T-junction
- ☐ No through road
- ☐ Give way

This type of sign warns you of hazards ahead. Make sure you look at each sign and road marking that you pass, so that you don't miss any vital instructions or information. This sign shows there's a T-junction with priority over vehicles from the right.

11.34 Mark one answer **DES s6, HC p109, KYTS p13**

What does this sign mean?

- ☐ Multi-exit roundabout
- ☐ Risk of ice
- ☐ Six roads converge
- ☐ Place of historical interest

It will take up to 10 times longer to stop when it's icy. Where there's a risk of icy conditions, you need to be aware of this and take extra care. If you think the road may be icy, don't brake or steer harshly, as your tyres could lose their grip on the road.

11.35 **Mark one answer** **DES s6, HC p108, KYTS p10**

What does this sign mean?

- ☐ Crossroads
- ☐ Level crossing with gate
- ☐ Level crossing without gate
- ☐ Ahead only

The priority through the junction is shown by the broader line. You need to be aware of the hazard posed by traffic crossing or pulling out onto a major road.

11.36 **Mark one answer** **DES s6, HC p108, KYTS p10**

What does this sign mean?

- ☐ Ring road
- ☐ Mini-roundabout
- ☐ No vehicles
- ☐ Roundabout

As you approach a roundabout, look well ahead and check all signs. Decide which exit you wish to take and move into the correct position as you approach the roundabout, signalling as required.

11.37 **Mark one answer** **DES s6, HC p108–109, KYTS p10–14**

What information would be shown in a triangular road sign?

- ☐ Road narrows
- ☐ Ahead only
- ☐ Keep left
- ☐ Minimum speed

Warning signs are there to make you aware of potential hazards on the road ahead. Take note of the signs so you're prepared and can take whatever action is necessary.

11.38 **Mark one answer** **DES s6, HC p109, KYTS p36**

What does this sign mean?

- ☐ Cyclists must dismount
- ☐ Cycles aren't allowed
- ☐ Cycle route ahead
- ☐ Cycle in single file

Where there's a cycle route ahead, a sign will show a bicycle in a red warning triangle. Watch out for children on bicycles and cyclists rejoining the main road.

11.39 **Mark one answer** **DES s6, HC p109, KYTS p13**

Which sign means that pedestrians may be walking along the road?

☐  ☐ 

☐  ☐ 

When you pass pedestrians in the road, leave plenty of room. You might have to use the right-hand side of the road, so look well ahead, as well as in your mirrors, before pulling out. Take great care if a bend in the road obscures your view ahead.

11.40 **Mark one answer** **DES s6, HC p108, KYTS p10**

Which sign means there's a double bend ahead?

☐  ☐ 

☐  ☐ 

Triangular signs give you a warning of hazards ahead. They're there to give you time to prepare for the hazard; for example, by adjusting your speed.

11.41 Mark one answer — DES s6, KYTS p30

What does this sign mean?

- ☐ Wait at the barriers
- ☐ Wait at the crossroads
- ☐ Give way to trams
- ☐ Give way to farm vehicles

Obey the 'give way' signs. Trams are unable to steer around you if you misjudge when it's safe to enter the junction.

11.42 Mark one answer — DES s6, HC p109, KYTS p72

What does this sign mean?

- ☐ Hump bridge
- ☐ Humps in the road
- ☐ Entrance to tunnel
- ☐ Soft verges

These humps have been put in place to slow the traffic down. They're usually found in residential areas. Slow down to an appropriate speed.

11.43 Mark one answer — DES s6, HC p108, KYTS p11

Which sign means the end of a dual carriageway?

☐  ☐ 

☐  ☐ 

If you're overtaking, make sure you move back safely into the left-hand lane before you reach the end of the dual carriageway.

11.44 Mark one answer

DES s6, HC p108, KYTS p11

What does this sign mean?

- ☐ End of dual carriageway
- ☐ Tall bridge
- ☐ Road narrows
- ☐ End of narrow bridge

Don't wait until the last moment before moving into the left-hand lane. Plan ahead and don't rely on other traffic letting you in.

11.45 Mark one answer

DES s6, HC p109, KYTS p12

What does this sign mean?

- ☐ Side winds
- ☐ Road noise
- ☐ Airport
- ☐ Adverse camber

A warning sign with a picture of a windsock indicates that there may be strong side winds. This sign is often found on exposed roads.

11.46 Mark one answer

DES s6, HC p109, KYTS p13–14

What does this traffic sign mean?

- ☐ Slippery road ahead
- ☐ Tyres liable to punctures ahead
- ☐ Danger ahead
- ☐ Service area ahead

This sign is there to alert you to the likelihood of danger ahead. It may be accompanied by a plate indicating the type of hazard. Be ready to reduce your speed and take avoiding action.

11.47 **Mark one answer** **DES s6, HC p109, KYTS p13–14**

You're about to overtake. What should you do when you see this sign?

- ☐ Overtake the other driver as quickly as possible
- ☐ Move to the right to get a better view
- ☐ Switch your headlights on before overtaking
- ☐ Hold back until you can see clearly ahead

You won't be able to see any hazards that might be hidden in the dip. As well as oncoming traffic, the dip may conceal

- cyclists
- horse riders
- parked vehicles
- pedestrians

in the road.

11.48 **Mark one answer** **DES s6, HC p108, KYTS p26**

What does this sign mean?

- ☐ Level crossing with gate or barrier
- ☐ Gated road ahead
- ☐ Level crossing without gate or barrier
- ☐ Cattle grid ahead

Some crossings have gates but no attendant or signals. You should stop, look both ways, listen and make sure that no train is approaching. If there's a telephone, contact the signal operator to make sure it's safe to cross.

11.49 **Mark one answer** **DES s6, HC p108, KYTS p30**

What does this sign mean?

- ☐ No trams ahead
- ☐ Oncoming trams
- ☐ Trams crossing ahead
- ☐ Trams only

This sign tells you to beware of trams. If you don't usually drive in a town where there are trams, remember to look out for them at junctions and look for tram rails, signs and signals.

11.50 **Mark one answer** **DES s6, HC p108, KYTS p12**

What does this sign mean?

- ☐ Adverse camber
- ☐ Steep hill downwards
- ☐ Uneven road
- ☐ Steep hill upwards

This sign gives you an early warning that the road ahead will slope downhill. Prepare to alter your speed and gear. Looking at the sign from left to right will show you whether the road slopes uphill or downhill.

11.51 **Mark one answer** **DES s6, HC p109, KYTS p12**

What does this sign mean?

- ☐ Uneven road surface
- ☐ Bridge over the road
- ☐ Road ahead ends
- ☐ Water across the road

This sign is found where a shallow stream crosses the road. Heavy rainfall could increase the flow of water. If the water looks too deep or the stream has spread over a large distance, stop and find another route.

11.52 **Mark one answer** **DES s6, KYTS p114**

What does this sign mean?

- ☐ Turn left for parking area
- ☐ No through road on the left
- ☐ No entry for traffic turning left
- ☐ Turn left for ferry terminal

This sign shows you that you can't get through to another route by turning left at the junction ahead.

11.53 **Mark one answer** **DES s6, HC p113, KYTS p114**

What does this sign mean?

- ☐ T-junction
- ☐ No through road
- ☐ Telephone box ahead
- ☐ Toilet ahead

You won't be able to find a through route to another road. Use this road only for access.

11.54 **Mark one answer** **DES s6, HC p111**

Which is the sign for a ring road?

☐  ☐ 

☐ 

☐ 

Ring roads are designed to relieve congestion in towns and city centres.

11.55 **Mark one answer** **DES s6, HC p113, KYTS p129**

What does this sign mean?

- ☐ The right-hand lane ahead is narrow
- ☐ Right-hand lane for buses only
- ☐ Right-hand lane for turning right
- ☐ The right-hand lane is closed

Yellow-and-black temporary signs may be used to inform you about roadworks or lane restrictions. Look well ahead. If you have to change lanes, do so in good time.

11.56 **Mark one answer** **DES s6, HC p113, KYTS p130**

What does this sign mean?

- ☐ Change to the left-hand lane
- ☐ Leave at the next exit
- ☐ Contraflow system
- ☐ One-way street

If you use the right-hand lane in a contraflow system, you'll be travelling with no permanent barrier between you and the oncoming traffic. Observe speed limits and keep a good distance from the vehicle ahead.

11.57 **Mark one answer** **DES s6, 11, HC r139**

What does this sign mean?

- ☐ Leave motorway at next exit
- ☐ Lane for heavy and slow vehicles
- ☐ All lorries use the hard shoulder
- ☐ Rest area for lorries

Where there's a long, steep, uphill gradient on a motorway, a crawler lane may be provided. This helps the traffic to flow by diverting the slower heavy vehicles into a dedicated lane on the left.

11.58 **Mark one answer** **DES s6, HC p102, KYTS p119**

What does a red traffic light mean?

- ☐ You should stop unless turning left
- ☐ Stop, if you're able to brake safely
- ☐ You must stop and wait behind the stop line
- ☐ Proceed with care

Whatever light is showing, you should know which light is going to appear next and be able to take appropriate action. For example, when amber is showing on its own, you'll know that red will appear next. This should give you ample time to anticipate and respond safely.

11.59	Mark one answer	DES s6, HC p102, KYTS p119

At traffic lights, what does it mean when the amber light shows on its own?

- ☐ Prepare to go
- ☐ Go if the way is clear
- ☐ Go if no pedestrians are crossing
- ☐ Stop at the stop line

When the amber light is showing on its own, the red light will follow next. The amber light means stop, unless you've already crossed the stop line or you're so close to it that stopping may cause a collision.

11.60	Mark one answer	DES s6, HC p102, KYTS p119

You're at a junction controlled by traffic lights. When should you wait at a green light?

- ☐ When pedestrians are waiting to cross
- ☐ When your exit from the junction is blocked
- ☐ When you think the lights may be about to change
- ☐ When you intend to turn right

As you approach the traffic lights, look into the road you wish to take. Only proceed if your exit road is clear. If the road is blocked, hold back, even if you have to wait for the next green signal.

11.61	Mark one answer	DES s6, HC p102, KYTS p119

You're in the left-hand lane at traffic lights, waiting to turn left. Which signal means you must wait?

- ☐ 
- ☐ 
- ☐ 
- ☐ 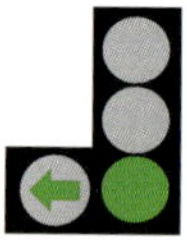

At some junctions, there may be separate signals for different lanes. These are called 'filter' lights. They're designed to help traffic flow at major junctions. Make sure that you're in the correct lane and proceed if the way is clear and the green light shows for your lane.

11.62 Mark one answer

DES s6, HC p108, KYTS p139

What does this sign mean?

- ☐ Traffic lights out of order
- ☐ Amber signal out of order
- ☐ Temporary traffic lights ahead
- ☐ New traffic lights ahead

You might see this sign where traffic lights are out of order. Proceed with caution, as nobody has priority at the junction.

11.63 Mark one answer

DES s6

Who has priority when traffic lights are out of order?

- ☐ Traffic going straight on
- ☐ Traffic turning right
- ☐ Nobody
- ☐ Traffic turning left

When traffic lights are out of order, you should treat the junction as an unmarked crossroads. Be cautious, as you may need to give way or stop. Look for traffic attempting to cross the junction, unaware that it doesn't have priority.

11.64 Mark one answer

DES s6, HC p102, KYTS p13, 26, 120

Where would you find these flashing red light signals?

- ☐ Pelican crossings
- ☐ Motorway exits
- ☐ Zebra crossings
- ☐ Level crossings

These signals are found at level crossings, swing or lifting bridges, some airfields and emergency access sites. The flashing red lights mean stop whether or not the way seems to be clear.

11.65 **Mark one answer** **DES s6, HC r191, KYTS p122**

What do these zigzag white lines mean?

- ☐ No parking at any time
- ☐ Parking allowed only for a short time
- ☐ Slow down to 20 mph
- ☐ Sounding horns isn't allowed

The approach to, and exit from, a pedestrian crossing is marked with zigzag lines. You mustn't park on them or overtake the leading vehicle when approaching the crossing. Parking here would block the view for pedestrians and approaching traffic.

11.66 **Mark one answer** **DES s6, HC r129, p114, KYTS p64**

When may you cross a double solid white line in the middle of the road?

- ☐ To pass traffic that's queuing back at a junction
- ☐ To pass a car signalling to turn left ahead
- ☐ To pass a road maintenance vehicle travelling at 10 mph or less
- ☐ To pass a vehicle that's towing a trailer

You may cross the solid white line to pass a stationary vehicle or to pass a pedal cycle, horse or road maintenance vehicle if it's travelling at 10 mph or less. You may also cross the solid white line to enter a side road or access a property.

11.67 **Mark one answer** **DES s6, HC r127, p114, KYTS p62**

What does this road marking mean?

- ☐ Don't cross the line
- ☐ No stopping allowed
- ☐ You're approaching a hazard
- ☐ No overtaking allowed

A single broken line along the centre of the road, with long markings and short gaps, is a hazard warning line. Don't cross it unless you can see that the road is clear well ahead.

11.68 **Mark one answer** **DES s6, KYTS p73**

Where would you see this road marking?

- ☐ At traffic lights
- ☐ On road humps
- ☐ Near a level crossing
- ☐ At a box junction

Because the road has a dark colour, changes in level aren't easily seen. White triangles painted on the road surface give you an indication of where there are road humps.

11.69 **Mark one answer** **DES s6, HC r127, p114, KYTS p62**

Which diagram shows a hazard warning line?

☐  ☐ 

☐  ☐ 

You need to know the difference between the normal centre line and a hazard warning line. If there's a hazard ahead, the markings are longer and the gaps shorter. This gives you advance warning of an unspecified hazard.

11.70 **Mark one answer** **DES s6, HC p114, KYTS p9, 67**

Why does this junction have a 'stop' sign and a stop line on the road?

- ☐ Speed on the major road is derestricted
- ☐ It's a busy junction
- ☐ Visibility along the major road is restricted
- ☐ The junction is on a downhill gradient

Where emerging traffic has a very restricted view of the main road, you may find a 'stop' sign and a solid white stop line. You must stop at the line and then check carefully before you emerge.

11.71 **Mark one answer** **DES s6, HC p114, KYTS p68**

What does this line across the road at the entrance to a roundabout mean?

- ☐ Give way to traffic from the right
- ☐ Traffic from the left has right of way
- ☐ You have right of way
- ☐ Stop at the line

Slow down as you approach the roundabout and check for traffic from the right. If you need to stop and give way, stay behind the broken line until it's safe to emerge onto the roundabout.

11.72 **Mark one answer** **DES s6, HC r106**

How will a police officer in a patrol vehicle signal for you to stop?

- ☐ Flash the headlights, indicate left and point to the left
- ☐ Overtake and give a slowing down arm signal
- ☐ Use the siren, overtake, cut in front and stop
- ☐ Pull alongside you, use the siren and wave you to stop

You must obey signals given by the police. If a police officer in a patrol vehicle wants you to pull over, they'll indicate this without causing danger to you or other traffic.

11.73 **Mark one answer** **DES s6, HC p104**

You're approaching a junction where the traffic lights aren't working. What should you do when a police officer gives this signal?

- ☐ Turn left only
- ☐ Turn right only
- ☐ Continue ahead only
- ☐ Stop at the stop line

When a police officer or traffic warden is directing traffic, you must obey them. They'll use the arm signals shown in The Highway Code. Learn what these signals mean and obey them.

11.74 **Mark one answer** **DES s6, HC p103**

What does this arm signal mean?

- ☐ The driver is slowing down
- ☐ The driver intends to turn right
- ☐ The driver wishes to overtake
- ☐ The driver intends to turn left

There might be an occasion where another driver uses an arm signal. This may be because the vehicle's indicators are obscured by other traffic. In order for such signals to be effective, all drivers should know their meaning. Be aware that the 'left turn' signal might look similar to the 'slowing down' signal.

11.75 **Mark one answer** **DES s6, HC p102, KYTS p90**

What does this motorway sign mean?

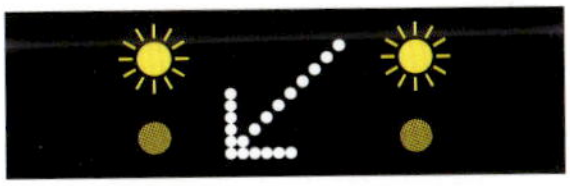

- ☐ Change to the lane on your left
- ☐ Leave the motorway at the next exit
- ☐ Change to the opposite carriageway
- ☐ Pull up on the hard shoulder

On the motorway, signs sometimes show temporary warnings due to traffic or weather conditions. They may be used to indicate

- lane closures
- temporary speed limits
- weather warnings.

11.76 **Mark one answer** **DES s6, HC p102, KYTS p91**

What does this motorway sign mean?

- ☐ Temporary minimum speed 50 mph
- ☐ No services for 50 miles
- ☐ Obstruction 50 metres (164 feet) ahead
- ☐ Temporary maximum speed 50 mph

Look out for signs above your lane or on the central reservation. These will give you important information or warnings about the road ahead. To allow for the high speed of motorway traffic, these signs may light up some distance from any hazard. Don't ignore the signs just because the road looks clear to you.

11.77 **Mark one answer** **DES s6, HC p102, KYTS p90**

What does this sign mean?

- ☐ Through traffic to use left lane
- ☐ Right-hand lane T-junction only
- ☐ Right-hand lane closed ahead
- ☐ 11 tonne weight limit

You should change lanes as directed by the sign. Here, the right-hand lane is closed but the left-hand and centre lanes are available. Merging in turn is recommended when it's safe and traffic is going slowly; for example, at roadworks or a road traffic incident. When vehicles are travelling at speed, this isn't advisable and you should move into the appropriate lane in good time.

11.78 **Mark one answer** **DES s6, HC p110, KYTS p79**

What does '25' mean on this motorway sign?

- ☐ The distance to the nearest town
- ☐ The route number of the road
- ☐ The number of the next junction
- ☐ The speed limit on the slip road

Before you set out on your journey, use a road map to plan your route. When you see an advance warning of your junction, make sure you get into the correct lane in plenty of time. Last-minute harsh braking and cutting across lanes at speed is extremely hazardous.

11.79 **Mark one answer** **DES s6**

How should the right-hand lane of a three-lane motorway be used?

- ☐ As a high-speed lane
- ☐ As an overtaking lane
- ☐ As a right-turn lane
- ☐ As an acceleration lane

You should stay in the left-hand lane of a motorway unless you're overtaking another vehicle. The right-hand lane of a motorway is an overtaking lane; it isn't the 'fast lane'. After overtaking, move back to the left when it's safe to do so.

11.80 **Mark one answer** **DES s6, HC r132, KYTS p71**

Where can you find reflective amber studs on a motorway?

☐ Separating the slip road from the motorway
☐ On the left-hand edge of the road
☐ On the right-hand edge of the road
☐ Separating the lanes

At night or in poor visibility, reflective studs on the road help you to judge your position on the carriageway.

11.81 **Mark one answer** **DES s6, HC r132, KYTS p71**

Where would you find green reflective studs on a motorway?

☐ Separating driving lanes
☐ Between the hard shoulder and the carriageway
☐ At slip-road entrances and exits
☐ Between the carriageway and the central reservation

Knowing the colours of the reflective studs on the road will help you judge your position, especially at night, in foggy conditions or when visibility is poor.

11.82 **Mark one answer** **DES s6, HC p102, KYTS p90**

What should you do when you see this sign as you travel along a motorway?

☐ Leave the motorway at the next exit
☐ Turn left immediately
☐ Change lane
☐ Move onto the hard shoulder

You'll see this sign if the motorway is closed ahead. Pull into the left-hand lane as soon as it's safe to do so. Don't wait until the last moment before you move across, because the lane may be busy and you'll have to rely on another driver making room for you.

11.83 Mark one answer | DES s6, HC p112, KYTS p89

What does this sign mean?

- ☐ No motor vehicles
- ☐ End of motorway
- ☐ No through road
- ☐ End of bus lane

When you leave the motorway, make sure that you check your speedometer. You may be going faster than you realise. Slow down and look for speed-limit signs.

11.84 Mark one answer | DES s6, HC p106, KYTS p20

Which sign means that the national speed limit applies?

☐  ☐ 

☐  ☐ 

You should know the speed limit for the road on which you're travelling and for your vehicle. The different speed limits are shown in The Highway Code.

11.85 Mark one answer | DES s6, HC p40

What's the national speed limit on a single carriageway road?

- ☐ 50 mph
- ☐ 60 mph
- ☐ 40 mph
- ☐ 70 mph

If you're travelling on a dual carriageway that becomes a single carriageway road, reduce your speed gradually so that you aren't exceeding the limit as you enter. There might not be a sign to remind you of the limit, so make sure you know the speed limits for different types of road and vehicle.

11.86 **Mark one answer** **DES s6, HC p102, KYTS p91**

What does this sign mean?

- ☐ End of motorway
- ☐ End of restriction
- ☐ Lane ends ahead
- ☐ Free recovery ends

Temporary restrictions on motorways are shown on signs that have flashing amber lights. At the end of the restriction, you'll see this sign without any flashing lights.

11.87 **Mark one answer** **DES s6, HC p111, KYTS p107**

What does this sign indicate?

- ☐ A diversion route
- ☐ A picnic area
- ☐ A pedestrian zone
- ☐ A cycle route

When a diversion route has been put in place, drivers are advised to follow a symbol, which may be a black triangle, square, circle or diamond shape on a yellow background.

11.88 **Mark one answer** **DES s6, HC p113, KYTS p138**

What does this traffic sign mean?

- ☐ Compulsory maximum speed limit
- ☐ Advisory maximum speed limit
- ☐ Compulsory minimum speed limit
- ☐ Advised separation distance

The sign gives you an early warning of a speed restriction. If you're travelling at a higher speed, slow down in good time. You could come across queuing traffic due to roadworks or a temporary obstruction.

11.89 **Mark one answer** **DES s6, HC p108, KYTS p139**

What should you do when you see this sign at a crossroads?

- ☐ Maintain the same speed
- ☐ Carry on with great care
- ☐ Find another route
- ☐ Telephone the police

When traffic lights are out of order, treat the junction as an unmarked crossroads. Be very careful and be prepared to stop; no-one has priority.

11.90 **Mark one answer** **DES s6, KYTS p17**

What does this sign mean?

- ☐ Motorcycles only
- ☐ No cars
- ☐ Cars only
- ☐ No motorcycles

You must comply with all traffic signs and be especially aware of those signs that apply specifically to the type of vehicle you're using.

11.91 **Mark one answer** **DES s6, HC p113, KYTS p135**

You're on a motorway. A lorry has stopped in the right-hand lane. What should you do when you see this sign on the lorry?

- ☐ Move into the right-hand lane
- ☐ Stop behind the flashing lights
- ☐ Pass the lorry on the left
- ☐ Leave the motorway at the next exit

Sometimes work is carried out on the motorway without closing the lanes. When this happens, signs are mounted on the back of lorries to warn other road users of the roadworks ahead.

11.92 Mark one answer **DES s6, HC p102, KYTS p91**

You're on a motorway. What should you do if there's a red cross showing on the signs above your lane only?

- ☐ Continue in that lane and look for further information
- ☐ Don't continue in that lane
- ☐ Pull onto the hard shoulder
- ☐ Stop and wait for an instruction to proceed

A red cross above your lane shows that your lane is closed. You should move into another lane as soon as you can do so safely.

11.93 Mark one answer **DES s6, HC r112**

When may you sound your vehicle's horn?

- ☐ To give you right of way
- ☐ To attract a friend's attention
- ☐ To warn others of your presence
- ☐ To make slower drivers move over

Never sound your vehicle's horn aggressively. You mustn't sound it in a built-up area between 11.30 pm and 7.00 am, or when you're stationary, unless another road user poses a danger. Don't scare animals by sounding your horn.

11.94 Mark one answer **DES s6, HC r112**

Your vehicle is stationary. When may you use its horn?

- ☐ When another road user poses a danger
- ☐ When the road is blocked by queuing traffic
- ☐ When it's used only briefly
- ☐ When signalling that you've just arrived

When your vehicle is stationary, only sound the horn if you think there's a risk of danger from another road user. Don't use it just to attract someone's attention. This causes unnecessary noise and could be misleading.

11.95 **Mark one answer** **DES s6, HC p107, KYTS p55**

What does this sign mean?

- ☐ You can park on the days and times shown
- ☐ No parking on the days and times shown
- ☐ No parking at all from Monday to Friday
- ☐ End of the urban clearway restrictions

Urban clearways are provided to keep traffic flowing at busy times. You may stop only briefly to set down or pick up passengers. Times of operation will vary from place to place, so always check the signs.

11.96 **Mark one answer** **DES s6, HC p109, KYTS p12**

What does this sign mean?

- ☐ Quayside or river bank
- ☐ Steep hill downwards
- ☐ Uneven road surface
- ☐ Road liable to flooding

You should be careful in these locations, as the road surface is likely to be wet and slippery. There may be a steep drop to the water, and there may not be a barrier along the edge of the road.

11.97 **Mark one answer** **DES s6, HC r127, p114, KYTS p62**

What do the long white lines along the centre of the road mean?

- ☐ Bus lane
- ☐ Hazard warning
- ☐ Give way
- ☐ Lane marking

The centre of the road is usually marked by a broken white line, with lines that are shorter than the gaps. When the lines become longer than the gaps, this is a hazard warning line. Look well ahead for these, especially when you're planning to overtake or turn off.

11.98 Mark one answer | DES s6, HC r130, p114, KYTS p64

What's the reason for the hatched area along the centre of this road?

- ☐ It separates traffic flowing in opposite directions
- ☐ It marks an area to be used by overtaking motorcyclists
- ☐ It's a temporary marking to warn of the roadworks
- ☐ It separates the two sides of the dual carriageway

Areas of 'hatched markings' such as these separate traffic streams that could be a danger to each other. They're often seen on bends or where the road becomes narrow. If the area is bordered by a solid white line, you mustn't enter it except in an emergency.

11.99 Mark one answer | DES s6, HC r110

Other drivers may sometimes flash their headlights at you. What's the official meaning of this signal?

- ☐ There's a radar speed trap ahead
- ☐ They're giving way to you
- ☐ They're warning you of their presence
- ☐ There's a fault with your vehicle

If other drivers flash their headlights, this isn't a signal to show priority. The flashing of headlights has the same meaning as sounding the horn: it's a warning of their presence.

11.100 Mark one answer | DES s6, HC p102, KYTS p31

What does this signal mean?

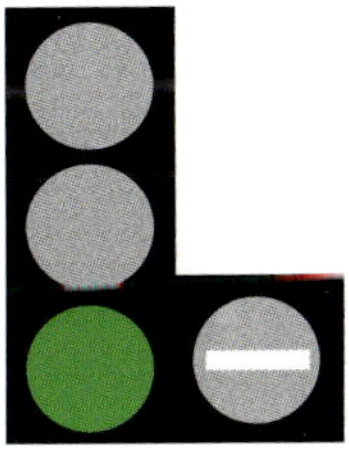

- ☐ Cars must stop
- ☐ Trams must stop
- ☐ Both trams and cars must stop
- ☐ Both trams and cars can continue

The white light shows that trams must stop. The green light shows that other vehicles can go if the way is clear. Trams are being introduced into more cities, so you're likely to come across them and you should learn which signs apply to them.

11.101 Mark one answer DES s6, KYTS p69

Where would you find these road markings?

- ☐ At a railway crossing
- ☐ At a mini-roundabout
- ☐ On a motorway
- ☐ On a pedestrian crossing

These markings show the direction in which the traffic should go at a mini-roundabout.

11.102 Mark one answer DES s6, HC r106

A police car is following you. What should you do if the police officer flashes the headlights and points to the left?

- ☐ Turn left at the next junction
- ☐ Pull up on the left
- ☐ Stop immediately
- ☐ Move over to the left

You must pull up on the left as soon as it's safe to do so and switch off your engine.

11.103 Mark one answer DES s6, HC p102, KYTS p119

You see this amber traffic light ahead. Which light, or lights, will come on next?

- ☐ Red alone
- ☐ Red and amber together
- ☐ Green and amber together
- ☐ Green alone

At junctions controlled by traffic lights, you must stop behind the white line until the lights change to green. A red light, an amber light, and red and amber lights showing together all mean stop.

You may proceed when the light is green unless your exit road is blocked or pedestrians are crossing in front of you.

If you're approaching traffic lights that are visible from a distance and the light has been green for some time, be ready to slow down and stop, because the lights are likely to change.

11.104 **Mark one answer** **DES s6, HC p102, KYTS p90**

What does it mean if you see this signal on the motorway?

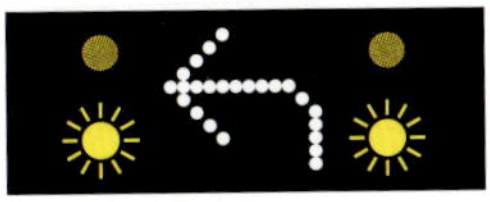

- ☐ Leave the motorway at the next exit
- ☐ All vehicles use the hard shoulder
- ☐ Sharp bend to the left ahead
- ☐ Stop: all lanes ahead closed

You'll see this sign if there has been an incident ahead and the motorway is closed. You must obey the sign. Make sure that you prepare to leave in good time.

Don't cause drivers to take avoiding action by cutting in at the last moment.

11.105 **Mark one answer** **DES s6, HC p106, KYTS p16**

What must you do when you see this sign?

- ☐ Stop only if traffic is approaching
- ☐ Stop even if the road is clear
- ☐ Stop only if children are waiting to cross
- ☐ Stop only if a red light is showing

'Stop' signs are situated at junctions where visibility is restricted or where there's heavy traffic. They must be obeyed: you must stop. Look carefully before moving off.

11.106 **Mark one answer** **DES s6, HC p108, KYTS p9–10**

Which shape is used for a 'give way' sign?

☐  ☐ 

☐  ☐ 

Other warning signs are the same shape and colour, but the 'give way' triangle points downwards. When you see this sign, you must give way to traffic on the road that you're about to enter.

11.107 **Mark one answer** **DES s6, HC p107, KYTS p19**

What does this sign mean?

- ☐ Buses turning
- ☐ Ring road
- ☐ Mini-roundabout
- ☐ Keep right

When you see this sign, look out for any direction signs and judge whether you need to signal your intentions. Do this in good time so that other road users approaching the roundabout know what you're planning to do.

11.108 **Mark one answer** **DES s6, HC p108, KYTS p11**

What does this sign mean?

- ☐ Two-way traffic straight ahead
- ☐ Two-way traffic crosses a one-way road
- ☐ Two-way traffic over a bridge
- ☐ Two-way traffic crosses a two-way road

Be prepared for traffic approaching from junctions on either side of you. Try to avoid unnecessary changing of lanes just before the junction.

11.109 **Mark one answer** **DES s6, HC p108, KYTS p11**

What does this sign mean?

- ☐ Two-way traffic crosses a one-way road
- ☐ Traffic approaching you has priority
- ☐ Two-way traffic straight ahead
- ☐ Motorway contraflow system ahead

This sign may be at the end of a dual carriageway or a one-way street. It's there to warn you of oncoming traffic.

11.110 **Mark one answer** **DES s6, HC p109, KYTS p12**

What does this sign mean?

- ☐ Hump bridge
- ☐ Traffic-calming hump
- ☐ Low bridge
- ☐ Uneven road

You'll need to slow down. At hump bridges, your view ahead will be restricted and the road will often be narrow. If the bridge is very steep, sound your horn to warn others of your approach. Going over the bridge too fast is highly dangerous to other road users and could even cause your wheels to leave the road, with a resulting loss of control.

11.111 **Mark one answer** **DES s6, KYTS p106**

What does this sign mean?

- ☐ Direction to park-and-ride car park
- ☐ No parking for buses or coaches
- ☐ Direction to bus and coach park
- ☐ Parking area for cars and coaches

To ease the congestion in town centres, some cities and towns provide park-and-ride schemes. These allow you to park in a designated area and ride by bus into the centre.

Park-and-ride schemes are usually cheaper and easier than car parking in the town centre.

11.112 **Mark one answer** **DES s6, HC p102, KYTS p119**

What should you do when you're approaching traffic lights that have red and amber showing together?

- ☐ Pass the lights if the road is clear
- ☐ Take care because there's a fault with the lights
- ☐ Wait for the green light
- ☐ Stop because the lights are changing to red

Be aware that other traffic might still be clearing the junction as you approach. A green light means you may go on, but only if the way is clear.

11.113 **Mark one answer** **DES s6, HC r293, p102**

You've stopped at a railway level crossing. What should you do if the red lights continue to flash after a train has gone by?

- ☐ Phone the signal operator
- ☐ Alert drivers behind you
- ☐ Wait
- ☐ Proceed with caution

You must always obey red flashing stop lights. If a train passes but the lights continue to flash, another train will be passing soon. Cross only when the lights go off and the barriers open.

11.114 **Mark one answer** **DES s6, KYTS p116**

You're in a tunnel and you see this sign. What does it mean?

- ☐ Direction to an emergency pedestrian exit
- ☐ Beware of pedestrians: no footpath ahead
- ☐ No access for pedestrians
- ☐ Beware of pedestrians crossing ahead

If you have to leave your vehicle and get out of a tunnel by an emergency exit, do so as quickly as you can. Follow the signs directing you to the nearest exit point. If there are several people using the exit, don't panic but try to leave in a calm and orderly manner.

11.115 **Mark one answer** **DES s6, HC p107, KYTS p19**

Which sign shows that you're entering a one-way system?

☐  ☐ 

☐  ☐ 

If the road has two lanes, you can use either lane and overtake on either side. Use the lane that's more convenient for your destination unless signs or road markings indicate otherwise.

11.116 Mark one answer — DES s6, HC p107, KYTS p32

What does this sign mean?

- ☐ With-flow bus and cycle lane
- ☐ Contraflow bus and cycle lane
- ☐ No buses and cycles allowed
- ☐ No waiting for buses and cycles

Buses and cycles can travel in this lane. In this example, they'll flow in the same direction as other traffic. If it's busy, they may be passing you on the left, so watch out for them. Times on the sign will show the lane's hours of operation; if no times are shown, or there's no sign at all, this means the lane is in operation 24 hours a day. In some areas, other vehicles, such as taxis and motorcycles, are allowed to use bus lanes. The sign will show if this is the case.

11.117 Mark one answer — DES s6, HC p109, KYTS p13

What does this sign mean?

- ☐ School crossing patrol
- ☐ No pedestrians allowed
- ☐ Pedestrian zone – no vehicles
- ☐ Zebra crossing ahead

Look well ahead and be ready to stop for any pedestrians crossing, or about to cross, the road. Also check the pavements for anyone who looks like they might step or run into the road.

11.118 Mark one answer — DES s6, HC r103, p103

Which arm signal tells you that the car you're following is going to pull up?

☐ 

☐ 

☐ 

☐ 

There may be occasions when drivers need to give an arm signal to confirm their intentions. This could include in bright sunshine, at a complex road layout, when stopping at a pedestrian crossing or when turning right just after passing a parked vehicle. You should understand what each arm signal means. If you give arm signals, make them clear, correct and decisive.

11.119 Mark one answer

DES s6, HC p107, KYTS p19

Which sign means turn left ahead?

- [ ] 
- [ ] 
- [ ] 
- [ ] 

Blue circles tell you what you must do and this sign gives a clear instruction to turn left ahead. You should be looking out for signs at all times and know what they mean.

11.120 Mark one answer

DES s6, HC p102, KYTS p119

You're approaching traffic lights and the red light is showing. What signal will show next?

- [ ] Red and amber
- [ ] Green alone
- [ ] Amber alone
- [ ] Green and amber

If you know which light is going to show next, you can plan your approach accordingly. This can help prevent excessive braking or hesitation at the junction.

11.121 Mark one answer

DES s6, HC p108, KYTS p12

What does this sign mean?

- [ ] Low bridge ahead
- [ ] Tunnel ahead
- [ ] Ancient monument ahead
- [ ] Traffic danger spot ahead

When approaching a tunnel, switch on your dipped headlights. Be aware that your eyes might need to adjust to the sudden darkness. You may need to reduce your speed.

11.122 Mark one answer

DES s6, HC p114, KYTS p65

What does the white line along the side of the road indicate?

- ☐ The edge of the carriageway
- ☐ The approach to a hazard
- ☐ No parking
- ☐ No overtaking

A continuous white line is used on many roads to indicate the edge of the carriageway. This can be useful when visibility is restricted. The line is discontinued at junctions, lay-bys, and entrances to or exits from private drives.

11.123 Mark one answer

DES s6, HC r128, KYTS p63

What does this white arrow on the road mean?

- ☐ Entrance on the left
- ☐ All vehicles turn left
- ☐ Return to your side of the road
- ☐ Road bends to the left

The arrow indicates the direction in which to pass hatch markings or double white lines. If you're overtaking, you must return to the left-hand side of the road.

11.124 **Mark one answer** **DES s6, HC r103, p103**

How should you give an arm signal to turn left?

There may be occasions when other road users are unable to see your indicator, such as in bright sunlight or at a busy, complicated junction. In these cases, an arm signal will help others to understand your intentions.

11.125 **Mark one answer** **DES s6, HC r104, 170**

You're waiting at a T-junction. What should you do if a vehicle is coming from the right, with its left indicator flashing?

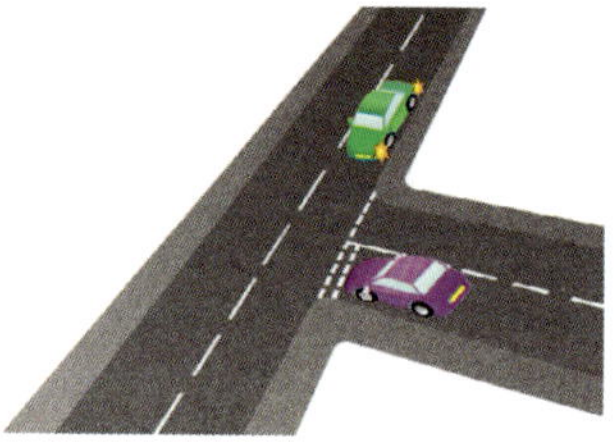

- ☐ Move out and accelerate hard
- ☐ Wait until the vehicle starts to turn in
- ☐ Pull out before the vehicle reaches the junction
- ☐ Move out slowly

Other road users may give misleading signals. When you're waiting at a junction, don't emerge until you're sure of their intentions.

11.126 **Mark one answer** **DES s6, HC r116**

When may you use hazard warning lights while you're driving?

- ☐ Instead of sounding the horn in a built-up area between 11.30 pm and 7.00 am
- ☐ On a motorway or unrestricted dual carriageway, to warn of a hazard ahead
- ☐ On rural routes, after a sign warning of animals
- ☐ On the approach to toucan crossings, where cyclists are waiting to cross

When there's queuing traffic ahead and you have to slow down or even stop, briefly showing your hazard warning lights will help alert the traffic behind to the hazard.

11.127 Mark one answer DES s6, HC r103

Why should you make sure that your indicators are cancelled after turning at a junction?

- ☐ To avoid flattening the battery
- ☐ To avoid misleading other road users
- ☐ To avoid dazzling other road users
- ☐ To avoid damage to the indicator relay

Leaving your indicators on could confuse other road users and may even lead to a crash. Be aware that if you haven't turned sharply, your indicators may not self-cancel and you'll need to turn them off manually.

11.128 Mark one answer DES s6, HC r103

You're driving in busy traffic. You want to pull up just after a junction on the left. When should you signal?

- ☐ As you're passing or just after the junction
- ☐ Just before you reach the junction
- ☐ Well before you reach the junction
- ☐ It would be better not to signal at all

You need to signal to let other drivers know your intentions. However, if you indicate too early, they may think you're turning left into the junction. Correct timing of the signal is very important to avoid misleading others.

Case study practice – 11 Road and traffic signs

You're driving through an area where there are many pedestrians.

There's a turning ahead with a red-bordered round sign, showing a car with a motorcycle above it.

Outside town, the single carriageway road has double unbroken white centre lines.

You see several signs with brown backgrounds.

You approach a traffic light that's showing green. The signal changes just before you reach it.

11.1 What's meant by the round sign described above?

Mark **one** answer

- ☐ No large vehicles
- ☐ No motor vehicles
- ☐ No through road
- ☐ No vehicle parking

HC p106

11.2 What do the lines along the centre of the road tell you?

Mark **one** answer

- ☐ No speeding
- ☐ No reversing
- ☐ No parking
- ☐ No turning

HC r240, p114 KYTS p64

11.3 What's the national speed limit on the road outside of town?

Mark **one** answer

- ☐ 40 mph
- ☐ 50 mph
- ☐ 60 mph
- ☐ 70 mph

HC p40

11.4 What details would you find on the brown signs?

Mark **one** answer

- ☐ Tourist information
- ☐ Safety information
- ☐ Cyclist information
- ☐ Weather information

DES s6 KYTS p101–104

11.5 As the traffic lights change, what colour signal would you see next?

Mark **one** answer

- ☐ A red light on its own
- ☐ Red and amber together
- ☐ An amber light on its own
- ☐ Green and amber together

HC p102 DES s6

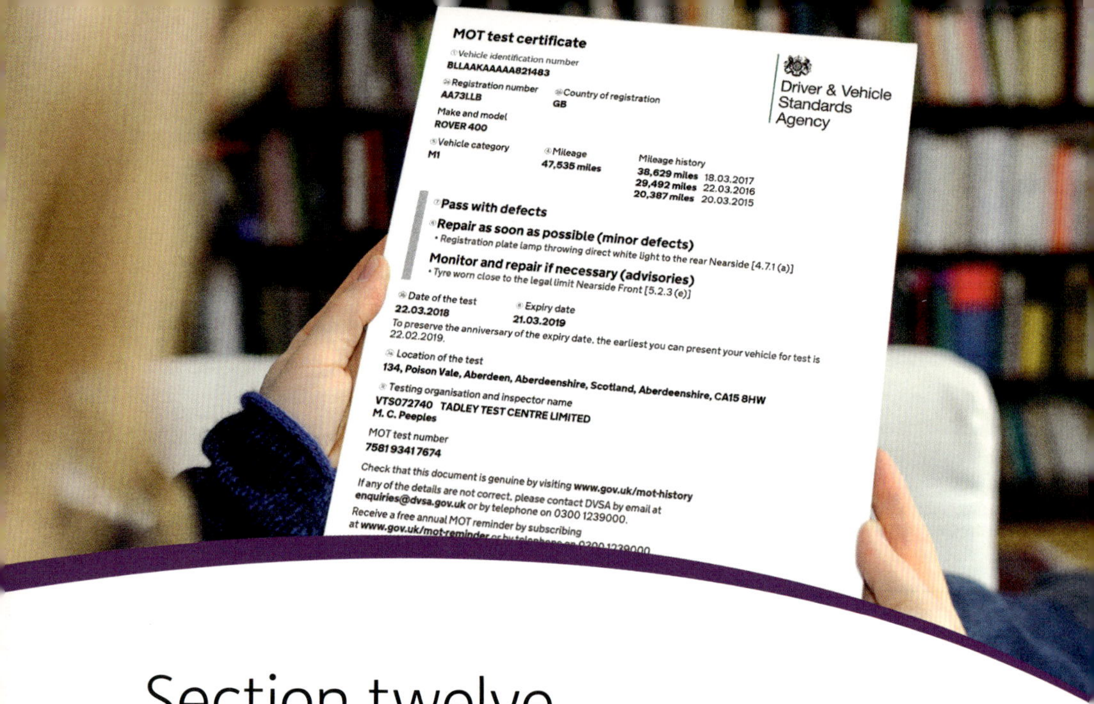

Section twelve

Essential documents

In this section, you'll learn about

- the documents you need when owning and keeping a car
- the driving licence
- buying insurance
- the MOT test.

Essential documents

Before you can legally drive on a public road, you **MUST**

- check that the vehicle tax has been paid on the vehicle you're driving
- hold a valid driving licence
- have valid insurance cover
- ensure the vehicle you're driving has a valid MOT certificate if it requires one.

You won't be able to tax your vehicle unless you have

- a valid MOT certificate (if your vehicle requires one)
- appropriate, current insurance cover.

HC p120–123 DES s2

Registering and owning a car

The vehicle registration certificate (V5C) contains details of

- the vehicle, including make, model, engine size and year of registration
- the registered keeper.

If you're the registered keeper, you **MUST** tell the Driver and Vehicle Licensing Agency (DVLA) when you change

- your vehicle
- your name
- your permanent address.

If you buy a second-hand vehicle, tell DVLA immediately that the keeper of the vehicle has changed.

Find out more about the V5C at this website.

www.gov.uk

Vehicle tax **MUST** be paid on all motor vehicles used or kept on public roads (unless the vehicle is exempt – see **www.gov.uk** for more details).

HC p122 DES s2

If you're not going to use your vehicle on public roads, you won't have to pay vehicle tax as long as you tell DVLA in advance. This is called a Statutory Off-Road Notification (SORN) and lasts until you tax, sell or scrap your vehicle.

DES s2

Your driving licence

Before driving on a public road, a learner **MUST** have a valid provisional driving licence.

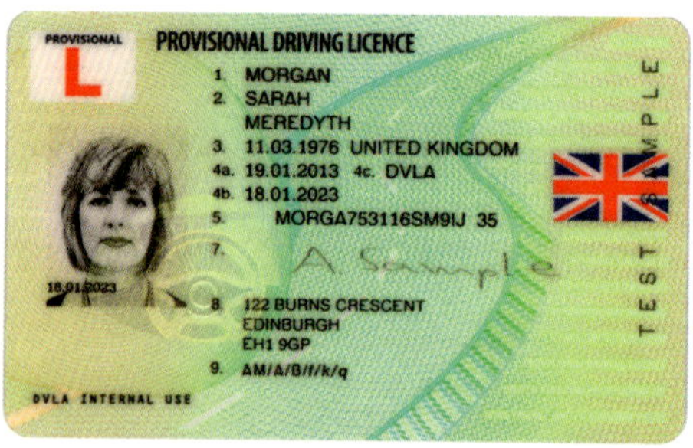

You **MUST** tell the licensing authority if

- your health is likely to affect your driving
- your eyesight doesn't meet the required standard.

HC r90 DES s1

Eyesight: to be able to drive you **MUST** be able to read in good daylight, with glasses or contact lenses if you wear them, a vehicle number plate from 20 metres (about 66 feet).

Tip

If you want to practise driving before you pass your test, you MUST be accompanied by someone who's at least 21 years old and has held (and still holds) a full licence for the category of vehicle you're driving, for three years.

HC p122 DES s2

For two years after you pass your first practical test (car or motorcycle), there's a probation period. This means that if you get six or more penalty points within this two-year probation period, you'll lose your licence. You'll then have to

- reapply for a provisional licence
- pass your theory and practical tests again.

Any points on your provisional licence will be transferred to your new licence when you pass your test.

HC p127, 134

Insurance

You **MUST** have at least third-party insurance cover before driving on public roads. This covers

- injury to another person
- damage to someone else's property
- damage to other vehicles.

Driving without insurance is a criminal offence. It can lead to an unlimited fine, and possibly disqualification.

HC p121–122 DES s2

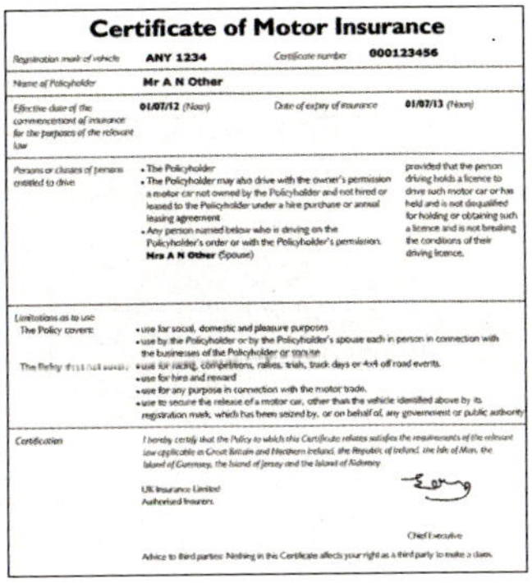
Certificate of Motor Insurance

Registration mark of vehicle **ANY 1234** Certificate number **000123456**

Name of Policyholder **Mr A N Other**

Effective date of the commencement of insurance for the purposes of the relevant law **01/07/12** (Noon) Date of expiry of insurance **01/07/13** (Noon)

Persons or classes of persons entitled to drive
- The Policyholder
- The Policyholder may also drive with the owner's permission a motor car not owned by the Policyholder and not hired or leased to the Policyholder under a hire purchase or annual leasing agreement
- Any person named below who is driving on the Policyholder's order or with the Policyholder's permission. **Mrs A N Other** (Spouse)

provided that the person driving holds a licence to drive such motor car or has held and is not disqualified for holding or obtaining such a licence and is not breaking the conditions of their driving licence.

Limitations as to use
The Policy covers:
- use for social, domestic and pleasure purposes
- use by the Policyholder or by the Policyholder's spouse each in person in connection with the businesses of the Policyholder or spouse

The Policy does not cover:
- use for racing, competitions, rallies, trials, track days or 4x4 off road events.
- use for hire and reward
- use for any purpose in connection with the motor trade.
- use to secure the release of a motor car, other than the vehicle identified above by its registration mark, which has been seized by, or on behalf of, any government or public authority

Certification
I hereby certify that the Policy to which this Certificate relates satisfies the requirements of the relevant law applicable in Great Britain and Northern Ireland, the Republic of Ireland, the Isle of Man, the Island of Guernsey, the Island of Jersey and the Island of Alderney

UK Insurance Limited
Authorised Insurers

Chief Executive

Advice to third parties: Nothing in this Certificate affects your right as a third party to make a claim.

You'll need to show your insurance certificate when you're taxing your vehicle or if a police officer asks you for it. Your insurer may give you a temporary cover note until you receive your insurance certificate.

Remember, if your vehicle is unused or off the road it **MUST** have either a SORN or valid insurance. If you have neither, and ignore any subsequent reminders sent to you as the registered keeper, you risk

- a fixed-penalty fine of £100
- court prosecution and a fine of up to £1000
- having the vehicle clamped, seized and destroyed.

DES s2

Tip

If a police officer asks to see your documents and you don't have them with you, you can produce them at a police station within seven days.

HC p122 DES s16

Your insurance policy may have an excess of, for example, £100. This means you'll have to pay the first £100 of any claim for damage to your vehicle. The cost of your insurance is generally lower if you're over 25 years old.

Before you drive anyone else's vehicle, make sure it's insured for you to drive.

HC p121–122 DES s2

MOT test

The MOT test makes sure your vehicle meets road safety and environmental standards. Cars **MUST** first have an MOT test when they're three years old (four in Northern Ireland). MOT certificates are valid for one year.

HC p121 DES s2

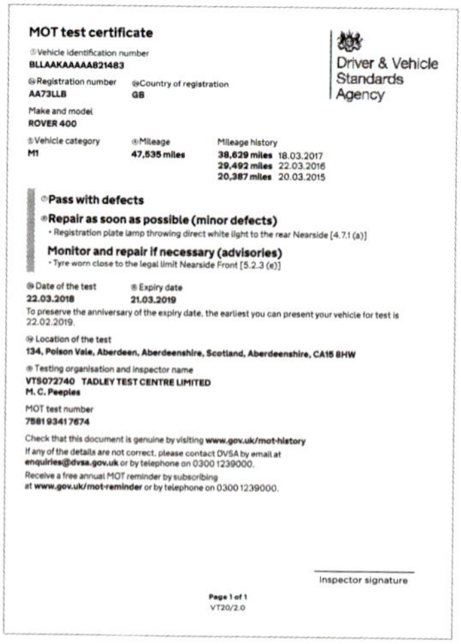
MOT test certificate

Driver & Vehicle Standards Agency

Vehicle identification number
BLLAAKAAAAAB21483

Registration number
AA73LLB

Country of registration
GB

Make and model
ROVER 400

Vehicle category
M1

Mileage
47,535 miles

Mileage history
38,629 miles 18.03.2017
29,492 miles 22.03.2016
20,387 miles 20.03.2015

Pass with defects

Repair as soon as possible (minor defects)
- Registration plate lamp throwing direct white light to the rear Nearside [4.7.1 (a)]

Monitor and repair if necessary (advisories)
- Tyre worn close to the legal limit Nearside Front [5.2.3 (e)]

Date of the test
22.03.2018

Expiry date
21.03.2019

To preserve the anniversary of the expiry date, the earliest you can present your vehicle for test is 22.02.2019.

Location of the test
134, Polson Vale, Aberdeen, Aberdeenshire, Scotland, Aberdeenshire, CA15 8HW

Testing organisation and inspector name
VTS072740 TADLEY TEST CENTRE LIMITED
M. C. Peeples

MOT test number
7581 9341 7674

Check that this document is genuine by visiting **www.gov.uk/mot-history**

If any of the details are not correct, please contact DVSA by email at **enquiries@dvsa.gov.uk** or by telephone on 0300 1239000.

Receive a free annual MOT reminder by subscribing at **www.gov.uk/mot-reminder** or by telephone on 0300 1239000.

Inspector signature

Page 1 of 1
VT20/2.0

Trailers and caravans don't need an MOT, but they do need to be kept in good order.

HC p121

Unless your car is exempt from MOT testing (see **www.gov.uk** for rules exempting vehicles from MOT testing), the only time when you can drive your car without an MOT certificate is when you're driving to or from an appointment at an MOT centre or to have MOT repairs carried out.

If your vehicle needs an MOT certificate and you don't have one

- you won't be able to renew your vehicle tax
- you could be prosecuted
- your insurance may be invalid.

HC p121 DES s2

For more information about MOT tests, see this website.

www.gov.uk

Meeting the standards

You must be able to
make sure that your driving licence is valid for the category of vehicle that you're driving
make sure that the vehicle is registered and the vehicle tax has been paid
make sure that you have valid insurance for your use of the vehicle
make sure that the vehicle has a current MOT certificate (if necessary).

You must know and understand
that you must have a valid driving licence for the vehicle you drive. You must also comply with any restrictions on your licence
that the vehicle must be registered with DVLA
that you must tell DVLA/DVA if you • change your name • change your address • have or develop a medical condition that will affect your ability to drive
the MOT requirements for vehicles being used on the road.

Notes

You can use this page to make your own notes or diagrams about the key points you need to remember.

Think about

- What documents do you need when taxing your vehicle?
- You must tell DVLA/DVA when certain details change: what are they?
- What's a SORN?
- What's the minimum level of insurance you must have before driving on public roads?
- What does an MOT test cover?

Your notes

Things to discuss and practise with your instructor

These are just a few examples of what you could discuss with your instructor. Read more about essential documents to come up with your own ideas.

Discuss with your instructor

- what will happen if you accumulate six or more penalty points on your licence within two years of passing your test
- what the letters 'SORN' stand for and what this means to the keeper of a vehicle
- what you **MUST** have to use a vehicle legally on the road; for example, a valid driving licence.

Practise with your instructor

It's difficult to practise your knowledge and understanding of documents. Just remember that the safer and more responsibly you drive, the less likely you are to

- cause high wear and tear to your car
- accumulate penalty points
- be involved in an incident and damage your car.

Meaning that

- your car will be more likely to be roadworthy and pass its MOT test
- you'll be able to find cheaper car insurance
- you won't lose your licence, under the New Driver's Act and beyond.

12.1 Mark one answer — DES s2, HC p121

For how long is an MOT certificate normally valid?

- ☐ Three years after the date it was issued
- ☐ 10,000 miles
- ☐ One year after the date it was issued
- ☐ 30,000 miles

Some garages will remind you that your vehicle is due for its annual MOT test, but not all do. To ensure continuous cover, you may take your vehicle for its MOT up to one month before its existing MOT certificate expires. The expiry date on the new certificate will be 12 months after the expiry date on the old certificate.

12.2 Mark one answer — DES s2, HC p121–122

What's a cover note?

- ☐ A document issued before you receive your driving licence
- ☐ A document issued before you receive your insurance certificate
- ☐ A document issued before you receive your registration document
- ☐ A document issued before you receive your MOT certificate

Sometimes an insurance company will issue a temporary insurance certificate called a cover note. It gives you the same insurance cover as your certificate but lasts for a limited period, usually one month.

12.3 Mark one answer — HC p127, 134

You've just passed your first practical driving test. What will you have to do if you get six penalty points on your licence in the next two years?

- ☐ Retake only your theory test
- ☐ Retake your theory and practical tests
- ☐ Retake only your practical test
- ☐ Reapply for your full licence immediately

If you accumulate six or more penalty points within two years of gaining your first full licence, it will be revoked. The six or more points include any gained due to offences you committed before passing your test. If this happens, you may only drive as a learner until you pass both the theory and practical tests again.

12.4 Mark one answer — DES s2, HC p122

For how long is a Statutory Off-Road Notification (SORN) valid?

- ☐ Until the vehicle is taxed, sold or scrapped
- ☐ Until the vehicle is insured and MOT'd
- ☐ Until the vehicle is repaired or modified
- ☐ Until the vehicle is used on the road

A SORN allows you to keep a vehicle off-road and untaxed. SORN will end when the vehicle is taxed, sold or scrapped.

12.5 | **Mark one answer** | **DES s2, HC p122**

What's a Statutory Off-Road Notification (SORN)?

- ☐ A notification to tell DVSA that a vehicle doesn't have a current MOT
- ☐ Information kept by the police about the owner of a vehicle
- ☐ A notification to tell DVLA that a vehicle isn't being used on the road
- ☐ Information held by insurance companies to check a vehicle is insured

If you want to keep a vehicle untaxed and off the public road, you must make a SORN. It's an offence not to do so. Your SORN is valid until your vehicle is taxed, sold or scrapped.

12.6 | **NI EXEMPT** | **Mark one answer** | **DES s2, HC p126**

What's the maximum fine for driving or riding without insurance?

- ☐ Unlimited
- ☐ £500
- ☐ £1000
- ☐ £5000

Driving or riding without insurance is a serious offence. As well as an unlimited fine, you may be disqualified or incur penalty points.

12.7 | **Mark one answer** | **DES s2, HC p122**

Who's legally responsible for ensuring that a vehicle registration certificate (V5C) is updated?

- ☐ The registered vehicle keeper
- ☐ The vehicle manufacturer
- ☐ Your insurance company
- ☐ The licensing authority

It's your legal responsibility to keep the details on your vehicle registration certificate (V5C) up to date. You should tell the licensing authority about any changes. These include your name, address or vehicle details. If you don't do this, you may have problems when you try to sell your vehicle.

12.8 | **Mark one answer** | **DES s2, HC p122**

Your insurer will issue you with an insurance certificate. When must you produce this document for inspection?

- ☐ When making a SORN
- ☐ When buying or selling a vehicle
- ☐ When a police officer asks you for it
- ☐ When your vehicle is having an MOT test

You must produce a valid insurance certificate when requested by a police officer. If you can't do this immediately, you may be asked to take it to a police station. Other documents you may be asked to produce are your driving licence and the vehicle's MOT certificate.

12.9 Mark one answer — DES s2, HC p120–122

What do you need before you can legally use a motor vehicle on the road?

- ☐ An appropriate driving licence
- ☐ Breakdown cover
- ☐ Proof of your identity
- ☐ A vehicle handbook

Using a motor vehicle on the road illegally carries a heavy fine and can lead to penalty points on your driving licence. You must

- hold a valid driving licence for the class of vehicle you're using
- be insured to drive the vehicle.

If required, the vehicle must have a current MOT test certificate and be taxed for use on the road.

12.10 Mark one answer — DES s2

What must you have when you apply to renew your vehicle tax?

- ☐ Valid insurance
- ☐ The vehicle's chassis number
- ☐ The handbook
- ☐ A valid driving licence

You can renew your vehicle tax online, at post offices and by phone using the DVLA vehicle tax service. When applying, make sure you have all the relevant valid documents, including a valid MOT test certificate where applicable.

12.11 Mark one answer — DES s2, HC p122

A police officer asks to see your documents. You don't have them with you. How many days do you have to produce them at a police station?

- ☐ 5 days
- ☐ 7 days
- ☐ 14 days
- ☐ 21 days

You don't have to carry your vehicle's documents wherever you go. If a police officer asks to see them and you don't have them with you, you may be asked to produce them at a police station within 7 days.

12.12 Mark one answer DES s2

What must you check before you drive someone else's vehicle?

- ☐ That the vehicle owner has third-party insurance cover
- ☐ That your own vehicle has insurance cover
- ☐ That the vehicle is insured for your use
- ☐ That the insurance documents are in the vehicle

Driving a vehicle without insurance cover is illegal, so be sure that, whoever's car you drive, you're insured – whether on their policy or on your own. If you need to take out insurance, it's worth comparing several quotes before you decide which insurance provider best meets your needs.

12.13 Mark one answer DES s2, HC p121

Your car needs to pass an MOT test. What may be invalidated if you drive the car without a current MOT certificate?

- ☐ The vehicle service record
- ☐ The vehicle insurance
- ☐ The vehicle tax
- ☐ The vehicle registration document

If your vehicle requires an MOT certificate, it's illegal to drive it without one and your insurance may be invalid if you do so. The only exceptions are that you may drive to a pre-arranged MOT test appointment, or to a garage for repairs required for the test.

12.14 Mark one answer DES s2, HC p121–122

What legal requirement must be met by a newly qualified driver?

- ☐ They must display green L plates
- ☐ They must have a new photograph taken for their full licence
- ☐ They must be accompanied on their first motorway journey
- ☐ They must have valid motor insurance

It's your responsibility to make sure you're properly insured for the vehicle you're driving. This is the case regardless of whether you're a newly qualified driver or one with more experience.

12.15 Mark one answer DES s2, HC p121

What's covered by third-party insurance?

- ☐ Damage to your vehicle
- ☐ Fire damage to your vehicle
- ☐ Flood damage to your vehicle
- ☐ Damage to other vehicles

Third-party insurance doesn't cover damage to your own vehicle or injury to yourself. If you have a crash and your vehicle is damaged, you might have to carry out the repairs at your own expense.

12.16 **Mark one answer** **DES s2, HC p122**

Who's responsible for paying the vehicle tax?

- ☐ The driver of the vehicle
- ☐ The registered keeper of the vehicle
- ☐ The car dealer
- ☐ The Driver and Vehicle Licensing Agency (DVLA)

The registered keeper of the vehicle is responsible for paying the vehicle tax or making a Statutory Off-Road Notification (SORN) if the vehicle is to be kept untaxed and off the road.

12.17 **Mark one answer** **DES s2, HC p122**

What information is found on a vehicle registration document?

- ☐ The registered keeper
- ☐ The type of insurance cover
- ☐ The service history details
- ☐ The date of the MOT

Every vehicle used on the road has a registration document. This shows the vehicle's details, including date of first registration, registration number, registered keeper, previous keeper, make of vehicle, engine size, chassis number, year of manufacture and colour.

12.18 **Mark one answer** **DES s2, HC p120, 122**

When must you contact the Driver and Vehicle Licensing Agency (DVLA)?

- ☐ When you get a parking ticket
- ☐ When you change your vehicle
- ☐ When you use your vehicle for work
- ☐ When your vehicle's insurance is due

DVLA needs to keep its records up to date. It sends out a reminder when a vehicle's tax is due for renewal. To do this, it needs to know the name and address of the registered keeper. Every vehicle in the country is registered, so it's possible to trace its history.

12.19 **Mark one answer** **DES s1, HC r90**

What circumstances require you to notify the Driver and Vehicle Licensing Agency (DVLA)?

- ☐ When your health affects your driving
- ☐ When you have to work abroad
- ☐ When you lend your vehicle to someone
- ☐ When your vehicle needs an MOT certificate

DVLA holds the records of all vehicles, drivers and riders in Great Britain and Northern Ireland. They need to know if you have a medical condition that might affect your ability to drive safely. You must tell them if your health deteriorates and you become unfit to drive.

12.20 NI EXEMPT Mark one answer DES s1, 11

When could the cost of your insurance be reduced?

- ☐ When you're under 25 years old
- ☐ When you don't wear glasses
- ☐ When you pass the driving test first time
- ☐ When you complete the Pass Plus scheme

The cost of insurance varies with your age and how long you've been driving. Usually, the younger you are, the more expensive it is, especially if you're under 25.

Pass Plus provides additional training to newly qualified drivers. The scheme is recognised by many insurance companies, and taking this extra training could give you reduced insurance premiums, as well as improving your skills and experience.

12.21 Mark one answer DES s2, HC p122

In order to supervise a learner driver you need to have held a full driving licence for the same category of vehicle, for at least three years. What other requirement must you meet?

- ☐ To have a car with dual controls
- ☐ To be at least 21 years old
- ☐ To be an approved driving instructor
- ☐ To hold an advanced driving certificate

Learner drivers benefit by combining professional driving lessons with private practice. However, you need to be at least 21 years old and have held your driving licence for at least 3 years before you can supervise a learner driver.

12.22 Mark one answer DES s2, HC p121

Your car requires an MOT certificate. When is it legal to drive it without an MOT certificate?

- ☐ Up to seven days after the old certificate has run out
- ☐ When driving to an MOT centre to arrange an appointment
- ☐ When driving the car with the owner's permission
- ☐ When driving to an appointment at an MOT centre

When a car is three years old (four years old in Northern Ireland), it must pass an MOT test and have a valid MOT certificate before it can be used on the road. Exceptionally, you may

- drive to a pre-arranged test appointment or to a garage for repairs required for the test
- drive vehicles that are more than 40 years old without an MOT test, but they must be in a roadworthy condition before being used on the road. See GOV.UK for more details.

12.23 NI EXEMPT **Mark one answer** **DES s2, HC p121**

When will a new car need its first MOT test?

- ☐ When it's one year old
- ☐ When it's three years old
- ☐ When it's five years old
- ☐ When it's seven years old

The vehicle you drive must be roadworthy and in good condition. If it's over three years old, it must pass an MOT test to remain in use on the road (unless it's exempt from the MOT test – see GOV.UK).

12.24 **Mark one answer** **DES s2, HC p121**

What does third-party insurance cover?

- ☐ Damage to your vehicle
- ☐ Damage to other vehicles
- ☐ Injury to yourself
- ☐ All damage and injury

Third-party insurance cover is usually cheaper than comprehensive cover. However, it doesn't cover any damage caused to your own vehicle or property. It only covers damage and injury you cause to others.

12.25 **Mark one answer** **DES s2, HC p121**

What's the legal minimum insurance cover you must have to drive on public roads?

- ☐ Third party, fire and theft
- ☐ Comprehensive
- ☐ Third party only
- ☐ Personal injury cover

The minimum insurance required by law is third-party cover. This covers your liability to others involved in a collision but not damage to your vehicle. Basic third-party insurance also won't cover theft or fire damage. Ask your insurance company for advice on the best cover for you and make sure that you read the policy carefully.

12.26 **Mark one answer** **DES s2**

What does it mean if your insurance policy has an excess of £500?

- ☐ The insurance company will pay the first £500 of any claim
- ☐ You'll be paid £500 if you don't claim within one year
- ☐ Your vehicle is insured for a value of £500 if it's stolen
- ☐ You'll have to pay the first £500 of the cost of any claim

Having an excess on your policy will help to keep the premium down. However, if you make a claim, you'll have to pay the excess yourself – in this case, £500.

Case study practice – 12 Essential documents

You've just bought your first car, a good second-hand vehicle. It has passed its MOT but the vehicle tax needs to be paid.

You arrange and pay for the highest level of insurance cover available. You receive a cover note from your insurance company.

You then go to the local post office to pay the vehicle tax.

12.1 What's meant when a vehicle passes its MOT?

Mark **one** answer

- ☐ The vehicle meets the minimum legal safety standards
- ☐ The vehicle's engine capacity is suitable for your needs
- ☐ The vehicle is a good bargain and the seats recline properly
- ☐ The vehicle registration document is properly filled out

DES s2

12.2 When would you need to contact DVLA?

Mark **one** answer

- ☐ If you change your employment status
- ☐ If you change your name or address
- ☐ If you choose to go abroad for a holiday
- ☐ If you're told to do so by a traffic officer

HC p122 DES s2

12.3 What's the highest level of insurance cover available?

Mark **one** answer

- ☐ Complimentary
- ☐ Comprehensive
- ☐ Complicated
- ☐ Compromising

HC p122 DES s2

12.4 What does the cover note give you?

Mark **one** answer

- ☐ Temporary cover
- ☐ Permanent cover
- ☐ Comprehensive cover
- ☐ No cover; it's a receipt

DES s2

12.5 Which document must you show at the post office to tax your car?

Mark **one** answer

- ☐ Birth certificate
- ☐ Driving licence
- ☐ Insurance certificate
- ☐ New keeper supplement

DES s2

Section thirteen

Incidents, accidents and emergencies

In this section, you'll learn about

- what to do if your car breaks down
- how to drive safely in a tunnel, and what to do if you have an emergency
- what to do if you're the first to arrive at an incident
- first aid and how to help casualties at an incident
- reporting an incident to the police.

Incidents, accidents and emergencies

If you're involved in an incident on the road, such as your car breaking down or arriving first at the scene of a crash, knowing what to do can prevent a more serious situation from developing.

Tip
It's useful to carry a first aid kit, a warning triangle and a fire extinguisher in your car for use in an emergency. This equipment could help to prevent or lessen an injury. You may be able to tackle a small fire if you have a fire extinguisher, but don't take any risks.

Breakdowns

Knowing what to do if your car breaks down will help keep you and your passengers safe, and avoid creating problems for other road users, such as traffic jams.

If a warning light shows on the instrument panel of your vehicle, you may have a problem that affects the safety of the vehicle. If necessary, stop as soon as you can do so safely and check the problem.

HC p128 DES s15

If your tyre bursts or you get a puncture while you're driving

- hold the steering wheel firmly
- pull up slowly or roll to a stop at the side of the road.

Tip
If you smell petrol while you're driving, stop and investigate as soon as you can do so safely. Don't ignore it.

If an emergency happens while you're on a motorway, try to get onto the hard shoulder and call for help from an emergency telephone. Marker posts show you the way to the nearest phone. An operator will answer and ask you

- the number on the phone, which will tell the services where you are
- details of yourself and your vehicle
- whether you belong to a motoring organisation.

Wait near your vehicle, well away from the carriageway and hard shoulder.

HC r270, 275 DES s15

Driver location signs can help you give the emergency services precise information about where you are. See this link for more details.

direct.gov.uk/prod_consum_dg/groups/dg_digitalassets/@dg/@en/documents/digitalasset/dg_185820.pdf

A person who has a disability that affects their mobility may display a 'help' pennant if they can't reach an emergency phone.

HC r278

If you break down on a level crossing

- get everyone out of the vehicle and clear of the crossing
- call the signal operator from the phone provided
- only move your vehicle if the operator tells you to do so.

If you're waiting at a level crossing and the red light signal continues to flash after a train has gone by, you **MUST** wait, as another train may be coming.

HC r293, 299 DES s6 KYTS p27

Watch the Think! 'Van of Elvises' video to find out what to do if you break down on a motorway.

youtube.com/thinkuk

Warning others of a breakdown or incident

Use your hazard warning lights

- if you need to suddenly slow down or stop on a motorway or unrestricted dual carriageway because of an incident or hazard ahead; as soon as the traffic behind you has reacted to your hazard lights, you should turn them off
- when your vehicle has broken down and is temporarily obstructing traffic.

HC r116, 274

If you have a warning triangle, place it at least 45 metres (147 feet) behind your vehicle. This will warn other road users that you've broken down. Never place a warning triangle on a motorway: there's too much danger from passing traffic.

HC r274 DES s15, 16

Tip

If you're driving on a motorway and you see something fall from another vehicle, or if anything falls from your own vehicle, stop at the next emergency telephone and report the hazard. Don't try to retrieve it yourself.

Safety in tunnels

You need to take extra care when driving in a tunnel because

- when you enter the tunnel, visibility is suddenly reduced
- the confined space can make incidents difficult to deal with.

Before driving through a tunnel, remove your sunglasses if you're wearing them and switch on dipped headlights. It's particularly important to keep a safe distance from the vehicle in front when driving in a tunnel, even if it's congested.

DES s7

Look out for signs that warn of accidents or congestion.

If your vehicle is involved in an incident or breaks down in a tunnel

- switch off the engine
- switch on your hazard warning lights
- go and call for help immediately from the nearest emergency telephone point.

If your vehicle catches fire while you're driving through a tunnel, drive it out of the tunnel if you can do so without causing further danger. If this isn't possible then you should

- stop
- switch on your hazard warning lights
- try to put out the fire – but only if it's a small fire
- call for help at the nearest emergency point.

DES s16

Tip

If your engine catches fire while you're driving, pull up as quickly and safely as possible. Get yourself and any passengers out and away from the vehicle. Then call the fire brigade. Don't open the bonnet, as this will make the fire worse.

Stopping at an incident

If you're the first to arrive at the scene of an incident or crash, stop and warn other traffic. Switch on your hazard warning lights. Don't put yourself at risk.

- Make sure that the emergency services are called as soon as possible.
- Ensure that the engines of any vehicles at the scene are switched off.
- Move uninjured people away from the scene.

HC r283 DES s16

A vehicle carrying dangerous goods will display an orange label or a hazard warning plate on the back. If a vehicle carrying something hazardous is involved in an incident, report what the label says when you call the emergency services. The different plates are shown in *The Official Highway Code*.

HC p117 DES s16

Helping others and giving first aid

Even if you don't know any first aid, you can help any injured people by

- calling the emergency services on 999 or 112
- keeping them warm and comfortable
- keeping them calm by talking to them reassuringly
- making sure they're not left alone.

HC p131–132 DES s16

Don't move an injured person if the area is safe. Only move them if they're in obvious danger, and then with extreme care. If a motorcyclist is involved, never remove their helmet unless it's essential in order to keep them alive, because removing the helmet could cause more serious injury. Always get medical help and never offer a casualty any food or drink, or a cigarette to calm them down.

HC p131–133 DES s16

If the casualty is unconscious, check that they can breathe normally. If they can, place them in the recovery position until medical help arrives. Keep checking them and make sure their airway remains clear.

If you need to provide emergency care, follow the **DR ABC** code.

Danger

Check that it's safe to approach.

Response

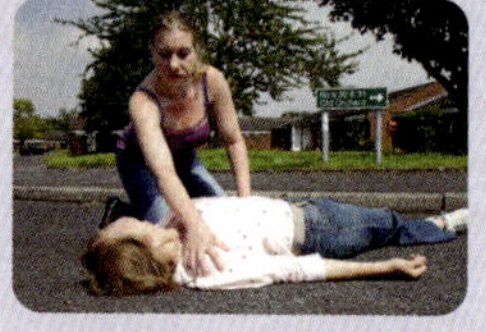

Try to get a response by gently shaking the casualty's shoulders and asking loudly 'Are you all right?' If they respond, check for injuries.

Airway

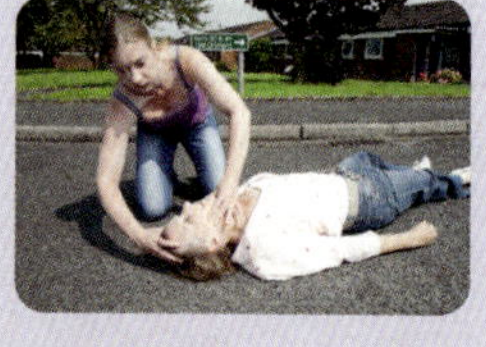

If there's no response, open the casualty's airway by placing your fingers under their chin and lifting it forward.

Breathing

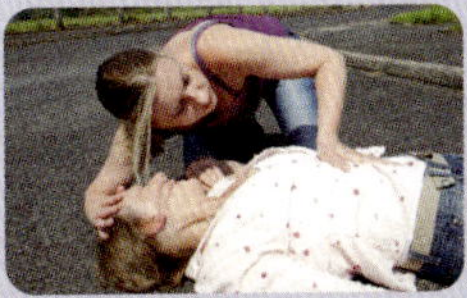

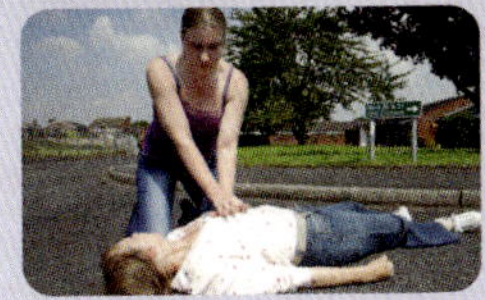

Check that the casualty is breathing normally. Look for chest movements, look and listen for breathing, and feel for breath on your cheek.

If there are no signs of breathing, start CPR. Interlock your fingers, place them in the centre of the casualty's chest and press down hard and fast – around 5–6 centimetres and about twice a second. You may only need one hand for a child and shouldn't press down as far. For infants, use two fingers in the middle of the chest and press down about a third of the chest depth. Don't stop until the casualty starts breathing again or a medical professional takes over.

Circulation

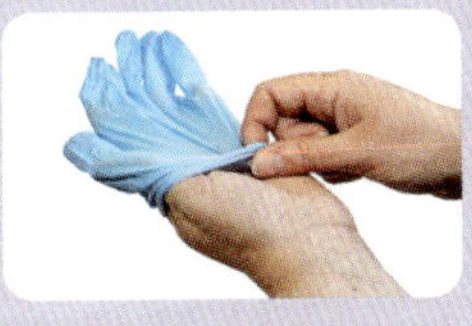

If the casualty is responsive and breathing, check for signs of bleeding. Protect yourself from exposure to blood and check for anything that may be in the wound, such as glass. Don't remove anything that's stuck in the wound. Taking care not to press on the object, build up padding on either side of the object. If nothing is embedded, apply firm pressure over the wound to stem the flow of blood. As soon as practical, fasten a pad to the wound with a bandage or length of cloth. Use the cleanest material available.

People at the scene may be suffering from shock: signs include a rapid pulse, sweating and pale grey skin.

To help someone suffering from shock

- reassure them confidently
- keep them warm
- make them as comfortable as you can
- avoid moving them unless it's necessary
- make sure they're not left alone.

If someone is suffering from burns

- douse the burns thoroughly with cool water for at least 20 minutes
- don't remove anything sticking to the burn.

Reporting an incident

You **MUST** stop and give your name and address if you're involved in an incident. If there's damage to another vehicle, property or animal, report it to the owner. If you don't do this at the time, you **MUST** report the incident to the police as soon as is reasonably practicable, and in any case within 24 hours (immediately in Northern Ireland).

If another person is injured and you don't produce your insurance certificate at the time of the incident, you **MUST** report the incident to the police as soon as is reasonably practicable, and in any case within 24 hours (immediately in Northern Ireland).

HC r286, 287 DES s16

If another vehicle is involved, find out

- who owns the vehicle
- the make and registration number of the vehicle
- the other driver's name, address and telephone number and details of their insurance.

Following an incident (or at any other time), the police may ask you for

- your insurance certificate
- the MOT certificate for the vehicle you're driving
- your driving licence.

HC r286, p122

Meeting the standards

At the scene of an incident, you must be able to

stop and park your vehicle in a safe place, if necessary

make sure that warning is given to other road users

give help to others if you can

where possible, record information about what you saw or the scene that you found. It may be helpful to take photographs and draw sketch plans.

You must know and understand

how to keep control of the vehicle, where possible, if it breaks down

how and when to use a warning triangle or hazard warning lights

what the law says about stopping if you're involved in an incident that causes damage or injury to

- any other person
- another vehicle
- an animal
- someone's property

This includes what to do about

- stopping
- providing your details
- giving statements
- producing documents

how to contact the emergency services and how important it is to give them accurate information.

Notes

You can use this page to make your own notes or diagrams about the key points you need to remember.

Think about

- What should you do if your car breaks down on the motorway?
- How can you warn other road users if you've broken down on the road?
- If you're the first person to arrive at the scene of a crash, what should you do?
- If a motorcyclist is involved in the crash, should you remove their helmet?
- What does DR ABC stand for?
- If you're involved in an incident with another vehicle, what must you do?

Your notes

Things to discuss and practise with your instructor

These are just a few examples of what you could discuss and practise with your instructor. Read more about incidents, accidents and emergencies to come up with your own ideas.

Discuss with your instructor

- what it means if you see a driver displaying a 'help' pennant
- when you may and may not use your hazard warning lights
- what you should do if you arrive at the scene of a crash and find
  - someone bleeding badly with nothing embedded in their wound
  - someone with a burn
  - someone who isn't breathing normally
  - an injured motorcyclist wearing a helmet.

Practise with your instructor

Hopefully, you won't have the opportunity to practise what to do in the event of an incident or emergency during your driving lesson. Instead, practise with your instructor

- learning the rules relating to
  - breakdowns on all roads, including motorways
  - obstructions
  - incidents, warning signs and flashing lights
  - passing and being involved in a crash
  - incidents involving dangerous goods
  - which documents you'll need to produce if you're involved in a crash
  - incidents in tunnels.

13.1 Mark one answer — HC r116

You're on a motorway. When can you use hazard warning lights?

- ☐ When a vehicle is following too closely
- ☐ When you slow down quickly because of danger ahead
- ☐ When you're being towed by another vehicle
- ☐ When you're using the hard shoulder as a running lane

Briefly using your hazard warning lights will warn the traffic behind you that there's a hazard ahead. Turn them off again when following drivers have seen and responded to your signal.

13.2 Mark one answer — DES s3, 11, 15, 16, HC r116

When are you allowed to use hazard warning lights?

- ☐ When stopped and temporarily obstructing traffic
- ☐ When travelling during darkness without headlights
- ☐ When parked on double yellow lines to visit a shop
- ☐ When travelling slowly because you're lost

You mustn't use hazard warning lights while moving, except to warn traffic behind when you slow suddenly on a motorway or unrestricted dual carriageway.

Never use hazard warning lights to excuse dangerous or illegal parking.

13.3 Mark one answer — DES s7, HC r126

What should you do if you have to stop while you're going through a congested tunnel?

- ☐ Pull up very close to the vehicle in front to save space
- ☐ Ignore any message signs, as they're never up to date
- ☐ Keep a safe distance from the vehicle in front
- ☐ Make a U-turn and find another route

It's important to keep a safe distance from the vehicle in front at all times. This still applies in congested tunnels, even if you're moving very slowly or have stopped. If the vehicle in front breaks down, you may need room to manoeuvre past it.

13.4 Mark one answer — DES s16, HC p133

You arrive at the scene of a crash where someone is bleeding heavily from a wound in their arm. Nothing is embedded in the wound. What could you do to help?

- ☐ Walk them around and keep them talking
- ☐ Dab the wound
- ☐ Get them a drink
- ☐ Apply pressure over the wound

If possible, lay the casualty down. Protect yourself from exposure to blood and, when you're sure there's nothing in the wound, apply firm pressure using clean material.

13.5 Mark one answer — DES s16, HC p132

You're at an incident. What could you do to help an unconscious casualty?

- ☐ Take photographs of the scene
- ☐ Check that they're breathing normally
- ☐ Move them to somewhere more comfortable
- ☐ Splash their face with cool water

If a casualty is unconscious, you need to check that they're breathing normally. Look for chest movements, look and listen for breathing, and feel for breath on your cheek.

13.6 Mark one answer — DES s16, HC p132

A casualty isn't breathing normally and needs CPR. At what rate should you press down and release on the centre of their chest?

- ☐ 10 times per minute
- ☐ 120 times per minute
- ☐ 60 times per minute
- ☐ 240 times per minute

If a casualty isn't breathing normally, cardiopulmonary resuscitation (CPR) may be needed to maintain circulation. Place two hands on the centre of the chest and press down hard and fast – around 5–6 centimetres and about twice a second.

13.7 Mark one answer — DES s16

Following a collision, a person has been injured. What would be a warning sign for shock?

- ☐ Flushed complexion
- ☐ Warm dry skin
- ☐ Slow pulse
- ☐ Rapid shallow breathing

The effects of shock may not be immediately obvious. Warning signs to look for include

- a rapid pulse
- sweating
- pale grey skin
- rapid shallow breathing.

13.8	Mark one answer	DES s16, HC p132

An injured person has been placed in the recovery position. They're unconscious but breathing normally. What else should be done?

- ☐ Press firmly between their shoulders
- ☐ Place their arms by their side
- ☐ Give them a hot sweet drink
- ☐ Check their airway remains open

After a casualty has been placed in the recovery position, make sure their airway remains open and monitor their condition until medical help arrives. Where possible, don't move a casualty unless there's further danger.

13.9	Mark one answer	DES s16, HC p132

An injured motorcyclist is lying unconscious in the road. The traffic has stopped and there's no further danger. What could you do to help?

- ☐ Remove their safety helmet
- ☐ Seek medical assistance
- ☐ Move the person off the road
- ☐ Remove their leather jacket

If someone has been injured, the sooner proper medical attention is given the better. Ask someone to phone for help or do it yourself. An injured person should only be moved if they're in further danger. An injured motorcyclist's helmet shouldn't be removed unless it's essential.

13.10	Mark one answer	DES s11, HC r280

What should you do if you see a large box fall from a lorry onto the motorway?

- ☐ Go to the next emergency telephone and report the hazard
- ☐ Catch up with the lorry and try to get the driver's attention
- ☐ Stop close to the box until the police arrive
- ☐ Pull over to the hard shoulder, then remove the box

Lorry drivers can be unaware of objects falling from their vehicles. If you see something fall onto a motorway, look to see if the driver pulls over. If they don't stop, don't attempt to retrieve the object yourself. Pull onto the hard shoulder near an emergency telephone and report the hazard.

13.11 Mark one answer DES s7

You're going through a long tunnel. What will warn you of congestion or an incident ahead?

- ☐ Hazard warning lines
- ☐ Other drivers flashing their lights
- ☐ Variable message signs
- ☐ Areas with hatch markings

Follow the instructions given by the signs or by tunnel officials. In congested tunnels, a minor incident can soon turn into a major one, with serious or even fatal results.

13.12 Mark one answer DES s16, HC p132

An adult casualty isn't breathing. To maintain circulation, CPR should be given. What's the correct depth to press down on their chest?

- ☐ 1 to 2 centimetres
- ☐ 5 to 6 centimetres
- ☐ 10 to 15 centimetres
- ☐ 15 to 20 centimetres

An adult casualty isn't breathing normally. To maintain circulation, place two hands on the centre of the chest. Then press down hard and fast – around 5–6 centimetres and about twice a second.

13.13 Mark one answer DES s16, HC p131-132

You're the first person to arrive at an incident where people are badly injured. You've switched on your hazard warning lights and checked all engines are stopped. What else should you do?

- ☐ Make sure that an ambulance has been called
- ☐ Stop other cars and ask the drivers for help
- ☐ Try and get people who are injured to drink something
- ☐ Move the people who are injured clear of their vehicles

If you're the first to arrive at a crash scene, the first concerns are the risk of further collision and fire. Ensuring that vehicle engines are switched off will reduce the risk of fire. Use hazard warning lights so that other traffic knows there's a need for caution. Make sure the emergency services are contacted; don't assume it's already been done.

13.14 **Mark one answer** **DES s16, HC p132**

You arrive at the scene of a motorcycle crash. The rider is injured. When should their helmet be removed?

- ☐ Only when it's essential
- ☐ Always straight away
- ☐ Only when the motorcyclist asks
- ☐ Always, unless they're in shock

Don't remove a motorcyclist's helmet unless it's essential. Remember they may be suffering from shock. Don't give them anything to eat or drink, but do reassure them confidently.

13.15 **Mark one answer** **DES s16, HC p132**

You arrive at an incident. There's no danger from fire or further collisions and the emergency services have been called. What's your first priority when attending to an unconscious motorcyclist?

- ☐ Check whether they're breathing normally
- ☐ Check whether they're bleeding
- ☐ Check whether they have any broken bones
- ☐ Check whether they have any bruising

At the scene of an incident, always be aware of danger from further collisions or fire. The first priority when dealing with an unconscious person is to ensure they can breathe. This may involve clearing their airway if you can see an obstruction or if they're having difficulty breathing.

13.16 **Mark one answer** **DES s16, HC p132**

At an incident, someone is unconscious and you want to help. What would be the first thing to check?

- ☐ Whether their vehicle is insured
- ☐ Whether they have any allergies
- ☐ Whether they're comfortable
- ☐ Whether their airway is open

Remember this procedure by saying DR ABC. This stands for Danger, Response, Airway, Breathing, Circulation. Give whatever first aid you can and stay with the injured person until a medical professional takes over.

13.17 — Mark one answer — DES s16, HC p131–132

What could you do to help injured people at an incident?

- ☐ Keep them warm and comfortable
- ☐ Give them something to eat
- ☐ Keep them on the move by walking them around
- ☐ Give them a warm drink

There are a number of things you can do to help, even without expert training. Be aware of further danger from other traffic and fire; make sure the area is safe. People may be in shock. Don't give them anything to eat or drink. Keep them warm and comfortable and reassure them. Don't move injured people unless there's a risk of further danger.

13.18 — Mark one answer — DES s16, HC r132

There's been a collision. How can you help a driver who's suffering from shock?

- ☐ Give them a drink
- ☐ Reassure them confidently
- ☐ Ask who caused the incident
- ☐ Offer them a cigarette

A casualty suffering from shock may have injuries that aren't immediately obvious. Call the emergency services, then stay with the person in shock, offering reassurance until the experts arrive.

13.19 — Mark one answer — DES s16, HC p131–132

You arrive at the scene of a motorcycle crash. No other vehicle is involved. The rider is unconscious and lying in the middle of the road. What's the first thing you should do at the scene?

- ☐ Move the rider out of the road
- ☐ Warn other traffic
- ☐ Clear the road of debris
- ☐ Give the rider reassurance

The motorcyclist is in an extremely vulnerable position, exposed to further danger from traffic. Approaching vehicles need advance warning in order to slow down and safely take avoiding action or stop. Don't put yourself or anyone else at risk. Use the hazard warning lights on your vehicle to alert other road users to the danger.

13.20 Mark one answer DES s16, HC p132

At an incident, how could you help a small child who isn't breathing?

- ☐ Find their parents and explain what's happening
- ☐ Open their airway and begin CPR
- ☐ Put them in the recovery position and slap their back
- ☐ Talk to them confidently until an ambulance arrives

If a young child has stopped breathing, first check that their airway is open and then begin CPR. With a young child, you may only need to use one hand and you shouldn't press down as far as you would with an adult. Continue the procedure until the child is breathing again or until a medical professional takes over.

13.21 Mark one answer DES s16, HC p132

At an incident, a casualty isn't breathing. What should you do while helping them to start breathing again?

- ☐ Put their arms across their chest
- ☐ Shake them firmly
- ☐ Roll them onto their side
- ☐ Open their airway

It's important to ensure that the airway is open before you start CPR. To open the casualty's airway, place your fingers under their chin and lift it forward.

13.22 Mark one answer DES s16, HC p133

At an incident, someone is suffering from severe burns. How could you help them?

- ☐ Apply lotions to the injury
- ☐ Burst any blisters
- ☐ Remove anything sticking to the burns
- ☐ Douse the burns with clean, cool water

Your priority is to cool the burns with clean, cool water. Its coolness will help take the heat out of the burns and relieve the pain. Keep the wound doused for at least 20 minutes. If blisters appear, don't attempt to burst them, as this could lead to infection.

13.23 Mark one answer DES s16, HC p133

You arrive at an incident. A pedestrian is bleeding heavily from a leg wound. The leg isn't broken and there's nothing in the wound. How could you help?

- ☐ Dab the wound to stop the bleeding
- ☐ Keep the casualty's legs flat on the ground
- ☐ Give them a warm drink
- ☐ Apply firm pressure over the wound

You should protect yourself from exposure to blood, and then apply firm pressure over the wound to stem the flow of blood. As soon as practical, fasten a pad to the wound with a bandage or length of cloth. Use the cleanest material available.

13.24 **Mark one answer** **DES s16, HC p131–132**

At an incident, a casualty is unconscious but breathing. When should you move them?

- ☐ When an ambulance is on its way
- ☐ When bystanders tell you to move them
- ☐ When there's a risk of further danger
- ☐ When bystanders offer to help you

Don't move a casualty unless there's further danger; for example, from other traffic or fire. They may have unseen or internal injuries. Moving them unnecessarily could cause further injury. Don't remove a motorcyclist's helmet unless it's essential.

13.25 **Mark one answer** **DES s16, HC p131–132**

At an incident, it's important to look after any casualties. What should you do with them when the area is safe?

- ☐ Move them away from the vehicles
- ☐ Ask them how it happened
- ☐ Give them something to eat
- ☐ Keep them where they are

When the area is safe and there's no danger from other traffic or fire, it's better not to move casualties. Moving them may cause further injury.

13.26 **Mark one answer** **DES s16, HC p117**

Which sign shows that a tanker is carrying dangerous goods?

☐ 

☐ 

☐ 

☐ 

Tankers will display a hazard warning plate on the side and rear of the vehicle. Details of hazard warning symbols are given in The Highway Code. If a tanker is involved in a collision, you may need to report the tanker's hazard labelling to the emergency services.

13.27 **Mark one answer** **HC r286, p122**

Which document may the police ask you to produce after you've been involved in a collision?

- ☐ Your vehicle registration document
- ☐ Your driving licence
- ☐ Your theory test certificate
- ☐ Your vehicle service record

You must stop if you've been involved in a collision that results in injury or damage. The police may ask to see your driving licence and insurance details at the time or later at a police station.

13.28 **Mark one answer** **DES s16, HC p131**

After a collision, someone is unconscious in their vehicle. When should you call the emergency services?

- ☐ Only as a last resort
- ☐ As soon as possible
- ☐ After you've woken them up
- ☐ After checking for broken bones

It's important to make sure that the emergency services arrive as soon as possible. When a person is unconscious, they could have serious injuries that aren't immediately obvious.

13.29 **Mark one answer** **DES s16, HC p131**

A collision has just happened. An injured person is lying in a busy road. What's the first thing you should do?

- ☐ Treat the person for shock
- ☐ Warn other traffic
- ☐ Place them in the recovery position
- ☐ Make sure the injured person is kept warm

The most immediate danger is further collisions and fire. You could warn other traffic by switching on hazard warning lights, displaying an advance warning triangle or sign (but not on a motorway), or by any other means that doesn't put you or others at risk.

13.30 **Mark one answer** **DES s16, HC p132**

At an incident, how could you help a casualty who has stopped breathing?

- ☐ Keep their head tilted forwards as far as possible
- ☐ Follow the DR ABC code
- ☐ Raise their legs to help with circulation
- ☐ Try to give them something to drink

The DR ABC code has been devised by medical experts to give the best outcome until the emergency services arrive and take care of casualties.

13.31 **Mark one answer** **DES s16, HC p132**

You're at the scene of an incident. How could you help someone who's suffering from shock?

- ☐ Reassure them confidently
- ☐ Offer them a cigarette
- ☐ Give them a warm drink
- ☐ Offer them some food

If someone is suffering from shock, try to keep them warm and as comfortable as you can. Don't give them anything to eat or drink but reassure them confidently and try not to leave them alone.

13.32 **Mark one answer** **DES s16, HC p132**

There's been a collision. A motorcyclist is lying injured and unconscious. Why should you only remove their helmet if it's essential?

- ☐ They might not want you to remove it
- ☐ Removing it could make any injuries worse
- ☐ Removing it could let them get cold
- ☐ You could scratch the helmet as you remove it

When someone is injured, any movement that isn't absolutely necessary should be avoided, since it could make the injuries worse. Unless it's essential to remove a motorcyclist's helmet, it's generally safer to leave it in place.

13.33 **Mark one answer** **DES s15, HC r274**

You've broken down on a two-way road. You have a warning triangle. At least how far from your vehicle should you place the warning triangle?

- ☐ 5 metres (16 feet)
- ☐ 25 metres (82 feet)
- ☐ 45 metres (147 feet)
- ☐ 100 metres (328 feet)

Advance warning triangles fold flat and don't take up much room. Use one to warn other road users if your vehicle has broken down or if there has been an incident. Place it at least 45 metres (147 feet) behind your vehicle (or the incident), on the same side of the road or verge. Place it further back if the scene is hidden by, for example, a bend, hill or dip in the road. Don't use warning triangles on motorways.

13.34 **Mark one answer** **DES s6, HC r299, KYTS p27**

Your car breaks down on a level crossing. What's the first thing you should do?

- ☐ Tell drivers behind what's happened
- ☐ Leave your vehicle and get everyone clear
- ☐ Walk down the track and signal the next train
- ☐ Stay in your car until you're told to move

If your vehicle breaks down on a level crossing, your first priority is to get everyone out of the vehicle and clear of the crossing. Then use the railway telephone, if there is one, to tell the signal operator. If you have time before the train arrives, move the vehicle clear of the crossing, but only do this if the alarm signals aren't activated.

13.35 Mark one answer DES s15, HC p129

What should you do if a tyre bursts while you're driving?

- ☐ Pull on the parking brake
- ☐ Brake as quickly as possible
- ☐ Pull up slowly at the side of the road
- ☐ Continue on at a normal speed

A tyre bursting can lead to a loss of control, especially if you're travelling at high speed. Using the correct procedure should help you to stop the vehicle safely.

13.36 Mark one answer DES s15, HC r275, p129

What should you do if your vehicle has a puncture on a motorway?

- ☐ Drive slowly to the next service area to get assistance
- ☐ Pull up on the hard shoulder or in an emergency refuge area. Change the wheel as quickly as possible
- ☐ Pull up on the hard shoulder or in an emergency refuge area and call for assistance
- ☐ Switch on your hazard warning lights. Stop in your lane

Pull up on the hard shoulder or in an emergency refuge area and call for assistance.

Don't attempt to repair your vehicle while it's on the hard shoulder, because of the risk posed by traffic passing at high speeds.

13.37 Mark one answer DES s6, HC r299

Your vehicle has stalled in the middle of a level crossing. What should you do if the warning bells start to ring while you're trying to restart the engine?

- ☐ Get out of the car and clear of the crossing
- ☐ Run down the track to warn the signal operator
- ☐ Carry on trying to restart the engine
- ☐ Push the vehicle clear of the crossing

If the warning bells ring, leave the vehicle and get any passengers well clear of the crossing immediately.

13.38 Mark one answer DES s7, HC r94

What should you do before driving into a tunnel?

- ☐ Switch off your radio
- ☐ Take off your sunglasses
- ☐ Close your sunroof
- ☐ Switch on your windscreen wipers

If you're wearing sunglasses, you should remove them before driving into a tunnel. If you don't, your vision will be restricted, even in tunnels that appear to be well lit.

13.39 Mark one answer — DES s7

Which lights should you use when you're driving in a tunnel?

- ☐ Sidelights
- ☐ Front spotlights
- ☐ Dipped headlights
- ☐ Rear fog lights

Before entering a tunnel, you should switch on your dipped headlights, as this will allow you to see and be seen. In many tunnels, it's a legal requirement.

Don't wear sunglasses while you're driving in a tunnel.

13.40 Mark one answer — DES s16, HC p130

What should you do to reduce the risk of your vehicle catching fire?

- ☐ Keep water levels above maximum
- ☐ Check out any strong smell of fuel
- ☐ Avoid driving with a full tank of fuel
- ☐ Use fuel additives

The fuel in your vehicle can be a dangerous fire hazard. If you smell fuel, check out where it's coming from. Never

- use a naked flame near the vehicle if you can smell fuel
- smoke when refuelling your vehicle.

13.41 Mark one answer — DES s11, HC r279–280

You're driving on the motorway. What should you do if luggage falls from your vehicle?

- ☐ Stop at the next emergency telephone and report the incident
- ☐ Stop on the motorway and switch on hazard warning lights while you pick it up
- ☐ Walk back up the motorway to pick it up
- ☐ Pull up on the hard shoulder and wave traffic down

If any object falls onto the motorway carriageway from your vehicle, pull onto the hard shoulder near an emergency telephone and call for assistance. Don't stop on the carriageway or attempt to retrieve anything.

13.42 Mark one answer — DES s3, HC p128

What should you do if an instrument panel warning light comes on while you're driving?

- ☐ Continue if the engine sounds all right
- ☐ Hope that it's just a temporary electrical fault
- ☐ Deal with the problem when there's more time
- ☐ Check out the problem quickly and safely

Make sure you know what the different warning lights mean. An illuminated warning light could mean that your car is unsafe to drive. If you aren't sure about the problem, get a qualified mechanic to check it.

13.43 **Mark one answer** **DES s16**

What should you do if your vehicle breaks down in a tunnel?

- ☐ Stay in your vehicle and wait for the police
- ☐ Stand in the lane behind your vehicle to warn others
- ☐ Stand in front of your vehicle to warn oncoming drivers
- ☐ Switch on hazard warning lights, then go and call for help

A broken-down vehicle in a tunnel can cause serious congestion and danger to other road users. If your vehicle breaks down, get help without delay. Switch on your hazard warning lights, then go to an emergency telephone to call for help.

13.44 **Mark one answer** **DES s16**

What should you do if your vehicle catches fire while you're driving through a tunnel?

- ☐ Leave it where it is, with the engine running
- ☐ Pull up, then walk to an emergency telephone
- ☐ Park it away from the carriageway
- ☐ Drive it out of the tunnel if it's safe to do so

If it's possible, and you can do so without causing further danger, it may be safer to drive a vehicle that's on fire out of a tunnel. The greatest danger in a tunnel fire is smoke and suffocation.

13.45 **Mark one answer** **DES s6, HC r299, KYTS p27**

What should you do first if your vehicle has broken down on an automatic railway level crossing?

- ☐ Get everyone out of the vehicle and clear of the crossing
- ☐ Telephone your vehicle recovery service to move it
- ☐ Walk along the track to give warning to any approaching trains
- ☐ Try to push the vehicle clear of the crossing as soon as possible

First, get yourself and anyone else well away from the crossing. If there's a railway telephone, use that to get instructions from the signal operator. Then, if there's time, move the vehicle clear of the crossing.

13.46 Mark one answer — DES s16, HC r286

What's the first thing you must do if you have a collision while you're driving your car?

- ☐ Stop only if someone waves at you
- ☐ Call the emergency services
- ☐ Stop at the scene of the incident
- ☐ Call your insurance company

If you're in a collision that causes damage or injury to any other person, vehicle, animal or property, by law you must stop. Give your name, the vehicle owner's name and address, and the vehicle's registration number to anyone who has reasonable grounds for requesting them.

13.47 Mark one answer — DES s16, HC r286

What information should you share if you're involved in a collision that causes damage to another vehicle?

- ☐ Your occupation and reason for your journey
- ☐ Your name, address and vehicle registration number
- ☐ Your national insurance number
- ☐ Your internet service provider

Try to keep calm and don't rush. Make sure that you've shared all the relevant details with the other driver before you leave the scene. If possible, take pictures and note the positions of all the vehicles involved.

13.48 NI EXEMPT Mark one answer — DES s16, HC r286

You lose control of your car and damage a garden wall. What must you do if the property owner isn't available?

- ☐ Report the incident to the police within 24 hours
- ☐ Go back to tell the house owner the next day
- ☐ Report the incident to your insurance company when you get home
- ☐ Find someone in the area to tell them about it immediately

If the property owner isn't available at the time, you must inform the police about the incident. This should be done as soon as possible, and in any case within 24 hours.

Case study practice – 13 Incidents, accidents and emergencies

You witness a road traffic incident involving three vehicles. You stop your vehicle and quickly place a warning triangle on the road. Then you telephone the emergency services.

You check on the people involved. Two people are slightly injured and another is in shock. You stay with them until the emergency services arrive.

While paramedics check the three casualties, you explain the situation to the police and offer your own contact details. The officers then speak to the casualties.

13.1 How else could you have used your own vehicle to warn other traffic?

Mark **one** answer

- ☐ By parking it in the middle of the road
- ☐ By switching on hazard warning lights
- ☐ By leaving headlights on main beam
- ☐ By constantly sounding the horn

HC r283 DES s16

13.2 Apart from casualty information, what details would you need to give to the emergency services?

Mark **one** answer

- ☐ Location of the incident
- ☐ Time and date of your call
- ☐ Driving licence details
- ☐ Insurance information

HC r283 DES s16

13.3 How should you deal with the person suffering from shock?

Mark **one** answer

- ☐ Find out their full name, then leave them alone
- ☐ Offer them a cigarette and get them a hot drink
- ☐ Offer some water, then sit them down somewhere
- ☐ Stay with them and reassure them confidently

HC p132 DES s16

13.4 Why would you provide your own details?

Mark **one** answer

- ☐ You might be required to supply a witness statement
- ☐ You want to get your triangular warning sign back later
- ☐ You need the police to keep you informed of progress
- ☐ You're interested in becoming involved in emergency work

DES s16

13.5 Which documents would police officers normally ask to see from the people involved in the incident?

Mark **one** answer

- ☐ Vehicle registration certificate and MOT certificate
- ☐ Driving licence and insurance certificate
- ☐ Insurance certificate and birth certificate
- ☐ MOT certificate and driving licence

HC r286–287 DES s16

Section fourteen

Vehicle loading

In this section, you'll learn about

- how to carry loads safely in your car
- carrying passengers and animals safely
- towing a caravan or trailer
- the effect of carrying a load on your vehicle's fuel consumption.

Vehicle loading

Loading your vehicle carefully will help to ensure that you can travel safely, whether your load is passengers, animals, a caravan or simply rubbish for the tip.

Keeping your car stable

You need to make sure that your vehicle isn't overloaded. Overloading can seriously affect the vehicle's handling, especially the steering and braking.

HC r98 DES s2

When you're carrying or towing a heavy load, you may need to make adjustments to your vehicle, such as

- increasing the air pressure in the tyres
- adjusting the aim of the headlights.

You should load your vehicle carefully to avoid upsetting the vehicle's stability.

- Distribute the weight evenly.
- Make sure that the load is fastened so that it can't move when you're cornering or braking.
- Ensure loads don't obstruct your view when you're driving, or stick out where they could be dangerous for other road users.

Carrying a load on a roof rack

- will increase wind resistance
- may make your vehicle less stable.

As the load is exposed to the weather, you may need to cover it to protect it from rain. Specially designed roof boxes are available, which cut down the wind resistance and keep loads secure and dry.

DES s2

Tip

You should inflate your tyres to a higher pressure than normal

- when you're carrying a heavy load
- if you're driving for a long distance on a dual carriageway or motorway at the speed limit for these roads.

Your vehicle handbook should tell you the correct pressure for different circumstances.

DES s14

Passengers

All passengers **MUST** wear seat belts if they're fitted. The driver is responsible for ensuring all children (under 14 years) wear a suitable restraint. The type of restraint varies with the age of the child but it **MUST** be suitable for the child's weight and size.

HC r99–101 DES s2

Baby carrier

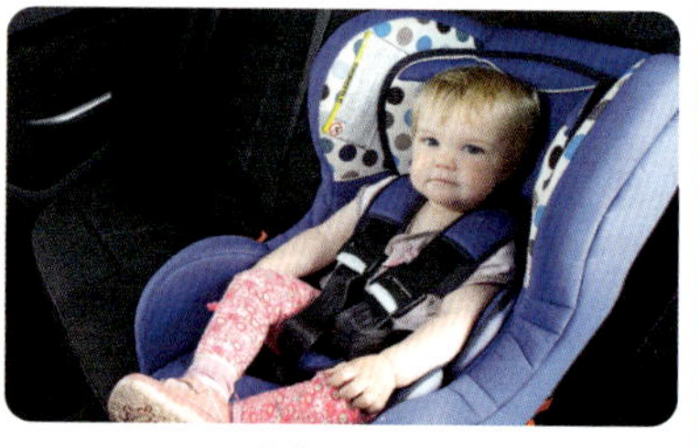

Child seat

See section 3, Safety and your vehicle, for more information.

Watch the various car seat videos on the RoSPA YouTube channel to find out more.

youtube.com/user/RoSPATube

Never allow a passenger to travel in a caravan while it's being towed.

DES s19

Animals

Animals should be restrained to ensure that they don't interfere with the driver or block the driver's view.

Dogs may travel in a special cage or behind a dog guard, and may be strapped in using a harness for added security. Other animals should travel in cages or in pet carriers that can be secured with a seat belt.

Towing

If you're planning to tow a caravan, it'll help the handling of your vehicle if you have a stabiliser fitted to your tow bar. This will be particularly helpful when it's windy.

If your caravan or trailer has a braking system, it must be fitted with a device to stop the trailer automatically in the event of separation of the main coupling. This is normally achieved by a breakaway cable attached to the parking-brake mechanism; it applies the brakes if the trailer becomes detached from the towing vehicle.

DES s19

If a trailer or caravan starts to swerve or snake as you're driving along

- ease off the accelerator
- reduce your speed gradually to regain control.

Tip

The maximum weight that can be put on your vehicle's tow bar (called the 'noseweight') can normally be found in your vehicle handbook.

DES s19

Find out more about towing a caravan or trailer at this website.

www.gov.uk

There's a lower national speed limit for all vehicles towing trailers.

On a dual carriageway or motorway

Maximum speed 60 mph (96 km/h)

A vehicle towing a trailer on a motorway that has more than two lanes **MUST NOT** be driven in the right-hand lane.

On a single carriageway

Maximum speed 50 mph (80 km/h)

HC r98, p40 DES s19

Saving fuel

Carrying a load will increase your vehicle's fuel consumption because of the extra weight. Carrying a load on a roof rack will increase the fuel consumption even more because of the wind resistance and drag created by the load.

When you've finished using a roof rack or box, remove it from the vehicle.
Even when it's empty, it will increase the fuel consumption because of the drag it creates.

Meeting the standards

You must be able to

make sure that passengers are seated legally, correctly and securely

make sure that loads are secure and distributed correctly, depending on the vehicle

allow for the effect that any extra load may have on how the vehicle handles.

You must know and understand

what the law says about the fitting and use of seat belts

what the vehicle handbook says about safely loading the vehicle

how to adjust the vehicle to allow for extra weight. For example, you may need to put more air in the tyres

how to change your driving to allow for extra weight. You may also need to think about how weight in different places can affect your driving; for example

- in the boot
- in a roof box
- on the back seat
- in a trailer.

Notes

You can use this page to make your own notes or diagrams about the key points you need to remember.

Think about

- What sorts of load might you carry in your vehicle that could affect its stability?
- When might you need to increase the tyre pressures?
- Are you likely to carry animals in your car? If so, what sort of carrier or restraint do you need?
- If you wanted to tow a trailer or caravan, what preparation would you need to do on your car?

Your notes

Things to discuss and practise with your instructor

These are just a few examples of what you could discuss and practise with your instructor. Read more about vehicle loading to come up with your own ideas.

Discuss with your instructor

- the effects that carrying a heavy load, such as a roof rack, might have on your car and your driving
- the motorway regulations for vehicles towing trailers
- the safety checks you should carry out before starting a journey towing a caravan.

Practise with your instructor

- driving with passengers in the car. Ask your instructor whether they would mind if you took along some friends for part of the lesson, so you can get used to
  - how the car handles differently with more weight in the back
  - how the presence of passengers can distract you.

14.1 Mark one answer | **DES s19, HC r124, 265**

What restrictions apply if you're towing a trailer on a three-lane motorway?

- ☐ You mustn't exceed 50 mph
- ☐ You mustn't overtake
- ☐ You must have a stabiliser fitted
- ☐ You mustn't use the right-hand lane

The motorway regulations for towing a trailer state that you mustn't

- use the right-hand lane of a three-lane motorway unless directed to do so (for example, at roadworks or due to a lane closure)
- exceed 60 mph.

14.2 Mark one answer | **DES s19, HC r98**

What should you do if you're towing a trailer and it starts to swing from side to side?

- ☐ Ease off the accelerator to reduce your speed
- ☐ Let go of the steering wheel and let it correct itself
- ☐ Brake hard and hold the pedal down
- ☐ Accelerate until it stabilises

Strong winds or buffeting from large vehicles can cause a trailer or caravan to swing from side to side ('snake'). If this happens, ease off the accelerator. Don't brake harshly, steer sharply or increase your speed.

14.3 Mark one answer | **DES s14**

When would you increase the pressure in your tyres so that it's above the normal value?

- ☐ When the roads are slippery
- ☐ When the vehicle is fitted with anti-lock brakes
- ☐ When the tyre tread is worn below 2 mm
- ☐ When carrying a heavy load

Check the vehicle handbook. This should give you guidance on the correct tyre pressures for your vehicle and when you may need to adjust them. If you're carrying a heavy load, you may need to adjust the headlights as well. Most cars have a switch on the dashboard to do this.

14.4 Mark one answer | **DES s2, HC r98**

How will a heavy load on your roof rack affect your vehicle's handling?

- ☐ It will improve the road holding
- ☐ It will reduce the stopping distance
- ☐ It will make the steering lighter
- ☐ It will reduce stability

A heavy load on your roof rack will reduce the stability of the vehicle because it moves the centre of gravity away from that designed by the manufacturer. Be aware of this when you drive round bends and corners. If you change direction at speed, your vehicle and/or load could become unstable and you could lose control.

14.5 Mark one answer — DES s2, HC r98

What would be affected if you carry a very heavy load on your vehicle?

- ☐ The vehicle's gearbox
- ☐ The vehicle's ventilation
- ☐ The vehicle's handling
- ☐ The vehicle's battery

Any load will have an effect on the handling of your vehicle, and this becomes worse as you increase the load. You need to be aware of this when carrying passengers or heavy loads, fitting a roof rack or towing a trailer.

14.6 Mark one answer — DES s2, HC r98

Who's responsible for making sure that a vehicle isn't overloaded?

- ☐ The driver of the vehicle
- ☐ The owner of the items being carried
- ☐ The person who loaded the vehicle
- ☐ The licensing authority

Carrying heavy loads will affect control and the vehicle's handling characteristics. If the vehicle you're driving is overloaded, you'll be held responsible.

14.7 Mark one answer — DES s19

You're planning to tow a caravan. What will help the handling of the combination?

- ☐ A jockey wheel fitted to the tow bar
- ☐ Power steering fitted to the towing vehicle
- ☐ Anti-lock brakes fitted to the towing vehicle
- ☐ A stabiliser fitted to the tow bar

Towing a caravan or trailer affects the way the towing vehicle handles. A stabiliser device isn't designed to overcome instability caused by incorrect loading but it can give added security in side winds and from buffeting caused by large vehicles.

14.8 Mark one answer — DES s19

Are passengers allowed to ride in a caravan that's being towed?

- ☐ Yes, if they're over 14
- ☐ No, not at any time
- ☐ Only if all the seats in the towing vehicle are full
- ☐ Only if a stabiliser is fitted

Riding in a towed caravan is highly dangerous. The safety of the entire unit is dependent on the stability of the trailer. Moving passengers would make the caravan unstable and could cause loss of control.

14.9 Mark one answer DES s19

What safety device must be fitted to a trailer braking system?

- ☐ Stabiliser
- ☐ Jockey wheel
- ☐ Corner steadies
- ☐ Breakaway cable

In the event that the trailer becomes detached from the towing vehicle, the breakaway cable activates the trailer brakes before snapping. This allows the towing vehicle to get free of the trailer and out of danger.

14.10 Mark one answer DES s19

You wish to tow a trailer. Where would you find the maximum noseweight for your vehicle's tow hitch?

- ☐ In the vehicle handbook
- ☐ In The Highway Code
- ☐ In your vehicle registration certificate
- ☐ In your licence documents

You must know how to load your trailer or caravan so that the hitch exerts an appropriate downward force on the tow ball. Information about the maximum permitted noseweight can be found in your vehicle handbook or obtained from your vehicle manufacturer's agent.

14.11 **Mark one answer** **DES s2, HC r98**

How should a load be carried on your roof rack?

- ☐ Securely fastened with suitable restraints
- ☐ Loaded towards the rear of the vehicle
- ☐ Visible in your exterior mirror
- ☐ Covered with plastic sheeting

Any load must be securely fastened to the vehicle. The safest way to carry items on the roof is in a specially designed roof box. This will help to keep your luggage secure and dry, and it also has less wind resistance than loads carried exposed on a roof rack.

14.12 **Mark one answer** **DES s2, HC r99**

You're carrying a child under three years old in your car. Which restraint is suitable for a child of this age?

- ☐ A child seat
- ☐ An adult holding a child
- ☐ An adult seat belt
- ☐ An adult lap belt

It's your responsibility to ensure that all children in your car are secure. Suitable restraints include a child seat, baby seat, booster seat or booster cushion. It's essential that any restraint used is suitable for the child's size and weight, and fitted according to the manufacturer's instructions.

Case study practice – 14 Vehicle loading

You and your family are going on holiday. You'll be driving.

You're loading a newly purchased roof rack on your estate car.

Your partner is helping two young children with their seat belts in the rear seats.

The family dog, Shadow, will be travelling in the rear compartment of the car.

Once ready to go, you call at the service station to buy fuel and make final checks.

14.1 How could the full roof rack affect the vehicle's handling?

Mark **one** answer

- ☐ Increase the road holding
- ☐ Reduce the stability
- ☐ Protect the paintwork
- ☐ Improve the journey time

HC r98 DES s2

14.2 How should Shadow be secured for safety?

Mark **one** answer

- ☐ In a child's seat belt
- ☐ In a cardboard box
- ☐ In a special harness
- ☐ In a plastic dog bed

HC r57 DES s2

14.3 Who's responsible for making sure that the children wear the appropriate seat belt or child restraint?

Mark **one** answer

- ☐ The police
- ☐ The parent
- ☐ The driver
- ☐ The children

HC r99–102 DES s2

14.4 Which one of these actions could help reduce the estate car's fuel consumption?

Mark **one** answer

- ☐ Removing the roof rack when it isn't being used
- ☐ Braking and accelerating as quickly as possible
- ☐ Fitting extra spoilers and larger wing mirrors
- ☐ Increasing tyre pressures and opening windows

DES s17

14.5 What should you check at the filling station?

Mark **one** answer

- ☐ For any spilt fuel around the vehicle on the station forecourt
- ☐ That none of your luggage has been left behind
- ☐ That the weather forecast for the journey is good
- ☐ That there's appropriate pressure in all four tyres plus the spare

HC p128–130 DES s5

Section fifteen

Case study practice

Case study practice

Some of the questions within the test will be presented as a case study.

You'll be presented with a scenario – the case study – which will appear on the left-hand side of the screen. The scenario will be presented in a text format and may be accompanied by a supporting picture or diagram. As you move within the case study, the questions will appear, one by one, on the right-hand side of the screen, and you'll be asked to respond. You can re-read the scenario throughout the case study should you wish to do so.

A case study example is shown below and on the following pages.

In this section, you'll also find five mixed-topic, practice case studies similar to the ones in the actual test. Use these to help you prepare for the real thing.

Answers to all the case studies in this book are in section 16, Answers.

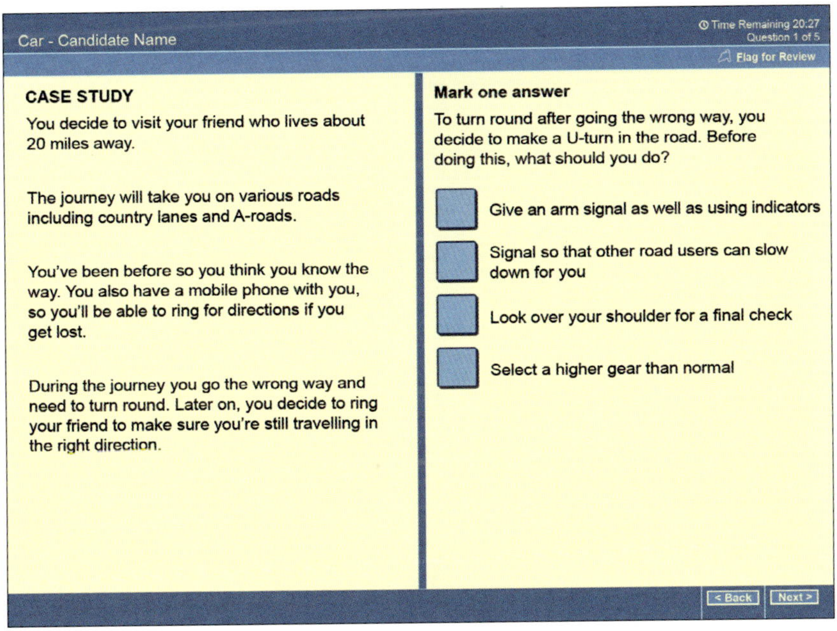

We'll soon be replacing the case study questions in the car theory test. Instead, after the multiple choice questions, you'll watch a computer-generated image (CGI) video clip. Then you'll have to answer three more multiple choice questions based on that clip. To see a sample clip and find out more, visit: **safedrivingforlife.info/driving-theory-test-booking-and-taking-your-test**

Car - Candidate Name

Time Remaining 18:38
Question 2 of 5
Flag for Review

CASE STUDY

You decide to visit your friend who lives about 20 miles away.

The journey will take you on various roads including country lanes and A-roads.

You've been before so you think you know the way. You also have a mobile phone with you, so you'll be able to ring for directions if you get lost.

During the journey you go the wrong way and need to turn round. Later on, you decide to ring your friend to make sure you're still travelling in the right direction.

Mark one answer

What should you do as you approach this bridge on your journey?

- Move to the right
- Slow down
- Change gear
- Keep to 30 mph

< Back | Next >

Car - Candidate Name

Time Remaining 15:52
Question 3 of 5
Flag for Review

CASE STUDY

You decide to visit your friend who lives about 20 miles away.

The journey will take you on various roads including country lanes and A-roads.

You've been before so you think you know the way. You also have a mobile phone with you, so you'll be able to ring for directions if you get lost.

During the journey you go the wrong way and need to turn round. Later on, you decide to ring your friend to make sure you're still travelling in the right direction.

Mark one answer

During your journey, you ring your friend. What's the safest way for you to use your mobile phone?

- Use hands-free equipment
- Make the call when you've stopped in a suitable place
- Travel slowly on a quiet road
- Direct your call through the operator

< Back | Next >

Car - Candidate Name

Time Remaining 14:09
Question 4 of 5
Flag for Review

CASE STUDY

You decide to visit your friend who lives about 20 miles away.

The journey will take you on various roads including country lanes and A-roads.

You've been before so you think you know the way. You also have a mobile phone with you, so you'll be able to ring for directions if you get lost.

During the journey you go the wrong way and need to turn round. Later on, you decide to ring your friend to make sure you're still travelling in the right direction.

Mark one answer

You're travelling along a country road. A horse and rider are approaching. What should you do?

- Increase your speed
- Sound your horn
- Flash your headlights
- Go slowly past

< Back | Next >

Car - Candidate Name

Time Remaining 13:40
Question 5 of 5
Flag for Review

CASE STUDY

You decide to visit your friend who lives about 20 miles away.

The journey will take you on various roads including country lanes and A-roads.

You've been before so you think you know the way. You also have a mobile phone with you, so you'll be able to ring for directions if you get lost.

During the journey you go the wrong way and need to turn round. Later on, you decide to ring your friend to make sure you're still travelling in the right direction.

Mark one answer

Near the end of your journey, you come to a pedestrian crossing, with pedestrians who are hesitating to cross. Why should you never wave people across at pedestrian crossings?

- There may be another vehicle coming
- They may not be looking
- It is safer for you to carry on
- They may not be ready to cross

< Back | Next >

Case study practice – A

You plan to visit a friend who lives in a town a full day's drive away. You'll be away for a week.

Two weeks before the journey, you realise that your vehicle tax will expire while you're away.

At the beginning of your journey, you reach a roundabout. Another car cuts in front of you, causing you to do an emergency stop.

Later, you join the motorway, where a red X is flashing above the outside lane.

While travelling along the motorway, you start to feel tired and stop at a service station.

It's just after 11 pm when you park outside your friend's house.

1 What should you do two weeks before you leave?

Mark **one** answer

- ☐ Tell your insurance company when the vehicle tax expires
- ☐ Notify DVLA that the vehicle is off the road
- ☐ Make a note to renew the vehicle tax on your return
- ☐ Renew your vehicle tax immediately

HC p122 DES s2

2 What should you do at the roundabout?

Mark **one** answer

- ☐ Flash your lights and change lanes
- ☐ Sound your horn at the other car
- ☐ Stay calm and continue when it's safe
- ☐ Continue on your journey immediately

HC r147 DES s1

3 What must you do on the motorway?

Mark **one** answer

- ☐ Drive down the outside lane
- ☐ Overtake in the outside lane
- ☐ Pull over in the outside lane
- ☐ Stay out of the outside lane

HC r258 DES s11

4 What should you do at the service station?

Mark **one** answer

- ☐ Drink two cups of coffee and rest for 15 minutes
- ☐ Drink a bottle of mineral water and leave immediately
- ☐ Drink two cups of coffee and leave immediately
- ☐ Drink a bottle of mineral water and rest for 5 minutes

HC r91 DES s1, 11

5 Why must you avoid using your horn when parked outside your friend's house?

Mark **one** answer

- ☐ Because they have children
- ☐ Because it's before midnight
- ☐ Because it's after 10.30 pm
- ☐ Because you're stationary

HC r112 DES s13

Case study practice – B

You're taking your 14-year-old nephew on a day trip.

You drive through town and reach a zebra crossing. A man carrying a white cane with a red band is waiting to cross.

You join a dual carriageway and see a sign which has a white circle with a diagonal black stripe.

As you drive across a roundabout, you're involved in a collision with a cyclist. You and your nephew aren't injured. The cyclist is conscious but is lying at the side of the road and their leg is bleeding heavily.

1 Who's responsible for your nephew wearing a seat belt?

Mark **one** answer

- ☐ He is
- ☐ You are
- ☐ His parents
- ☐ The police

HC r99 DES s2

2 What do the markings on the man's cane mean?

Mark **one** answer

- ☐ He's blind
- ☐ He's deaf and blind
- ☐ He's deaf
- ☐ He has mobility problems

HC r207 DES s10

3 What does the sign mean?

Mark **one** answer

- ☐ Pedestrian zone ends
- ☐ End of goods-vehicle restriction
- ☐ End of minimum speed requirement
- ☐ National speed limit applies

HC p106 DES s6 KYTS p20

4 What should you do at the roundabout?

Mark **one** answer

- ☐ Take your nephew to the hospital
- ☐ Drive to the nearest police station
- ☐ Put on your hazard warning lights
- ☐ Flag down passing drivers for help

HC r283 DES s16

5 What should you do about the cyclist?

Mark **one** answer

- ☐ Leave them for the emergency services
- ☐ Restrict the blood flow from their leg
- ☐ Help them back onto their bike
- ☐ Give them a drink of water

HC r283, p133 DES s16

Case study practice – C

You're driving into the town centre. The weather is cold and wet.

There are several cars parked down either side of the main road.

It's market day and there are many pedestrians around.

Ahead of you, a large van is being unloaded on your side of the road and there's oncoming traffic.

Later, you reach a junction with some traffic lights that aren't working. There are several other vehicles in the area.

On your way home, your steering begins to feel a little heavy. You stop at a nearby filling station.

1 What's the recommended time gap that should be left between vehicles in these weather conditions?

Mark **one** answer

- ☐ Two seconds
- ☐ Four seconds
- ☐ Six seconds
- ☐ Eight seconds

HC r126, p41 DES s7

2 What should you watch out for in this area?

Mark **one** answer

- ☐ Sale posters going up in any of the shop windows
- ☐ The next available free parking space on the road
- ☐ Pedestrians stepping out from between vehicles
- ☐ Traffic wardens who may be working in the area

HC r152 DES s7

3 How should you react to the van?

Mark **one** answer

- ☐ Stop and wait until the way ahead is clear
- ☐ Move out and pass as quickly as possible
- ☐ Find another route to your destination
- ☐ Wait until the van is unloaded and moved

HC r163 DES s7

4 Who has right of way at the lights?

Mark **one** answer

- ☐ No-one
- ☐ Oncoming drivers
- ☐ Drivers in large vehicles
- ☐ Drivers in fast vehicles

HC r146, 176 DES s6, 8

5 What might cause the steering to feel this way?

Mark **one** answer

- ☐ Being very low on fuel
- ☐ Engine oil level is low
- ☐ Driving at a slow speed
- ☐ Tyre pressure is too low

HC p129 DES s7

Case study practice – D

You're driving to work on a single carriageway road.

It's early morning and there's patchy fog, which is very thick in places.

A sports car is travelling too closely behind you.

Later, you reach a roundabout where you need to turn right. The approach road is still a single carriageway. There's only one line of traffic.

When you get to work, you find that the car park is full. You have to park on the main road, facing downhill.

You need to leave some camera equipment in your vehicle until later.

1 What lights would you use under these weather conditions?

Mark **one** answer

- ☐ Headlights with fog lights as necessary
- ☐ Full-beam headlights at all times on the journey
- ☐ No lights at all during the whole journey
- ☐ Sidelights and hazard warning lights

HC r226, 234–236 DES s12

2 What should you do about the sports car?

Mark **one** answer

- ☐ Brake sharply and allow the other vehicle past
- ☐ Pull over to the side of the road and then stop
- ☐ Increase speed and pull away from the vehicle
- ☐ Slowly drop back to allow more room in front

HC r235 DES s10, 12

3 How should you position your vehicle when approaching the roundabout?

Mark **one** answer

- ☐ Move closer to the centre line but give no signal at all
- ☐ Stay close to the left-hand kerb and signal to go right
- ☐ Move nearer to the centre line and signal to go right
- ☐ Stay in the middle of the lane but don't signal

HC r184–190 DES s8

4 How should you position your front wheels when parking here?

Mark **one** answer

- ☐ Turned in towards the kerb
- ☐ Aligned alongside the kerb
- ☐ Turned away from the kerb
- ☐ Mounted up onto the kerb

HC r252 DES s9

5 What should you do with the equipment?

Mark **one** answer

- ☐ Put it on the back seat in a bag
- ☐ Lock it away securely out of sight
- ☐ Cover it with a blanket or jacket
- ☐ Put it in the passenger footwell

HC p131 DES s20

Case study practice – E

You're taking a friend and their two children to the coast. The children are aged two and six.

With fuel and tyre pressures done, you make other final checks.

After helping the children into the vehicle, you set off.

It rained heavily overnight and the roads are still wet in places. However, the sun is now shining and the day is very warm and bright.

Once on the motorway, the traffic is very heavy. A large goods vehicle is travelling in front of you.

Further on, you see an overhead gantry with the number 40 in a red circle showing above all lanes, including the hard shoulder.

1 What else should you check before your journey?

Mark **one** answer

- ☐ Oil and water levels
- ☐ The ashtray is empty
- ☐ The central locking is working
- ☐ Interior temperature

DES s14

2 How must you seat the younger child?

Mark **one** answer

- ☐ On a cushion with a lap belt
- ☐ In a normal adult seat belt
- ☐ On a booster cushion only
- ☐ In a suitable child restraint

HC r99–102, p32 DES s2

3 What hazards would you expect to encounter in these weather conditions?

Mark **one** answer

- ☐ Puddles making the tyres muddy
- ☐ Glare from the sun on wet roads
- ☐ Road surface drying out too fast
- ☐ Mud on the road

HC r93 DES s12

4 What position should you take behind the goods vehicle?

Mark **one** answer

- ☐ Well back, so you can see ahead and be seen
- ☐ Close enough to stay out of the sun's glare
- ☐ Just far enough back to stay in its slipstream
- ☐ Close enough to prevent another vehicle pulling into the gap

HC r221–222 DES s7, 11

5 What does the sign on the overhead gantry mean?

Mark **one** answer

- ☐ There's an obstruction on the hard shoulder 40 yards ahead
- ☐ Only 40 vehicles can use the hard shoulder until further notice
- ☐ This lane can be used as a running lane at a maximum speed of 40 mph
- ☐ Traffic must merge in turn back onto the motorway in 40 minutes

HC r269 DES s11, 18

Section sixteen

Answers

1. Alertness

1.1	☐ Look over your shoulder for a final check
1.2	☐ Slow down
1.3	☐ Approaching a dip in the road
1.4	☐ Overtaking traffic should move back to the left
1.5	☐ Leave it until you have stopped in a safe place
1.6	☐ To make you aware of your speed
1.7	☐ Be ready to stop
1.8	☐ Use the mirrors
1.9	☐ You'll give the driver a chance to see you in their mirrors
1.10	☐ To assess how your actions will affect the traffic behind
1.11	☐ Stop and then move forward slowly and carefully for a clear view
1.12	☐ Your view could be obstructed
1.13	☐ Leave the motorway and stop in a safe place
1.14	☐ So others can see you more easily
1.15	☐ Using a mobile phone
1.16	☐ When you've parked safely
1.17	☐ Keep both hands on the steering wheel
1.18	☐ Look around before moving off
1.19	☐ Leave them plenty of room as you pass
1.20	☐ When you're approaching bends and junctions
1.21	☐ Ask someone to guide you
1.22	☐ An area not visible to the driver
1.23	☐ It will divert your attention
1.24	☐ Check that the central reservation is wide enough for your vehicle
1.25	☐ Motorcyclists
1.26	☐ Set it before starting your journey

1. Case study practice

1.1 Information about the medicine causing drowsiness

1.2 To maximise your visibility to others

1.3 You become drowsy

1.4 Stop in a service area, drink a caffeinated drink and then rest

1.5 Open the window

2. Attitude

2.1	☐ Give way to pedestrians already on the crossing
2.2	☐ Another vehicle may be coming
2.3	☐ Your view of the road ahead will be restricted
2.4	☐ Your view ahead will be reduced
2.5	☐ Four seconds
2.6	☐ Slow down
2.7	☐ Bomb disposal
2.8	☐ Pull over as soon as it's safe to do so
2.9	☐ Doctor's car
2.10	☐ Tram drivers
2.11	☐ Cycles
2.12	☐ To alert others to your presence
2.13	☐ In the right-hand lane
2.14	☐ To help other road users know what you intend to do
2.15	☐ Toucan
2.16	☐ Allow the vehicle to overtake
2.17	☐ When letting them know that you're there
2.18	☐ Slow down and look both ways
2.19	☐ When checking your gap from the vehicle in front
2.20	☐ Steady amber
2.21	☐ Slow down, gradually increasing the gap between you and the vehicle in front
2.22	☐ Dipped headlights
2.23	☐ Slow down and let the vehicle turn
2.24	☐ Drop back to leave the correct separation distance
2.25	☐ Use the parking brake and release the footbrake
2.26	☐ Keep a steady course and allow the driver behind to overtake
2.27	☐ The lane is in operation 24 hours a day
2.28	☐ Stop and switch off your engine
2.29	☐ Go past slowly and carefully
2.30	☐ Slow down and prepare to stop
2.31	☐ Slow down and be ready to stop
2.32	☐ When the pedestrians have cleared the crossing
2.33	☐ 
2.34	☐ When it's dry

2.35	☐ Use dipped headlights
2.36	☐ Pull in when you can, to let the vehicles behind overtake
2.37	☐ It can make the roads slippery for other road users
2.38	☐ Check that your filler cap is securely fastened
2.39	☐ Competitive

2. Case study practice

2.1 Slow down and, if necessary, stop

2.2 Remain calm, slow down and increase the gap

2.3 In the left-hand lane while signalling left

2.4 The vehicle needs more room to turn

2.5 Stop and wait for the pedestrians to cross

3. Safety and your vehicle

3.1	☐ The vehicle's stopping distance would increase
3.2	☐ Between 11.30 pm and 7.00 am in a built-up area
3.3	☐ It's powered by electricity
3.4	☐ To help the traffic flow
3.5	☐ To reduce traffic speed
3.6	☐ To reduce harmful exhaust gases
3.7	☐ When tyres are cold
3.8	☐ When its tyres are under-inflated
3.9	☐ Take it to a local-authority disposal site
3.10	☐ Harsh braking and accelerating
3.11	☐ Distilled water
3.12	☐ When the speed limit exceeds 30 mph
3.13	☐ Keep engine revs low
3.14	☐ A faulty braking system
3.15	☐ Just above the cell plates
3.16	☐ You'll have an easier journey
3.17	☐ Your journey will have fewer delays
3.18	☐ Your original route may be blocked
3.19	☐ Allow plenty of time for the trip
3.20	☐ Increased fuel consumption
3.21	☐ Brake-fluid level
3.22	☐ Have the brakes checked immediately
3.23	☐ A fault in the braking system
3.24	☐ To maintain control of the pedals

3.25	☐ A properly adjusted head restraint
3.26	☐ The shock absorbers are worn
3.27	☐ Fuel consumption will increase
3.28	☐ If they have any large, deep cuts in the side wall
3.29	☐ 1.6 mm
3.30	☐ You, the driver
3.31	☐ By accelerating gently
3.32	☐ By having your vehicle serviced regularly
3.33	☐ Walk or cycle on short journeys
3.34	☐ Under-inflated tyres
3.35	☐ The seat belts
3.36	☐ About 30%
3.37	☐ Have the brakes checked as soon as possible
3.38	☐ The steering will vibrate
3.39	☐ The tyres
3.40	☐ Lock them out of sight
3.41	☐ Etching the registration number on the windows
3.42	☐ The vehicle registration document
3.43	☐ Lock it and remove the key
3.44	☐ Driving more slowly
3.45	☐ Take it to a local-authority site
3.46	☐ To help protect the environment against pollution
3.47	☐ Anticipate well ahead
3.48	☐ Your vehicle will remain reliable
3.49	☐ Maintain a reduced speed throughout
3.50	☐ Before a long journey
3.51	☐ No, not under any circumstances
3.52	☐ Lock it and remove the key
3.53	☐ It helps deter thieves
3.54	☐ In front of a property entrance
3.55	☐ To help you avoid neck injury
3.56	☐ Avoid making a lot of short journeys
3.57	☐ Walk or cycle
3.58	☐ Take all valuables with you
3.59	☐ Install a security-coded radio
3.60	☐ Leave it in a well-lit area
3.61	☐ Registering with a Vehicle Watch scheme
3.62	☐ On the exhaust system
3.63	☐ Reduction in fuel consumption by about 15%
3.64	☐ Missing out some gears

3.65	☐ By reducing exhaust emissions
3.66	☐ Improved road safety
3.67	☐ 1.6 mm
3.68	☐ When you're accelerating
3.69	☐ When they're exempt for medical reasons
3.70	☐ You, the driver
3.71	☐ The oil seals will leak
3.72	☐ Using an adult seat belt
3.73	☐ They must use a suitable child restraint
3.74	☐ Switch off the engine
3.75	☐ Deactivate the airbag
3.76	☐ Never if you're away from the vehicle
3.77	☐ The ESC system has activated

3. Case study practice

3.1 Reduced travel time

3.2 No stopping at any time

3.3 Proceed with care, as with an unmarked junction

3.4 Tyres that are under-inflated

3.5 Lock it away securely out of sight

4. Safety margins

4.1	☐ Ten times
4.2	☐ Passing pedal cyclists
4.3	☐ To improve your view of the road
4.4	☐ Go slowly while gently applying the brakes
4.5	☐ The tyre grip
4.6	☐ On an open stretch of road
4.7	☐ Drop back to regain a safe distance
4.8	☐ Pass widely
4.9	☐ Increase your distance from the vehicle in front
4.10	☐ Keep a safe distance from the vehicle in front
4.11	☐ Choose an appropriate lane in good time
4.12	☐ Drive at a slow speed in the highest gear possible
4.13	☐ The driver
4.14	☐ Slow down gently
4.15	☐ The windows
4.16	☐ Using a higher gear than normal
4.17	☐ Brake gently in plenty of time
4.18	☐ Improved grip on the road

4.19	☐ Select a low gear and use the brakes carefully
4.20	☐ Turn the steering wheel towards the kerb
4.21	☐ Check your mirror and slow down
4.22	☐ Loose
4.23	☐ Rapidly and firmly
4.24	☐ Test your brakes
4.25	☐ There's less tyre noise
4.26	☐ The steering will feel very light
4.27	☐ In the rain
4.28	☐ A two-second time gap
4.29	☐ By changing to a lower gear
4.30	☐ Brake promptly and firmly until you've stopped
4.31	☐ Dipped headlights
4.32	☐ Reduction in control
4.33	☐ Allow more time

4. Case study practice

4.1	Allow more time
4.2	Gently and slowly
4.3	The road could be icy
4.4	Steer gently to the right
4.5	Amber

5. Hazard awareness

5.1	☐ On a large goods vehicle
5.2	☐ The cyclist crossing the road
5.3	☐ The parked car (arrowed A)
5.4	☐ Slow down and get ready to stop
5.5	☐ Doors opening on parked cars
5.6	☐ The road will bend sharply to the left
5.7	☐ Slow down and allow the cyclist to turn
5.8	☐ The view is restricted
5.9	☐ Buses
5.10	☐ Lorry
5.11	☐ Stop behind the line, then edge forward to see clearly
5.12	☐ Ignore the error and stay calm
5.13	☐ They'll take longer to react to hazards
5.14	☐ Yes, regular stops help concentration
5.15	☐ Stop before the barrier
5.16	☐ Be prepared to stop for any traffic
5.17	☐ Wait for the pedestrian in the road to cross

5.18	☐ Only consider overtaking when you're past the junction
5.19	☐ Be prepared to give way to large vehicles in the middle of the road
5.20	☐ They give a wider field of vision
5.21	☐ Approach with care and overtake on the left of the lorry
5.22	☐ Stay behind and don't overtake
5.23	☐ The bus may move out into the road
5.24	☐ A school bus
5.25	☐ Children running out between vehicles
5.26	☐ The cyclist may swerve into the road
5.27	☐ Stop and take a break
5.28	☐ At a reduced speed
5.29	☐ Because of the level crossing
5.30	☐ To help you select the correct lane in good time
5.31	☐ Traffic in both directions can use the middle lane to overtake
5.32	☐ A tractor
5.33	☐ Stop
5.34	☐ People may cross the road in front of it
5.35	☐ Approaching a junction
5.36	☐ Your ability to judge speed will be reduced
5.37	☐ Edge of the carriageway
5.38	☐ A steady amber light
5.39	☐ Allow the cyclist time and room
5.40	☐ Check for bicycles on your left
5.41	☐ A staggered junction is ahead
5.42	☐ Traffic will move into the left-hand lane
5.43	☐ The two left lanes are open
5.44	☐ Don't drink any alcohol at all
5.45	☐ Insurance premiums
5.46	☐ Go home by public transport
5.47	☐ Avoid driving and check with your doctor
5.48	☐ Get someone else to drive
5.49	☐ Stop driving until you're fit to drive again
5.50	☐ Stop and rest as soon as possible
5.51	☐ Leave the motorway at the next exit and rest
5.52	☐ Wait until you're fit and well before driving
5.53	☐ Take regular refreshment breaks

5.54	☐ Check the label to see if the medicine will affect your driving
5.55	☐ Continue and find another route
5.56	☐ Looking at road maps
5.57	☐ Sound your horn and be prepared to stop
5.58	☐ Calm down
5.59	☐ There are roadworks ahead of you
5.60	☐ Keep a safe gap
5.61	☐ Find a way of getting home without driving
5.62	☐ It increases confidence
5.63	☐ Some types of medicine can affect your ability to drive safely
5.64	☐ Whenever you're driving
5.65	☐ Tinted
5.66	☐ Drugs
5.67	☐ Tell the driver licensing authority
5.68	☐ When your vehicle has broken down and is causing an obstruction
5.69	☐ Approach slowly and edge out until you can see more clearly
5.70	☐ To accelerate quickly
5.71	☐ Be aware of spray reducing your vision
5.72	☐ Pedestrians walking towards you
5.73	☐ Slow down, keeping a safe separation distance
5.74	☐ When driving on a motorway to warn traffic behind of a hazard ahead
5.75	☐ Reflections of traffic in windows
5.76	☐ Inform the licensing authority
5.77	☐ To allow vehicles to enter and emerge
5.78	☐ Open a window and stop as soon as it's safe and legal

5. Case study practice

5.1 By showing reflections of any unseen vehicles approaching

5.2 Pedestrians or cyclists could be hidden from view

5.3 Stop and wait until the way is clear ahead

5.4 Stop and wait patiently until signalled to go on

5.5 Not at any time

6. Vulnerable road users

6.1	☐ 
6.2	☐ Give way to them
6.3	☐ Pedestrians
6.4	☐ They may be overtaking on your right
6.5	☐ Cyclists can use it
6.6	☐ By displaying a 'stop' sign
6.7	☐ On the rear of a school bus or coach
6.8	☐ A route for pedestrians and cyclists
6.9	☐ They're deaf and blind
6.10	☐ Be patient and allow them to cross in their own time
6.11	☐ Be careful; they may misjudge your speed
6.12	☐ Give the cyclist plenty of room
6.13	☐ Bicycle
6.14	☐ They're harder to see
6.15	☐ Motorcycles can easily be hidden behind obstructions
6.16	☐ So that the rider can be seen more easily
6.17	☐ To make them more visible
6.18	☐ To check for traffic in their blind area
6.19	☐ Motorcyclist
6.20	☐ Give them plenty of room
6.21	☐ Wait patiently while they cross
6.22	☐ Reduce speed until you're clear of the area
6.23	☐ To allow children to see and be seen when they're crossing the road
6.24	☐ On a school bus
6.25	☐ Any direction
6.26	☐ Stay behind until the moped has passed the junction
6.27	☐ Stay well back
6.28	☐ Be patient and prepare for them to react more slowly
6.29	☐ Be patient, as you expect them to make mistakes
6.30	☐ Pedestrians
6.31	☐ Hold back until the cyclist has passed the junction
6.32	☐ In any direction
6.33	☐ Flashing amber beacon
6.34	☐ The vehicle is slow moving
6.35	☐ With-flow cycle lane
6.36	☐ Slow down and be ready to stop

6.37	☐ To ensure children can see and be seen when they're crossing the road
6.38	☐ Watch out for pedestrians walking in the road
6.39	☐ Allow extra room in case they swerve to avoid potholes
6.40	☐ Cycle route ahead
6.41	☐ Allow them space to turn
6.42	☐ Prepare to slow down and stop
6.43	☐ The pedestrian is deaf
6.44	☐ Cyclists and pedestrians
6.45	☐ To allow cyclists to position in front of other traffic
6.46	☐ The cyclist might be unsettled if you pass too near them
6.47	☐ Go very slowly
6.48	☐ You're approaching an organised walk
6.49	☐ By taking further training
6.50	☐ Get out and check
6.51	☐ Give way to the pedestrian
6.52	☐ Children
6.53	☐ Stop, then move forward slowly until you have a clear view
6.54	☐ To check for overtaking vehicles
6.55	☐ Give way to any pedestrians on the crossing
6.56	☐ Wait for them to finish crossing
6.57	☐ Slow down and be prepared to stop for children
6.58	☐ Check for traffic overtaking on your right
6.59	☐ Look for motorcyclists filtering through the traffic
6.60	☐ Pedestrians might come from behind the bus
6.61	☐ Drive slowly and leave plenty of room
6.62	☐ The rider may be blown in front of you
6.63	☐ At junctions
6.64	☐ You shouldn't wait or park your vehicle here
6.65	☐ Slow down and be prepared to stop for a cyclist
6.66	☐ Set your mirror to the anti-dazzle position
6.67	☐ Be prepared to stop

6. Case study practice

6.1	Swerve
6.2	Go in any direction
6.3	Children may be crossing the road
6.4	30 mph
6.5	They're deaf and blind

7. Other types of vehicle

7.1	☐ 
7.2	☐ Anything overtaking the lorry will be hidden from view
7.3	☐ Stay well back and give it room
7.4	☐ Wait behind the long vehicle
7.5	☐ Keep well back
7.6	☐ To get the best view of the road ahead
7.7	☐ Look for pedestrians
7.8	☐ Drop back until you can see better
7.9	☐ Drop back further
7.10	☐ Allow it to pull away, if it's safe to do so
7.11	☐ Keep well back so that you get a good view of the road ahead
7.12	☐ Cars
7.13	☐ Slow down and be prepared to wait
7.14	☐ Wait for the vehicle to finish turning
7.15	☐ It will take longer to overtake a large vehicle
7.16	☐ Keep well back
7.17	☐ Watch carefully for the sudden appearance of pedestrians
7.18	☐ Slow down and give way
7.19	☐ Because trams can't steer to avoid obstructions
7.20	☐ Extended-arm side mirrors
7.21	☐ Dipped headlights
7.22	☐ Allow extra room

7. Case study practice

7.1 60 mph

7.2 They could be blown off course

7.3 Drop back so you can see more of the road ahead

7.4 Trams are unable to steer round obstructions

7.5 Give way as long as it's safe to do so

8. Road conditions and vehicle handling

8.1	☐ When you're in a one-way street
8.2	☐ It will be doubled
8.3	☐ Beware of bends in the road ahead
8.4	☐ When oncoming traffic prevents you turning right
8.5	☐ 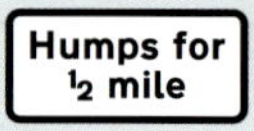
8.6	☐ To slow traffic down
8.7	☐ Red
8.8	☐ Alert you to a hazard
8.9	☐ Leave plenty of time for your journey
8.10	☐ Make sure you don't dazzle other road users
8.11	☐ Slow down and stay behind
8.12	☐ To make you aware of your speed
8.13	☐ Stop at a passing place
8.14	☐ To prevent the motorcycle sliding on the metal drain covers
8.15	☐ Your brakes will be wet
8.16	☐ It's more difficult to see what's ahead
8.17	☐ The engine will work harder
8.18	☐ Be wary of a sudden gust
8.19	☐ In case it stops suddenly
8.20	☐ Leave parking lights switched on
8.21	☐ Slow down or stop
8.22	☐ When visibility is seriously reduced
8.23	☐ Switch them off as long as visibility remains good
8.24	☐ To prevent dazzling drivers behind
8.25	☐ They'll dazzle other drivers
8.26	☐ To help prevent skidding in deep snow
8.27	☐ By changing to a lower gear
8.28	☐ You'll have less steering and braking control
8.29	☐ Ten times the normal distance
8.30	☐ Use your headlights
8.31	☐ Dipped headlights
8.32	☐ The condition of the tyres
8.33	☐ When you change to a lower gear
8.34	☐ Dipped headlights
8.35	☐ To make them more visible in thick fog

8.36	☐ Whether your journey is essential
8.37	☐ The windows and lights are clean and clear
8.38	☐ Switch off your fog lights
8.39	☐ They may be confused with brake lights
8.40	☐ It will reduce your control
8.41	☐ The vehicle will gain speed more quickly
8.42	☐ Use a low gear and drive slowly
8.43	☐ There won't be any engine braking
8.44	☐ When you're driving in poor visibility

8. Case study practice

8.1 It could be doubled
8.2 Visibility is below 100 metres
8.3 The vehicle ahead may stop suddenly
8.4 Wait until the road ahead is clear
8.5 A reminder to make you aware of your speed

9. Motorway driving

9.1	☐ Match your speed to traffic in the left-hand lane and filter into a safe gap
9.2	☐ 70 mph
9.3	☐ Any vehicle that isn't overtaking
9.4	☐ Vehicles towing a trailer
9.5	☐ It allows easy location by the emergency services
9.6	☐ Gain speed on the hard shoulder before moving out onto the carriageway
9.7	☐ On a steep gradient
9.8	☐ They're countdown markers to the next exit
9.9	☐ Between the central reservation and the carriageway
9.10	☐ White
9.11	☐ Green
9.12	☐ In the direction shown on the marker posts
9.13	☐ To allow you to fit safely into the traffic flow in the left-hand lane
9.14	☐ Face the oncoming traffic
9.15	☐ Red
9.16	☐ Left
9.17	☐ Keep a good distance from the vehicle ahead

9.18	☐ In the left-hand lane
9.19	☐ Obey the speed limit
9.20	☐ Powered mobility scooters
9.21	☐ Look much further ahead than you would on other roads
9.22	☐ Stay in the left-hand lane
9.23	☐ When you're overtaking
9.24	☐ When you're stopping in an emergency
9.25	☐ Move to the left and reduce your speed to 50 mph
9.26	☐ When you're signalled to do so by traffic signals
9.27	☐ Adjust your speed or change lane if you can do so safely
9.28	☐ Keep to the left-hand lane unless you're overtaking
9.29	☐ When in queues and traffic to your right is moving more slowly than you are
9.30	☐ In cases of emergency or breakdown
9.31	☐ Stop and direct anyone on a motorway
9.32	☐ You shouldn't travel in this lane
9.33	☐ The hard shoulder can be used as a running lane
9.34	☐ By using variable speed limits
9.35	☐ Variable speed limits
9.36	☐ In an emergency or breakdown
9.37	☐ 70 mph
9.38	☐ Stop and wait
9.39	☐ The hard shoulder is for emergency or breakdown use only
9.40	☐ Use all the lanes, including the hard shoulder
9.41	☐ At the nearest service area
9.42	☐ 60 mph
9.43	☐ When the road ahead is clear
9.44	☐ Switch on your hazard warning lights
9.45	☐ Use an emergency telephone and call for help
9.46	☐ Carry on to the next exit
9.47	☐ Switch on your hazard warning lights
9.48	☐ Continuous high speeds increase the risk of your vehicle breaking down
9.49	☐ Traffic ahead is slowing or stopping suddenly
9.50	☐ The left-hand lane

9.51	☐ They can't drive unaccompanied
9.52	☐ Check your location from the nearest marker posts beside the hard shoulder
9.53	☐ When there are lane closures
9.54	☐ Lower speed limits

9. Case study practice

9.1 Vehicles already travelling in the left-hand lane

9.2 Green/yellow

9.3 The left-hand lane

9.4 60 mph

9.5 Continue on until you reach the next exit

10. Rules of the road

10.1	☐ National speed limit applies
10.2	☐ 70 mph
10.3	☐ By street lighting
10.4	☐ 30 mph
10.5	☐ End of minimum speed
10.6	☐ Stay behind it if you're in any doubt
10.7	☐ Long vehicle
10.8	☐ Never
10.9	☐ Waiting restrictions
10.10	☐ When you're in a one-way street
10.11	☐ When you're overtaking or turning right
10.12	☐ Continue in that lane
10.13	☐ On either the right or the left
10.14	☐ Signal left before leaving the roundabout
10.15	☐ Long vehicle
10.16	☐ When your exit road is clear
10.17	☐ When oncoming traffic prevents you from turning right
10.18	☐ A police officer
10.19	☐ Be ready to slow down or stop to let them cross
10.20	☐ Cyclists and pedestrians
10.21	☐ Give way to pedestrians on the crossing
10.22	☐ To pick up or set down passengers
10.23	☐ You'll have a clearer view of any approaching traffic
10.24	☐ Children may run out from between the vehicles
10.25	☐ Give way to oncoming traffic

10.26	☐ When you're turning right or overtaking
10.27	☐ No-one has priority
10.28	☐ 10 metres (32 feet)
10.29	☐ More than 10 metres (33 feet) from a junction
10.30	☐ Carry on waiting
10.31	☐ End of controlled parking zone
10.32	☐ Obey the speed limit
10.33	☐ So that you can be easily seen by others
10.34	☐ Wait until the road is clear in both directions
10.35	☐ 60 mph
10.36	☐ Leave parking lights switched on
10.37	☐ Approaching a concealed level crossing
10.38	☐ When signalled to stop by a traffic officer
10.39	☐ Signal left just after you pass the exit before the one you're going to take
10.40	☐ To gain access to a property
10.41	☐ 50 mph
10.42	☐ 60 mph
10.43	☐ Park in a bay and pay
10.44	☐ They mustn't drive along the lane
10.45	☐ Keep well to the left of the road
10.46	☐ Continue to wait
10.47	☐ Keep going and clear the crossing
10.48	☐ Turn around in a side road
10.49	☐ When you're carrying out a manoeuvre that includes reversing
10.50	☐ No further than is necessary
10.51	☐ Get out and check
10.52	☐ Your view will be restricted
10.53	☐ Wait in the box junction if your exit is clear
10.54	☐ When the front of your vehicle swings out
10.55	☐ In a garage
10.56	☐ To set down and pick up passengers
10.57	☐ Wait for a regular parking space to become free
10.58	☐ Pull into a passing place on your left
10.59	☐ As soon as the vehicle passes you
10.60	☐ Outside its hours of operation
10.61	☐ By using brake lights
10.62	☐ Turn around in a quiet side road
10.63	☐ In a well-lit area
10.64	☐ Move to the left in good time

10.65	☐ You shouldn't drive in the lane unless it's unavoidable
10.66	☐ When you have a Blue Badge
10.67	☐ If you're involved in an incident that causes damage or injury

10. Case study practice

10.1 There are regularly spaced street lights in the area

10.2 Short dashes with long spaces

10.3 Amber

10.4 It's for vehicles that have two or more occupants

10.5 Because you mustn't park there

11. Road and traffic signs

11.1	☐ They're circular with a red border
11.2	☐ 
11.3	☐ 
11.4	☐ Maximum speed limit with traffic calming
11.5	☐ End of 20 mph zone
11.6	☐ No motor vehicles
11.7	☐ No entry
11.8	☐ No right turn
11.9	☐ 
11.10	☐ Route for trams only
11.11	☐ High vehicles
11.12	☐ 
11.13	☐ No overtaking
11.14	☐ Waiting restrictions apply
11.15	☐ End of restricted parking area
11.16	☐ 
11.17	☐ No stopping
11.18	☐ Distance to parking place ahead
11.19	☐ Vehicles may park fully on the verge or footway
11.20	☐ Give priority to oncoming traffic

11.21	☐ You have priority over vehicles coming towards you
11.22	☐ 
11.23	☐ Stop
11.24	☐ Minimum speed 30 mph
11.25	☐ Pass either side to get to the same destination
11.26	☐ Route for trams
11.27	☐ They give mandatory instructions
11.28	☐ On a one-way street
11.29	☐ Contraflow bus lane
11.30	☐ Tourist directions
11.31	☐ Tourist attraction
11.32	☐ To give warnings
11.33	☐ T-junction
11.34	☐ Risk of ice
11.35	☐ Crossroads
11.36	☐ Roundabout
11.37	☐ Road narrows
11.38	☐ Cycle route ahead
11.39	☐ 
11.40	☐ 
11.41	☐ Give way to trams
11.42	☐ Humps in the road
11.43	☐ 
11.44	☐ End of dual carriageway
11.45	☐ Side winds
11.46	☐ Danger ahead
11.47	☐ Hold back until you can see clearly ahead
11.48	☐ Level crossing with gate or barrier
11.49	☐ Trams crossing ahead
11.50	☐ Steep hill downwards
11.51	☐ Water across the road
11.52	☐ No through road on the left
11.53	☐ No through road
11.54	☐ 
11.55	☐ The right-hand lane is closed
11.56	☐ Contraflow system
11.57	☐ Lane for heavy and slow vehicles

11.58	☐ You must stop and wait behind the stop line
11.59	☐ Stop at the stop line
11.60	☐ When your exit from the junction is blocked
11.61	☐ 
11.62	☐ Traffic lights out of order
11.63	☐ Nobody
11.64	☐ Level crossings
11.65	☐ No parking at any time
11.66	☐ To pass a road maintenance vehicle travelling at 10 mph or less
11.67	☐ You're approaching a hazard
11.68	☐ On road humps
11.69	☐ 
11.70	☐ Visibility along the major road is restricted
11.71	☐ Give way to traffic from the right
11.72	☐ Flash the headlights, indicate left and point to the left
11.73	☐ Stop at the stop line
11.74	☐ The driver intends to turn left
11.75	☐ Change to the lane on your left
11.76	☐ Temporary maximum speed 50 mph
11.77	☐ Right-hand lane closed ahead
11.78	☐ The number of the next junction
11.79	☐ As an overtaking lane
11.80	☐ On the right-hand edge of the road
11.81	☐ At slip-road entrances and exits
11.82	☐ Leave the motorway at the next exit
11.83	☐ End of motorway
11.84	☐ 
11.85	☐ 60 mph
11.86	☐ End of restriction
11.87	☐ A diversion route
11.88	☐ Compulsory maximum speed limit
11.89	☐ Carry on with great care
11.90	☐ No motorcycles
11.91	☐ Pass the lorry on the left
11.92	☐ Don't continue in that lane
11.93	☐ To warn others of your presence
11.94	☐ When another road user poses a danger

11.95	☐ No parking on the days and times shown
11.96	☐ Quayside or river bank
11.97	☐ Hazard warning
11.98	☐ It separates traffic flowing in opposite directions
11.99	☐ They're warning you of their presence
11.100	☐ Trams must stop
11.101	☐ At a mini-roundabout
11.102	☐ Pull up on the left
11.103	☐ Red alone
11.104	☐ Leave the motorway at the next exit
11.105	☐ Stop even if the road is clear
11.106	☐ 
11.107	☐ Mini-roundabout
11.108	☐ Two-way traffic crosses a one-way road
11.109	☐ Two-way traffic straight ahead
11.110	☐ Hump bridge
11.111	☐ Direction to park-and-ride car park
11.112	☐ Wait for the green light
11.113	☐ Wait
11.114	☐ Direction to an emergency pedestrian exit
11.115	☐ 
11.116	☐ With-flow bus and cycle lane
11.117	☐ Zebra crossing ahead
11.118	☐ 
11.119	☐ 
11.120	☐ Red and amber
11.121	☐ Tunnel ahead
11.122	☐ The edge of the carriageway
11.123	☐ Return to your side of the road
11.124	☐ 
11.125	☐ Wait until the vehicle starts to turn in
11.126	☐ On a motorway or unrestricted dual carriageway, to warn of a hazard ahead

11.127	☐ To avoid misleading other road users
11.128	☐ As you're passing or just after the junction

11. Case study practice

11.1 No motor vehicles
11.2 No parking
11.3 60 mph
11.4 Tourist information
11.5 An amber light on its own

12. Essential documents

12.1	☐ One year after the date it was issued
12.2	☐ A document issued before you receive your insurance certificate
12.3	☐ Retake your theory and practical tests
12.4	☐ Until the vehicle is taxed, sold or scrapped
12.5	☐ A notification to tell DVLA that a vehicle isn't being used on the road
12.6	☐ Unlimited
12.7	☐ The registered vehicle keeper
12.8	☐ When a police officer asks you for it
12.9	☐ An appropriate driving licence
12.10	☐ Valid insurance
12.11	☐ 7 days
12.12	☐ That the vehicle is insured for your use
12.13	☐ The vehicle insurance
12.14	☐ They must have valid motor insurance
12.15	☐ Damage to other vehicles
12.16	☐ The registered keeper of the vehicle
12.17	☐ The registered keeper
12.18	☐ When you change your vehicle
12.19	☐ When your health affects your driving
12.20	☐ When you complete the Pass Plus scheme
12.21	☐ To be at least 21 years old
12.22	☐ When driving to an appointment at an MOT centre
12.23	☐ When it's three years old

12.24	☐ Damage to other vehicles
12.25	☐ Third party only
12.26	☐ You'll have to pay the first £500 of the cost of any claim

12. Case study practice

12.1 The vehicle meets the minimum legal safety standards

12.2 If you change your name or address

12.3 Comprehensive

12.4 Temporary cover

12.5 New keeper supplement

13. Incidents, accidents and emergencies

13.1	☐ When you slow down quickly because of danger ahead
13.2	☐ When stopped and temporarily obstructing traffic
13.3	☐ Keep a safe distance from the vehicle in front
13.4	☐ Apply pressure over the wound
13.5	☐ Check that they're breathing normally
13.6	☐ 120 times per minute
13.7	☐ Rapid shallow breathing
13.8	☐ Check their airway remains open
13.9	☐ Seek medical assistance
13.10	☐ Go to the next emergency telephone and report the hazard
13.11	☐ Variable message signs
13.12	☐ 5 to 6 centimetres
13.13	☐ Make sure that an ambulance has been called
13.14	☐ Only when it's essential
13.15	☐ Check whether they're breathing normally
13.16	☐ Whether their airway is open
13.17	☐ Keep them warm and comfortable
13.18	☐ Reassure them confidently
13.19	☐ Warn other traffic
13.20	☐ Open their airway and begin CPR
13.21	☐ Open their airway
13.22	☐ Douse the burns with clean, cool water

13.23	☐ Apply firm pressure over the wound
13.24	☐ When there's a risk of further danger
13.25	☐ Keep them where they are
13.26	☐ 
13.27	☐ Your driving licence
13.28	☐ As soon as possible
13.29	☐ Warn other traffic
13.30	☐ Follow the DR ABC code
13.31	☐ Reassure them confidently
13.32	☐ Removing it could make any injuries worse
13.33	☐ 45 metres (147 feet)
13.34	☐ Leave your vehicle and get everyone clear
13.35	☐ Pull up slowly at the side of the road
13.36	☐ Pull up on the hard shoulder or in an emergency refuge area and call for assistance
13.37	☐ Get out of the car and clear of the crossing
13.38	☐ Take off your sunglasses
13.39	☐ Dipped headlights
13.40	☐ Check out any strong smell of fuel
13.41	☐ Stop at the next emergency telephone and report the incident
13.42	☐ Check out the problem quickly and safely
13.43	☐ Switch on hazard warning lights, then go and call for help
13.44	☐ Drive it out of the tunnel if it's safe to do so
13.45	☐ Get everyone out of the vehicle and clear of the crossing
13.46	☐ Stop at the scene of the incident
13.47	☐ Your name, address and vehicle registration number
13.48	☐ Report the incident to the police within 24 hours

13. Case study practice

13.1 By switching on hazard warning lights

13.2 Location of the incident

13.3 Stay with them and reassure them confidently

13.4 You might be required to supply a witness statement

13.5 Driving licence and insurance certificate

14. Vehicle loading

14.1	☐ You mustn't use the right-hand lane
14.2	☐ Ease off the accelerator to reduce your speed
14.3	☐ When carrying a heavy load
14.4	☐ It will reduce stability
14.5	☐ The vehicle's handling
14.6	☐ The driver of the vehicle
14.7	☐ A stabiliser fitted to the tow bar
14.8	☐ No, not at any time
14.9	☐ Breakaway cable
14.10	☐ In the vehicle handbook
14.11	☐ Securely fastened with suitable restraints
14.12	☐ A child seat

14. Case study practice

14.1 Reduce the stability

14.2 In a special harness

14.3 The driver

14.4 Removing the roof rack when it isn't being used

14.5 That there's appropriate pressure in all four tyres plus the spare

15. Case study practice

Case study on pages 459–461

1 Look over your shoulder for a final check
2 Slow down
3 Make the call when you've stopped in a suitable place
4 Go slowly past
5 There may be another vehicle coming

Case study practice A

1 Renew your vehicle tax immediately
2 Stay calm and continue when it's safe
3 Stay out of the outside lane
4 Drink two cups of coffee and rest for 15 minutes
5 Because you're stationary

Case study practice B

1 He is
2 He's deaf and blind
3 National speed limit applies
4 Put on your hazard warning lights
5 Restrict the blood flow from their leg

Case study practice C

1 Four seconds
2 Pedestrians stepping out from between vehicles
3 Stop and wait until the way ahead is clear
4 No-one
5 Tyre pressure is too low

Case study practice D

1 Headlights with fog lights as necessary
2 Slowly drop back to allow more room in front
3 Move nearer to the centre line and signal to go right
4 Turned in towards the kerb
5 Lock it away securely out of sight

Case study practice E

1 Oil and water levels
2 In a suitable child restraint
3 Glare from the sun on wet roads
4 Well back, so you can see ahead and be seen
5 This lane can be used as a running lane at a maximum speed of 40 mph